Labor in a New Land

Labor in a New Land

ECONOMY AND SOCIETY IN SEVENTEENTH-CENTURY SPRINGFIELD

Stephen Innes

Princeton University Press
Princeton, New Jersey

Copyright © 1983 by Princeton University Press

Published by Princeton University Press, 41 William Street,
Princeton, New Jersey 08540

In the United Kingdom: Princeton University Press, Guildford, Surrey

This book has been composed in Linotron Baskerville

Clothbound editions of Princeton University Press books are printed on
acid-free paper, and binding materials are chosen for strength and durability.
Paperbacks, although satisfactory for personal collections, are not usually
suitable for library rebinding.

Printed in the United States of America by Princeton University Press
Princeton, New Jersey

Library of Congress Cataloging in Publication Data

Innes, Stephen.
   Labor in a new land.

   Includes index.
   1. Springfield (Mass.)—Economic conditions.   2. Springfield (Mass.)—
Social conditions.   3. Springfield (Mass.)—History—17th century.   I. Title.
HC108.S83I56   1983   330.9744'26   82–61369
ISBN 0–691–04698–0
ISBN 0–691–00595–8 (pbk.)

In Memory of Roberta
and
for Julie

Contents

Acknowledgments

MANY generous friends have helped me to write this book. T. H. Breen supervised it in dissertation form and was throughout a model advisor. Stanley N. Katz and Josef Barton provided guidance and support at a number of critical stages of the enterprise. Robert A. Gross, Thomas Slaughter, John M. Murrin, Edward Ayers, W. W. Abbot, Erik Midelfort, Robert Stanley, James Schmotter, Christine Leigh Heyrman, John J. McCusker, and Jean Lee all offered discriminating (and repeated) readings of the manuscript, often at considerable personal sacrifice. Professors Gross and Slaughter, in particular, were tireless in helping me formulate and sharpen my argument, a role also ably played by the two readers for Princeton University Press, Russell Menard and Douglas Greenberg. James A. Henretta penetratingly critiqued the chapter on land while it was at an early stage of gestation, as did Michael McGiffert. Juliette Tomlinson, as Director of the splendid Connecticut Valley Historical Museum, helped me enter the thicket of the Pynchon account books with as little harm as possible. Ruth A. McIntyre's transcription of volume three was equally helpful. Lottie McCauley and Kathleen Miller typed an exceedingly difficult manuscript more times than they would like to recall—both on a typewriter and a word processor. It's impossible to imagine more competent, or more forebearing, typists and proofreaders. Alice Calaprice showed unerring judgment as a copyeditor and was a pleasure to work with besides.

I must reserve special thanks for four people. Gail Filion, Social Sciences Editor at Princeton University Press, saw the virtues of a manuscript still in very rough form and helped immeasurably in bringing it to fruition. Olivier Zunz, while trying to complete his own book, guided mine through the countless arcane procedures needed to computerize the text for printing. My debt to him is immense. Fred V. Carstensen, both in his several readings of the text and in our many conversations about it, was instrumental in clarifying my theoretical assertions, especially in the epilogue. Finally, William M. Daly, as a scholar and a teacher, showed me some years ago that the historian's craft could be an ennobling one. Without his example, this book would never have been written.

Quotations from manuscripts appear as originally written, except that abbreviations have been expanded, certain archaic usages modernized, and punctuation added when necessary. All dates in the text are rendered in New Style (with the year beginning on January 1 rather than March 25, as it did prior to 1752). Readers of the paperback edition are advised to consult the clothbound edition for the Dependency Tables and Wage Tables that form much of the documentary basis for chapters three and four.

Abbreviations

Account Books	John Pynchon's Account Books, 1652–1702, 6 vols. Connecticut Valley Historical Museum, Springfield
CVHM	Connecticut Valley Historical Museum, Springfield
HCPC Rec.	Hampshire County Probate Court Records, Hampden County Courthouse, Springfield
Mass. Archives	Massachusetts Archives, Boston State House
Mass. Recs.	*Records of the Governor and Company of the Massachusetts Bay in New England, 1628–1686*, ed. Nathaniel B. Shurtleff. 5 vols. in 6. Boston, 1853–1854
Pynchon Court Rec.	*Colonial Justice in Western Massachusetts (1639–1702): The Pynchon Court Record . . .*, ed. Joseph H. Smith. Cambridge, Mass., 1961
William Pynchon Account Book	William Pynchon's Record of Accounts with Early Settlers and Indians, 1645–1650. Forbes Library, Northampton, Mass.
Springfield Town Recs.	*The First Century of the History of Springfield: The Official Records from 1636–1736*, ed. Henry M. Burt. 2 vols. Springfield, 1898–1899
WMQ	*William and Mary Quarterly*, 3rd Series
Winthrop's Journal	John Winthrop, *The History of New England from 1630 to 1649*, ed. James Savage. 2 vols. Boston, 1853
Winthrop Mss.	Winthrop Papers, Massachusetts Historical Society Library, Boston
Winthrop Papers	*Winthrop Papers, 1498–1649*, ed. Allyn B. Forbes. 5 vols. Boston, 1929–1947

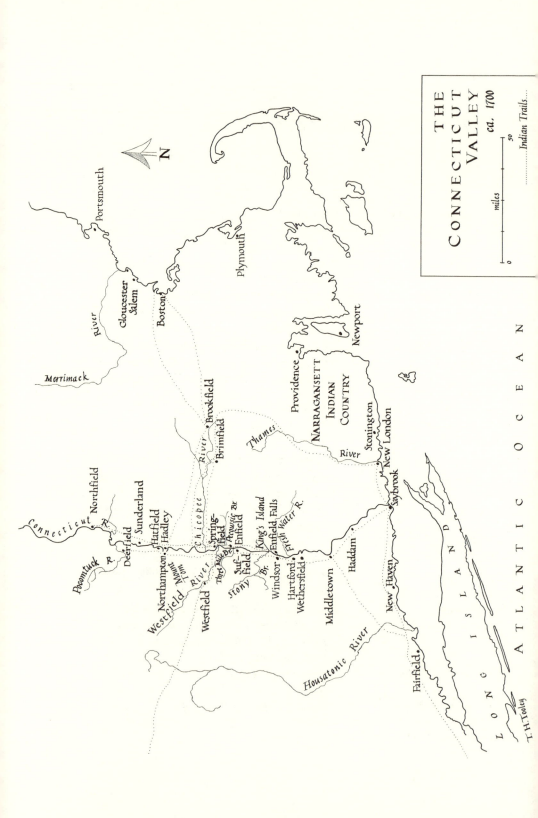

THE
CONNECTICUT
VALLEY
ca. 1700

miles
50
0
Indian Trails ....

N

Portsmouth

Gloucester
Salem

Boston

Merrimack

River

Plymouth

Brookfield
Brimfield

River

Chicopee

Thames

Providence

NARRAGANSETT
INDIAN
COUNTRY

Newport

Stonington

River

New London

Saybrook

Northfield

Connecticut R.

Deerfield

Sunderland

Hatfield
Hadley

Pocomtuck R.

Northampton

Mount Tom

Westfield River

Springfield

Three Mile Br.

Prioung Br.

Enfield

King's Island

Fresh Water R.

Enfield Falls

Westfield

Stony Br.

Suffield

Windsor

Hartford
Wethersfield

Middletown

Haddam

New Haven

Fairfield

Housatonic River

LONG ISLAND

ATLANTIC OCEAN

T. H. Tooley

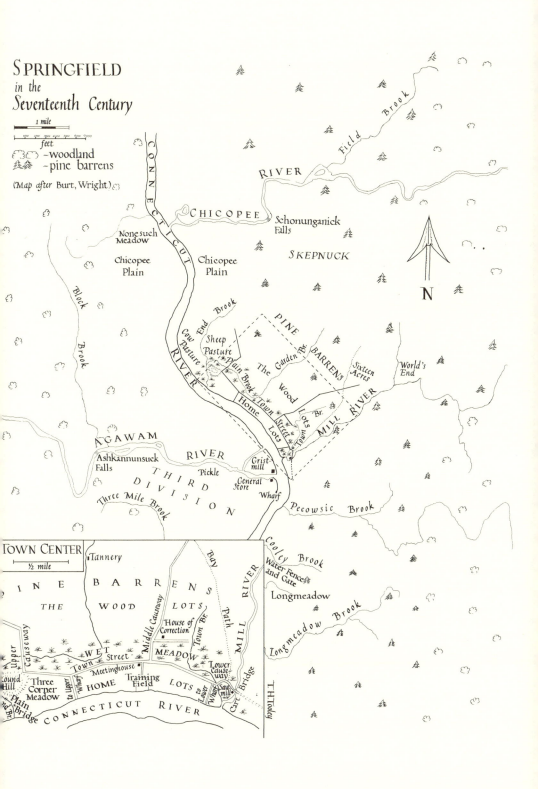

SPRINGFIELD
in the
Seventeenth Century

1 mile

feet

- woodland
- pine barrens

(Map after Burt, Wright)

CONNECTICUT

RIVER

CHICOPEE

Schonunganick
Falls

Nonesuch
Meadow

Chicopee
Plain

Chicopee
Plain

SKEPNUCK

Block

Brook

End Brook

Sheep
Pasture

Cow
Pasture

Plain Brook

The

Garden Br.

PINE

BARRENS

Sixteen
Acres

World's
End

Wood

Lots

Home

Town
Lots

Town
Street

Br.

MILL RIVER

AGAWAM

RIVER

THIRD

DIVISION

Ashkannunsuck
Falls

Three Mile Brook

Pickle

Grist
mill

General
Store

Wharf

Pecowsic   Brook

Cooley

Brook

N

Field

Brook

RIVER

TOWN CENTER

½ mile

Tannery

P I N E

B A R R E N S

THE

W O O D

L O T S

House of
Correction

Bay

Path

Middle Causeway

Town Br.

MILL

RIVER

Water Fence
and Gate

Longmeadow

Longmeadow   Brook

WET

Town
Street

Upper
Causeway

MEADOW

Three
Corner
Meadow

Meetinghouse

HOME

Training
Field

LOTS

Lower
Cause-
way

Saw
mill

Cart Bridge

T. Hooley

to Upper Wharf

to Lower Wharf

Round
Hill

Plain
and Br.

Bridge

CONNECTICUT   RIVER

"[T]he growing good of the world is partly dependent on unhistoric acts; and that things are not so ill with you and me as they might have been, is half owing to the number who lived faithfully a hidden life and rest in unvisited tombs."

George Eliot, *Middlemarch*

• *Introduction* •

Social Diversity and Social Change in Seventeenth-Century New England

FEW TOPICS have rivaled the colonial New England town as an object of fascination for the most recent generation of American historians. Since the simultaneous appearance of important community studies by Kenneth A. Lockridge, Philip J. Greven, John Demos, and Michael Zuckerman in the banner year of 1970, scholars have been reformulating the entire panorama of United States history in the light of the experience of early New Englanders.[1] The studies of Dedham and Andover have been particularly influential, and their portrayal of a communal, egalitarian, harmonious society has not yet been brought into serious question. A new study of Salem, Massachusetts, published in 1980, begins by invoking the current "consensus" regarding the early New England town: "Homogeneous, closed, corporate and cohesive, the pattern has been established and documented."[2] Scholars dealing with topics as diverse as social change during the Revolution and changes in the law of contract and the law of negligence in the early national period have built on the quietistic models of seventeenth-century Dedham and Andover. Historians of the stature of Richard Hofstadter substantially reformulated their own work in response to the findings of the new demographic studies.[3] Building on the communal and "one-class" images of the seventeenth century, these interpretations have linked the apparent disharmony and stratification of the eighteenth century to the coming of the American Revolution. This view sees the rising incidence of land scarcity, religious strife, and "un-

[1] Kenneth A. Lockridge, *A New England Town, The First Hundred Years: Dedham, Massachusetts, 1636–1736*, New York, 1970; Philip J. Greven, Jr., *Four Generations: Population, Land, and Family in Colonial Andover, Massachusetts*, Ithaca, 1970; John Demos, *A Little Commonwealth: Family Life in Plymouth Colony*, New York, 1970; Michael Zuckerman, *Peaceable Kingdoms: New England Towns in the Eighteenth Century*, New York, 1970.

[2] Christine Alice Young, *From 'Good Order' to Glorious Revolution: Salem, Massachusetts, 1628–1689*, Ann Arbor, 1980, p. 1.

[3] *America at 1750: A Social Portrait*, New York, 1971, p. 7.

neighborly" behavior by the villagers as preconditions for the Revolutionary crisis.

In their depiction of the process of cultural change, therefore, the new social historians ironically found themselves in close agreement with the old intellectual historians. For Lockridge and Greven, as for Perry Miller, the story was one of erosion after a heroic first generation—whether the word used to describe this process was "decline" or "declension" or whether the villain was factionalism or secularism. In either case, the end result was the same: the communalistic ideology of Puritanism gave way to the individualistic ethos of republicanism. Insuring godly behavior became less important than protecting private property. Access to markets became more desirable than access to the sacraments. Deferential politics gave way to participatory democracy, and selectmen surrendered up their power to the town meeting. But as politics became more egalitarian, the distribution of wealth became less so, as "the rich" and "the poor" made their first appearance in New England. Well before the first bloodletting at Lexington and Concord, these scholars all agree, Puritans had been transformed into Yankees, and an ascriptive society had given way to one based on achievement.

Surprisingly few historians have questioned this so-called "modernization" thesis, or queried whether the experiences of Dedham and Andover really typified early New England. Particularly striking is the willingness to generalize with such confidence from the examples of two subsistence farming communities, especially since both towns have as many reasons to argue against typicality as for it. The majority of seventeenth-century New Englanders lived either in ocean ports or in major river towns. Dedham and Andover were neither. They were somewhat isolated, backwater farming communities whose very parochialism warns against assumptions of normative behavior.

In point of fact, early New England contained not one but three distinct settlement zones: an urbanized coastal region, typified by Boston and Salem; a subsistence farming region comprised of towns like Dedham and Andover; and an area of highly commercialized agriculture, such as the towns of the colony's breadbasket—the Connecticut River Valley. Each region had different patterns of social relations, economic opportunity, and political behavior. Throughout the seventeenth century, the levels of communal harmony, social stratification, and political elitism displayed a wide diversity in each of the three zones. To use the words of J. M. Cameron, each zone had a distinct "ensemble of social relations."

Scholars have acknowledged this high level of diversity for the eighteenth century, but for the earlier period the Dedham and Andover models continue to command almost universal acceptance. This unanimity is not entirely the result of a dearth of scholarship. Several historians who have closely examined the coastal ports of Boston and Salem have discovered mercantilist, faction-ridden, stratified, and contentious communities rather than peasant utopias. To date, however, there has been no similar treatment of one of the highly commercialized agricultural towns.[4]

This study attempts to remedy that deficiency. It focuses on socioeconomic relationships in Springfield, Massachusetts during the seventeenth century. As a highly commercialized, developmental community, Springfield typified many of the experiences of towns in the Merrimack Valley, in Plymouth, on Cape Cod, and in the remainder of the Connecticut Valley. This study demonstrates that the findings drawn from the subsistence farming regions cannot be generalized to the entire colony. By all measures, Springfield was a more individualistic, less communal and egalitarian place than early New England is usually thought to have been.

Material opportunity, not organic unity, governed the inhabitants' behavior. Men came to the town to seek their fortune—as fur traders, artisans, teamsters, laborers, or farmers—not to establish a godly community. These individualistic goals produced a society where a man's worth was measured largely in economic, not religious, terms. Court records show convincingly that the town's inhabitants were willing to countenance various forms of antisocial behavior, often of a decidedly non-Puritan character, if the culprit was a skilled artisan or a hard-working laborer. The ability to curry leather, join a houseframe, or last a shoe was more highly prized than was personal probity.

These materialistic goals were reflected in Springfield's high level of economic diversification. Here again the town presents a sharp contrast to the Dedham and Andover depiction of a homogeneous society of subsistence farmers. In Springfield, rather than being simply agriculturalists, over two-thirds of the community's men possessed a marketable skill which they used to earn their daily bread. Many inhabitants displayed competence in as many as three or more crafts. Some highly skilled workers rarely, if ever, performed major field labor. These included: carpenters, smiths, coop-

[4] Darrett B. Rutman, *Winthrop's Boston: Portrait of A Puritan Town, 1630–1649*, Chapel Hill, 1965; Paul Boyer and Stephen Nissenbaum, *Salem Possessed: The Social Origins of Witchcraft*, Cambridge, Mass., 1974.

ers, tailors, millers, and brickmakers. And almost every man worked periodically as a canoeman, teamster, mill hand, sawyer, stone-mason, drover, or day-laborer.

Equally diversified was the town's manufacturing base. Throughout the seventeenth century Springfield's economy displayed a highly developed commercial orientation. Financed and controlled largely by the town's founding family, the Pynchons, these commercial enterprises encompassed gristmills, sawmills, lead mines, turpentine manufactures, ironworks, and housing construction. These projects provided either full-time or seasonal employment to the roughly one-third of the town's male population who lacked sufficient land to make farming their sole means of livelihood. Such enterprises also served as magnets to draw itinerant artisans and laborers from elsewhere in the valley and colony. Of critical importance here was Springfield's function as what geographers describe as a "central place." It stood at the nexus of an economic region comprised of a network of producing areas and local trading centers which served as feeders to the community's marketing system.[5] Hadley and Westfield were the principal producing areas, Northampton the next largest trading center. The surplus wheat provided by the valley's farmers allowed the Pynchons to export downriver as many as two thousand bushels annually.[6]

Springfield's economic orientation produced a society that was far from being a peasant utopia. It was for many of its inhabitants a depressing place in which to live. Throughout the seventeenth century, it was characterized by inequality, bankruptcy, and social conflict. Two Old World phenomena rarely associated with early New England—land tenancy and wage labor—were everyday realities for half the town's population. In many ways Springfield was not a social community, but an economic community, and the weakness of communal bonds brought a high level of discord. Far from revealing a peasant utopia, court records testify to both the frequency and virulence of antisocial behavior. Throughout the period, the community experienced disruptive levels of physical assault, family feuds, slander, witchcraft accusations, and drunkenness. In their social conduct, as in their economic activities, the inhabitants behaved as self-assertive individuals, not as other-directed communitarians. If a resident found himself enraged at a fellow villager, he was not constrained from venting this anger by an

[5] Edward M. Cook, Jr., *The Fathers of the Towns: Leadership and Community Structure in Eighteenth-Century New England*, Baltimore, 1976, pp. 77–79, 183.

[6] Account Books, 1–6; Howard S. Russell, *A Long, Deep Furrow: Three Centuries of Farming in New England*, Hanover, N.H., 1976, p. 42.

overriding need to preserve communal harmony. In Springfield the most important social bonds were not those of the neighborhood, but those of the marketplace. And the most important market ties were those that led to the Pynchon family.

Nothing illustrates Springfield's contrast with Dedham so vividly as does the position of the Pynchons. Despite Kenneth Lockridge's depiction of seventeenth-century New England as a "one-class" society and Michael Zuckerman's assertion that the development of a distinct social elite was a "virtual impossibility in provincial Massachusetts," Springfield from the beginning was dominated by the Pynchons.[7] William Pynchon founded the town as a fur-trading post in 1636 and soon oversaw the embryonic community much like an English manorial lord. The largest landholder, principal merchant, and employer of almost every citizen, he also held all important civil and judicial power. When he returned to England in 1652, following a theological dispute with the General Court, William's privileges and status devolved upon his twenty-six-year-old son John. The younger Pynchon quickly became the most powerful figure in western Massachusetts. He retained his father's fur monopoly, expanded the family's landholdings, served as the financier for most of the region's settlements, and continued to be the valley's largest employer. In Springfield itself, some forty men worked on an approximately full-time basis for Pynchon, and about half the town's population at any one time was financially dependent in some fashion—rental of land or animals, employment, or debt—on the resources and good graces of Pynchon. As a result of his viselike economic grip on the community, the processes of getting work or getting land routinely began with a trek to the Pynchon general store.[8]

Not surprisingly, by 1665 John Pynchon held virtually every significant leadership position. He was simultaneously magistrate, judge of the county court, permanent moderator of the town meeting, and captain of the militia. Equally important, the townsmen habitually relied on Pynchon's initiative and financial wherewithal, rather than common taxation, for funding community projects. When it came time to build a new gristmill or sawmill, or to purchase a flock of sheep for the community's wool, he supplied the necessary capital and in return received ownership rights as well as toll privileges.

John Pynchon's economic, familial, and political connections with

---

[7] Lockridge, *A New England Town*, p. 76; Zuckerman, *Peaceable Kingdoms*, p. 219.
[8] Account Books, 1–6.

the outside world served as the linchpin to his dominance. This power derived from his position as mediator or "gatekeeper" between the valley and Boston. As Springfield's spokesman in Boston and as the instrument of General Court policy in western Massachusetts, Pynchon commanded enormous influence in both locales. This dominance remained unchallenged until New England's version of the Glorious Revolution dramatically modified the sources of his power. Until this time, Pynchon's economic hegemony, enhanced by his monopoly of political and judicial offices, created a proliferating set of dependency relationships which undermined traditional Puritan concepts of the organic, classless society.[9]

Dependence, of course, does not necessarily connote exploitation. Some men used their association with the Pynchons to improve their standard of living. Joseph Parsons, beginning as a fur agent for the Pynchons, ended his life with an estate valued at £2,088, the second largest inventory probated in seventeenth-century Hampshire County.[10] Others were not so fortunate. They used the resources Pynchon had to offer—work, developmental leases, credit—in an effort to get ahead. The price to *taking* this gamble was dependency on Pynchon, the price of *losing* it was often financial ruin. The tanner Griffith Jones lost his house and lands through indebtedness to the Pynchons, as did the blacksmith John Stewart, the cooper John Mathews, the agricultural laborer and tenant Jonathan Taylor, and the merchant-tailor Samuel Marshfield. Their stories were more typical than was Parsons's.[11]

The particulars of this dependency are laid out in remarkable detail in the Pynchon account books, the principal source used for this study. These volumes reveal how and at what cost men became associated with the Pynchons. When renting land and livestock, buying manufactured goods, or simply transferring credit to a fellow villager, men paid their accounts at the family's general store with the fruits of their labor—whether they were farmers, craftsmen, or laborers. Accordingly, the account books contain a wide variety of information relating to the distribution of goods and services, occupations, credit, indebtedness, prices, tenancy, labor patterns, mortgages, and foreclosures. Better than any similar seventeenth-century documents, the account books illuminate the substance and rhythms of day-to-day existence. They show how often and at what tasks men and women worked in the Pynchons' fields, mills, or canoes.

[9] Lockridge, *A New England Town*, pp. 57–78.
[10] HCPC Rec., 1 (1660–1690), pp. 235–236.
[11] Account Books, 1–6.

By tracing some two hundred individual work careers through the account books, a complex and multifarious portrayal of Springfield's economy emerges—one that calls into question a number of long-standing scholarly assumptions. Among these are: the scarcity of labor, high wage levels, the concentration of skilled artisans in major coastal ports, the ready availability of land, and the universality of fee-simple land tenure. This analysis likewise suggests that the prevailing emphasis on the eighteenth century as a period of declining opportunity and increasing social conflict is in need of modification. In Springfield, it appears, something very near the opposite occurred. Rather than moving toward economic stratification and increased intercommunal strife, the town was growing more egalitarian and harmonious as the Revolution approached. For ordinary inhabitants, access to both land and political power came easier in the eighteenth century than before.

Finally, the account books and the Hampshire court records allow for a humanization of the individual settlers. The new social historians have brought us closer to the everyday life of the "common sort" than most ever imagined possible. But this was often done at the cost of reducing the inhabitants to statistical abstractions, faceless peasants, or Weberian ideal types. The Springfield records reveal that this tendency is not unavoidable. Throughout the seventeenth century the town clearly had its share of vivid personalities, individuals who even at the remove of three hundred years come across in stark and recognizable tones. Theirs is the story this book seeks to tell.

LABOR IN A NEW LAND

· *Chapter 1* ·

A Company Town

"Laborare est orare"

SPRINGFIELD began as a commercial enterprise and remained such throughout the seventeenth century. Founded in 1636 by William Pynchon as a fur-trading post, the town quickly became the major merchandising center in the upper Connecticut Valley. The fur trade enriched the Pynchon family and brought large numbers of artisans, teamsters, and laborers to the community. Within a generation of settlement, the relationships between the Pynchons and the laboring classes had produced a society that can best be described as a company town.

The commercial orientation that William Pynchon brought to the Connecticut Valley reflected the economic individualism of his native Essex County. Pynchon had been born in 1590 into a family on the periphery of the English gentry class, and he grew to maturity in the modest Essex County village of Springfield.[1] This was the region to which the enclosure movement had come earliest and, as a result, by the time of Pynchon's youth the manor was "little more than a rent-collecting machine." The growth of enclosed-field farming commercialized land exchange and fostered an environment of economic individualism. Most Essex County landholders—whether of free, lease, or copyhold lands—rationalized their production of cereal grains, wool, and livestock for export to the London market. Augmenting this increased market orientation was the transfer of day-to-day administrative and judicial functions from the courts leet and courts baron to the parish and justice of the peace. By the beginning of the seventeenth century, the manor did not play a significant role in regulating farming activities in Essex and men were left to make their own decisions.[2]

---

[1] *Pynchon Court Rec.*, p. 6.

[2] David Grayson Allen, *In English Ways: The Movement of Societies and the Transferal of English Local Law and Custom to Massachusetts Bay in the Seventeenth Century*, Chapel Hill, 1981, pp. 151–153.

Or at least they were until the centralizing policies of Charles I brought higher levels of taxation, outside control, and religious persecution.[3] William Pynchon, like many of the gentry of the eastern counties, became a zealous convert to the Puritan reform movement, and the King's new policies threatened his religious as well as his economic autonomy. By 1629, with Parliament suspended, higher taxes promised, and wool prices plummeting because of the Thirty Years War, Pynchon decided to leave England. He became one of the patentees of the Massachusetts Bay Company and set sail with the fleet that brought John Winthrop to New England.[4] Accompanying him were his wife Anna and three daughters, and his son John would follow shortly.[5] Already one of the luminaries in the company, William received a midvoyage invitation to dine with Governor Winthrop. The governor entered into his journal that "About eleven of the clock, our captain sent his skiff and fetched aboard us the masters of the other two ships, and Mr. Pynchon, and they dined with us in the round-house."[6]

Upon arrival in America—displaying the energy and purposefulness characteristic of all he did—Pynchon began trafficking in furs, raising livestock, and farming. His boats plied the New England coast as far north as Sagadahock, Maine, sometimes with untoward results. In the fall of 1631, as Winthrop's journal relates, "Mr. Pynchon's boat, coming from Sagadahock, was cast away at Cape Ann, but the men and chief goods saved, and the boat recovered."[7] Such mishaps aside, these voyages brought Pynchon into contact with fur traders and inspired him to concentrate most of his resources on this activity. He remembered the heavy demand for beaver pelts in the London hatmaking industry, and he possessed the right contacts on Fleet Street to begin immediately merchandising furs there. As early as 1621, Pynchon was engaged in a business partnership with Thomas Brocke, "Citizen and Mercer of London," sharing with him a £202 judgment in the Court of Common Pleas against a certain Thomas Elliot of Roxwell.[8] By 1634, with the help of his London agents, Pynchon was the leading fur trader in Massachusetts with a volume of pelts tenfold that of

[3] T. H. Breen, "Persistent Localism: English Social Change and the Shaping of New England Institutions," *WMQ*, 32 (1975), p. 9.

[4] Samuel Eliot Morison, *Builders of the Bay Colony*, Boston, 1962, p. 339; George C. Homans, "The Puritans and the Clothing Industry in England," *New England Quarterly*, 13 (1940), pp. 519–529.

[5] *Pynchon Court Rec.*, p. 9.

[6] *Winthrop's Journal*, 1, p. 14.

[7] *Ibid.*, 1, p. 76.

[8] CVHM Ms.

his nearest competitor.[9] He subsequently moved from Dorchester to the less densely settled town of Roxbury to maximize his advantage.

At the same time, Pynchon entered into a trading consortium with Governor Winthrop and his son John. The London merchant, Francis Kirby, alluded to this connection when he wrote John Winthrop, Jr., on March 26, 1633: "I understand how you have dealt with mr. Pinchen for the Cloth, which bargain is not amisse, but may produce reasonable profit if he deale well with you in the Condicion of the beaver that he shall deliver to you." The magnitude of this trade is suggested by the younger Winthrop's payment to Pynchon of £197 1s. 8d. for imported cloth in March of 1636. Four months later this order was followed by one for 225 yards of cloth valued at £90; and in September of that year Pynchon "Reckoned with mr. John Winthrop Junior . . . for the fraight of 16 Tunn in the [ship] Blessinge at 35 shillings per Tunn . . . [and] for 24 Tunn in the Batchelor for 45 shillings per Tunn."[10]

Yet with the proliferation of traders around Massachusetts Bay, Pynchon recognized that his days of fur trading preeminence were numbered unless he moved west. By far the most promising region for fur trapping was the Connecticut Valley, and the lure of expanding his trade in such a bountiful environment induced Pynchon to move his family for the third time within six years.[11]

The Connecticut Valley had long been known for the abundance of its fur resources. In 1614 the Dutch trader Adrian Block had traveled fifty miles up the river to reconnoiter its commercial potential. So successful was the subsequent Dutch intrusion that during the decade from 1623 to 1633 their traders obtained an average of ten thousand beaver skins annually.[12] The forested valleys of the Connecticut River and its capillary system of tributary rivers and streams provided an ideal habitat for beaver, moose, otter, muskrat, marten, and lynx. Pynchon's decision to tap these resources was made easier by the large migration from Massachusetts Bay of the settlers who established the towns of Hartford, Windsor, and Wethersfield. But while the other migrants made the trek

[9] "Pincheon Papers," *Collections of the Massachusetts Historical Society*, 2nd Ser., 8 (1819), pp. 231–232.

[10] Francis Kirby to John Winthrop, Jr., March 26, 1633, *Winthrop Papers*, 3, p. 116; see also pp. 238, 285–286, 314.

[11] *Pynchon Court Rec.*, p. 11; Ruth A. McIntyre, *William Pynchon: Merchant and Colonizer, 1590–1662*, Springfield, 1962.

[12] Francis X. Moloney, *The Fur Trade in New England, 1620–1676*, Cambridge, Mass., 1931, p. 46.

primarily for religious reasons, Pynchon went to the valley as a merchant, not a Puritan. The community he built reflected this priority.

For his trading post, Pynchon selected a site located immediately above the highest navigable point on the Connecticut River. Not only was it north of the three newly settled towns, but it also stood at the nexus of several major Indian trails. Most important, it bisected the principal Indian path from Narragansett and Pequot country in the southeast to Mohawk territory in the Hudson Valley. His intention to build the settlement on the lush alluvial lands near the confluence of the Agawam and Connecticut Rivers was thwarted when the Indians refused to leave. "[T]he best ground at Agawam [was so] incombred with Indians," Pynchon wrote John Winthrop, Jr., "that I shall loose halfe the benefit thereby: and am compelled to plant on the opposite side to avoid trespassing of them."[13] He thereupon built his settlement on the less promising east side which, while it could not rival the opposite shore in agricultural potential, more than sufficed as a trading post.

In April 1636 Pynchon purchased the site from the Agawam Indians for "eighteen fathams of Wampam, eighteen coates, 18 hatchets, 18 hoes, [and] 18 knives."[14] The deed divided the purchase into three separate sections: (1) the Agawam meadows, located southwest of the Agawam River; (2) the land on the east bank where the Springfield town center was eventually situated; and (3) the "Long Meadow" located four miles to the south on the east bank. The deed allowed that the Agawams, who were hunter-gatherers and primitive agriculturalists, "shal have and enjoy all that cottinackeesh, or ground that is now planted; And have liberty to take Fish and Deer, ground nuts, walnuts, akornes, and sasachiminesh or a kind of pease, And also if any of our cattle spoile their corne, to pay as it is worth; and that hogs shall not goe on the side of Agawam but in akorne time."[15]

The commercial potential of the Connecticut Valley location appeared unlimited. William Pynchon doubtless was struck, as observers have been ever since, by the lushness and natural beauty of the valley. Formed out of the remains of a glacial lake dating back to the late Wisconsin period, the Connecticut basin comprises some 11,320 square miles of fertile and variegated countryside.

[13] William Pynchon to John Winthrop, Jr., June 2, 1636, *Winthrop Papers*, 3, p. 267.

[14] *Springfield Town Recs.*, 1, pp. 17–19.

[15] H. A. Wright, ed., *Indian Deeds of Hampden County*, Springfield, 1905, pp. 11–12.

The river itself meanders along a 410-mile course from the Canadian border down to Saybrook, Connecticut.[16] In the colonial period, the plains and lower terraces flanking the river provided rich alluvial soil, the result of periodic flooding. Rising gently on either side of the valley were the mountainous remains of the perimeter of the lake; these were now covered with both deciduous and evergreen trees. As the first Indian cultivators discovered, the upper terraces of the valley, particularly the bluffs and plateaus extending eastward from the future site of Springfield toward the mountains, offered considerably less promising farmland than did the meadows and plains near the river. The bluffs and plateaus of the east, in addition to their irregular and difficult topography, possessed soil covered by a thin acid litter that severely diminished its fertility.[17] The English settlers later referred to this area as the "pine barrens." The most desirable farmland within the corporate confines of Springfield was found at the confluence of the Agawam and Connecticut Rivers. Here the annual spring floods washed up silt deposits from the rivers to replenish the soil's nitrogen. Not surprisingly, this was the location William Pynchon found "incombred with Indians" upon his initial visit to the valley.

In addition to its obvious potential as a transportation center, the valley location offered the best environment in Massachusetts for cereal grain cultivation. While soil conditions elsewhere in the colony forced the settlers to rely on a combination of rye and Indian corn, in the Connecticut Valley wheat, oats, and barley all flourished. English grains grew successfully in New England only on the alluvial terraces bordering the Connecticut River from Middletown north.[18] Wheat (always the favored grain for bread), barley (needed for bread and broth as well as beer), and oats (for fodder) all were thriving in the upper valley towns well before 1660.[19] The region's climate offered particularly ideal growing conditions for wheat—wet springs followed by long, dry summers. If the climate of twentieth-century Springfield has not changed appreciably over the past three hundred years, the growing season usually averaged between 150 and 170 days, with average annual precipitation of

[16] For an overall description of the Connecticut River, see William F. Steke and Evan Hill, *The Connecticut River*, Middletown, Conn., 1972.

[17] Louis Seig, "Concepts of Change and the Historical Method in Geography: The Case of Springfield, Massachusetts," Ph.D. dissertation, University of Minnesota, 1968, pp. 55–57.

[18] Russell, *A Long, Deep Furrow*, p. 42; Robert A. Gross, "Culture and Cultivation: Agriculture and Society in Thoreau's Concord," *Journal of American History*, 69 (1982), pp. 59–60.

[19] Account Books, 1–2.

just under fifty inches. The first frost rarely came before the mid-October displays of resplendent foliage. The only real drawback for agriculturalists and traders alike was that winters could be severe; and even in normal years, freezing temperatures usually prevailed for at least four months. During particularly frigid winters, even the wide and swift-flowing Connecticut River froze solid. This may have occurred with unusual frequency in the settlement period, as some geographers now believe that the seventeenth century was a quasi ice age, with exceptionally cold and prolonged winters. Under normal conditions, the ground began to thaw after mid-March and the area was usually frost-free by mid-April.[20]

In addition to its potential as a trading post and an environment for raising cereal grains, Springfield offered equally promising conditions for livestock husbandry. The area's extensive pasturage meant that beef, pork, and horses could profitably be raised for the export market. Having grown up in the livestock-orientated wood pastures of East Anglia, Pynchon was determined to recreate in America the dual foundation of English farming: livestock, with grassland to feed it; and bread-grain for the family.[21] Springfield's original incorporation agreement underscored the importance accorded to raising livestock. The first inhabitants alloted two acres of new mowing land for each head of neat cattle and twice that for every horse, "because estate is like to be improved in cattell, and such ground is aptest for theyr use."[22] As with any livestock husbandry, the problems of spring feed, summer grass, and winter fodder all required quick resolution. Wheat and rye straw make excellent cattle fodder, but barley straw does not. Most important of all, however, were the summer grasses. And, as the "starving time" of Springfield's first years revealed, the valley soil's richness would remain largely untapped without the introduction of the superior English grasses.

The paltry harvest of 1637 brought home this lesson to Pynchon. The following spring he described the famine's effect on man and beast alike: "In regard to the great straits the whole population was in, both of persons and cattle for 2 or 3 months together: The wants of the Plantation were such, that som were forced to give malt to piggs to save their lives, and those that had som English meale, and would have kept it, were faine to spend it for want of corne . . . and 3 or 4 were in Consultation to leave the Plantation

---

[20] Government Printing Office, *Climatic Atlas of the U.S.*, Washington, D.C., 1968, pp. 27–31.

[21] Russell, *A Long, Deep Furrow*, pp. 24–25.

[22] Morison, *Builders of the Bay Colony*, p. 345.

for a while, to earne their bread elsewhere, till corne might be had here." Writing in both the third and first persons, he related that: "Mr. Pynchon's wants were often soe great, that divers times he hath not had half a bushell of corne in his house for his family . . . Alsoe, my wife, walking more amongst my Cattle . . . professed that It was her dayly grief to see them in that poore starveing condition."[23] Soon thereafter Pynchon began the process of converting to English grasses. His account books show that he brought up thirty bushels of "Flanders grass seed" from Hartford. This was presumably red clover and it was later supplemented with white clover. (Both were eventually replaced by Timothy grass in the early eighteenth century.)[24]

The successful introduction of English grasses by the early 1650s allowed Springfield to become the first major livestock-producing area in colonial Massachusetts. The Pynchons raised both hogs and cattle for market, stall-feeding the latter.[25] The hogs were usually slaughtered and packed in Springfield itself, while the cattle were taken on the hoof to Warehouse Point at Hartford. The brackish water at Hartford was used to pack the beef for overseas shipment. After midcentury, the Pynchons' drovers also herded cattle from the rich pastures of Hadley and Hatfield and took them overland to markets in Boston.[26]

William Pynchon was equally methodical in building up the town's labor supply. With the departure before 1641 of all but two of the original signatories to the town covenant, he immediately began to recruit indentured servants from Boston and London. Typically these servants arrived under direct consignment to the founder. He thereupon sold their remaining terms of service to one of his fellow villagers, often one of his sons-in-law, Henry Smith or Elizur Holyoke. On September 9, 1650, Hugh Dudley signed an indenture with Pynchon. In the agreement, Dudley, apparently captured in Scotland during the Cromwellian wars, "did covenant promise and grant to and with William Pynchon of Springfield in New England merchant . . . for and duringe the tearme of five yeares."[27] His new master then "assigned and set [Dudley] over to Mr. Henry Smith of Springfield for the said tearme of 5 yeeres." Smith agreed to "allow [Dudley] three pounds and ten shillings per yeare, to find him apparell: and to endevor at the end of his tyme to provide

---

[23] Mason Green, *Springfield, 1636–1886*, Springfield, 1888, pp. 29–30.
[24] Russell, *A Long, Deep Furrow*, pp. 29–30, 130.
[25] *Ibid.*, p. 61.
[26] Account Books, 1, p. 273; 5, pp. 19, 415.
[27] *Pynchon Court Rec.*, p. 224.

him a convenient allottment of land." On the same day another Scot, James Wells, signed an indenture with Pynchon for "the tearme of nine yeares."[28] This contract was likewise turned over to Smith. A third Scot, Edward Foster, was indentured to Pynchon for a term of nine years. Elizur Holyoke received this contract. Pynchon also apprenticed out other servants for the purpose of learning a trade. Hoping one day to become a weaver, on October 15, 1650, Samuel Terry "with the consent of my present master, William Pynchon of Springfield, gentleman, have put my self an apprentense to Benjamin Cooly of Springfield weaver . . . [for] three yeeres 6 months."[29]

Upon completion of their apprenticeships, these men—and most of the town's other inhabitants as well—became employees of William Pynchon. The labor needs of Springfield's founder were manifold. His fur-trading activities demanded the placement of agents throughout the valley, and marketing required extensive use of canoemen, teamsters, coopers, blacksmiths, and common laborers. Almost all men worked at least occasionally at one or more of these tasks. Pynchon constructed a warehouse at Enfield falls immediately below the highest point of navigation on the east side of the Connecticut River, approximately seven miles south of Springfield. He likewise built or rented warehouses in Hartford, Middletown, and New London. [See Connecticut Valley map.] The canoemen who carried goods to and from the warehouses usually traveled by canoes made either from birchbark or a hollowed-out log.[30] Pynchon also needed coopers to build barrels in which to ship furs, pork, and beef, as well as smiths to construct agricultural implements, and common laborers to string the wampum used as Indian currency. Moreover, his burgeoning fields increasingly needed farmhands and tenants, particularly by the late 1640s.[31] Pynchon revealed the scope of his work force in a letter written in 1644 to Stephen Day, who at the time was a mining prospector in the employ of John Winthrop, Jr.: "you write for butter and cheese [but] it is not to be had in all our plantation. I spend it as fast as I make it, because I have much resort and many workmen, which eate it as soone as I have it."[32]

A group profile of the inhabitants entered on the 1646 tax list

[28] *Ibid.*, p. 225.

[29] *Ibid.*, pp. 226–227.

[30] Harold Roger King, "The Settlement of the Upper Connecticut River Valley to 1675," Ph.D. dissertation, Vanderbilt University, 1965, pp. 225–226.

[31] William Pynchon Account Book.

[32] William Pynchon to Stephen Day, October 8, 1644, *Winthrop Papers*, 4, p. 495.

underscores the central importance of William Pynchon to the town's economy. Of the thirty-nine men on this list (out of an overall town population of one hundred men, women, and children), twenty-five remained in Springfield permanently. Three died within the next decade. Of the fourteen who emigrated, one later returned. Fifteen of the twenty-two men who remained in the town derived a substantial portion of their income as employees of either William Pynchon or his son John. Moreover, twelve of those who stayed would at one time or another experience serious indebtedness problems with the Pynchons.

As these men became the Pynchons' employees, they became their customers as well. The general store opened by William quickly became the central wholesale and retail outlet in the upper valley. The store consisted of a palisaded warehouse built on the west side "over agaynst Agawam."[33] Indians canoed down the river and its tributaries with the furs they had trapped to exchange them for wampum, blankets, coats, cotton cloth, axes, knives, and the like. Pynchon's workers then packed the furs into hogsheads, which were either teamed or taken by canoe to the warehouse at Enfield falls. At the falls, coasting vessels picked up the furs for shipment to Boston, whence they were forwarded by sailing packet to the fur market in London. In return, Pynchon imported textiles, tools, and medicines for sale in his general store.[34] As his entrepôt expanded, Pynchon's economic hold over the village's inhabitants grew to the point where, according to Bernard Bailyn, "he could rightly have considered his role that of a manorial lord."[35]

In 1641 this authority was enhanced by Springfield's secession from the colony of Connecticut. Pynchon had been charged by the Connecticut General Court with the task of purchasing badly needed corn from the neighboring Nonotuck Indians. He believed that the Indians' asking price was too high and refused to deal with them until it was lowered. With the colony's half-starved inhabitants clamoring for the corn, the General Court rebuked Pynchon for the delay. Following an opinion the magistrates had solicited from the Reverend Thomas Hooker of the Hartford Church, they fined him forty bushels of corn. The Court also publicly accused him of trying to monopolize the Indian trade. Hooker declared that Pynchon deferred the sale "that he should have all the trade to himselfe, and have all the corne in his owne hands . . . and so rack the country

---

[33] Morison, *Builders of the Bay Colony*, p. 357.

[34] William Pynchon Account Book.

[35] Bernard Bailyn, *The New England Merchants in the Seventeenth Century*, New York, 1964, pp. 54–55.

at his pleasure."[36] Pynchon defended his actions by citing passages from Sir John Fortescue's *On the Laws of England*. He had earlier attacked the granting of fur monopolies as an unreasonable restraint of trade; now he again preached free market principles in ridiculing the ancient "just price" doctrine. The Indians, he argued, knew full well that the demand for corn was great after the poor harvest in 1637. They intended, therefore, to hold out for as high a price as they thought the market would bear—regardless of the General Court's preoccupation with inherent value and the unlawfulness of usury.[37] But all these arguments were of no avail; the magistrates refused to abate the fine or retract the condemnation. Their rigidity, however, proved costly. It provoked Pynchon into seeking and gaining formal readmission into Massachusetts. On February 14, 1639, "the Inhabitants of Agawam uppon Quinnettecot" asserted that they had "by Gode's providence fallen into the line of the Massachusets Jurisdiction."[38] The reentry of Agawam, the settlement's initial name, henceforth gave the community an east-west rather than a north-south axis. Instead of simply being one of several rising towns in Connecticut, Springfield became the westernmost outpost of Massachusetts. This location afforded Pynchon an autonomy he would not have enjoyed in Connecticut and, more significant, conferred new importance on the plantation as the sole representative of Massachusetts in the valley for almost two decades.[39]

The community's first official act after reentering Massachusetts proved prophetic. William Pynchon was named magistrate and given extraordinary powers. The normal authority magistrates possessed included power to probate wills, hold petty sessions, and try all causes not involving loss of life or limb. Magistrates performed the judicial functions of discovery, indictment, trial, and sentencing. They also inflicted corporal punishment and administered oaths. Puritan jurisprudence, like that of England itself, had not yet arrived at a clear-cut distinction between the prosecutorial and adjudicative functions of the bench. And, as John M. Murrin has pointed out, "To judge from their behavior, New England magistrates consciously imitated what they evidently regarded as the

---

[36] Morison, *Builders of the Bay Colony*, pp. 352–353; William Pynchon to John Haynes, May 2, 1639, *Proceedings of Mass. Hist. Soc.*, 48 (1915), pp. 40–41.

[37] Morison, *Builders of the Bay Colony*, p. 354.

[38] *Pynchon Court Rec.*, p. 203; Simeon E. Baldwin, "The Secession of Springfield from Connecticut," *Publications of the Colonial Society of Massachusetts*, 12 (1908), pp. 55–82.

[39] Seig, "Concepts of Change," p. 96.

most progressive and efficient feature of the whole system, the trend toward summary justice. In a culture as addicted to guilt as Puritan New England, they succeeded overwhelmingly in criminal law, but they had to yield ground over civil disputes which lacked comparable internalized sanctions." While England was "groping toward an adversarial system of justice," in the "strict technical sense of the term, criminal justice in the orthodox colonies was inquisitorial." The criminal law in Massachusetts sought not only to protect against forcible seizure of goods and violence to the person, but to punish sins as well. Seventeenth-century New England jurisprudence, as a conflation of common law and scriptural injunctions (the Ten Commandments), made adultery and blasphemy capital crimes, but not the crimes against property that constituted the overwhelming majority of English capital offenses. Magistrates, accordingly, punished sinners as well as criminals.[40]

In addition to these already impressive traditional magisterial duties, William Pynchon, also received domain over "what ever else may tend to the Kinges peace, and the manifestation of our fidelity to the Bay Jurisdiction and the restraining of any that shall molest Gode's lawes: or lastely whatsoever else may fall within the power of an assistant." Both the execution and substance of this act were illegal under Massachusetts law. According to legal historian Joseph H. Smith, "the sole power to establish courts or grant judicial powers resided in the General Court."[41] Moreover, the enlarging clause, "what ever else may tend to the Kinge's peace," is not customarily included in magistracy authorizations. Pynchon proceeded to hold courts with no *de jure* status for the next two-and-one-half years. In June 1641 the Massachusetts General Court officially validated his actions. In May 1642 he was chosen to be an assistant to the General Court, thereby rendering the town's 1639 commission superfluous.[42] Pynchon had no formal legal training to aid him in fulfilling his judicial functions, and the only law books we know he owned were Michael Dalton's *Country Justice* and Sir John Fortescue's *On the Laws of England*.[43]

Pynchon likewise organized and led the area's militia and served as moderator for all the town meetings of Springfield, as the settlement was officially renamed in 1641. In 1648 the General Court

[40] John M. Murrin, "Magistrates, Sinners, and a Precarious Liberty: Trial by Jury in Seventeenth–Century Massachusetts," in David D. Hall, John M. Murrin, and Thad W. Tate, eds., *Essays in Honor of Edmund S. Morgan*, New York, 1983.

[41] *Pynchon Court Rec.*, pp. 90, 203.

[42] *Mass. Recs.*, 1, p. 345; 2, p. 2; 3, p. 230; 4, Part 1, p. 49.

[43] *Pynchon Court Rec.*, p. 31.

authorized him "to make freemen, in the towne of Springfield, of those that are in covenant and live according to their profession." Believing his daily presence necessary for Springfield's survival, Pynchon petitioned the Court to release him from compulsory attendance at its sessions. On May 9, 1649, "Att the request of Mr. William Pinchon, the [General Court] consented with [him] for his dismission from the further attending on the services of this Courte."[44]

Whether or not Pynchon's continued presence was necessary for the town's survival, his taxes were. He regularly paid over half of the annual tax load and also served as the credit agency of first access for the local government. Of the "voluntary rate" of £41 in January 1639, he paid £21. For an additional levy at the same time, he contributed £24 out of £40. He likewise furnished the necessary capital to build the meetinghouse and the gristmills, as well as to pay the Indians for the town plot. In return, he received land grants and other emoluments for persevering "at greate personall adventures" in establishing the town while others "fell off for feare of the difficulties."[45]

By 1646 these grants, in addition to Pynchon's normal allotments, gave him and his kinsmen command over the town's best available land. Although the community possessed some of the most fertile and productive land in the Connecticut Valley, this acreage was concentrated in a few relatively small areas. These included four square miles on the west side of the Connecticut River, two square miles south of the town center, and something less than two square miles north of the center. As we have seen, much of the remainder of the land, especially on the east side, was composed of woodlands, unimprovable pine barrens, marshes, and terrain so rugged as to be useless for farming. Within a decade of the town's founding, most of the acreage that was both tillable and accessible—in particular the lush alluvial meadows of the west side—was in the hands of William Pynchon and his two sons-in-law. The three men held 510 acres, roughly a quarter of the alloted lands. Of the forty-two landowners in Springfield, Pynchon, with 237 acres, had the largest holding. William Vaughan's six acres were the smallest allotment. After the holdings of Pynchon, Smith, and Holyoke, the next largest holding was the Reverend George Moxon's sixty-seven acres. The median holding was less than sixty acres.[46]

William Pynchon's tenure as lord of this emerging manorial economy was cut short by his return to England in 1652. The catalyst

[44] *Mass. Recs.*, 2, p. 224; 3, p. 158.
[45] *Springfield Town Recs.*, 1, pp. 157, 160–161.
[46] *Ibid.*, 1, pp. 157, 190–191.

to his departure, surprisingly, was a theological dispute with the Massachusetts General Court. While Pynchon's actions in the New World had been predominantly those of a hard-driving merchant, he returned in the early 1650s to the religious preoccupations of his youth. He penned a tract that was published in 1650 under the title, *The Meritorious Price of Our Redemption*. In it Pynchon attempted to explain his understanding of the atonement, arguing that man's salvation had been achieved through the perfect obedience of Christ, not by the Passion. The crucifixion was the work of men, not a result of the wrath of God. Christ did not, therefore, descend into Hell for the purpose of universal redemption—His perfect life had been sufficient to that end. By emphasizing the redemptive nature of Christ's life instead of His death, Pynchon undercut orthodox Puritanism's central tenet: that by taking men's sins upon himself and dying for them, Christ had saved the elect from Adam's curse. The Springfield leader thus placed himself in accord with the English latitudinarian or "Socinian" writers whose works were widely regarded as antitrinitarian. The Socinians, as Philip F. Gura has recently pointed out, "claimed that trinitarians abused the gift of reason in their arguments for a triune God and insisted that a mind unshackled by ecclesiastical authority would find in the Bible a Christ who, rather than being a part of the godhead, was a mere man, albeit one whom God had greatly exalted so that his moral example would inspire emulation."[47] Pynchon followed the lead of these religious rationalists, demanding greater toleration for heterodox opinions and less stringent tests of faith, tests always rendered suspect by the innate fallibility of all men, ministers and magistrates included. This individualistic and antiauthoritarian biblicism was scarcely calculated to set well with the coastal magistrates, acutely aware as they were about being caught in the crossfire between English Presbyterians and Congregationalists. Immediately upon reading *The Meritorious Price*, the members of the General Court branded it heretical and ordered Pynchon to recant. Publicly declaring that they did "utterly dislike it and detest it as erronious and daingerous," the assistants ordered that the tract be

[47] Gura, " 'The Contagion of Corrupt Opinions' in Puritan Massachusetts: The Case of William Pynchon," *WMQ*, 39 (1982) p. 479. That early New England was religiously, as well as socially, diverse is highlighted by Gura's observation that there is "little doubt that the Connecticut Valley harbored a small but active group of Puritan rationalists . . . whose presence suggests that historians have underestimated the great variety of Puritan thought in New England." *Ibid.*, p. 490. This comment also suggests a link between religious toleration and commercial orientation, two themes that would continue to be linked in Springfield for the remainder of the colonial period.

burnt by the colony's marshal in the Boston marketplace. So implacable was the Court that it refused even to record the objections of Pynchon's few defenders.[48] Attempting to find some common ground, at the next General Court session in May 1651 Pynchon "conferred with the Reverend Mr. Cotton, Mr. Norrice, and Mr. Norton, about some points of the greatest consequence in my booke, and I hope I have so explained my meaning to them as to take off the worst construction."[49] Still not satisfied, the Court deferred judgment, an action which was repeated the following October. At that time the magistrates made it clear that Pynchon would have to recant his views before the May session or be officially censured. Rather than submit to this indignity, the Springfield leader chose to go back to England. His son-in-law Henry Smith and the minister George Moxon made the same decision.[50]

William Pynchon's return to England did not sever his ties with Springfield. His son John remained in Massachusetts and quickly stepped into the leadership vacuum left by William's departure. The valley's fur trade was booming as never before, and the elder Pynchon could now coordinate the merchandising of beaver in the London marketplace. From his new home in the Buckinghamshire County village of Wraysbury, William (while continuing his theological ruminations) worked at the always difficult problem of securing credit.[51] The magnitude of the trade is suggested by a bond signed on May 24, 1662. In it he wrote "I, William Pynchon . . . gentleman, am firmly bound to William Bower of London . . . for three hundred pounds, legal money of England." Two days earlier, Pynchon had given Bower a bond for £80, also for the purpose of obtaining credit on Fleet Street.[52] With William superintending the family's trading activities in England, John Pynchon expanded both his marketing network and his domain over the now nearly 120 Springfield inhabitants. What William sowed, John would reap.

---

[48] *Mass. Recs.*, 4, Part 1, p. 29; Morison, *Builders of the Bay Colony*, pp. 370–373.

[49] *Mass. Recs.*, 4, Part 1, pp. 29–30, 48–49.

[50] *Pynchon Court Rec.*, p. 29.

[51] Morison, *Builders of the Bay Colony*, p. 375.

[52] Bond, William Pynchon to William Bower, May 24, 1662, photoduplicated copy, CVHM; Bond, William Pynchon to William Bower, May 22, 1662, photoduplicated copy, CVHM.

- *Chapter 2* •

Dominance

"Come, come, I'll show unto thy sense
Industry hath its recompense."
Anne Bradstreet, "The Flesh and the Spirit"

WHEN JOHN PYNCHON died in 1703, the Reverend Solomon Stoddard of Northampton eulogized him as a "Father to the Country." In a moving oration, the Northampton divine lamented that "a great man is fallen this day in our Israel. . . . God has removed one that has been a long while Serviceable. That has been improved about Public Service for above *Fifty Years*: he has been Serviceable unto the Country in general, and in special among our selves. He hath had the principal management of our Military Affairs, and our Civil Affairs: and laboured much in the setling of most of our Plantations, [he] has managed things with Industry, Prudence and Moderation. He hath been careful, in time of War, and as there has been occasion, he has been a Peace Maker among us, and helpfull in composing of differences: he has discountenanced Rude and Vicious Persons, bearing his Testimony against them." Stoddard concluded his memorial by observing that Pynchon "had great influence upon men in Authority Abroad, and upon the People at home, and had more experience by far, than any among us."[1]

Solomon Stoddard's paternalistic metaphor was well-taken. John Pynchon had indeed been a "Father of the Country" during the preceding half-century. While William Pynchon's efforts brought Springfield into being, John's developmental activities did likewise for the remainder of the upper valley settlements. He founded, financed, and helped govern every community established in western Massachusetts during the second half of the seventeenth century. These developmental activities and his generally decent and even-handed treatment of those financially dependent upon him allowed Pynchon to solidify and extend the control over Springfield

---

[1] Solomon Stoddard, *God's Frown in the Death of Usefull Men*, Boston, 1703, pp. 21–24.

that his father had bequeathed to him. Known to his fellow towns-men as the "Worshipful Major Pynchon," he dominated his town in ways utterly incompatible with "one-class" and communal images of early New England. Whether the measure was wealth, power, and status, or dress, bearing, and world-view, he stood visibly apart from the remaining inhabitants. The ornate and prepossessing Pynchon mansion gave architectural expression to this disparity. Consciously modeled on the country homes of the seventeenth-century English gentry, the mansion stood in stark contrast to the modest two and one-half-room dwellings that most villagers inhabited. As the town's physical appearance proclaimed, in Springfield the class structure was essentially two-tiered: John Pynchon and everyone else.[2]

And Stoddard's Mosaic allusion notwithstanding, Pynchon achieved this dominance not as a patriarch but as a patron. It was not so much Elizabethan Puritanism as it was mercantile capitalism that gave birth to the world of John Pynchon. As the manor economy was replaced by the market economy, master-servant ties were supplanted by those of employer and employee.[3] The transition from the world of the manor to the world of the market, as Pynchon's experience reveals, came through the agency of the patron-client bond. The patron-client relationship harkened back to the manor by its emphasis on person-to-person ties, but even more it anticipated the triumph of contractualism and the cash nexus by its preeminently economic nature. Patron-client ties occupied the middle ground between feudalism and capitalism, and they allowed the peasants of the sixteenth century to become the wage-earners of the eighteenth.

John Pynchon's success derived from his ability to forge both corporate and private patronage bonds. He simultaneously dominated public life in Springfield (and in the upper valley generally) while establishing strong financial claims over more than half the town's individual citizens. In 1652, after he assumed ownership of his father's approximately three hundred acres and lucrative fur-trading network, the General Court selected Pynchon to serve on the magistrate's commission.[4] By 1665 he had parlayed these early advantages into positions of economic and political dominance. He

---

[2] The most palpable expression of this disparity was the £8,446 estate left by Pynchon at his death in 1703. As we will see below, almost half of Springfield's 17th-century decedents left estates valued at less than £100; for Pynchon's estate, see HCPC Rec., Box 19, no. 40.

[3] Allen, *In English Ways*, p. 151.

[4] *Pynchon Court Rec.*, pp. 227–228.

simultaneously filled the positions of magistrate, judge of the county court of Hampshire, permanent moderator of the town meeting, and captain of the militia. First elected as Springfield's deputy to the General Court in 1659, Pynchon followed this selection with appointment as judge of the newly created Hampshire County court in 1662. Three years later he was elected magistrate and held that position until the colony's first charter was suspended in 1684. In 1661, during their annual meeting to choose officers for the forthcoming year, Springfield's inhabitants selected Pynchon as "Moderator for all Towne meetings the yeare ensueing"—a procedure that continued without break until 1694.[5] In equally rapid succession he received commissions in the militia: lieutenant in 1653, captain in 1657, sergeant major in 1671, and elevation to the rank of colonel during King Philip's War (1675–76).[6]

Militia leaders in the Connecticut Valley commanded much greater authority than they did in eastern towns. Because of the almost continuous threat of Indian attack after 1675, the decisions of militia officers directly affected the safety and well-being of all inhabitants. In a letter requesting gunpowder from Boston in 1690, Pynchon emphasized that "we are dayly alarmed of" possible Indian assaults. In a similar letter eight years later, he underscored the extent to which the Indian threat disrupted the rhythms of daily existence: "we Cannot with safety follow out ourselves in the Fields. We dare not live upon our Lands that lie a little Remote from the body of our Towne; the Countrye is putt to Great Charge in maintaining Garrison Souldiers, and also for pursueing after them when they have done hurt."[7] The Indians and their French allies were fully aware of the valley settlers' reliance on Pynchon's leadership. He told his cousins in Hartford, Samuel Willys and John Allyn, that "Stephen Lee reported here that the French and Indians had a special aime to this Towne and a particular designe against me."[8]

The Indians' view of Pynchon's importance was not misplaced. He was the essential cog in the governmental machinery of western Massachusetts. This role derived from Pynchon's position as mediator or "gatekeeper" between the Connecticut Valley and Boston.

[5] *Springfield Town Recs.*, 1, p. 281; 2, pp. 197, 339. Michael Zuckerman explores the moderator's power over town meetings in *Peaceable Kingdoms*, pp. 162–165.

[6] *Pynchon Court Rec.*, p. 37.

[7] John Pynchon to Major General Wait Winthrop, July 17, 1690, Winthrop Mss.; John Pynchon and Samuel Patrigg to Governor Bellomont, July 26, 1698, British Public Record Office, C.O. S/1041 1 (1v) 639, typescript copy, CVHM.

[8] John Pynchon to Samuel Willys and John Allyn, February 24, 1690, Edes Ms., Mass. Hist. Soc.

Mediators, according to anthropologists, are those who link the local world to the outside world, guarding and controlling access each way. Those in the locality desiring access to the metropolis, or those at the provincial level needing to implement public policy in the village, must deal through—and reward—the mediator. Much like the gentry of seventeenth-century England, land magnates in nineteenth-century Italy, or "padrones" in twentieth-century Andalusia or Castile, John Pynchon served as the indispensable middleman in implementing public policy. As magistrate, he held the highest position in the local community and also sat on the governor's council in Boston. Local and provincial power reinforced each other. Because he alone occupied the formal offices that linked the local and provincial systems, Pynchon functioned as a mediator between the community and the rest of New England until the Crown suspended the first charter in 1684.[9]

This role was available to Pynchon because of the parochial nature of seventeenth-century New England towns, even those as highly commercialized as Springfield. The locus of men's daily actions—and thoughts—rarely extended beyond the community's boundaries. Few villagers who were not teamsters or canoemen had reason to travel to other towns, newspapers were few, and communications by letter were usually the prerogative of the gentry. As Kenneth Lockridge's study of literacy in colonial New England has revealed, less than 60 percent of men in seventeenth-century Massachusetts could read fluently. Moreover, less than 60 percent could write, 20 percent were semiliterate, and 20 percent were illiterate. Commenting on the implications of these findings, Lockridge emphasizes that access to the written word allowed elites to act as intermediaries between their illiterate fellow villagers and the outside world: "These data open the way to a new understanding of the respect shown for the sermon, for the minister, and indeed for any highly literate man in seventeenth-century New

[9] The anthropological literature which deals with mediators is extensive. See Sydel F. Silverman, "Patronage and Community-Nation Relationships in Central Italy," *Ethnology,* 4 (1965), pp. 172–188; Eric R. Wolf, "Aspects of Group Relations in a Complex Society: Mexico," *American Anthropologist,* 58 (1956), pp. 1065–1078; Clifford Geertz, "The Javanese Kijaji: The Changing Role of a Cultural Broker," *Comparative Studies in Society and History,* 2 (1960), pp. 228–249; also see T. H. Breen, "Persistent Localism," *WMQ* (1975), p. 9; Peter Laslett, "The Gentry of Kent in 1640," *Cambridge Historical Journal,* 9 (1947–1949), pp. 148–164. For an analysis of the magistrate's power, see John M. Murrin "Anglicizing an American Colony: The Transformation of Provincial Massachusetts," Ph.D. dissertation, Yale University, 1966; and Barbara A. Black, "The Judicial Power and the General Court in Early Massachusetts, 1634–1686," Ph.D. dissertation, Yale University, 1975.

England. They suggest that New Englanders once lived closer than
we have imagined to the credulous word-of-mouth world of the
peasant, closer to its absorbing localism, closer to its dependency
on tradition and on the informed few."[10] In addition, because it
was separated from Boston by over one hundred miles of forested,
often inaccessible terrain, Springfield's isolation from its colonial
government was even more complete.

John Pynchon, and mediators like him elsewhere in the colony,
bridged this distance by personal communications as well as official
correspondence with other gentry leaders. Unlike most villagers,
whose perceptions of their world were shaped by the immediacies
of what they saw and heard, the gentry actively followed and reported on colony-wide and even international developments. In
February of 1668 Pynchon thanked Connecticut Governor John
Winthrop for several (borrowed) London newspapers which
Winthrop had sent the Springfield leader to apprise him of affairs
in the mother country. During the 1680s Pynchon and Robert
Livingston of Albany exchanged information on the military ex-
ploits of Prince Louis of Baden, commander of the armies of the
Holy Roman Empire in Hungary against the Turks in 1689–1690.
Praising Prince Louis's daring, Pynchon noted that "The Imperi-
alists have taken Belgium and other places so that the Turks are
almost outed of Hungaria," which was "A Notable exploit of Prince
Louis, who with 3,000 horses attacked the Turks that Proved to be
. . . 15,000."[11] In like manner, Springfield learned of wars with the
Dutch and the machinations of rival political groups in London
from letters Pynchon received from Winthrop and Captain Sylvester Salisbury, Commander-in-Chief at Fort Albany.[12]

In concepts as basic as time, a perceptual gap stood between the
informed few and the remainder of the inhabitants. The annual
cycles of planting and harvesting grain governed most villagers'
comprehension of time. When Sarah Clark, unwed, testified before
the magistrate during an inquiry aimed at discovering the paternity

---

[10] Kenneth A. Lockridge, *Literacy in Colonial New England*, New York, 1974, p.
15.

[11] John Pynchon to Robert Livingston, January 16, 1689, Livingston Family Papers, Franklin Delano Roosevelt Library, Hyde Park, New York.

[12] John Winthrop, Jr. to John Pynchon, November 9, 1674, Winthrop Mss.; John
Pynchon to Captain Sylvester Salisbury, July 20, 1678, in E. B. O'Callaghan and
J. H. Brodhead, eds., *Documents Relating to the Colonial History of the State of New York*,
Albany, 1881, 13, p. 511. Darrett B. Rutman examines the problems of vertical and
horizontal spheres of integration in "The Social Web: A Prospectus for the Study
of the Early American Community," in W. L. O'Neill, ed., *Insights and Parallels:
Problems and Issues of American Social History*, Minneapolis, 1973, pp. 57–88.

of her child, she declared that Richard Barnard had "carnall knowledge of her Body last English harvest at the very beginning of Reaping Ry."[13] By contrast, specific months, days, and even hours—rather than agricultural seasons—formed John Pynchon's concept of time. He invariably wrote the exact calendar date and sometimes the time of day on all his correspondence. In Springfield, he was usually the only link between the Sarah Clarks and the outside world.[14]

John Pynchon's position of mediator was the necessary precondition for his role as patron. He became the instrument of General Court policy in western Massachusetts and his community's agent in Boston as well. When the Court wanted new plantations established in the Connecticut Valley, negotiations with Connecticut or the Mohawk Indians, or boundaries perambulated, John Pynchon was inevitably its choice. When, for example, the General Court voted to construct a new highway to Connecticut, the magistrates "refferd to Major Pynchon to order the said way to be laid out and well marked."[15] Similarly, in Boston, Pynchon articulated local issues. His townsmen knew that his access to provincial authorities could be translated into palpable benefits for Springfield in the form of land grants, tax abatements, or favorable rulings on boundary disputes. And because the colonial officials in Boston recognized Pynchon's influence in the Connecticut Valley, they heeded his recommendations.

In his memorial oration, Solomon Stoddard underscored the fundamentally reciprocal nature of Pynchon's mediating role as well as the enormous influence it brought at both the provincial and local levels. He asserted that Pynchon "had great influence upon men in Authority abroad, and upon the People at home." Men like Pynchon are "well respected, and upon that account capable to do abundance of Service; their proposals are much hearkened to by those that are in Supream Authority in the Country." The eulogist emphasized that this influence directly benefited all of the valley's inhabitants: "If [useful men] make a motion for the good of the places where they live, they are readily hearkened unto, their judgment and fidelity is relied on; they can do a man a kindness with their word" because "They can have access to those in

---

[13] *Pynchon Court Rec.*, p. 272.

[14] Pynchon lost this exclusivity of access after the Glorious Revolution. See Chapter 6.

[15] *Mass. Recs.*, 5, p. 394.

Chief Authority when others cannot; their word will be regarded when the word of others will not."[16]

Pynchon's principal task as the instrument of General Court policy in the valley—the coordination of relations with Connecticut—was greatly facilitated by his close friendship with Connecticut Governor John Winthrop. Pynchon's wife Amy, the daughter of former Connecticut Governor John Willys, spent over a year in Winthrop's care while recovering from an illness during the early 1650s. In expressing his gratitude for Winthrop's services as a physician, Pynchon wrote "my wife hath now been a Tabler with you above a yeare, besides all your Phisick and paines, I pray Sir let me know what the one and the other is worth, that I may sattisfie accordingly, and yet shall acknowledge my selfe as long as I live ingaged to you."[17] Pynchon continued in the following decades to turn to his friend for medical help. On December 19, 1660, he wrote that "my Son Joseph . . . is much trobled with a kind of hoarsness and dryness in his throate and yet not with any Cold that we can preceive. But a continuall kind of hemming and harsh dryness." In May 1661 the Springfield leader needed orthopedic advice regarding his daughter and the son of one of his workers. He asked Winthrop what to do about the "Lame boy" and "my daughter . . . [to] bring her legg to rights and straite."[18] Sometimes a note of grave concern accompanied these requests. On July 24, 1663, he wrote, "Sir we are bold to crave your advice concerning our young daughter about or neere one yeare and three quarters old, God having pleased to visit her with Illness: shee hath not been very well these 3 or 4 days but especially yesterday morning was taken with a greate looseness and vomiting which doth Continue much and exceedingly weaken her."[19]

John Pynchon and Governor Winthrop were also trading partners and often pooled their resources on joint economic ventures. Winthrop, along with Pynchon's influential cousins in Hartford, Samuel Willys and John Allyn, oversaw the transshipment of the Springfield merchant's grain and livestock. On April 6, 1658, Pynchon wrote Winthrop, "If Goodman Rogers should send any vessell for Corne before I returne hom, that you would please to direct them to have recourse to my Cousin Allyn."[20] On another occasion,

---

[16] *Usefull Men*, pp. 12–13.

[17] John Pynchon to John Winthrop, Jr., May 28, 1655, Winthrop Mss.

[18] John Pynchon to John Winthrop, Jr., May 23, 1661, Winthrop Mss.

[19] John Pynchon to John Winthrop, Jr., July 24, 1663, Boston Medical Library, typescript copy, CVHM.

[20] John Pynchon to John Winthrop, Jr., April 6, 1658, Winthrop Mss.

Pynchon expressed enthusiasm over a pending livestock deal, but, having no marketable animals, he told Winthrop that "for your position about Calves, I like well of it, if I could procure any worth the sending."[21]

These personal and commercial ties between Pynchon and Winthrop, combined with geographic proximity and the common threat of Indian danger, made the two men the spokesmen of their respective colonies. The Massachusetts General Court habitually called on Pynchon to act as an intermediary between the two governments. In March 1674 the Springfield leader wrote Winthrop for the purpose of "conveying it to you whereby you will understand what our Court [has] done."[22] Pynchon also personally oversaw negotiations aimed at resolving long-standing boundary disputes. Most important of all, when beleaguered Massachusetts needed military assistance from Connecticut during King Philip's War, it was "left with Major John Pynchon to treat with the Governour and council there for effecting the same."[23] The ferocious Indian assaults of the 1690s brought another request from the General Court for Pynchon to appeal to Connecticut's "friendly neighbourlyness" in an effort to secure more military aid. He wrote the Connecticut General Court that his government had "direct[ed me] to apply to your Honors . . . to supply with 60 men."[24]

Pynchon likewise served as the General Court's principal emissary to New York. In August 1664 he received a commission from the Court to travel to New York in order to coordinate military activities against the Dutch.[25] In 1689 he made a "long and tedious" journey to Albany, this time for the purpose of coordinating the New England and New York explanations of the overthrow of Governor Edmund Andros during the Glorious Revolution. Upon returning to Springfield, Pynchon informed the officials in Boston that "We have Indeavoured with al faithfulness to Manage the Negotiation you Imployed us about" and presented the colony with a bill for expenses of £219.[26]

Pynchon was equally indispensable as the Massachusetts colony's agent to the western Indians. Springfield's location and Pynchon's commercial ties with the Indians again made him the natural choice

[21] John Pynchon to John Winthrop, Jr., June 24, 1656, Winthrop Mss.

[22] John Pynchon to John Winthrop, Jr., March 23, 1674, Winthrop Mss.

[23] *Mass. Recs.*, 5, p. 171.

[24] John Pynchon to the Governor and Council of Connecticut, January 18, 1692, Edes Ms., Mass. Hist. Soc.

[25] *Mass. Recs.*, 4, Part 2, pp. 123–125.

[26] Mass. Archives, 35, p. 32.

for this position. As with Connecticut, whenever the Court needed to negotiate with the Indians, it turned to Pynchon. Most important in the wake of King Philip's War was the need to secure an alliance with the Mohawks against the hostile Wampanoags and Narragansetts. In April 1677 Pynchon and James Richards embarked on a "long, troublesome and hazardous journey" to Albany to negotiate with the Mohawks on behalf of both Massachusetts and Connecticut. Pynchon calculated his service and expenses to be valued at £128 and charged the colony accordingly.[27] By 1680, the Mohawk alliance still unconsummated, the Springfield leader once more travelled to Albany, "in order to the stopping of any invassions, depredation, and insolencys toward our neighbors, Indians and friends, that live within this jurisdiction."[28]

While negotiations with neighboring colonies and with the Indians were Pynchon's major diplomatic responsibilities, his principal domestic task was plantation-founding. In his eulogy of the Springfield magistrate, Solomon Stoddard emphasized that Pynchon had "laboured much in the setling of most of our Plantations," and rightly so. The General Court appointed him to head the commission of every town founded in western Massachusetts during the period from 1653 to 1702. In May 1653 the Court empowered Pynchon and two other men to organize the town of Northampton.[29] Six years later he formed a commission to establish the new settlement of Hadley.[30] During the same period, he also organized a commission to oversee settlement at Woronoco, the future Westfield. In May 1667 the magistrates called on Pynchon to superintend the founding of a new community, this time at Quabaug.[31] In similar fashion he was empowered to organize the settlements of Suffield in 1670, Northfield in 1671, Deerfield and Sunderland in 1673, Enfield in 1683, and Brimfield in 1701.[32]

The powers of these founding commissions were considerable. The commission members received authority to lay out the new settlements, admit inhabitants, grant lands, appoint selectmen, administer the freeman's oath, and govern the community until it was officially incorporated by the General Court. In 1656 Westfield's founding commission received authorization to "dispose of the land . . . to such men as they Saw fit, and what quantity they

---

[27] *Pynchon Court Rec.*, p. 43; *Mass. Recs.*, 5, pp. 138, 165–168.
[28] *Mass. Recs.*, 5, p. 299.
[29] *Usefull Men*, p. 22; *Mass. Recs.*, 4, Part 1, p. 136.
[30] *Mass. Recs.*, 4, Part 1, p. 368.
[31] *Ibid.*, 4, Part 2, p. 342.
[32] *Ibid.*, 4, Part 2, pp. 469, 528–529, 557; 5, pp. 410–411.

should give to any person whomsoever they in theire best discretion saw fit."[33] The Quabaug (Brookfield) commission likewise was empowered to "admitt inhabitants, grant lands, and to order all the prudentiall affayres of the place" until "the place shall be so farr setled with able men as that this Court may judge meete to give them full liberty of a township."[34] Of all these powers, easily the most significant was the authority to grant land to the prospective inhabitants. By determining the amount of acreage each man would receive, Pynchon and his fellow commission members directly fashioned the social structure of each new community.

The lifespans of the founding commissions, the interval between a town's settlement and its incorporation, averaged approximately ten years. When the General Court received an official petition for incorporation, the magistrates sought John Pynchon's opinion of its merits and, if he acquiesced, the petition was approved.[35]

While Pynchon was organizing the new valley towns in his public capacity, as a private citizen he was financing them. The only valley resident with significant credit resources, Pynchon routinely was called upon by prospective inhabitants to buy land from the Indians. He paid for this acreage with wampum, textiles, or tools from his general store. In turn, the patentees gave him a conveyance of lands in trust until they repaid the principal. More important, for his services, each new community also granted the Springfield entrepreneur extensive lands and allowed him to erect gristmills and sawmills within the settlement. In this manner Pynchon financed the establishment of the towns of Northampton, Hadley, Westfield, Deerfield, Northfield, Brookfield, Enfield, and Suffield.[36]

Many communities remained in Pynchon's debt for extended periods. He did not formally assign a settlement title to its land until he had received payment in full. Accordingly, it was in the settlers' best interest to repay their debt as quickly as possible—or risk erosion of their corporate autonomy. The fact that the period in which the loans were outstanding was usually coterminous with the life of the founding commissions made this autonomy especially precarious. Many communities were simultaneously economically and politically dependent on Pynchon for over a decade. He bought lands for Westfield during the mid-1660s, paying £50 to an Indian squaw named Paupsunnick for acreage on the south side of the

[33] *Springfield Town Recs.*, 1, p. 245.
[34] *Mass. Recs.*, 4, Part 2, p. 342.
[35] *Ibid.*, 4, Part 2, pp. 469, 528–529, 557; 5, pp. 410–411.
[36] *Ibid.*

Woronoco River.[37] An interval of twenty years passed, however, before the loan was repaid. On February 11, 1685, he formally assigned the title to the Westfield inhabitants: "I John Pynchon . . . Several yeeres since made a purchase of Lands at Westfield of the Indians for the Inhabitants of Westfield . . . to Paupsunnick I did truly pay for the same about fifty pounds which sum . . . I have [now] received of the Inhabitants . . . according to Each man's Proportion."[38] In September 1653 Pynchon paid 150 fathom of wampum, ten coats, and assorted small gifts for the purchase of Northampton's land. A decade later, the settlers having completed repayment, he assigned them title.[39] On three separate occasions between 1658 and 1662, the inhabitants of Hadley called on Pynchon to buy Indian lands. His expenses, totalling £78, were not fully repaid until eleven years after the initial transaction. It took Suffield's settlers fifteen years to complete their repayment. In 1670 Pynchon paid the Indian owner £40 for six square miles of land. It was not until April 10, 1685, however, that he closed out the account book entry: "For al Lands which I [bought] for the Inhabitants of Suffeild [for] forty pounds, and do hereby acknowledge . . . to be fully satisfied."[40] Nearly eleven years passed between purchase and assignment of the land for the town of Enfield. Pynchon bought the land for the settlers in 1683, but by 1694, £3 10s. of the £30 principal remained unpaid.[41]

In addition to his specific responsibilities as diplomat and plantation-founder, the General Court expected Pynchon to act on his own initiative on any issue touching the colony's interest. These initiatives often included a wide array of problems: supplying provisions for the royal fleet, paying bribes to Indian informants, or hiring mercenaries in time of war. In 1667 during the Anglo-Dutch wars, "by his oune voluntary contribution," Pynchon expressed "his sence of the then present distressed condition of his majestie's fleet in his plantations in the [Caribbean] Islands" by "put[ting] on board [an embarking ship] sixteen barrells of pork."[42] In 1673, in order to elicit intelligence on possible hostilities from neighboring Indians, Pynchon gave "[re]wards . . . [among] our Indians to Effect

[37] Wright, ed., *Indian Deeds*, p. 97; Hampden County Deeds, Volume AB (1636–1704), p. 53, Hampden County Court, Springfield.
[38] Hampden Co. Deeds, Volume AB, p. 53.
[39] *Ibid.*, Volume A (1638–1699), p. 15.
[40] Account Books, 2, p. 248.
[41] *Ibid.*, 6, Index, p. 15.
[42] *Mass. Recs.*, 4, Part 2, pp. 547–548.

it."[43] When faced with an insufficient number of troops to meet the Indian threat in the 1690s, he was "forced to Imploy . . . private Soldiers."[44] On a more prosaic level, when a carpenter proposed to build a bridge over the Quabaug River in Brookfield, Pynchon and John Winthrop collaborated in arranging its construction. Pynchon informed Winthrop that the carpenter "desired me to write to your Worship about it," as "he will Ingage to make a good Bridge for £20 . . . if he may be sure of his pay." In a request that emphasizes the conflation of public and private spheres in early New England, Pynchon asserted that "for my owne part I will willingly give 4 or 5£ toward it" if Winthrop could come up with a similar amount.[45]

John Pynchon did not go unrewarded for these services. Because both the local community and the provincial hierarchy saw Pynchon as the indispensable man, they rewarded him with land—the most highly prized commodity in seventeenth-century Massachusetts. This in turn increased his power, in both the local community and beyond. Local and provincial power reinforced each other, and the result was a spiral effect where power brought land and land brought more power. When Pynchon's home town allocated new acreage to its inhabitants, for example, he invariably received a disproportionate share. In a typical allotment, for the "inner commons" in 1699, Springfield awarded Pynchon 133 rods of mile-long strips; the next largest grantee, his nephew John Holyoke, received only 26 rods.[46] Through these land grants and by private purchase and mortgage foreclosures, Pynchon expanded his family's monopoly over Springfield's best land. He eventually owned over two thousand acres, including most of the town's genuinely first-rate land.[47] Similarly, other Connecticut Valley towns indebted to Pynchon for services rendered paid him back in lucrative land allotments. Usually, but not always, these grants were a direct result of his organization of the respective founding committees. And, as we saw earlier, these grants were often made in tandem with privileges for building gristmills and sawmills within the new community. In the

[43] John Pynchon to Gerrt Van Slichtenhorst, December 12, 1673, Livingston Family Papers, Roosevelt Library.

[44] Mass. Archives, 36, p. 439.

[45] John Pynchon to John Winthrop, Jr., December 24, 1666, Winthrop Mss.

[46] "Coppy of Mens' Lots in the 2d Division," April, 1699, Manuscripts Collection, Springfield Public Library.

[47] 1685 tax list, inscribed "Anno Dom. 1685. An Estimate of the Plantation, both of Mens' Houses and Lands, in Springfield," Tax Collector's Office, Springfield City Hall, hereafter cited as 1685 Tax List.

1680s the town of Enfield granted Pynchon 314 acres of land "for Severall years pains and Services as Committee for said Enfield."[48]

At the provincial level, Pynchon found the General Court equally generous. During the period from 1659 to 1685, he received over 8,170 acres from the Court for mediating services performed by him or his father William.[49] On November 12, 1659, "In answer to the petition of Capt. John Pynchon, the Court judgeth it meete to grant him one thousand acres." Seven years later, "for severall services past," he received an additional 500 acres.[50] On October 17, 1681, "in consideration of his paines formerly in runing our patent line," the Court awarded Pynchon an island on the Connecticut River below Enfield falls.[51] The fourth of June, 1685, was a particularly good day for the Springfield leader. First, the Court granted William Avery, Hezekiah Usher, and Pynchon 1,000 acres in the Connecticut Valley. Later that day, in answer to his petition, the Court granted "the quantity of eight miles square [5,120 acres] to Major John Pynchon."[52] Pynchon eventually owned extensive tracts in every Massachusetts town in the Connecticut Valley. In addition to his 2,000 acres in Springfield itself, he held 510 acres and both a sawmill and a gristmill at Suffield, 200 acres and a gristmill at Brookfield, 314 acres and both a sawmill and a gristmill at Enfield, and 120 acres at Deerfield.[53] Outside of the colony, Pynchon owned 2,788 acres at Groton, Connecticut, and part of the island of Antigua in the West Indies.[54]

After land grants, the most valuable emoluments available to mediators were trading monopolies, and one of these—the fur-trading franchise—played a decisive role in Pynchon's stunning

[48] Hampden Co. Deeds, Volume AB, p. 86.

[49] *Mass. Recs.*, 4, Part 1, p. 402; Part 2, p. 306; *ibid.*, 5, pp. 482–486; Mass. Archives, 45, p. 82. Pynchon also may have received an additional 1,000 acres from the Court after his extensive losses sustained during King Philip's War in 1675; see J. G. Holland, *History of Western Massachusetts*, Springfield, 1845, 1, p. 309. Moreover, Pynchon and two other men received a grant of ten square miles in 1659 during the abortive effort to establish a fur-trading post 40 miles west of Springfield; see Arthur H. Buffington, "New England and the Western Fur Trade, 1629–1675," *Transactions of the Col. Soc. Mass.*, 18 (1917), pp. 176–177. Theodore B. Lewis underestimates Pynchon's landholdings in "Land Speculation and the Dudley Council of 1686," *WMQ*, 31 (1974), pp. 255–272.

[50] *Mass. Recs.*, 4, Part 1, p. 402; Part 2, p. 306.

[51] *Ibid.*, 5, pp. 329–330.

[52] *Ibid.*, 5, pp. 482, 486.

[53] Hampden Co. Deeds, Volume AB, p. 86.

[54] Account Books, 2, pp. 238–239; Samuel Willys to Connecticut General Court, October 1687, "Private Controversies, 1642–1716," Ser. 1, Volume 3, Document 258, Connecticut State Library, Hartford.

commercial rise. Before the depletion of beaver in the late 1660s, the most lucrative monopoly in the Connecticut Valley was the fur trade. Because of their influence in the colonial government, William Pynchon and later John received fur monopoly rights. They in turn farmed out these privileges to selected agents at various locations throughout the valley.[55] Furs received by the agents were then sent to the Pynchon general store for eventual shipment to London.

John Pynchon's account books testify to the extraordinary magnitude of the fur trade. During the period from 1652 to 1674, he transshipped over 23,930 pounds of beaver to the London market. With the price of beaver skins averaging ten shillings per pound, he realized gross receipts during these years of approximately £11,965. Calculating his profit margin at one shilling per pound, John's total earnings for this period exceeded £1,196. In a society where the daily wage for a farm laborer averaged between sixteen and twenty pence, these profits represented an enormous sum. In addition to the beaver, Pynchon shipped over 7,000 pounds of moose skins, 400 otter skins, 718 muskrat, 315 "Foxes and Raccons," and lesser amounts of mink, marten, and lynx. In 1654 alone, Pynchon sent 3,723 pounds of beaver to his London agents—giving him gross receipts that year of £1,860.[56]

The halcyon days of the fur trade in the Connecticut Valley were over by the late 1650s. The volume of the trade declined somewhat sporadically thereafter, until King Philip's War brought an abrupt end to all commercial exchange between whites and Indians. Again, statistics tell the story. Between 1652 and 1658, John Pynchon shipped 13,917 pounds of beaver, or 58.2 percent of the total amount he merchandised. By 1663, he had exported 19,778 pounds or 82.6 percent of all the beaver he sent to England in the seventeenth century.[57]

Pynchon, as magistrate, enforced the monopoly rights he enjoyed as a private trader. Poachers risked the exceedingly punitive fines that the law allowed for these infractions. Samuel Fellows and Joseph Leonard learned this lesson to their dismay on March 28, 1671. Pynchon brought the two men before the county court over which he presided as quorum judge. He accused Fellows and Leon-

---

[55] Ruth A. McIntyre, "John Pynchon, Merchant and Colonizer of the Upper Connecticut Valley in the Seventeenth Century, A Study of the Business Practices of John Pynchon," unpublished Ms., CVHM.

[56] Account Books, 3, pp. 319–321.

[57] *Ibid.*

ard of two offenses: "buying of the Indians One Skin of Beaver against [the] Law" and selling the Indians "Strong Liquors." The respective punishments for the two offenses underscore the severity with which Pynchon and the General Court viewed unlicensed fur trading. The defendants received fines of £10 for violating the ordinance against selling liquor to the Indians—always considered a grave offense because it was "famously known how the Indians abuse themselves by excessive drinking of strong liquors." For "buying One Skin of Beaver" without a license, however, the two men were fined the immense sum of £100. Joseph Leonard may have pointed out Pynchon's conflict of interest in the proceedings, as the court slapped him with an additional £5 fine for his "contemptuous carriage particularly towards the Worshipfull Captain Pynchon."[58]

By the late 1650s, fur merchants in Massachusetts recognized that long-term survival of the trade depended on expansion into the Hudson Valley. With the eastern rivers almost entirely depleted and the Connecticut Valley nearly so, the New Englanders would have to tap the fur domains then controlled by the Dutch. No one understood this reality better than did John Pynchon, and he set out to do something about it. In 1659 he and Major William Hawthorne of Salem and a number of merchants in Boston formed a company designed to establish overland trading routes to the upper Hudson Valley. The company attempted to combine Boston capital with Pynchon's trapping network, friendly relations with the western Indians, and proximity to Fort Orange (Albany). Expecting opposition from the Dutch fur traders, the Hawthorne Company, as it was eventually named, resorted to subterfuge. They told the (presumably incredulous) Dutch that the company intended to settle a small plantation midway between Springfield and the Hudson River for the sole purpose of raising cattle to supply the Dutch at Fort Orange. In August 1659 Pynchon accompanied Hawthorne to Fort Orange in a vain attempt to convince the Dutch of their good intentions. In 1662 the company made an abortive effort to revive the plan, and this time they succeeded in constructing a small trading post on the Housatonic River. But the Dutch were still unyielding and again made clear their determination to keep New England merchants out of New Netherland. By this time Pynchon had wearied of his fellow members' general lack of resolve, and he withdrew from the project. He charged the company £60

---

[58] *Pynchon Court Rec.*, pp. 235, 271.

for his journey to Fort Orange and for the "loss of tyme and disappointment."[59]

England's conquest of New Netherland in 1664 removed the threat of Dutch opposition to the expansion of the Massachusetts fur trade, and in the early 1670s Pynchon tried again. He joined forces with Governor John Leverett and William Paine, one of the Boston merchants involved in the Hawthorne project, and petitioned the General Court for an extensive land grant in western Massachusetts. The Court ruled favorably on the petitioners' request, granting them ten square miles of land near the colony's western border. But with the fury of King Philip's War about to explode on the New Englanders, the time was not propitious for new fur-trading schemes.[60] The failure of the Hawthorne and Paine projects to secure entry into the Hudson Valley sounded the death knell for the Massachusetts fur trade.[61]

The abrupt termination of the fur trade wreaked havoc with John Pynchon's economic enterprises. Because most of his wealth was in the form of fixed capital investments—land, mills, ships, mines—he relied on the fur trade for needed liquid assets. Pelts could quickly and easily be converted into specie, wampum, or bills of exchange and thus represented the seventeenth-century equivalent of ready cash. In February 1672 Pynchon emphasized the severe limitations on his trading imposed by this money shortage. In a letter to his son Joseph, then beginning a career as a physician in Uxbridge, England, he wrote: "I am forced not to send to England for any goods this yeare: I have noe trade as formerly and am altogither out of that capacity of helping with Monny."[62] Three years later, his commercial affairs still in disarray, Pynchon again wrote his son, reiterating that he was unable to send any money and in fact might need to borrow some: "it may be you are in expectations of some help from me, which I should readily afford If I could, but am noe ways able to doe any thing, having been wholy out of Trade ever since you went from this Country [and I] am now reduced to our best Contrivance for our Comfortable Living and much adoe to make things hold out. So that I am sometimes almost ready to send to you for some of that I reserved

[59] McIntyre, "John Pynchon," pp. 55–57.

[60] Douglas Edward Leach, *Flintlock and Tomahawk: New England in King Philip's War*, New York, 1966.

[61] Bailyn, *New England Merchants*, pp. 54–55.

[62] John Pynchon to Joseph Pynchon, February 1, 1672, Wetmore Family Papers, Yale University Library.

to be paid me yearly."[63] But while the fur trade was gone, Pynchon still had his landholdings and the general store. As things turned out, these would be more than enough.

Even before the final depletion of the beaver, Pynchon had made a major decision—to shift the basis of his exports from furs to agricultural products. By the mid-1660s, because of its capacity for large-scale production of both wheat and livestock, the Connecticut Valley was becoming the breadbasket of New England. And because of his extensive commercial network, it was Pynchon who did most of the merchandising of these foodstuffs. Farmers from as far north as Deerfield, as far east as Brookfield, and as far west as Westfield brought their surplus pork and grain to his general store. He also accumulated the pork, wheat, and barley from his own farms and from the fields of his tenants. Unlike his earlier tendency to send most of his exports to Hartford or Boston, Pynchon now increasingly turned toward the sugar islands of the West Indies.[64]

The explosive growth of the British West Indies—Barbados, Jamaica, and the Leeward Islands—allowed Pynchon to reestablish his commercial preeminence by trading foodstuffs for rum. The radically labor-intensive nature of sugar cane cultivation induced planters to import massive quantities of flour and livestock rather than detailing precious slave labor for raising food. The rum, molasses, and sugar Pynchon received in exchange for his foodstuffs likewise afforded him a monopoly of these products back in the Connecticut Valley.[65]

Recognizing that the profits to be made from rum rivaled those made earlier in the fur trade, Pynchon attempted to establish his own sugar colony in the early 1680s. Together with his Hartford associates, Samuel Willys and Richard Lord, Pynchon founded what was called the "Cabbage Tree Plantation" on the island of Antigua.[66] The three men went to considerable pains in setting up their incongruously named colony with slaves, foodstuffs, and livestock. Antigua had long been among the least promising of the Leeward Islands, both because of its aridity and proximity to the French sugar islands.[67] These barriers, along with some internecine quarreling over financing between Willys and Lord, eventually

[63] John Pynchon to Joseph Pynchon, June 30, 1675, Historical Society of Pennsylvania, Philadelphia, typescript copy, CVHM.

[64] Account Books, 3, 5.

[65] Richard S. Dunn, *Sugar and Slaves: The Rise of the Planter Class in the English West Indies, 1624–1713*, New York, 1973.

[66] Wyllys Ms., 2, p. 60, Connecticut Historical Society, Hartford.

[67] Dunn, *Sugar and Slaves*, pp. 117–148.

doomed the colony's prospects.[68] But despite this setback, the West Indies market remained a bonanza for New England merchants, and by the mid-1680s the sugar islands were the destination for the major portion of John Pynchon's exports.[69]

Land speculation was an equally attractive source of revenue for Pynchon in the waning days of the fur trade. Here he engaged in speculative ventures with men as highly placed in the Massachusetts political structure as Governor John Leverett. Together the two men purchased extensive tracts in the Connecticut Valley for subsequent resale to private individuals.[70] Dealings between the two men were doubtless eased by kinship ties. Pynchon's son John married Margaret Hubbard of Ipswich, whose brother had married Ann Leverett, the governor's daughter.[71] In Connecticut, Pynchon and James Rogers collaborated in purchasing between three thousand and five thousand acres in Rogers's home town of New London during the mid-1660s.[72]

But it was the control of both Springfield's export trade and its domestic economy, particularly the mills, that provided John Pynchon with his most secure and predictable sources of income. As on the English manor, the most symbolic expression of local preeminence was ownership of the community's mills. In an agricultural society that relied heavily on cereal grains for food, gristmills were especially important. Because grain was a staple in the diet of all early New Englanders, mill owners were invariably powerful figures within the township. Unlike Virginians, who relied on mortar and pestle well into the eighteenth century, northern settlers ground almost all their grain in gristmills from the mid-seventeenth century onward. Springfield's dependence on its gristmill is highlighted by the often calamitous consequences brought by breakdowns. In August 1675, Pynchon dispatched a frantic note to the General Court asking that provisions immediately be sent to the town because "our Mill having been out of order renders it extreame difficult here."[73] When the Indians attacked two months later, their most devastating blow was putting Pynchon's gristmill to the torch. The hardships imposed by living without a mill brought some inhabitants to the brink of despair, with talk of abandoning

---

[68] Wyllys Ms., 2, p. 60, Conn. Hist. Soc.

[69] Account Books, 3, 5.

[70] Hampden Co. Deeds, Volumes A, AB.

[71] *Pynchon Court Rec.*, p. 42, n. 34.

[72] *Ibid.*, pp. 47–48.

[73] John Pynchon to unknown, August 7, 1675, Long Island Hist. Soc., Brooklyn, typescript copy, CVHM.

the town rampant. Pynchon wrote Leverett that "our People are under great discouragement, Talke of Leaving the Place . . . [We need] Provisions, I meane Bread, for want of a Mill is difficult." He emphasized the primacy of grain in the villagers' diet: "we have flesh enough . . . [but] noe Mill will drive many of our Inhabitants away, especially those that have noe Corn."[74]

Mill ownership, of course, brought profit as well as social influence. Millers were entitled to a fixed percentage of the corn they processed. For his gristmill, John Pynchon received "the eleventh partt of the bushell, for all Sorts of graine that shall be heere ground."[75] Characteristically, Pynchon sublet his mills to a tenant who tended the mill in exchange for a third of the annual tolls. On November 28, 1672, he agreed with Goodman Aires "to keepe the mill at Quabaug [Brookfield] and tend it to grind the Corne brought to it for one yeare: he to take the Tole allowed, viz. ½ a peck out of a bushel . . . and for his tending the Mill, he is to have one 3d of the Tole."[76]

The manner in which Springfield constructed its mills reveals both the weakness of corporate and the importance of patron-client ties. When the town was unable to secure sufficient funds to build a new mill, John Pynchon stepped in and provided the requisite funding. In exchange for these outlays, the town granted him land, mill ownership, toll privileges, and voluntary labor from the citizens. In 1666 a town *ad hoc* committee appointed to "consider what course they judge best to be taken for the supply of the Towne" recommended the construction of a new gristmill. The town meeting, however, soon found itself deadlocked over how to raise the necessary funds. Whereupon, "the case being long debated, Capt. Pynchon did promise . . . that Hee will be at £200 charge for the building of a new mill." Pynchon offered to finance the project, "Provided the Towne will disburse what estate more must be laid out which £200 will not discharge for the effecting such a worke." Despite his willingness to defray most of the expenses for the mill's construction, Pynchon's fellow villagers balked at paying the remaining costs. After an extended and frequently acrimonious debate, "the Plantation [was] not cheerfull to engage therein." Pynchon thereupon agreed to build the mill using his own resources and the voluntary labor of any willing inhabitants on condition that he receive in perpetuity a toll of one-twelfth of all grain ground at the mill. Their inability to cooperate on funding the mill resulted in the inhabitants' forfeiture of control of their community's single most important capital investment.[77]

Construction of Springfield's first sawmill followed a similar pattern, with an additional inducement of 150 acres for the entrepreneur. In January 1663 the town meeting voted to grant Pynchon "thirty acres of land . . . and . . . the priviledge of the said brook . . . on Condition that he build a Saw Mill . . . within five yeeres."[78] Three years later, the mill still unbuilt, the town tried to sweeten the pot by deciding that "Captain Pynchon shall have 50 acres of Upland and 30 acres of Meddow . . . Provided that he build a Saw Mill . . . within three yeeres from this tyme." As these grants failed to spur him to action, the town acted again six months later: "whereas Capt. Pynchon hath had and still hath intentions to sett up a Saw Mill within this Township . . . for his encouragement in the said work . . . To all other former grannts made to the said Capt. Pynchon in reference to such work, There is further granted unto him by the Plantation the free use of the said Streame . . . also free Liberty for felling and Sawing what trees he shal please that are upon the Comons . . . [also] thirty acres of land."[79]

Throughout the seventeenth century, Springfield turned to John Pynchon for its major capital improvements. When it came time to build a new mill, school, or house of correction, or when the inhabitants wanted to erect a storage chamber over the meetinghouse or establish sheep-raising or swine-raising projects, Pynchon acted as both financier and construction supervisor. Land grants, preemption rights, monopoly privileges, and free usage were the emoluments he received in return. When the town's population more than doubled during the two decades after midcentury— from just over one hundred to nearly three hundred people— construction of a new seating gallery in the meetinghouse became imperative. Pynchon agreed to "defray all the charge that concerns the work" if the town allowed him to sell seatrights in the proposed gallery. After a discussion, the town meeting acceded to his proposition, ordering that "Captayn Pynchon shal be paid by Such as shal be Seated there [at] 4s. a person."[80]

The action of Springfield in contracting with Pynchon to build a gallery in the meetinghouse and then charging for seatrights is richly emblematic of the community's system of values. The contrast is obvious between the accustomed practice in the communal towns

[77] *Springfield Town Recs.*, 1, pp. 352–355.
[78] *Ibid.*, 1, pp. 303–304.
[79] *Ibid.*, 1, pp. 354–355.
[80] *Ibid.*, 1, p. 303.

where everyone was assigned a place by virtue of membership in the community and the selling of seatrights in Springfield, where essentially users paid for the benefit and Pynchon profited from his service to the town. Similarly, when Springfield needed additional storage space for its corn, the meeting voted that "if mr. John Pynchon will make a [storage] chamber over the meeting howse and board it: he shall have the use of it Intirely to himselfe for Ten yeares." After the expiration of the ten-year period, "then if the Towne neede it and require it they may have it, Provided they allow the said mr. John Pynchon the charge that he hath [paid for] it."[81] Seeing need for a local smeltery in the mid-1690s, the town again turned to Pynchon. On December 5, 1696, he and Joseph Parsons "made some proposals in order to the setting up and carrying on an Iron Mill." After considering "the great benefitt [the iron mill] will bee to this place," the town granted Pynchon and Parsons monopoly rights over all iron ore within the township.[82] Continuing its deliberations the following month, the town granted the two men an eighty-acre site on which to locate the ironworks.[83]

Pynchon was also called upon to build up the town's vital livestock herds—particularly the sheep necessary to free the colonists from reliance on English woolen imports. As with livestock production generally, the Connecticut Valley pasturage was unsurpassed in Massachusetts for grazing sheep. In emphasizing the valley's unique congeniality for sheep-raising in New England, agricultural historian Howard S. Russell points out that "Sheep raising is a specialized calling. Sheep require good pasturage free from thickets and briers likely to catch and tear their wool coats, protection from predatory animals, and careful knowledgeable attention on the part of man. Much of New England's surface, even in the 1700s, was still too untamed for their somewhat fastidious appetites."[84] Recognizing their region's potential, in 1654 the town voters granted Pynchon twenty-one acres of the town's most highly assessed land on condition that he purchase "40 sheepe within the space of Six months." He agreed to "use his best endevoure to bring [the sheep] into Towne and there to dispose of them as hee shall se cause."[85] In 1660 the community resorted to similar procedures to augment its dwindling supply of hogs. Pynchon and two other well-heeled

[81] *Ibid.*, 1, p. 200.
[82] *Ibid.*, 2, p. 346.
[83] *Ibid.*, 2, p. 288.
[84] Russell, *A Long, Deep Furrow*, p. 154.
[85] *Springfield Town Recs.*, 1, p. 232.

inhabitants received forty acres of land "according as they carry on theire designe of keeping swine there."[86]

Reliance on John Pynchon's enterprise and resources became a habit in Springfield, and it could include the most routine obligations. In 1670, learning that the town's representative had not received his commissary payments, Pynchon again stepped in. The town meeting acknowledged its "neglect in providing for the deputy . . . to the General Corte . . . whereof many tymes his diet at Boston is too long unsatisfyed." Because of "the Towne's want of pay in hand, Capt. Pynchon proffers to give 20s. towards it."[87] When Springfield's gunpowder stocks became dangerously depleted in 1668, Pynchon "propounded to the Town, That if the Towne would grannt him [a] house lott . . . he would lett them have one halfe of [a] barrell of powder, which the Towne did yeeld unto."[88]

By "yeelding unto" John Pynchon with such frequency, the inhabitants of Springfield forfeited control over their own economic destinies. When corporate remedies failed, the residents looked to Pynchon rather than themselves to find a way out. Throughout the seventeenth century, when they asked him to finance new capital improvements, he usually agreed to do so—but always at a price. The concessions he exacted, in the forms of land grants, monopolies, and special privileges and immunities, ultimately served to enrich him at the expense of his fellow villagers. Without corporate self-reliance, it became only too easy to keep calling on Pynchon, even at such an obvious cost. The weakness of the town meeting was the mirror image, as well as the product, of the economic individualism typical of early Springfield. Reliance on Pynchon came easier than cooperation with one another, and his dominance of the public economy was the result.[89]

And while John Pynchon's sway over the public economy was considerable, his private power as an employer, landlord, and creditor was even more complete. During the period from 1652 to 1703, over two hundred men were personally dependent on Pynchon for employment, land, or credit—or some combination of the three. These dependent men usually included half of the adult male population at any time. Of the seventy-two men on the 1665 List of Springfield Inhabitants, forty (56%) were wage-laborers, tenants, or debtors of Pynchon. Of the seventy-six inhabitants entered on the 1672 List of Springfield Town Meeting Voters, thirty-two (42%)

[86] *Ibid.*, 1, p. 280.
[87] *Ibid.*, 2, p. 106.
[88] *Ibid.*, 2, pp. 95–96.
[89] See Chapter 5.

fulfilled one or more of these categories. Fifty-six (47%) of the 120 taxpayers in 1685 can be so classified.[90]

These men came to Pynchon on their own volition and with their eyes open. He had the land, the tools, the draft animals, and the jobs that they needed. This was particularly true for the large numbers of single and semi-impoverished men who had made their way to Springfield with little more than the clothes on their back. Pynchon offered them a chance to get established, to secure a leasehold, employment, and a line of credit for buying the first piece of land. Word doubtless got around that Pynchon had these things to offer, and many men whose indigence would have invited a warning-out from the covenanted communities hoped for better prospects in Springfield. In this expectation, they were rarely disappointed because Pynchon needed them as much as they needed him.

The dependency bond between Pynchon and these men was a dual one. Just as the word "bond" has a double meaning—a connection and, as in "bondage," a restraint—so too was this, as all relationships, subject to influence and constraints.[91] The authority figure, in this case John Pynchon, is never an autonomous figure. Neither the authority figure nor his dependent in Springfield was a free actor. Both in fact were dependent. Each exercised some measure of initiative.[92] Tenants, as well as landlords, had bargaining powers. Both understood that authority always has limits that are particular to place, person, and time. What, Pynchon might have asked, is a landlord without his tenants, a boss without underlings, a creditor without debtors? Tenants might have no choice but to rent, but they could go elsewhere. The same was true for those looking for work or credit. As Richard Hofstadter observes, "raw, idle land could be made profitable only when settlers were brought in to work, rent, or buy it." Hofstadter cites Sir Josiah Child's assertion that "Lands, though excellent, without hands proportionable will not enrich any kingdom."[93] It was Pynchon's recognition of this mutual dependence that gave the system its motive force. As the account books reveal, he actively sought out men and attempted to establish patron-client relationships.

These individual patron-client ties may be defined as an "informal contractual relationship between persons of unequal status and

[90] *Springfield Town Recs.*, 2, pp. 76–77, 115–116; 1685 Tax List.

[91] I am grateful to Thomas Slaughter of Rutgers University for emphasizing this point for me.

[92] Richard Sennett, *Authority*, New York, 1980, Chapters 1 and 2.

[93] *America at 1750*, p. 10.

power, which imposes reciprocal obligations of a different kind on each of the parties."[94] As patron, John Pynchon exchanged the fruits of his status, power, influence, and authority for the loyalty and political support of the client. Men sought out Pynchon because he was the only one who could help supply their economic needs. He rented them land, provided employment, or lent money. Most important, he showed selective flexibility in hiring, firing, and foreclosing. Clients could count on keeping their jobs, lands, or housing when others could not. In response, the clients accepted certain restrictions on their behavior. Those tenants whose rent was in arrears, men chronically indebted to Pynchon, or wage laborers dependent on him for long-term or seasonal employment were not likely to oppose his wishes in the town meeting, on the muster green, or anywhere else.

The Pynchon account books show vividly the myriad forms of the patron's favoritism. Pynchon often ignored contractual deadlines if the client found himself unable to meet them. Mortgages were not foreclosed, lands and housing were not seized, debts were not called on the day or even the month or year of maturity. Laborers, too, were hired when Pynchon had no genuine need or desire to take them on. Likewise, he seldom pursued his technical legal rights as a creditor, landlord, or employer in cases relating to clients. The strength of the particular patron-client bond determined whether Pynchon would modify, renegotiate, or postpone collection of debts. For the same reasons, some renters were able to secure significantly better terms than others. Some, for example, were entitled to one-half of all offspring born to cattle rented from Pynchon. Lesser clients or non-clients were contractually obliged to raise all calves to the age of two years and then forfeit them to Pynchon.

Because clientage, by its nature, is an informal, oral (even unspoken) relationship, it does not yield to easy identification. In many

---

[94] Silverman, "Patronage and Community-Nation Relationships," *Ethnology* (1965), p. 176. See also George M. Foster, "The Dyadic Contract: A Model for the Social Structure of a Mexican Village," *Am. Anthropologist*, 63 (1961), pp. 1173–1192, and "The Dyadic Contract in Tzintzuntzan, II: Patron-Client Relationships," *ibid.*, 65 (1963), pp. 1280–1294; Julian A. Pitt-Rivers, *The People of the Sierra*, Chicago, 1961, pp. 154–155; Morton H. Fried, *Fabric of Chinese Society: A Study of the Social Life of a Chinese County Seat*, New York, 1953, pp. 224, 227; Michael Kenny, "Patterns of Patronage in Spain," *Anthropological Quarterly*, 33 (1960), pp. 14–23, and *A Spanish Tapestry: Town and Country in Castile*, Bloomington, Ind., 1961, pp. 154–155. For a particularly suggestive discussion of the relationship of cliency to the formation of village factions, see Edit Fel and Tamas Hofer, "Tanyaket-s, Patron-Client Relations, and Political Factions in Atany," *Am. Anthropologist*, 75 (1973), pp. 787–800.

ways it is only discernible by an apparently routinized disruption of normal patterns of association that *may* be verified. To employ a metaphor from astronomy, clientage is very much like a black-hole argument. It must be there because of the strange way everything else behaves when passing through its orbit. Yet it itself remains invisible. An examination of John Pynchon's dealings with his tenants, workers, and debtors shows an inescapable pattern of separating these men into two camps: those for whom he would walk the extra mile, and those for whom he would not. For those whose skills he needed, and whose support in public affairs he could count upon, Pynchon showed a pronounced indulgence, particularly regarding debt collection. For others, too busy to help him at harvest, too irregular in their work habits, or simply too personally independent, he stuck inflexibly to the sovereign letter of the contract. The difference, for many men, ultimately was between success and failure.[95]

Pynchon's negotiations with William Brooks in early 1667 illustrate the bargaining process between patron and client. Brooks had approached his landlord to request a second year's grace on his mortgage. As Pynchon related in his account book: "William Brooks desyred me not to advantage against him of this agreement but to let him enjoy his [land] one yeare longer, he desyred but a yeares tyme more . . . though this tyme was out above a yeare since, and I might . . . now challenge the land for newly owned." But after this assertion of his legal rights, rights that both men recognized would be enforced in Pynchon's courtroom, the landlord relented. He vouchsafed that "yet I would settle to his desires in it and grant him one yeare's tyme longer to pay the debt per contract, and if he payd it not by this tyme 12 months then the land to be mine." This kind of ameliorating behavior paid dividends to both parties. Brooks gained still another year in which to raise the necessary funds; Pynchon secured the loyalty of the client.[96]

The trade-offs for this kind of favor, of course, were rarely stated explicitly. Contractually, Brooks offered Pynchon nothing in return for the foreclosure's extension. But as both the court records and account books reveal, Pynchon's subsequent claims on Brooks's loyalty could not be easily denied. When the magistrate needed support in the town meeting, help at harvest time, or intelligence regarding illegal gaming activities in the community, he could usu-

[95] I am obliged to John M. Murrin for helping me to refine these points, and for suggesting the metaphor.
[96] Account Books, 2, p. 215.

ally count on William Brooks.[97] Equally important, neither patron nor client found this kind of asymmetrical relationship unusual or demeaning. Brooks knew that he was joined by roughly half the town's men in dependency on Pynchon. All Springfield inhabitants recognized that those who hoped to establish a secure economic foothold usually found John Pynchon more forthcoming in meeting their material needs than was the town meeting.

But, as with the town meeting's habitual reliance on Pynchon's entrepreneurial resources, individual reliance on patron-client rather than corporate ties came at a price. Dependency relationships with Pynchon tended to become permanent and often, in the long run, disabling. William Brooks, for example, eventually lost his 150 acres to the creditor and ended up quitting the town.[98] As he learned, the dependency ties in Springfield—despite appearances—were not those of the medieval manor, but of the company town.

Springfield was an almost textbook example of the "hegemony" described with such brilliance by Antonio Gramsci, and used by Eugene Genovese to highlight the reciprocal obligations characteristic of slave society. As in the company towns of the postbellum South, the bottom line of paternalism was profit, not protection. Springfield was an avatar of the new capitalist world, for which the patron-client bond would serve as midwife. Clientage was a relationship that permitted the entrepreneur to rationalize production and maximize returns partly by relying upon premodern patterns of behavior among subordinates. Those with skills who responded in the expected way could expect indulgence. Those who behaved differently might get away with it, but if they foundered, they could expect no mercy. As Pynchon's use of clientage reveals, the emergence of a true capitalist type depended partly upon the continuing existence of others less modern than he. And the future would belong to the market, not the manor. For Pynchon, patron-client ties were preeminently a means of organizing labor, and, as Robert L. Heilbroner observes, "the driving force of capitalism [is] the accumulation of capital by means of wage labor." Heilbroner's definition of capitalism helps place Pynchon's use of patronage ties in context: "Capitalism . . . is quintessentially a means of organizing labor to produce a social surplus. By a surplus I mean the production of material wealth over and above whatever is needed to maintain ordinary life at its existing level. The line between surplus and mere replenishment is always blurred, as are most social dis-

[97] See Chapter 5.
[98] Account Books, 5, p. 27.

tinctions, but in the large there is no difficulty in distinguishing the form and extent of surplus in all surplus-producing systems."[99] Nothing betokens this surplus-orientation more vividly than does the highly commercialized nature of both land and labor. To invoke the Aristotelian distinction between "use value" and "exchange value" to determine whether an economy is capitalized or not, Springfield's was clearly in the latter camp. And it was so from the beginning.[100]

[99] Robert L. Heilbroner, "The Demand for the Supply Side," *The New York Review of Books* (June 11, 1981), pp. 37–41.

[100] E. J. Hobsbawm, "Pact with the Devil," *The New York Review of Books* (December 18, 1980), p. 3.

Chapter 3

Land

*"Somebody once said that capitalism
without bankruptcy is like Christianity without hell."*
Frank Borman, chairman and president of
Eastern Air Lines, *Forbes* (June 8, 1981)

LAND in seventeenth-century Springfield was less a communal bond than it was a fungible commodity. Unlike the subsistence farming communities, land in the Connecticut Valley town changed hands early and often. As the "Records of Possession" make clear, Springfield had an active land market as early as 1650. The weakness of corporate ties resulted in the town meeting's loss of primary control over land allocation. Rather than carefully rationing acreage in order to preserve social harmony and protect future generations, Springfield allowed most of the town's genuinely first-rate acreage to pass quickly into private hands. And, by a combination of allocation, purchase, and foreclosure, most of it ended up with John Pynchon. The result was twofold: a high level of social stratification and the prevalence of land tenancy.[1]

The amplitude of land and the absence of tenancy in seventeenth-century New England towns have become articles of faith among historians. The ready availability of land, we are told, minimized inequality and muted social tensions. In Dedham, Massachusetts, the "incomparable abundance of land" enabled sons to "expect a patrimony which would keep [them] from having to rent land or work for another man or beg in the streets."[2] In Andover, by 1662, land allotments provided the town's earliest settlers with "land on a scale impossible for most of them to have anticipated . . . in England."[3] A resident of such communities could expect to

---

[1] "Records of Possessions," 1651–1699, City Clerk's Office, Springfield.

[2] Lockridge, *A New England Town*, pp. 70–71.

[3] Greven, *Four Generations*, p. 59. For a sophisticated treatment of the relationship between land availability and communal solidarity, see Robert A. Gross, *The Minutemen and Their World*, New York, 1976, pp. 68–108.

receive approximately two hundred acres during his lifetime, and overall, according to Kenneth Lockridge, "an estimate of 150 acres for the typical early inhabitant of an eastern Massachusetts town is a reasonable figure."[4] Consequently, in these towns the "distribution of wealth [was] relatively even and the spectrum of social rank narrow." Or, to use Lockridge's forthright characterization, they composed a society of "One class, one interest, one mind."[5]

Springfield, however, was anything but a one-class society. Patterns of unequal land distribution appeared with the town's founding and intensified as the century progressed. The 1646 tax list, as we have seen, shows William Pynchon and his two sons-in-law monopolizing the best acreage in the community's three planting fields. Their combined holdings of 510 acres comprised 25 percent of the total land allocated.[6] By 1655 there were already so many landless men in Springfield that the meeting devised a separate system for taxing them.[7] In addition, unlike the subsistence towns where inhabitants were discouraged from leaving the village center, Springfield passed legislation designed to facilitate out-migration and thereby reduce the demand for land.[8] As early as 1664, the town meeting unhappily concluded that "there are diverse Persons in this Town who have but little land." Three years later, the meeting appointed a committee to "consider of the necessitous Condition of some familyes in the Plantation," who needed relief.[9] Fathers complained, presumably with some warmth, that they had insufficient acreage to provide an inheritance for their sons. In drawing

[4] Kenneth A. Lockridge, "Land, Population and the Evolution of New England Society, 1630–1790; and an Afterthought," in Stanley N. Katz, ed., *Colonial America: Essays in Politics and Social Development*, Boston, 1971, pp. 469–471. See also Greven, *Four Generations*, p. 59; Christopher Jedrey, *The World of John Cleaveland: Family and Community in Eighteenth-Century New England*, New York, 1979, pp. 58–94; Sumner Chilton Powell, *Puritan Village: The Formation of a New England Town*, Middletown, Conn., 1963, Appendices 6 and 7; Charles S. Grant, *Democracy in the Connecticut Frontier Town of Kent*, New York, 1961, pp. 97–103. For comparisons with English landholding practices, see Mildred Campbell, *The English Yeoman Under Elizabeth and the Early Stuarts*, New Haven, 1942, Chapters 3 and 4; Lawrence Stone, *Family and Fortune*, Oxford, 1973, pp. 288–291; W. G. Hoskins, *Provincial England*, London, 1963, pp. 151–160; Brian Manning, *The English People and the English Revolution, 1640–1649*, London, 1976, pp. 112–162; and Peter Laslett, *The World We Have Lost: England Before the Industrial Age*, New York, 1965, pp. 22–52.

[5] Lockridge, *A New England Town*, p. 76.

[6] *Springfield Town Recs.*, 1, pp. 190–191.

[7] *Ibid.*, 1, p. 245.

[8] *Ibid.*, 1, pp. 248–249. To encourage settlement of Woronoco (Westfield), then under Springfield's control, the town rebated one-half of the rates assessed there.

[9] *Springfield Town Recs.*, 1, pp. 318, 359.

up a petition for rate relief, the town asked the General Court to "consider our poverty."[10] Even Springfield's minister, Pelatiah Glover, wondered if the level of privation in the community would make it impossible for the residents to pay his salary. In discussing Glover's plans to move elsewhere, the selectmen observed that "he apprehends that Wee are not able comfortably to maynteyne him."[11] Because this privation was rooted in the inequitable land distribution, the committees responsible for land grants were in constant disarray. During its first three decades the town repeatedly vacillated over the question of which institution—the board of selectmen, a special *ad hoc* committee, or the entire town meeting—should control land allocation.[12]

This progressive stratification is plainly revealed by the remarkably detailed 1685 tax list. Drawn up amid the uncertainty over land titles arising from the Crown's *quo warranto* proceedings against Massachusetts, this list shows the size, location, and valuation of all land holdings. Anxious to demonstrate incontrovertible proof of ownership, the assessors designated which land already had been "broken up" for tillage, and they computed the overall worth of each tract of woodland, pasture, and upland. The 1685 list thus affords an unrivaled look at both the distribution of acreage and the relative worth of various holdings. Not surprisingly, on both counts—particularly the latter—John Pynchon comes out on top by a wide margin. Of a total of approximately 9,000 acres held by some 120 persons, Pynchon owned 1,800 (20%). The acreage of the next largest landowner, Japhet Chapin, was 365. Pynchon held more land than the collective acreage of the fifty-two smallest owners, or 43 percent of the total number of male freeholders. The bottom 10 percent possessed less than 1 percent of all the acreage; the bottom 20 percent, 4.2 percent; and the bottom 30 percent, 8.6 percent of the land granted. With Pynchon's holdings subtracted from the whole, the mean acreage was 60. Forty-nine men held estates smaller than 50 acres, and sixteen owned fewer than 25 acres. Still more important, these landholdings, in addition to being small, were often infertile or remote. Like his father before him, John Pynchon monopolized the holdings in the rich alluvial third division adjacent to the Agawam (Westfield) River. [See Springfield map.] Here land valuations averaged up to sixty shil-

---

[10] *Ibid.*, 2, p. 166; *Mass. Recs.*, 2, p. 270; 3, p. 154; 5, pp. 483–484.
[11] *Springfield Town Recs.*, 2, pp. 101–102; also see Chapter 5.
[12] *Springfield Town Recs.*, 2, p. 81.

lings per acre, in contrast to median valuations of twenty shillings per acre elsewhere.[13]

The distribution of wealth revealed by the 1685 tax list is paralleled to a striking degree in estate inventories. From 1650 to 1705 the town (or Hampshire County) probated the estates of seventy Springfield inhabitants. With adjustments made for encumbrances, the total value of probated estates was £22,843. Of this amount John Pynchon's estate totaled £8,446 (37%). Largely because of his extensive property, the top 5 percent of the decedents held £11,721, or 51 percent of the inventoried wealth. At the other extreme of the social spectrum, things were radically different. The bottom 20 percent held estates valued at a total of £243 (1%), and the bottom 50 percent owned £1,951 (8.5%). The poorest sixty-two men (89% of the decedents) held a total of £8,547 (37.4%). It took the combined holdings of almost 90 percent of the deceased townsmen, therefore, to equal the property owned by John Pynchon. Only three men other than the magistrate held estates valued in excess of £800. Ensign Benjamin Cooley owned holdings worth £1,241 when he died in 1684. Pynchon's brother-in-law, Elizur Holyoke, died eight years later leaving his heirs property worth £1,187. Quartermaster George Colton owned assets valued at £847 at his death in 1690. At the opposite end, thirty men (43%) died with estates worth less than £100; fifteen of these were valued below £50. Six men died owning assets amounting to less than £25, four of whom died as town charges. Only 24 percent of the decedents, seventeen men, left estates within the supposedly normative £200 to £400 range.[14]

These figures reveal that the specter of intermittent poverty stalked at least half of Springfield's seventeenth-century population. Estimates of the number of acres necessary to provide adequately for a family's needs vary greatly, largely because the relevant evidence is fragmentary and often ambiguous. Speculations regarding the requirements for the typical family of seven range from twenty-eight to one hundred acres, depending on such variables as soil

[13] 1685 Tax List.

[14] HCPC Rec., 1–4 (1660–1780). Many Springfield decedents never had their estates inventoried. Most quantitative historians believe that those dying young or poor were the most likely to be excluded. For a comparative view of another Connecticut Valley town, see Linda A. Bissell, "From One Generation to Another: Mobility in Seventeenth-Century Windsor, Connecticut," *WMQ*, 31 (1974), pp. 79–110. For a portrayal of similar divisions in Plymouth Colony, see John J. Waters, "The Traditional World of the New England Peasants: A View from Seventeenth-Century Barnstable," *New England Historical and Genealogical Register*, 129 (1976), pp. 3–21.

fertility, agricultural techniques, access to markets, and dietary habits.[15] The Springfield data suggest that a minimum of sixty accessible acres was needed to support a family of seven if the householder lived exclusively by farming.[16] Skilled artisans, depending on the profitability of their craft, could make do with somewhat less. But while they may have required less planting ground than did full-time farmers, artisans, like everyone else, needed a homelot, pasturage, and woodlots. Each household in colonial New England, for example, needed between fifteen and twenty cords of wood to get through an average winter.[17] Likewise, all inhabitants shared the common necessity of providing a patrimony for their male children.

For that half of Springfield's population with fewer than sixty acres, and much of this infertile or distant, the choice was to get a lease from John Pynchon or get out. Most chose the former. During any one year between 1650 and 1703, over one-third of the town's adult males were renting some or all of their land, housing, or livestock from Pynchon. In 1685, 49 out of the 120 inhabitants entered on the tax list leased land or livestock from Springfield's seigneur. Of that same 120, fully 113 rented from Pynchon at some point during their stay in the town. During the half-century after 1650, approximately 140 renters paid him over £4,000 for fifteen hundred contract years.[18] The landlord's annual income from rent receipts during this time ranged from £100 to £150, in addition to value derived from tenants' improvement of his property. Men

[15] A careful evaluation of land requirements for family subsistence is found in James T. Lemon, "Household Consumption in Eighteenth-Century America," *Agricultural History*, 41 (1967), pp. 59–70. For the land needs of communities primarily devoted to stock-raising, see Jedrey, *The World of John Cleaveland*, pp. 58–64.

[16] 1685 Tax List.

[17] Russell, *A Long, Deep Furrow*, p. 175.

[18] 1685 Tax List. The number of contract years has been calculated by totaling each contract year paid for every rental, even if some were coterminous; that is, if a man rented a 30-acre lot for 6 years and a yoke of oxen for the same 6 years, his total contract years would be 12. It is probable that the rental periods were considerably longer than the statistics cited suggest, because only the years in which Pynchon actually entered the payment for the rent in his account books were used in the sample. Repeatedly, in the account book, a contract was signed for a lease of 5, 7, 11 years, etc., but no subsequent payments are recorded. Although Pynchon was, for the period, an assiduous bookkeeper, it is likely that many payments were not recorded—or were recorded in day books that have not survived. To ensure the integrity of the statistics in this analysis, all contracts without recorded payments have been ignored. In addition to the 140 Springfield tenants, some 60 residents of other valley towns also rented from Pynchon. Usually they leased lands or housing within their own communities, although some rented within Springfield itself.

rented from Pynchon largely because he owned a disproportionate share of the town's alluvial meadows and bottom land in the third division. Men without allotments in these fields were usually consigned to pine barrens, rocky woodlands, and marshlands. Consequently, rather than work infertile lands or make the daily trek to distant fields, many approached Pynchon for a lease. In a telling 1676 petition to the General Court for relief from garrison duties, the town declared that "many are forced to hyre land here, there own being so remote."[19]

Tenancy in seventeenth-century Springfield, however, was often a swift route to economic hardship; and the reasons for this hardship are found in the complexities of the English common law notion of waste. In America, in sharp contrast to the mother country, the rule of waste was used developmentally. In England, the common law notion of waste barred the tenant from making any alterations of the leasehold, whether these changes involved clearing the land for cultivation or erecting buildings. At common law, "any fundamental alteration by a tenant of the condition of the land constituted waste for which he was liable."[20] And "a tenant who erected buildings on land had no right to remove them at the end of his term."[21] Legal historians have long mistakingly viewed the English law of waste as a dead letter in colonial America. Justice Joseph Story's famous ruling in *Van Ness v. Pacard* (1829) is the most frequently cited justification of this view. According to Story, the common law rule of waste had never been accepted in America because "The country was a wilderness, and the universal policy was to procure its cultivation and improvement. The owner of the soil as well as the public, had every motive to encourage the tenant to devote himself to agriculture, and to favor any erections which should aid this result; yet, in the comparative poverty of the country, what tenant could afford to erect fixtures of much expense or value, if he was to lose his whole interest therein by the very act of erection?"[22] But as the contractual terms of John Pynchon's ground rents make clear, the rule of waste *was* received—although used very differently—in America. In the New World, the rule of waste appears to have been stood on its head. Many of Pynchon's leases

---

[19] Springfield Petition to the Massachusetts General Court, August 30, 1676, CVHM; 1685 Tax List.

[20] Morton J. Horwitz, *The Transformation of American Law, 1780–1860*, Cambridge, Mass., 1977, p. 54; see also S.F.C. Milsom, *Historical Foundations of the Common Law*, London, 1969, pp. 252, 255.

[21] Horwitz, *Transformation of American Law*, p. 55.

[22] Cited in *ibid.*, p. 55.

required the tenant to clear and break up new land, and often included provisions for erecting buildings as well. But the tenant received neither equity nor the right to remove the buildings upon termination of the lease. Tellingly, the only area where the English use of waste did prevail in America was in regard to equity. Waste, as a time-honored landlord's remedy, protected against tenants' suits to recover equity by making the lessee in fact liable for such changes. Tenants in Springfield cleared and built only for the landlord's ultimate benefit.[23]

The rule of waste deprived the Springfield tenants of their most valuable capital asset—their labor. As Stuart Bruchey points out in his seminal *The Roots of American Economic Growth, 1607–1861*, the value of improved land was "by far the most important constituent of capital" in the colonies.[24] And according to economic historian William N. Parker, "Land clearing was the heaviest of the tasks [confronted by the colonists]. . . . Altogether it took a man as many as twenty to thirty-five days to make an acre of land reasonably free of its original cover and ready for first cultivation."[25] In a frontier agricultural society, the labor involved in clearing the land, erecting fences, and nurturing livestock was the most available means of capital formation. Only by this daily investment of time and sweat could most men appreciably better their standard of living. But labor for someone else's benefit was counterproductive, for if,

[23] Account Books, 6, p. 229. Because of the importance of contractual obligations in Springfield (see Chapter 4), when a contract existed, its terms would govern a dispute over property removal, not the doctrine of waste. But John Pynchon sometimes issued leases without a contract, or with an agreement so vague in its construction as to be open to conflicting interpretations. In disputable cases, and for those without written contracts, the cardinal function of waste was to frame men's *expectations*. The doctrine of waste as it was used in England, the only legal culture most colonists knew, predisposed them not to expect equitable recovery for improvements of the leasehold. In regard to the apparent unfairness of the developmental leases, Pynchon doubtless would have pointed to their modest rents and the large assumption of risk in being a frontier landlord. The fact that he supplied some of the construction materials would likewise support his position. Paradoxically, the modern law of contract, in some ways, has come full circle and returned to the "just price" theory so odious to the Pynchons. Today, a defendant might raise the argument that the lease/contract was unfair and a contract of adhesion. Thus it must be voided as "unconscionable." I am indebted to Rayman L. Solomon of the American Bar Foundation for these observations.

[24] Stuart Bruchey, *The Roots of American Economic Growth, 1607–1861*, New York, 1965, p. 23. This reference was brought to my attention by David Thomas Konig, *Law and Society in Puritan Massachusetts: Essex County, 1629–1692*, Chapel Hill, 1979, p. 65, n. 4.

[25] William N. Parker, "The American Farmer," in Jerome Blum, ed., *Our Forgotten Past: Seven Centuries of Life on the Land*, London, 1982, pp. 182–183.

after clearing, stubbing, and plowing the land, constructing fences and sometimes buildings, raising stock, and paying rent and taxes, a tenant surrendered up his lease, all money and labor were lost. One of the principal grievances in the Tenant Rising of 1766 in Dutchess County, New York, was the ejection of the tenants without "any manner of recompense for their labour, fatigue, and expense in cultivating, manuring, clearing, fencing, and improving said lands, nor for their buildings thereon erected."[26] A still more graphic indictment of tenancy's capacity to rob a man of the fruits of his labor is provided by Cadwallader Colden. He ascribed the depopulation of the Hudson Valley patroonships to this theft of a tenant's labor: "every year the Young people go from this Province and Purchase Land in the Neighbouring Colonies, while much better and every way more convenient Lands lie useless to the King and Country. The reason for this is that the [owners] themselves are not, nor never were in a Capacity to improve such large Tracts and other People will not become their Vassals or Tenants for one great reason, as people's (the better sort especially) leaving their native Country, was to avoid the dependence on landlords, and to enjoy in fee [simple] to descend to their posterity *that their children may reap the benefit of their labor and Industry.*"[27]

Tenancy in America only made sense for those who had nothing to lose to begin with. Men without sufficient capital to purchase the land, provisions, and equipment required to start their own freehold doubtless saw tenancy as an attractive alternative to the life of a wage laborer. There can be little question that many men came to Springfield specifically in order to rent from John Pynchon. In so doing, of course, they were simply following everyday practices in England where tenants constituted 80 percent of the working agricultural population. The Pynchon account books show that tenancy in Springfield enabled men to move up from laborer to husbandman—itself no small achievement. But because renters were not recompensed for their labor, their long-term prospects were limited by an inability to gain enough wealth to become independent. Tenancy in Springfield, therefore, was usually a dead-end street. It offered a certain kind of mobility to the landless, but only at the price of dependence on John Pynchon. For those tenants who were landholders, their labor for Pynchon precluded improvement of their own freeholds. Many in both categories became chronic

[26] Cited in Staughton Lynd, *Anti-Federalism in Dutchess County, New York: A Study of Democracy and Class Conflict in the Revolutionary Era*, Chicago, 1962, p. 47.

[27] Cited in Irving Mark, *Agrarian Conflicts in Colonial New York, 1711–1775*, New York, 1940, p. 14; emphasis mine.

debtors; some forty men lost sizable amounts of land, housing, or livestock to Pynchon for their debts.[28]

The forms of tenancy in Springfield varied greatly. Some tenants leased eighty-acre farms, complete with housing, orchards, livestock, and tools, for twenty years or longer—at rents sometimes exceeding £22 annually. Others rented a single acre of meadow for one year at six shillings. Most leases fell between these extremes. A typical renter might hold fifteen acres, some housing, and a yoke of oxen for between twelve and sixteen years. In addition to oxen, tenants rented draft horses, cows, sheep, pigs, and the stud services of Pynchon's bulls.[29] Other men leased gristmills and sawmills from the landlord, at charges up to £18 a year.[30] Heavy artisans such as blacksmiths, tanners, and millwrights leased the tools of their trade from him.[31] Those without a plow did likewise. To his more affluent tenants, Pynchon rented out fur-trading rights, warehouse space, and shares in ocean-going vessels.[32]

In addition to their rent, which was paid at "Michaelmas" in late September, tenants were usually responsible for fence maintenance, local taxes, and, as we have seen, the clearing of part of the leasehold.[33] Often, Pynchon required his tenants to "stub, clear, and bring to plowing" designated portions of the holding. Some contracts likewise specified the exact dimensions of any housing, barns, or out-buildings to be erected by the tenant. Livestock rentals provided that Pynchon receive half and sometimes all of the offspring—a significant requirement in that cows, horses, pigs, and sheep were valued as much for their ability to reproduce as for their daily utility.[34]

[28] For a discussion of the importance of rent in the transfer of wealth in preindustrial economies, see Eric R. Wolf, *Peasants*, Englewood Cliffs, N. J., 1966, pp. 9–10. Wolf also discusses caloric minima and villagers' efforts to curtail consumption. These problems are likewise explored in G. M. Foster, "Peasant Society and the Image of Limited Good," in J. M. Potter, M. N. Diaz, and G. M. Foster, eds., *Peasants: A Reader*, Boston, 1967, pp. 300–323.

[29] Account Books, 5, pp. 548–549.

[30] *Ibid.*, 5, p. 170.

[31] *Ibid.*, 2, p. 283.

[32] *Ibid.*, 6, pp. 230–231.

[33] Pynchon's willingness to retain the usage of such "popish" terms as Michaelmas, Whitsuntide, and Eastertide is itself instructive. Massachusetts Governor John Winthrop and most other coastal magistrates, by contrast, did their best to banish such terms, regarding them as relics of superstition. I am grateful to John M. Murrin for this observation.

[34] Account Books, 5, pp. 161, 307. For comparisons with tenancy practices elsewhere in the colonies, see Mark, *Agrarian Conflicts*; Gregory A. Stiverson, *Poverty in a Land of Plenty: Tenancy in Eighteenth-Century Maryland*, Baltimore, 1977; Aubrey

John Pynchon's account books make it possible to identify six classes of renters in Springfield: (1) fifteen tenant farmers (characterized by Pynchon as "My Farmers"); (2) fifty dependent renters; (3) thirty short-term dependent renters; (4) nine long-term independent renters; (5) thirty-one short-term independent renters; and (6) five who rented only animals. Of these, the tenant farmers were the most dependent.[35]

The tenant farmers leased self-contained, fully equipped farms for extended periods at high rents. Their only contribution to the arrangement was labor.[36] John Pynchon supplied the lands, housing, barns, dairy and draft animals, and tools. The cost was accordingly high: £18 yearly was the most common sum, an amount often equal to the value of half or more of the tenant's harvest. Collectively, the tenant farmers paid for a total of 226 contract years, with payments of £1,903. The average duration of their rental period was fifteen years. Most began renting from Pynchon while in their late twenties or early thirties, presumably after it had become evident that other avenues for obtaining land were closed. Virtually to a man, the tenant farmers continued in some kind of contractual relationship with him as long as they remained in Springfield.

Isaac Morgan's experience can stand as typical. The son of a Welsh immigrant who had been John Pynchon's most active canoeman, Morgan first rented land in March 1672. He started off with a lease for three and one-half acres in the Chicopee section

---

C. Land, "Economic Base and Social Structure: The Northern Chesapeake in the Eighteenth Century," *Journal of Economic History*, 25 (1965), pp. 639–654. The most benign portrayals of American tenancy are found in Sung Bok Kim, *Landlord and Tenant in Colonial New York: Manorial Society, 1664–1775*, Chapel Hill, 1978; Patricia U. Bonomi, *A Factious People: Politics and Society in Colonial New York*, New York, 1971, pp. 179–228. For continental and Latin American parallels, see Thomas F. Sheppard, *Lourmarin in the Eighteenth Century: A Study of a French Village*, Baltimore, 1971, Chapters 1 and 6; Laurence Wylie, *Chanzeaux, A Village in Anjou*, Cambridge, Mass., 1966; and William B. Taylor, *Landlord and Peasant in Colonial Oaxaca*, Stanford, 1972, pp. 67–163, 195–202.

[35] In his description of tenancy in a 20th-century Japanese village, Ronald P. Dore proposes the following categories: "*Landlords*—renting out more land than they farmed. *Owner-farmers*—owning at least 90 per cent of the land they farmed and some of them also renting out an acre or two. *Owner-tenants*—owning 50–90 per cent of the land they farmed. *Tenant-owners*—owning 10–50 per cent of the land they farmed. *Tenants*—owning less than 10 per cent of the land they farmed." See *Shinohata: A Portrait of a Japanese Village*, New York, 1978, p. 46. Such categorization makes sense for 17th-century Springfield as well, although insufficient data on yearly percentages of owned vs. leased land prevents the outright adoption of this scheme for the Massachusetts community.

[36] Account Books, 5, p. 524.

of town. The following year, at age twenty-one, he married Isabel Gardner and quickly sought additional land with which to support his new bride. On Christmas day he signed an agreement with Pynchon to lease a forty-two-acre farm for a term of eleven years. The obligations of both men were considerable. Pynchon bound himself to bog and clear five acres of land, to provide "sixty load of dung to mend the land," and to "Build at the round hill this next Summer, a house for the said Isack Morgan to dwell in to the End of the terme." The landlord also supplied "a Barne . . . Three cows, a yoake of oxen and a horse . . . togither with a Cart and wheeles, yoake, Plough and chaine, and all irons for the Teames" and "80 Apples trees for the said Isack's use." The tenant, for his part, agreed to clear and plow the remaining upland and to pay both the town rates on the livestock and rent graduated up to £22 yearly.[37]

The account books show that Morgan worked hard to make a go of his leasehold. In addition to raising his own crops, he also performed a variety of manual labor for Pynchon. Indeed, so active was Morgan after taking over the forty-two-acre farm that his labor credits rivaled the annual £15 salary Pynchon paid his farm hands. Morgan specialized in heavy field work and, like his father Miles, slaughtering. Most of his labor credits were for such tasks as digging ditches, draining marshes, gathering stones, carting goods, and either gelding or slaughtering livestock. In November 1672 he received credit for "mowing, haymaking . . . 58 Rod ditching [and carting up from Enfield falls] 17 bushels ½ Salt." The year Morgan took the farm, Pynchon paid him £9 for "Bogging And the 3 acres he formerly engaged to doe . . . and 2 acres he engaged to cleare . . . and for 35 Rod of ditching." The next year he earned £13 for a wide array of tasks: "digging stones . . . cutting calves . . . carting 2 load stone . . . raising house, Nayling up Bords . . . cutting a Bull . . . 7 load wood . . . 8 days [work] . . . Setting up Rayles . . . Mowing . . . carting clay and daubing, fencing . . . carting 1 load Posts . . . killing sheep . . . winter[ing] of 7 cattle and killing 2 [cattle] . . . killing hoggs."[38]

King Philip's followers destroyed most of the farm when they attacked Springfield in 1675, but they did not sever Isaac Morgan's ties to John Pynchon. During his sixteen-year rental career, he leased additional plowland, meadow, and oxen before he emigrated to Enfield in the early 1680s. There he also continued to work for

[37] *Ibid.*, 5, pp. 422–423.
[38] *Ibid.*, 5, pp. 189, 420–423.

his former landlord. On December 31, 1681, Pynchon "Agreed with Isack Morgan well to stub and break up with Plough 2 acres of land in my lot at Enfield. That is to say all the bredth of my lot there and 14 rod in the length of it and the place where he is to doe this is agreed to be about 40 rod from the front of my home lot there . . . [for] Three Pounds and a stubbing hoe." A year later Pynchon asked Morgan "to do 20 rod of good 5 Raile fence at fresh water [for] 37 shillings."[39]

Jonathan Ball's career illustrates a similar dependence on Pynchon. It also shows how day-laborers used tenancy as a vehicle for upward mobility. Ball was born in Springfield in 1645 and began working for John Pynchon as a field hand at the age of nineteen. Pynchon wrote in 1665 that "Jonathan Ball came to me the 21 March 1664/65 and he is to be with me 2 months for which I am to allow him 20s. per month." Ball continued to work primarily for Pynchon for the next dozen years, receiving payments for "carting dung 6 days . . . 2 months work in 1665 . . . a Journey to New London, and looking up cattle . . . 15 days worke . . . 11 days worke at the Mill . . . 2 days worke sawing . . . fencing at woronoke, Rayls 25s., ditching 9s., Log fence 10s."[40] During the early 1670s, Ball began to concentrate increasingly on canoe work, as account book entries credit him for "carrying Corne downe the falls May 22 1671, your share of all is £3 2s. . . . By bringing up wine, sugar, Cords and etc. . . . By goeing down the falls and bringing up goods with Goodman Miller [in] May and June 1675, your part is . . . £3 5s. 4d." Not giving up field work completely, however, Ball took 10 shillings in 1675 for "50 Rod of ditch[ing]."[41]

In 1677, at the age of thirty-two, Ball leased Pynchon's eighty-acre farm in joint tenancy with Samuel Taylor. Rent was set at £18. As the account books reveal, the tenants were starting from scratch. They brought almost nothing of their own to the farm and relied on the landlord to supply even the most elemental necessities, including fodder, foundation stock, and planting seed. On April 13, 1677, Pynchon sold them "[7] bushels pease . . . 1 load of hay, 19 bushels of oates, 1 pair of Cart wheels . . . Cart irons . . . [and] 6 rubstones." Presumably to celebrate their new lease, Ball and Taylor also bought "2 pints of Liquors." A year and a half later, Pynchon "put to my farmers besides a yoak of steeres which I let to Sam Taylor and 2 steers I had of Henry Chapin." After the tenants complained that they lacked sufficient pasturage, Pynchon also

[39] *Ibid.*, 5, p. 421.
[40] *Ibid.*, 3, pp. 128–129.
[41] *Ibid.*, 5, pp. 40–41.

"agreed with my farmers, they desyring . . . to fence in some ground for a pasture."[42]

As the prominence of oats in the planting seed suggests, Ball and Taylor planned their enterprise around animal fodder production. In the seventeenth century, as today, wheat, barley, and rye were for human consumption; oats were used as winter feed for livestock.[43] In this expectation, the two tenants were apparently successful. During their first year of operation, Pynchon paid them £12 for "80 bushels of oates [and another] 20 bushels of oates." Likewise, two years later he credited them £8 for "80 bushels of oates." To help meet operating expenses, both men continued to perform field labor for their landlord worth roughly £12 annually. But, despite these efforts, Ball and Taylor could not generate enough income to cover their overhead, particularly the £18 rental fee. After holding the farm seven years, they gave it up in 1684. Ball, however, continued to lease his meadowland and plowground from Pynchon. That year he rented two acres of meadow at sixteen shillings, and in 1688 he leased eleven acres of prime upland for £3 8s. yearly. Ball held this land until the landlord's death fifteen years later. By that time he had paid for a total of twenty-five contract years, with cumulative payments in excess of £145.[44] This period of extended tenancy, as the 1685 valuation list reveals, is attributable to insufficient lands. In that year Ball owned only twenty-nine acres, despite the fact that he was at that time over forty years old and had been married twelve years. Moreover, sixteen of his twenty-nine acres were located in a marshy and unproductive section of Springfield known as the "Pickle."[45]

---

[42] *Ibid.*, 5, p. 524.

[43] Russell, *A Long, Deep Furrow*, p. 42.

[44] Account Books, 5, pp. 524–525; 6, pp. 18–19.

[45] 1685 Tax List. The fact that Jonathan Ball was a tenant farmer did not bar him from full participation in the community's social and political life. He held a number of town offices, including those of both selectman and tithingman. His illiteracy was no barrier to service as a selectman. Boards of selectmen in 17th-century Springfield often included at least one member unable to read. Ball's selection as tithingman, however, may have raised a few eyebrows. Tithingmen were charged by the General Court with the responsibility for ensuring domestic peace and maintaining Puritan norms of personal rectitude within the villages. And on occasion, it seems, Ball's behavior was something less than exemplary. In the spring of 1667 he was fined five shillings for "unseasonable Night Metings." Typically these offenses related to Ball's penchant for nightly bouts of drinking with his friends Sam Owen and Josias Leonard. On one such occasion, in early January of 1686, Owen apparently had a bit too much, and Ball and Leonard failed to see that he got home safely—with somewhat calamitous consequences for the widow Sarah Barnard. Two weeks later, Mrs. Barnard stood before the court and testified that

With his tenant farmers paying annual rents as high as £22, John Pynchon fully appreciated their worth. In a letter to his son describing the devastation brought by the Indian attack, Pynchon underscored his growing reliance on income derived from tenants (and debtors as well). After relating the town's and his own losses, he cited the destruction visited on his tenants, especially the farmers: "Four of those houses and barns . . . which were burnt in this towne belongeth to me also. So God hath laid me low. My farmers are also undone, and many in this town that were in my debt utterly disabled, so that I am really reduced to great straits."[46] In a similar letter to the Reverend John Russell of Hadley, Pynchon again lamented the burning of the "houses and barnes I had let out to tenants."[47]

But it was the second class of tenants, the dependent renters, that provided Pynchon with his greatest sources of income. The fifty men in this group paid for some 890 contract years, with total recorded payments of £2,133. Their rental careers lasted an average of seventeen years, their average lifetime payments were £43—in addition to taxes and labor. Each dependent renter was in

---

the inebriated Owen had on that night invaded both her home and her bed. She told the court that "the 7th of this . . . January shee was much afrighted by a mans coming in to her House in the Night when she was in Bed and lying downe on her Bed wheruppon shee gat up and called when presently Thomas Lamb came in and speaking to him he gave noe answer to said Lamb till he Pulled him about to the fire and saw that it was Samuell Owen . . . at first [he] only opened his eyes and shut them again: I decerned that he had bene Drinking and smelled of it." Lamb and David Morgan attempted to resuscitate Owen, at first unsuccessfully. After an interval of fifteen minutes, Owen revived and "Labord to get up though he staggered a pritty while before he could recover himself, but at last he stood up." At this point Lamb proceeded to admonish the still-bewildered Owen: "I asked him Samuell what will your wife say to this that you come to another womans Bed." Under this questioning, Owen "made no answer for some time." As his head cleared, however, he began to wonder about the whereabouts of his drinking companions, and he then "askt after Josias Leanord and Jonathan Ball." When Lamb inquired "were they of your company," Owen again "made noe answer." Lamb then took it upon himself to see that Owen was started toward home: "Samuell: said I Come goe hom, and leading him as far as my House He Inquired the way Hom; I showed him and set him in it, and so parted." This parting was apparently premature, as "Goodman Foster told [Lamb] he gat but to his House that Night, and that with some difficulty having fallen in the Snow as he saw next morning." Jonathan Ball did make it home safely that night, possibly because his strong physical constitution allowed him to carry his liquor more easily than did Owen. His robustness enabled Ball to outlive his two drinking companions, his landlord, and most of the rest of his neighbors as well. He finally died in 1741, at the age of 96. Account Books, 3, p. 128; *Pynchon Court Rec.*, pp. 310–311.

[46] John Pynchon to Joseph Pynchon, October 20, 1675, CVHM.

[47] Mass. Archives, 67, p. 282.

some vital way reliant on his lease for economic sustenance. Unlike the tenant farmers, who were drawn almost entirely from the town's most marginal families, the dependent renters represented a broad spectrum of the population. They included both respected and venerable selectmen and the dispossessed. The career of Edward Foster illustrates the experiences of the latter.

Foster began and ended his stay in Springfield as a client of the Pynchon family. He was brought to the community from Scotland under an indenture to William Pynchon. Upon arrival, Foster's nine years of service were assigned to Elizur Holyoke.[48] After gaining his freedom, he went to work in John Pynchon's lead mine (which up until that time had been more promise than fulfillment). On March 30, 1659, Pynchon wrote that "The £3 which Edward Foster owes me below he engages to pay me out of his worke in the lead mines . . . noe pay to be made to [Foster] . . . till the debt is Satisfied." By the end of the decade of the 1650s, Foster had committed himself to full-time work for John Pynchon. After mining, his principal areas of concentration were canoe work, agricultural labor, and sawing. Various account book entries during the period from 1659 to 1674 credit him for "goeing downe the falls and carying 77½ bushels wheat with Goodman Mirick," "26 days ½ worke at the Mill Trench at 2s. 6d. [is] £3 6s.," "127 foote of boards," "making 8 rod of fence against the River," "By worke this Last Summer Mowing and about my Mill Dam and carting [12] days."[49]

Foster first rented land from Pynchon in 1668, and remained a tenant almost continuously until 1703. During this time, he paid for thirty-six contract years, with total payments of £153. In the late 1660s and early 1670s, Foster leased a 3½-acre homelot and 4½ acres of bottom land. His rent for these holdings was over £5 yearly—approximately half his former annual income as a laborer. In one of the leases, signed in March 1668, Pynchon "Lett out to Edward Foster my land in the Spring Bottom being about 4 acres for which he is to allow and pay me for this yeare coming the sum of thirty shillings . . . he is to take care of and repair the fence for the security of the field. Also let out to Edward Foster the hom lot of 3 acres and ½ . . . for 3 yeares, for which Edward Foster is to allow me 28s. per anum and repair the fence." The lease also included a proviso that if Pynchon decided to sell the land, "he shall have it before another at a meate price." In 1673 Foster signed

---

[48] *Pynchon Court Rec.*, p. 225.
[49] Account Books, 1, p. 217; 2, p. 209; 3, pp. 184–185, 247; 5, pp. 58–59, 474–475; 6, pp. 54–55; 1685 Tax List.

a contract with Pynchon that significantly altered his tenancy status. Now, rather than a two- or three-year lease, Foster agreed to a ten-year rental period. If he had envisioned his earlier leases as temporary expedients until he secured an adequate freehold, Foster evidently abandoned that hope in 1673. The new contract consolidated all the tenant's existing leases, along with additional meadowland, and called for rents of £7 yearly. He held this lease for the next eighteen years, until 1690. Foster subsequently rented five more acres in the rich Cold Spring bottom for thirty shillings annually, which he paid for the next seven years. Like the tenant farmers, he apparently rented because his own holdings were insufficient. In 1685 he owned only twenty-five acres, six of which were located in a distant and barren section with the ironic name of None Such. Because of these acreage deficiencies, Foster continued to rent from the third generation of Pynchons.[50]

The provisions of John Kilum's lease show graphically how tenancy could deprive a man of the fruits of his labor. The January 1689 contract committed Kilum to what in ordinary circumstances would be nearly a decade's worth of work. Pynchon "Agreed with John Kilum to have some of my Land over Agawam River for fifteen yeares . . . five acres . . . also he is to have my forty acres of upland in the Feild." The tenant was required to "cleare and break up at least fifteene acres," build "a good Timber House . . . at least 23 foote long [and] 18 foote wide," and "Plant an orchard." He also agreed to build and maintain all fences and pay rates up to ten shillings. The landlord agreed to provide boards for the floors and the exterior of the house. After Kilum fulfilled these obligations and paid an annual rent up to £5, he was expected to "Leave it . . . Tennentable" at the expiration of the lease.[51] Likewise, Philip Matoone's obligations in leasing Pynchon's eighteen cow commons and four sheep commons in Deerfield were considerable. In addition to a rent graduated up to £4, the tenant agreed to pay all rates, maintain the fences, and build "a good dwelling house strong substantial and well Built and Compleately furnished," with dimensions of 30-by-20-by-10 feet as well as a barn of at least 48-by-24-by-14 feet. The contract bound Matoone to "compleate and

---

[50] *Ibid.*

[51] Account Books, 6, pp. 228–229. Kilum held this land for 9 years, during which time he and Pynchon renegotiated the rent from £5 to £7 10s. annually. Kilum subsequently leased a total of over 30 acres of plowland and meadowland, some at joint tenancy. In 1693 he leased 11 acres in joint tenancy with Thomas Jones for £3 8s. yearly. By the time of John Pynchon's death in 1703, Kilum had paid for 16 contract years with lifetime payments of £66.

finish the same before the end of the terme, then leave and deliver all in good repaire."[52] Working on others' lands left men little time to work on their own. When Indians took his life in 1696, Philip Matoone's estate was valued at but £87, £23 of which was in real property.[53]

Such leading figures as selectmen and deputies to the General Court were numbered among the dependent renters. John Dumbleton, selectman for sixteen terms as well as a militia officer, paid £117 for sixty-six contract years during the period from 1652 to 1692. He leased at various times over fifty acres, oxen, bulls, and horses.[54] Lieutenant Abel Wright, selectman and representative to the General Court, paid £56 for leases of plowland, meadow, oxen and bulls during the years from 1668 to 1686. In 1668 Wright rented land which Pynchon two days earlier had taken for debts from Benjamin Dorchester. The contract provided that if, at the expiration of the term, Wright "can attain to buy the land he is to have it before another." Unfortunately for the tenant, he failed to come up with the purchase price and ended up paying the thirty-eight-shilling rent for the next eighteen years.[55] Wright owned 160 acres in 1685 and would appear, therefore, to be an unlikely candidate for tenancy. But, again, his holdings show the fallacy of equating land *ownership* with land *use*. Because of a combination of remoteness and infertility, Wright's 160 acres were valued at £47, an average of only six shillings per acre, roughly one-tenth of land valuations in the third division.[56]

Although the dependent renters included men drawn from both the town's leadership elite and the servant class, most tenants came from a large middle group composed of men who were usually freemen but rarely civic leaders. Lazarus Miller was typical of these men. During a rental career that was cut short by his death at the age of forty-two, he leased over seventy-seven acres of upland and meadow as well as housing, orchards, and oxen. As with Abel Wright, a lack of decent, accessible acreage led Miller to rent. The sixty-four acres he owned in 1685 were located several miles from the town center in "Block Bridge" where land values averaged five shillings per acre. In 1680 Miller rented an eleven-acre lot, an

[52] Account Books, 5, pp. 536–537.

[53] HCPC Rec., 3 (1692–1713), p. 27.

[54] *Pynchon Court Rec.*, p. 266; Account Books, 1, pp. 67–69; 2, p. 164; 3, p. 181; 5, pp. 50–51, 182–183, 540; 6, p. 196.

[55] *Pynchon Court Rec.*, pp. 313, 387; Account Books, 3, pp. 116–117; 5, pp. 102–103; 6, p. 174; 6, Index, p. 4.

[56] 1685 Tax List.

orchard, and a house in Chicopee plain for two years at £3 10s. annually. This lease was followed by one in 1684 for a twenty-four-acre lot in Chicopee field. In 1694, he leased a thirty-acre lot, ten acres of which had already been plowed. His rent was £1 15s. yearly, as well as fence maintenance and town rates; in addition the tenant was required to stub and clear all the remaining unbroken land and build a shelter.[57] Largely because he had spent his life's labors improving Pynchon's leaseholds, instead of his own, Miller left very little except debts when he died in the mid-1690s.[58] In a scene replete with patron-client overtones, his brothers Obadiah and John approached Pynchon to seek forgiveness of part of the balance. As Pynchon recounted the conversation after the two men had left: "Obadiah Miller and John Miller seeing this account and being satisfied in it: proposed that I would abate something or give something to the widow: which I yielded unto and we readyly and freely give to Lazarus Miller's widdow Thirty shillings out of this Debt and so reduce the Debt to £8 12s." Pynchon appended this entry with the comment that "This was in case the Estate proved Solvent to Incourage them to administer and for their benefit."[59] The estate, however, did not prove solvent. Miller's total assets were valued at £38, his debts at £39, of which—after a final recalculation—£18 were owed to Pynchon.[60]

The third class of tenants was the short-term dependent renters—men who relied on leases from Pynchon to help them through brief periods of economic dislocation. These thirty renters paid approximately £240 for 218 contract years. The average duration of their rental period was seven years; the average total payment was £8. Their dependency on Pynchon is illustrated by the scope and diversity of their contracts. Some men, clearly of adequate means, used short-term tenancy as the most expeditious way of getting a start in Springfield. Joseph Marks, for example, although he paid for only seven contract years, rented a twenty-acre lot in Chicopee field for £3 10s. yearly, as well as a shed, yoke of oxen, mare, and a gun.[61] Likewise, Miles Morgan's nine contract years included leases for a house, twenty-five acres, oxen, a bull, and a cow.[62] Men with the necessary skills sought to lease Pynchon's mills, doubtless aware of the highly remunerative tolls earned by millers.

[57] Account Books, 5, pp. 490–491; 6, pp. 190–191; 6, Index; 1685 Tax List.
[58] HCPC Rec., 3, p. 38.
[59] Account Books, 6, p. 190.
[60] *Ibid.*; HCPC Rec., 3, p. 38.
[61] Account Books, 6, pp. 130–131.
[62] *Ibid.*, 1, pp. 77, 265; 3, pp. 142–144, 240; 6, p. 26.

Thomas Copley rented both a sawmill and a gristmill between 1681 and 1685. The contract specified that the mills were to be held "at halves." Copley tended and maintained the mill, while Pynchon helped defray the cost of upkeep. The two men divided the tolls equally at year's end.[63] Other millers simply paid an annual rent of £16 and kept all the tolls to themselves.[64]

The short-term dependent renters included a high percentage of joint or multiple tenancies. Under these leases, the tenants divided expenses, profits, and labor according to a prearranged formula. John Burt, Benjamin Knowlton, and Thomas Mirrick rented an eleven-acre lot in the third division from 1689 to 1693 "at thirds."[65] Victory Sikes and George Granger leased meadowland over the Agawam River for £4 10s. yearly. Pynchon required the two tenants to "clear off all trees and bush from the mowing land."[66] Ebenezer Graves rented a twenty-one-acre lot in Chicopee in joint tenancy with his brother Daniel in 1689.[67] Because joint tenancies allowed marginal men to pool their meager resources, they were commonly utilized by Springfield's more impoverished inhabitants.[68]

The fourth category of tenants, the long-term independent renters, included nine men who leased moderately sized plots of land for extended periods, usually twelve to fourteen years.[69] In contrast to the dependent renters, leasing for this group was a supplemental activity. They rented because it was convenient and profitable, but not necessary, to do so. Many of these contracts suggest what anthropologists describe as "collegial relationships." These are largely symbolic economic ties between relative social equals whose purpose is to solidify friendship and loyalty.[70] For example, Henry Chapin, the son of Springfield's first deacon, leased 7½ acres of wet meadow from Pynchon for a period of twenty-two years.[71] Chapin, who

---

[63] *Ibid.*, 5, pp. 170–171; 6, p. 48.

[64] See Chapter 4.

[65] Account Books, 6, p. 178.

[66] *Ibid.*, 6, p. 106.

[67] *Ibid.*, 6, pp. 156, 172.

[68] It is not possible, however, simply to equate joint tenancies with impoverishment. The Graves brothers were clearly among Springfield's more marginal inhabitants. Both were landless on the 1685 Tax List. Similarly Benjamin Knowlton who, married for ten years by 1685, owned only 16 acres. At his death in 1690, Knowlton's land was valued at £13. HCPC Rec., 2 (1678–1716), p. 61. John Burt and Thomas Mirrick, by contrast, were obviously not among the town's poor. Burt owned 72 acres of prime land in 1685, Mirrick, 110 acres. 1685 Tax List.

[69] As a group, these renters paid for 118 contract years, with average payments of £11.

[70] Foster, "The Dyadic Contract," *Am. Anthropologist* (1961), pp. 1173–1192.

[71] Account Books, 3, pp. 156–157; 5, pp. 22–23, 208; 6, p. 44.

bought two hundred acres from Pynchon in 1659 and was the third largest landholder on the 1685 tax list, rented out of choice, not necessity.[72] So did Joseph Ashley, who leased three wharf lots between 1678 and 1687, two of them for at least nine years each. Ashley was a part-time merchant and rented primarily to foster his trading activities. He already had sufficient land on which to raise his crops. In 1685 Ashley owned eighty-six acres in the most highly assessed section of the town, and, at his death in 1711, his real estate was valued at £209.[73]

The fifth set of tenants, those least reliant on Pynchon, were the short-term independent renters. These were individuals who, like the long-term independent renters, leased for reasons of choice, not necessity. The thirty-one tenants in this group rented for limited periods, usually three years or less.[74] Predominantly from Springfield's more affluent families, they likewise possibly hoped to establish a symbolic bond with John Pynchon.[75] Japhet Chapin, a brother of Henry, held 365 acres in 1685, second only to Pynchon's 1,800 acres. During an intermittent rental career that extended from 1665 to 1695, Chapin leased a 5½-acre lot, a 4-acre lot, a meadow, and a bull.[76] George Colton, quartermaster in the militia, selectman, and representative to the General Court, died in 1690 leaving an estate worth £847. But he too rented, a "little red stonehorse" in 1654 and meadow on Freshwater River between 1663 and 1667.[77]

The sixth and last group of renters, those who leased animals exclusively, was composed predominantly of non-Springfield residents. Of the twenty-six men in this category, only five lived in John Pynchon's home town. Draft animals—oxen or stone horses—were the most frequently rented livestock, though leases of short-horned cattle, mares, swine, and sheep were not uncommon. Renters in this group were usually drawn from poorer families. Judah Trumble, for one, was a subsistence farmer who tilled his small plot with a yoke of oxen leased from Pynchon for £2 annually for

[72] Deed, John Pynchon to Henry Chapin, March 9, 1660, CVHM.

[73] Account Books, 5, pp. 444–445; 6, pp. 28–29; 1685 Tax List; HCPC Rec., 3, pp. 243–244.

[74] The short-term independent renters paid for a total of 85 contract years. In addition to the 31 Springfield renters, there were 20 short-term renters from other valley towns.

[75] Foster, "The Dyadic Contract," *Am. Anthropologist* (1961), pp. 1173–1192.

[76] 1685 Tax List; Account Books, 3, pp. 58–59; 5, p. 13; 6, p. 44.

[77] HCPC Rec., 3, pp. 68–70; Account Books, 1, p. 140; 2, pp. 246–247; 3, pp. 60–62.

seven years.[78] As with all livestock leases, Trumble paid all the rates and charges on the oxen and was responsible for replacing them if they were injured or destroyed while in his service. The option of what to do with the offspring—allow the renter to keep all or part of them, take them after two years while indemnifying the renter, or simply take them without compensation—made livestock leases fertile ground for patron-client relationships. John Crowfoot, for example, apparently was not a client. He leased a young mare for three years during the 1680s and was required to give Pynchon all foals that reached two years of age. Symon Rumnel, by contrast, rented a "sanded sow" for three years "at halves," and the owner received only one-half of the new piglets.[79] While most livestock leases stipulated three-year terms, some were for as many as seven. In 1692, Pynchon let out a cow to William Booth for seven years at ten shillings annually.[80] Because it was not possible for a family to subsist long in the absence of draft and dairy animals, (witness "Jack and the Bean Stalk") a note of urgency sometimes accompanied lease requests. After John Woodward had approached him several times during the early 1690s, Pynchon yielded to Woodward's "entreaties" for a yoke of oxen.[81] Both men recognized that Woodward had few alternatives. In Springfield, those who needed livestock, like those who needed land, turned to John Pynchon.

But for all these groups, the risk posed by increased dependence on Pynchon was serious and sometimes crippling indebtedness. The debit entries in the account books lay bare the process of wealth transfer in early Springfield. Because Pynchon's control of the local economy was so extensive, all residents found at least occasional indebtedness to him inescapable. Tenancy was the principal cause, but even those who avoided becoming indebted as tenants often saw their economic fortunes imperiled through chronically unbalanced ledgers at the store. Not all debt is detrimental, of course. In a barter economy, people became indebted to each other for the day-to-day exchange of goods and services, or for loans made for capital improvements. The critical distinction here, however, is between this constructive indebtedness and the kind of chronic, disabling indebtedness which is not redeemed through regular transactions. For those without clientage ties with Pynchon, chronic

---

[78] Account Books, 5, pp. 342–343.

[79] *Ibid.*, 5, p. 307; 6, p. 122.

[80] *Ibid.*, 6, p. 91.

[81] *Ibid.*, 6, p. 35.

indebtedness was likely to result in loss of lands, home, or live-stock—or possibly even debt peonage.[82]

Debt peonage, as Pete Daniel observes, "flourishes best in a prim-itive capitalistic economy that is adjusting its labor system." Daniel points to such transitional periods as the abolition of the *encomiendas* in South America and of chattel slavery in North America. In addition to a labor system in transition, he finds peonage resulting from "high illiteracy rates, a rural and isolated environment, an inviolate power structure, and corrupt or corruptible local law-enforcement officers." With the exception of official corruption, all of these elements apply with some degree to Springfield.[83] What the town didn't have, of course, was the *institutionalized* deprivation of disprivileged groups such as Indians or blacks by vagrancy laws, labor-contract statutes, criminal-surety systems, and convict leasing. In the post-Civil War South, the engine to the system of peonage was not paternalistic persuasion, but rather legal enforcement. As Daniel asserts, "The line that divided the cropper from the peon was a thin but crucial one. It depended on the compulsion that forced a man to remain on a plantation year after year," a com-pulsion provided by sheriffs, constables, local police, justices of the peace, and state legislators. "Peonage occurred," Daniel reports, "only when a planter forbade the cropper to leave the plantation because of debt." If, when the account books were balanced, "the planter told his cropper that he remained in debt and could not move from the plantation, then the system became peonage." Peon-age resulted from indebtedness, "but the debtor had to be re-strained for the legal definition to be fulfilled." When a peon fled, the creditor called on local law enforcement officials, who would "arrest [the] black laborers, hold them in jail until the planter ar-rived, and then allow the employer to deal with the prisoners as he would."[84] No such institutionalized collusion between the cred-itor and the law existed in Springfield. Equally important, the town lacked the general climate of violence, intimidation, and terrorism that provided the crucial extra-legal enforcement of the planter's will in both the post-bellum South and Latin America. Debt peon-

[82] Debtors could not expect much protection from colonial courts. As William E. Nelson observes, "Debtors in general were almost powerless" while "Creditors had broad remedies not only against their immediate debtors but against others as well." *Americanization of the Common Law: The Impact of Legal Change on Massachusetts Society, 1760–1830*, Cambridge, Mass., 1975, pp. 42–43.

[83] Pete Daniel, *The Shadow of Slavery: Peonage in the South, 1901–1969*, New York, 1973, p. x. See also William Cohen, "Negro Involuntary Servitude: A Preliminary Analysis," *Journal of Southern History*, 42 (1976), pp. 31–60.

[84] Daniel, *Shadow of Slavery*, pp. 24–25.

age in Springfield, as elsewhere, was a form of manipulating laborers; but John Pynchon called on personal obligation instead of the constable to achieve this end. Peonage in Springfield, as with tenancy and work, was a personal, not institutionalized, experience. Here again the key transitional device from manorial to capitalistic relationships was the patron-client bond. Nothing shows this so vividly as do the contrasts between John Pynchon's treatment of those debtors who were clients and those who were not.

For those men with whom Pynchon had forged a patron-client relationship, indebtedness was restrictive but not destructive; it curbed their political autonomy but it did not drive them under. The account books are replete with instances of long overdue debts. The carpenter Joseph Leonard, for example, owed Pynchon the sum of £98 in 1680. Seven years later the figure had grown to £116, and the creditor expressed his growing impatience but did not threaten or take legal action. In February 1689 the two men made an accounting and found £79 "of old account which hath been long due."[85] Leonard was the most highly skilled joiner in Springfield and was usually the first man Pynchon turned to when the landlord needed new houses constructed. Moreover, a large part of the reason Leonard was so indebted was the annual rent of £10 10s. the carpenter paid for five and a half acres of Pynchon's land in the third division.[86] Leonard, who died with an estate valued at £640, *needed* neither employment nor a lease from Pynchon in order to survive.[87] His skills and his lands gave him sufficient bargaining power. And Pynchon's recognition of this power made it prudent to forestall collection of Leonard's debts for so long. The same was true for the tavern-keeper Nathaniel Ely, whose ordinary served as the courtroom where Pynchon sat as magistrate.[88] Ely, who rented his house and lands from Pynchon for £8 yearly, was indebted to his landlord for more than £130 by 1664. Rather than hectoring Ely or threatening litigation, he allowed the tavern-keeper to get by simply by paying a 5 percent annual interest on the principal.[89] Possibly the most dramatic example of Pynchon's willingness to long defer debt collection was Thomas Cooper. A twenty-term selectman as well as one of Pynchon's fur agents, Cooper was in-

[85] Account Books, 5, pp. 66–67, 532; 6, pp. 62–63.
[86] *Ibid.*, 5, pp. 66–67, 532.
[87] HCPC Rec., 4 (1708–1780), pp. 14–15.
[88] John F. Whicher, "Criminal Procedures before the County Court for Hampshire County, Massachusetts, From 1658 to 1685," unpublished paper, January 6, 1947, CVHM.
[89] Account Books, 3, pp. 108–109.

debted to Pynchon for £1,000 in 1656. But despite the magnitude of the debt, Cooper was allowed to bring it down gradually; he had not fully repaid it by the time Indians killed him in 1675.[90]

For those men who were not clients of Pynchon, however, the consequences of indebtedness were often calamitous. For them, he showed little inclination to long ignore deadlines or forgive a portion of the balance. The choice was either to pay up or forfeit part of their freehold. Many were forced to take the latter route. Between 1655 and 1703, over forty Springfield residents lost a total of some one thousand acres, in addition to houses, mills, and livestock, for debts to Pynchon amounting to £1,134. Many who lost property in this way subsequently rented it back. The unhappy experiences of Jonathan Taylor, Obadiah Miller, and Samuel Marshfield illustrate this process. In October 1656, Taylor's debt to Pynchon stood at £19 19s. and he set his mark to a formal acknowledgment of this sum. Two years later, Taylor's mounting debt compelled him to give his "yoake of steeres" to offset £12 10s. of the balance due. As a replacement for his team Taylor purchased an ancient steer, well past the age when most draft animals had been put out to pasture. Broke, Taylor paid for the animal with a promise of future labor: "Sold to Jonathan Taylor 12½ [-year-old] flax steere for which he Ingages and promises me to reape and shock 2 acres of wheate and to cut one acre of pease when I call for it to be done next harvest and to doe it upon 2 days [notice]." Despite surrendering his oxen, and performing a wide array of tasks for Pynchon—"21 days worke . . . carting dung . . . haymaking . . . 10 days at the mill . . . milking my Cows this yeare 6 weeks"— Taylor failed to reduce his debt. Moreover, on March 10, 1668, he increased his financial dependence on Pynchon by leasing a house and 7½ acres of land. The landlord "Let out to Jonathan Taylor my house (on the west side of the River) and 7 acres and ½ of Ground . . . for 35s. and to repair the house by thatching it and etc. . . . and he is to repair all the fencing."[91]

Two days after signing the house lease Taylor dropped by the smithy, presumably to share a pipe and some conversation with the blacksmith, John Stewart; but he got more than he bargained for. John Pynchon arrived in the shop and straightaway lit into Taylor for non-performance. As the account books relate it: "meeting with Jonathan Taylor at the smith's shop I spake to him to bring in the Indian Corne and the wheate which he promised for the Sugar

[90] *Ibid.*, 1, p. 326; 5, pp. 258–259; HCPC Rec., 1, p. 167.
[91] Account Books, 1, pp. 125–126, 314; 2, pp. 228–229; 3, pp. 174–175.

per Contract: and told him that when he had all which was 2 Months agoe he promised Corne Spedyly and twas tyme now to pay it, which he Granted and so he would bring it in quickly." He then proceeded to admonish Taylor for also allowing his debts to remain unpaid: "I then wished him to pay what he owed me, viz. that per Contract and in old booke and told him it had bin due a great while and now it was tyme to pay it." Taylor agreed that the debt was well past due but "propounded noe way of pay." When the creditor proposed to "take your 4 acres of land which you offered me a while agoe," Taylor replied that he "knew not how to part with it." Pynchon's entry in his account book reveals the precarious state of Taylor's finances: "Noe said I, are you not willing to pay the debt[?] He said he could not doe it till next yeare: said I, I think it tyme you should pay it now, and though you have bin on my debt a long time yet, I will give you £12 for that land; he said he thought it was too little and would not let it goe so, and said he could not tell how to pay me till next yeare."[92]

Returning home with celerity to discuss the family's plight with his wife, Taylor decided that he had no alternative but to give up the land. One week later, Pynchon "Agreed with Jonathan Taylor for his land over the River by my meddow . . . by the black Pond, all which (as he says) it is above 5 acres and ½ for which I am to give him £13 17s. and the use of it this summer coming." The landlord also consented to "give him in 20 pounds of Sugar which he was to have into the bargaine."[93] Taylor continued to rent Pynchon's house and land until his death in 1681. Problems with indebtedness plagued him until the end. By March of 1680 his balance owed to Pynchon stood at £46.[94] Again, as with the earlier debt of £14, this was not an abnormally high sum. Pynchon habitually allowed clients with debts in excess of £100—and in Thomas Cooper's case in excess of £1,000—extraordinary flexibility in the repayment schedules. Not so for Taylor, however. Not having forged the necessary patron-client bond, he continued to forfeit land. The year before he died, Taylor lost an additional seven acres in Chicopee plain for debts of £36.[95] When his estate was probated in 1683, it was valued at £40, only £5 of which was in land. The estate's encumbrances amounted to £47.[96]

[92] *Ibid.*, 3, pp. 174–175.

[93] *Ibid.*; Deed, Jonathan Taylor to John Pynchon, March 22, 1682, Hampden Co. Deeds, Volume AB, pp. 61, 167.

[94] Account Books, 5, p. 53.

[95] Deed, Jonathan Taylor to John Pynchon, March 30, 1698, Hampden Co. Deeds, Volume AB, p. 167.

[96] HCPC Rec., 2, p. 39.

The experiences of Obadiah Miller are reminiscent of those of Jonathan Taylor to a striking degree. Like Taylor he worked as a day-laborer and rented from John Pynchon from the mid-1650s onward. In 1656, in what would be the first of many such accountings, Pynchon "Received by one acre and halfe of meddow" from Miller for debts. Seven years later the creditor wrote that "rests due to mee from Obadiah Miller the sum of Eight Pounds Ten shillings foure pence which is all now due to be paid in wheate at 3s. 6d. [per] bushel." But Miller could not come up with the necessary funds and told Pynchon that "he is unable to pay all this yeare and therefore only engages 20 bushels of wheate this yeare . . . and [the] rest he promises to pay some short tyme after." However, after the projected interval had passed, "he [had] failed of payment so owes me the whole [sum]." Part of Miller's problem resulted from the fact that his work for Pynchon was more than offset by his food purchases from him. In early January 1663, Pynchon wrote that "what worke he did for me this yeare 1662 was set off for corne he had of me." Moreover, in the spring of 1668 Miller decided that it was time for a new house, and he went to see what Pynchon had to offer. The entrepreneur had a frame ready for sale, and he agreed to subcontract the remaining work. On June 27, Pynchon "Sold to Obadiah Miller the Timber for a house frame over the River . . . for which he is to pay me the Sum of £3 10s. And I am to help him toward the getting it done, viz. to procure Thomas Coply to saw it which Obadiah is to pay me for as also I am to Sattisfie John Baker £3 for his worke to frame the house which Obadiah is to repay me."[97]

But even as Miller made plans to move into his new house, the family's indebtedness problems continued to mount. In December of 1665 he lost his "Six acres of Land which lys neere the cold Spring Bottom." Pynchon agreed to allow Miller "Liberty for this year to Mow that acre and ½ by my house which I bought of him in case John Henryson doth not hold it and he is Ingaged for this yeare to come to Looke to set up and sufficiently repair all the fencing which belongs to this 6 acres of land." In March 1668, Miller lost nine more acres for debts of £17. A month later, the process continued. Wearied by the accelerating erosion of the family's fortunes, Miller's wife Joanna decided to take matters into her own hands. According to the account book entry: "Goodwife Miller came to mee with her husband and said she was willing I should have the land. But she thought I gave too little, and in further

[97] Account Books, 1, p. 302; 2, pp. 134–135; 3, pp. 178–179; *Springfield Town Recs.*, 2, pp. 605–606.

discourseing and owning my debt to have been long due, she was willing to agree to the sale, if I would allow her 11s. she owes for kersey, which I yielded to, and so both of them were willing, and the price for the land is £18 1s."[98] Such modest favors failed to bring the Millers to solvency and their indebtedness problems became worse, not better. Finally, in 1682, they lost an additional eighty acres and a yoke of oxen to Pynchon "for the debts [of] £54."[99] Left with little more than a few household belongings, the Millers packed these up and departed the town forever.

The most spectacular example of the destructive effects of indebtedness was Samuel Marshfield. Born in England and one of the earliest settlers in Springfield, Marshfield quickly became a prosperous and esteemed member of the community. He served as the town's representative to the General Court for three terms and was a selectman for no less than thirteen years.[100] Something of a jack-of-all-trades, Marshfield earned his livelihood as a merchant, tailor, canoeman, teamster, drover, carpenter, sheep-shearer, smith, and agricultural worker.[101] He also kept the town ordinary from 1660 to 1665.[102] He first became a tenant of John Pynchon in 1665, leasing for varying periods thereafter 9 acres, a 7½-acre lot with an attached orchard, a 3½-acre lot, land in the "Pickle," and plowland over the Agawam River. He also periodically rented a yoke of oxen. By the late 1680s, Marshfield's annual rental payment stood at £7. In an apparent paradox, the number of his leases multiplied as he entered his declining years. Rather than moving from tenancy to freehold, he was doing the reverse. The explanation is found in his indebtedness records.[103]

By 1667, Marshfield's debt to John Pynchon stood at £54 and the creditor called it in. As with Taylor and Miller, the magnitude of the debt—when compared with the sums owed to Pynchon by many of his clients—was in no way excessive. But the flexibility over payment schedules enjoyed by clients did not extend to Marshfield. The creditor demanded immediate payment on pain of forfeiture of all of the debtor's land and housing on the east side of the Connecticut River. Marshfield confessed his inability to pay, and Pynchon thereupon took "his howse and land, viz. all his howsing and all his land on this side of the great River . . . To Cleare

[98] *Springfield Town Recs.*, 2, pp. 605–606.
[99] Account Books, 5, p. 543.
[100] *Pynchon Court Rec.*, p. 381; *Springfield Town Recs.*, 1, pp. 26–39.
[101] Account Books, 1, pp. 108, 110; 2, p. 109; 3, p. 111; 6, pp. 188–189.
[102] Whicher, "Criminal Procedures," p. 30.
[103] Account Books, 1, p. 108; 3, pp. 110–111; 5, pp. 36–37, 471; 6, pp. 188–189.

the debt."[104] Still a man of considerable means because of his property holdings on the west side, Marshfield appeared likely to survive even such a major land forfeiture. But the past was prologue. Two decades later, Marshfield's debts having grown to over £150, Pynchon demanded a similar reckoning. Again Marshfield could not raise the necessary funds and in September of 1686, the creditor took the surety of 124 acres and part ownership in a sawmill: "I accept as followeth: 15 acres of Land in the Medow over Agawam River more or less, 12 acres in the Pikle over the River more or less, 7 acres and ½ by my orchard over the River, 10 acres of Meddow and 10 acres of upland at Nonsuch: 20 acres more or less his due at Enfeild, 50 acres at the falls joining to that Land which I had of William Brookes. His part of the sawmil at Schonunganock . . . with the Saw wholy to be mine."[105] Even this transaction did not extricate Marshfield from the noose of indebtedness. At his death six years later, landless and with total assets of but £66, he still owed John Pynchon £72.[106] The debt was then remanded to Marshfield's son Josiah. Three years later, with an outstanding balance of £23, the creditor offered to abate the amount to £18 if it was paid "within 10 or 20 days."[107]

The lessons of these land forfeitures presumably were not lost on the rest of Springfield's inhabitants. Without a strong, communally oriented town meeting to protect their interests, the best route to survival in the town's perilous economy was a patron-client bond with John Pynchon. The experiences of Taylor, Miller, and Marshfield—and many more like them—could serve as cautionary tales, whether intended as such or not. In the company town that was Springfield, the financial destinies of half the population were sealed over the counter of the Pynchon general store. Those who needed land—and wanted to keep it—had to make an accommodation with John Pynchon. This also applied to those who needed work.

[104] *Ibid.*, 3, p. 111.
[105] *Ibid.*, 6, pp. 188–189, 230–231.
[106] *Ibid.*, 6, p. 188; HCPC Rec., 3, p. 2.
[107] Account Books, 6, pp. 230–231.

• Chapter 4 •

Work

"You see a man skillful in his craft:
he will serve kings, he will not serve common men"
Proverbs, XXII, 29

FOR MOST of the inhabitants of early Springfield, the process of "getting work" began with a trek to the Pynchon general store. Over half of the town's population at any given time was working a month or longer each year for John Pynchon, and for approximately forty seventeenth-century inhabitants he was their primary source of income. Men worked for Pynchon either by choice or necessity. Those who worked by choice were the skilled artisans—blacksmiths, coopers, tailors, and the like—who found in Pynchon a man eager for their services and well able to pay for them. Those who worked by necessity were the landless laborers or marginal tenant farmers, individuals who were forced to supplement their meager incomes by toiling in Pynchon's fields for sixteen to twenty pence per day.[1]

The necessity for a large and reliable labor force was Pynchon's chief incentive for forming patron-client ties with so many of the town's men. Throughout the seventeenth century, his new fields needed to be cleared, stubbed, and plowed. Likewise, weather permitting, few days passed without the continuous ringing of hammers as a town was formed out of a wilderness. Pynchon's mills needed to be tended, and so did his herds of livestock. When his wheat grew golden in the fields, he needed to be able to count on the labor of some forty-odd reapers during the always hectic days of harvest. Men who owned canoes or oxcarts found Pynchon always in need of their services, hauling goods to and from Enfield falls, carting logs to his sawmills, or gathering dung from the pasture. Those who had a way with animals broke his oxen to the yoke

[1] Still the standard work on labor and wage patterns in early America is Richard B. Morris, *Government and Labor in Early America*, New York, 1946; see also, Carl Bridenbaugh, *The Colonial Craftsman*, New York, 1950.

and his horses to the saddle. Those with sufficient barn space stall-fed his livestock from late November to early March, earning up to twenty shillings per head for their efforts. Finally, the Springfield entrepreneur needed men for his various extractive projects, including lead, iron ore, tar, turpentine, and resin.

While an age profile of John Pynchon's work force would reveal a preponderance of men between the ages of eighteen and thirty, most inhabitants continued to do at least occasional labor for him throughout their productive lives. It was not uncommon for fathers and sons to work side-by-side harvesting Pynchon's crops, clearing his upland, or tending his mills. Occupation patterns, like patterns of tenancy, tended to perpetuate themselves over several generations.[2]

Most work agreements were contracted orally, with payment coming upon completion of the task. Typically these were regularized procedures, with workers approaching Pynchon with similar job requests year after year. A predictable yet flexible system, it allowed the employer and his workers to adjust to the requirements of any particular year. Larger projects that would make a prolonged demand on either a worker's time or Pynchon's resources required written contracts. The same was true for contracts for the performance of highly specialized tasks. Contracts for carpentry work were the ones most often committed to writing. On December 2, 1657, for example, Pynchon "Agreed with Thomas Barber to Build me a Barne over the great River [of] 50 foote long and 24 feete wide with a leantoe, all along the back side." The project was "all to be compleated [by] Harvest next" for which "I am to allow him £21."[3] Similarly, in January 1677 Pynchon contracted with Jonathan and David Morgan "to Build me a house of 24 feet Long [and] 18 feet wide . . . they to doe all the worke from falling to finishing Except the Sawing . . . for which I am to allow and pay them fourteen Pounds; they well clapboarding the whole House ale Timber worke as well as above."[4] Likewise, an agreement signed with Sam Gaines in 1688 stipulated that the carpenter-millwright was "To

---

[2] The Strong family, tanners all, is one such example. In 1671 John Strong, Sr., received £8 3s. for "Taning per agreement (ox hides at 13s. and Cow hides at 8s. apeace) 7 Sole hides at 13s. pce . . . [and] 9 upper leather hides at 8s." His son Returne was credited at various times in John Pynchon's account books for "dressing 13 hides and 2 small ones . . . to 7 hides [and] taning 4 hides and a horse skin [and] by taning 6 hides." Another son, Ebenezer, received payments for "4 hides att 24s. apce, 1 ox hide 36s., the bull hide 27s. [is] £7 19s." Account Books, 3, pp. 205, 209, 219½.

[3] Account Books, 1, p. 176.

[4] *Ibid.*, 5, pp. 384–385.

Build my Mills at Suffeild New and compleate and substantial both Corne mil and Saw mil and Dam for them . . . in all respectes workmanlike done and after the securest manner, I am to allow and pay him the full Sum of Seventy-five Pounds."[5] Agricultural tasks that promised a prolonged expenditure of time also demanded written agreements. In December 1673 Pynchon "Agreed with Richard Waite to Bogg and cleare my meddow on the other side of the hill by the old ditch 8 rod broad."[6] On May 16, 1656, he contracted with Thomas Mirrick "for 30 load of dung, he promised me I should have good dung . . . (as good as any in New England) at 8d. per load."[7]

Pynchon paid his workers both by the day and by the project. Rowland Thomas received £8 2s. 6d. for "63 days worke . . . at 2s. 6d." for "stonning the celler" of the employer's son-in-law Joseph Whiting. But on another occasion he was paid by the load, receiving thirty-six shillings for carting "36 load of stone . . . at 12d." Back on a per diem basis in a subsequent account book entry, Thomas took twenty-seven shillings for "3 days Trimming Trees" and 8½ days "Levelling my ground and goeing after the Mares."[8] For major construction projects, Pynchon sometimes took on workers for up to a year or more at a predetermined salary. On August 27, 1677, he "Agreed with John Artsell . . . [to] serve me one yeare at Stony River about [righting] up my Saw mill setting it to worke sawing and etc., [and] doeing my corne mill." He promised to pay Artsell "Twenty Pounds and let him have Sixe weeks tyme to help out of it on the yeare."[9]

Regardless of the method of calibrating earnings, wages in Springfield—particularly for the unskilled—remained surprisingly low throughout the seventeenth century. Early American labor historians have long contended that wage levels were much higher in the colonies than they were in England. In his authoritative *Government and Labor in Early America*, Richard B. Morris writes that "The colonial workman commanded real wages which exceeded by from 30 to 100 per cent the wages of a contemporary English workman." But without a study of the relative wage levels and living costs in each society, such assertions are not persuasive.[10] More to

[5] *Ibid.*, 6, pp. 271, 273.
[6] *Ibid.*, 5, p. 391.
[7] *Ibid.*, 1, p. 100.
[8] *Ibid.*, 3, p. 197.
[9] *Ibid.*, 5, p. 205.
[10] Morris, *Government and Labor*, p. 45. What comparative data does exist fails to support contentions that American workmen received substantially higher wages.

the point, however, the Pynchon account books reflect low rather than high wage levels throughout the seventeenth century. They fail to support the universally cited contemporary assertion that "labor is deare [in Massachusetts], viz., 2s., and sometimes 2s., 6d. a day for a day labourer."[11] Rarely, in Springfield, did day-laborers average more than eighteen to twenty-four pence for summer work, and fourteen pence or sixteen pence for winter work. Likewise, we have been told that the abortive attempts by the Massachusetts General Court to establish wage and price controls during the decades of the 1630s and 1670s foundered because workers were accustomed to getting much higher wages than the guidelines prescribed—two shillings daily for common laborers, for example. But when wage levels of the 1630s ordinance and the proposed bills of the 1670s are compared with the payment schedules in the Pynchon account books, the Springfield levels are often *below* the standardized rates.[12] Workers in the American colonies did make more than English laborers, but they did so because they worked longer and harder, not because they received higher wages. As the conspicuous absence of the countless English feast days attests, work—not rest— was normative in America.[13]

As James E. Thorold Rogers's exhaustive study of wages and prices in preindustrial England reveals, English laborers during the second half of the 17th century received from twelve to fifteen pence per diem; craftsmen took between two shillings sixpence and three shillings. Day-laborers in Springfield received between eighteen and twenty-four pence for summer work during the same period. Craftsmen normally took between three shillings and four shillings sixpence, depending on their skill level. Because Massachusetts currency was inflated in relation to English currency in the ratio of £125 to £100 for most of the 17th century, the apparently higher wages in the colony, are brought closer to parity if inflation is allowed for. The fact that the Pynchons nearly universally paid wages in country pay (credit for goods and services) instead of specie—which usually exchanged at a rate 10 to 20 percent higher—likewise brings Springfield's wage levels more in line with those in England. James E. Thorold Rogers, *A History of Agriculture and Prices in England*, Oxford, 1887, 5, pp. 668–669, 817; John J. McCusker, *Money and Exchange in America, 1600–1775: A Handbook*, Chapel Hill, 1978, pp. 146–147. From comparisons with Essex County, Massachusetts, the Pynchons' accounts apparently exhibited considerably less fluctuation over time than did prices in the coastal towns; see William I. Davisson, "Essex County Price Trends: Money and Markets in 17th Century Massachusetts," *Essex Institute Historical Collections*, 102 (1967), pp. 144–185; see also Terry Lee Anderson, *The Economic Growth of Seventeenth Century New England: A Measurement of Regional Income*, New York, 1975, pp. 44–81.

[11] *Morris, Government and Labor*, p. 45.

[12] For the wage levels of the 1630s ordinance and the bills of the 1670s, as well as attempts at wage and price controls elsewhere in New England, see Morris, *Government and Labor*, pp. 55–84.

[13] E. P. Thompson, "Time, Work-Discipline, and Industrial Capitalism," *Past and Present*, 38 (1967), pp. 56–97. For a suggestion that the lack of sufficient work

The Pynchon account books show plainly that the settlers were persevering and tenacious in building their community. While, as in any agricultural society, there was always time for sitting in the sun, enjoying a pipe, or stealing a nap, the men and women of Springfield spent more time on the job than off it. Theirs was a frontier society, and the demands of building, cultivating, and repairing were unrelenting. The destruction of some fifty-odd buildings during King Philip's War merely called for a redoubling of these daily efforts. By way of contrast, historians such as Edward P. Thompson have emphasized the irregular work habits of the contemporary English population, with "alternate bouts of intense labour and of idleness [common] wherever men were in control of their working lives." He asserts that "Saint Monday . . . appears to have been honoured almost universally wherever small-scale, domestic, and outwork industries existed."[14] As the author points out, the reason for the working population's irregularity was lack of opportunities as well as lack of incentive. Richard Hakluyt observed in 1584 that the poor laws and proclamations against vagabonds had failed "for want of sufficient occasion of honest employment."[15] Gregory King's estimate that half the families in England did not earn enough to support themselves (without public relief) reveals the severity of the problem of underemployment. As Joyce Appleby asserts, "Capitalism required unrelenting personal effort in the market place" and could only work "if the poor, like the rich, were converted to possessive individualism and economic rationality." The laboring poor of England needed new opportunities *and* new aspirations. They needed more days in which to work than the disjointed English economy allowed them, and they needed to adapt the notion of expandable spending. In short, they had to experience "the propulsive power of envy, emulation, love of luxury,

opportunities provoked the massive emigration of indentured servants from early 17th-century England, see James Horn, "Servant Emigration to the Chesapeake in the Seventeenth Century," in Thad W. Tate and David L. Ammerman, eds., *The Chesapeake in the Seventeenth Century*, New York, 1979, pp. 51–95, esp. pp. 75–80. See also Edmund S. Morgan, "The Labor Problems at Jamestown, 1607–1618," in T. H. Breen, ed., *Shaping Southern Society: The Colonial Experience*, New York, 1976, pp. 17–31. For a general consideration of the relationship between preindustrial and industrial patterns of work, see Herbert G. Gutman, *Work, Culture, and Society in Industrializing America*, New York, 1976, esp. pp. 3–78; and Daniel T. Rogers, *The Work Ethic in Industrial America, 1850–1920*, Chicago, 1978, pp. 1–29.

[14] Thompson, "Time, Work-Discipline, and Industrial Capitalism," *Past and Present* (1967), pp. 73–74.

[15] Richard Hakluyt, "Discourse on Western Planting," in E.G.R. Taylor, ed., *The Writings and Correspondence of the Two Richard Hakluyts*, London, 1935, 2, p. 234.

vanity, and vaulting ambition."[16] But in England the idea of universal economic rationality always came to grief over the shortage of available land. England was not a frontier society, and few day-laborers or small craftsmen could realistically aspire to become freeholders or even husbandmen. Saving their meager wages would not lead to land ownership, so they patronized the grog shops instead.

In the American colonies, however, aspirations toward land ownership were not chimerical for laborers—even in such restrictive environments as seventeenth-century Springfield or Virginia.[17] As the Pynchon account books reveal, the laboring men and women of early Springfield hoped one day to become freeholders. The road to this goal was often fraught with peril and sudden reverses and chronic indebtedness always threatened to reduce the labors of a lifetime to ashes. But the vision lingered nonetheless, and the prospect of working for themselves made the town's laborers willing, even eager, to work for others. For those who were marginal, getting ahead meant getting work.[18]

[16] Joyce Appleby, "Ideology and Theory: The Tension between Political and Economic Liberalism in Seventeenth-Century England," *American Historical Review*, 81 (1976), pp. 500, 505, 515.

[17] For the charnel house that was early Virginia, see Edmund S. Morgan, *American Slavery-American Freedom: The Ordeal of Colonial Virginia*, New York, 1976, pp. 71–179.

[18] For a description of the negative attitudes toward work found in an environment with exceedingly limited opportunities for upward mobility, see David D. Gilmore, *The People of the Plain: Class and Community in Lower Andalusia*, New York, 1980, pp. 54–56. The author points out that in the rigidly stratified agricultural towns of southern Spain, "work is a curse." The laborers "view work not as a means for social mobility or personal satisfaction, but as a hateful burden to be avoided at all costs." This attitude arises "from the fact that trabajo [work] is thought to produce not wealth, but only *miseria*, or poverty; that is, the more you work, the poorer you become." As the townspeople explain to their American visitor: "if a man must work to live, then obviously, he owns no land and is thus dependent upon the vagaries of agrarian wage-labor. This dependency, in turn, means that this unfortunate is necessarily unemployed for half the year. Informants conclude, with unshakably circular logic, that when this man *does* work, his wages are used only to pay off old debts; he can never save and thus improve himself. The proceeds from work are immediately depleted and the round of debt and impoverishment begins anew. Or, as the laborers say proverbially, 'lo comido por lo servido'—'No sooner served than eaten.' The laborers express their intense hatred for work succinctly in statements like the following:
'The only man who *doesn't* earn money is the laborer!'
'The only way you *can't* get rich is by working!' " p. 55.
The 17th-century Springfield economy, of course, possessed all these perils and more. But it also offered real possibilities for advancement as well, a small but psychologically critical distinction.

The importance of work in Springfield was reflected in a contractually oriented legal system. For labor, as with land, the town adopted a philosophy of economic individualism. Court decisions in Springfield call into question recent claims that judges and juries in colonial Massachusetts did not order compliance for non-performance of contractual obligations.[19] Both the magistrate's court and the Hampshire County court systematically enforced contractual rights. Surprisingly, plaintiffs in special assumpsit cases did *not* have to plead performance (show that they had already fulfilled their part of the agreement by paying a consideration) to recover damages for either misfeasance or nonfeasance. All that needed to be demonstrated was a witnessed oral contract or a written instrument (covenant). In Springfield throughout the seventeenth century, a bargain made was a bargain enforced. Both judges and juries (the latter used with surprising infrequency in contract disputes) ordered that the terms of the agreement be upheld. Notions of a "just price" did not invalidate a bargain once made. In some cases, the court even went so far as to order specific performance for personal service contracts (believed unenforceable in colonial America). On April 2, 1655, Thomas Cooper brought an action against John Bliss for "non-performance of a bargayne of fetchinge the said Thomas some fencinge stuffe." Despite Bliss's denial, the commissioners ruled that "synce the bargayne is proved, the said John Bliss shall carry this fencinge stuffe soe soon as the way is fitt for cartinge, and whereas the tyme is come that fences should be sett up; it was adjudged that John Bliss should be liable, to pay such damages as accrew for want of the fencing beinge done, because he neglected to cart the stuffe when there was convenient opportunity to cart it."[20] Likewise, in 1660 Hugh Dudley brought suit against Thomas Mirrick for "not performinge Covenante in plowinge up ½ an acre of new ground, which should have been done in May last . . . the said Hugh pleadinge great damages and still expecting the ploughinge of the ground." After hearing the plaintiff, commissioners John Pynchon and Samuel Chapin ruled that "Thomas Mirack was adjudged to have damnified the said Hugh ten shillings, which he is to pay him, and also to plow up the ½ acre of ground by the first of May next."[21]

In a still more involved case of specific performance litigated in May 1661, Henry Burt complained "against John Henryson for

---

[19] Nelson, *Americanization of the Common Law*, p. 6; and Nelson, *Dispute and Conflict Resolution in Plymouth County, Massachusetts, 1725–1825*, Chapel Hill, 1981.

[20] *Pynchon Court Rec.*, p. 236.

[21] *Ibid.*, pp. 246–247.

not paying of Three bushells of wheate according to promise for spinning and knitting of Stockens." Henryson's defense was that "the debt which he owes Henry Burt is but 10s., and this he ingaged 2 bushells of wheate towards it and noe more: and he hath paid Henry Burt in worke so that Henry Burt owes him 8s. for worke." Plaintiff Burt admitted "his owing him 8s. which says he John Henryson was to have a shurt cloth for and John owning it is adjudged to take the shurt cloth." But for the remainder of the balance due Burt, commissioners Elizur Holyoke and John Pynchon ordered specific performance: "for the other 10s., John Henryson is adjudged to pay Henry Burt Two bushells of wheate (7s.) and Three shillings in a day and halfe worke."[22]

The dispositive nature of the bargain is also revealed by those cases in which it could *not* be proved. In September of 1680 joiner John Pope complained "against Leiutenant Thomas Stebbins for Taking him off from a peice of Joinery worke and promising him sattisfaction, which he now refuses: to the Damadge of said Pope 39s." But as magistrate Pynchon's investigations found "noe profe being made either of Damage nor yet of any promise made by Leiutenant Stebbins to make him sattisfaction," he ruled in the defendant's favor.[23]

Courts likewise enforced penalties for exceeding deadlines. In one such case, the commissioners ordered forfeiture payments for a delay of eleven days in the fulfillment of Thomas Mirrick's plowing obligations. On September 14, 1660, "John Lamb complaynes against Thomas Mirack for non-performance of a bargayne of ploughing for him the said John Lamb being bound thereto by Bill under penalty of 2s. per day for every day the land should be unploughed after the tyme prefixt in the Bond: John Lamb pleaded for the forfeiture mentioned in the said Bill or bond for that the Land was not ploughed till 11 dayes after the tyme limitted in the Bill." After considering the case, "The Commissioners apprehendinge the lateness in the yeere that the land was ploughed, and that the penalty mentioned in the bond was not unreasonable they adjudged that Thomas Mirack should pay John Lamb 20s. damage and 3s. 4d. for the entry of the action."[24]

While Mirrick was a plowman, most litigants involved in non-

---

[22] *Ibid.*, pp. 252–253.

[23] *Ibid.*, pp. 294–295.

[24] *Ibid.*, p. 247. It is not clear from the judgment what the court meant by "reasonable" in the *Lamb* case. From the context of the commissioners' other decisions, it is likely that it was a "liquidated damages" provision, not consideration that was questioned. I am grateful to Rayman L. Solomon for this observation.

performance suits were skilled artisans. On April 27, 1674, the carpenter David Morgan complained "against Charls Ferry for not weaving linnen yarne into cloth according to agreement: David affirming That Charls Ingaged to pay him for worke in building Charls a shop: Thirty shillings in weaving cloth, which now Charls refuseth to doe." After weighing the evidence, the court ruled "That Charls Ferry make good the Thirty shillings in weaving or otherwise pay him Thirty shillings, in Current Pay: together with Costs of Court, 3s. 6d."[25]

Although weaver Ferry lost this case, he, like all the town's artisans, depended for his livelihood on the assurance that the court would consistently order compliance.[26] In a similar case in 1680, the joiner John Pope complained against Nicholas Rust "for not paying five shillings etc: Pope declaring the debt to be for worke making tuggs etc. of cedar to serve instead of Cork for a net: which Pope's Servant says he wrought halfe a day about it: besides his Master turning the wood etc: which Pope affirmes to be about 3 quarters of a day." After his deliberations, magistrate Pynchon declared that "I find for the Plantiff five shillings and Costs of Court, only the small Bass fish which Pope had is to be accounted toward the five shillings."[27]

The most compelling evidence of the highly commercialized nature of work in early Springfield was the prominence of manufacturing-productive enterprises. Rather than simply being agriculturalists, over two-thirds of the town's men possessed some kind of manual skill, ranging from such highly demanding crafts as blacksmithing to the relatively accessible trade of the cobbler. The presence of so many skilled artisans in Springfield, of course, was no accident. Conceiving their settlement as a commercial enterprise, both William and John Pynchon actively recruited such men whenever possible. The maturation of the Pynchons' marketing enterprises after midcentury attracted still more skilled workers to the community. Many of these individuals displayed competence in several crafts, although usually only formally apprenticed in one. Most work careers included two or three and sometimes more areas of occupational specialization. Depending on how remunerative was a man's principal skill, or how many acres he held under cultivation, he supplemented his income by working as many days at more pedestrian tasks as was necessary.

Overall, using a base figure of £50 as the minimum annual in-

[25] *Pynchon Court Rec.*, p. 279.
[26] Grant Gilmore, *The Ages of American Law*, New Haven, 1977, pp. 44–48.
[27] *Pynchon Court Rec.*, p. 294.

come necessary to feed a family of seven without recourse to large-scale farming, one-sixth of Springfield's men were able to live by their craft alone, and another one-sixth were able substantially to supplement their income by their craft. If their per diem wages are multiplied by a 180-day work-year, the following craftsmen would have earned £50 or more: millers, blacksmiths, millwrights, tanners, house carpenters, coopers, resin workers, brickmakers, shoemakers, and tailors. Those workers who could have supplemented their income by yearly wages of up to £25 included: stonemasons, canoemen, teamsters, shinglers, sackmakers, cobblers, sowgelders, and slaughterers. Finally, those who earned from between £15 (the average yearly income for day-laborers) to £25 included: plowmen, stubbers, ditchers, reapers, and mill hands. To see these figures in the perspective of an exclusively agricultural economy, the annual income produced by raising twelve acres of wheat (based on optimum yields of twenty-five bushels per acre, and payments of 3 shillings 6 pence per bushel) would have been just over £50. Similar yields from barley or oats (at 2 shillings 4 pence per bushel) would have produced an income of £35.[28]

In Springfield's diversified economy, therefore, the labor involved in food growing was only one—and not always the dominant—form of work. Usually, more days per year were spent on farm formation, manufacturing, or commercial activities. As economic historian William N. Parker points out: "Even without a draft-animal and without wild game supplement, the labor of growing food for a family on a diet of rude abundance in corn meal, hog meat, vegetables, and poultry could not have occupied more than thirty working days a year for a frontier family. The rest of the time was spent in the tasks of farm formation, in hunting and fishing, for the men, and food preparation and preservation, for

[28] An intriguing—and fundamental—question relates to the proportion of a family's income ultimately consumed as food. Presently, as Kenneth J. Arrow points out, "in the poorer less-developed countries, roughly two-thirds of income goes for expenditures on food." The data from the Pynchon account books suggests (in very fragmentary form) that such a breakdown would not be out of line for 17th-century Springfield. The town's socioeconomic structure, likewise, appears to accord with Arrow's assertions that in agricultural societies a family's standard of living is usually shaped by the distribution of wealth, not the availability of food. See "Why People Go Hungry," *The New York Review of Books* (July 15, 1982), pp. 24–26; see also (for the source of Arrow's statistical formulations) T. T. Poleman, "Quantifying the Nutrition Situation in Developing Countries," *Food Research Institute Studies*, 18 (1981), p. 25; and Amartya Sen, *Poverty and Famines: An Essay on Entitlement and Deprivation*, Oxford, 1982.

the frontier women."[29] And in highly commercialized towns like Springfield, he might have added, manufacturing enterprises.

MANUFACTURING WORKERS

Manufacturing workers in seventeenth-century Springfield fell into four categories, each of which will be considered in turn. (1) heavy artisans: millers, millwrights, blacksmiths, tanners, and resin workers; (2) light artisans: shoemakers, tailors, and weavers; (3) building trades: house carpenters, shinglers, brickmakers, and stonemasons; and (4) sea trades: coopers and canoemen.

Heavy Artisans

Millers were the most important artisans in the development of early American communities. Because of the savings in labor offered by mills, their presence in a community could make the difference between success and failure. In the areas of both food preparation and farm formation, water-powered mills could cut labor expenditures as much as tenfold. Although rarely more than a few horsepower, waterwheels supplied the motive power for sawing planks, milling flour and sugar, forging iron, tanning hides, and carding wool. Most important were the gristmills. As we have seen, the destruction of Springfield's gristmill during King Philip's War provoked many inhabitants openly to consider quitting the town. The laborious process of using pestle and mortar to grind corn for a family's daily bread took a minimum of two hours' work, and the final product was often unappetizing. Only slightly less necessary for a community's well-being was the sawmill. Water-powered sawmills provided the uniformly flat planks that allowed settlers expeditiously to frame their houses and install level and durable floors. The presence of mills brought new members to a community and kept old ones from leaving. As a recent study by Louis C. Hunter points out, watermills allowed colonists to shift from subsistence to market-oriented agriculture and "often became the entering wedge of a slowly emerging market economy."[30]

Springfield's most successful miller was Anthony Dorchester. By mastering his craft, and working for John Pynchon, he rose from

[29] Parker, "American Farmer,"p. 183.

[30] Louis C. Hunter, *A History of Industrial Power in the United States, 1780–1930,* Volume 1: *Waterpower in the Century of the Steam Engine,* Charlottesville, Va., 1979, p. 41; Mark Rose, review of *Waterpower,* in "Watermills and the History of American Technology," *Reviews in American History,* 9 (1981), pp. 34–39; William Fox, Bill Brooks, and Jane Tyrwhitt, *The Mill,* Boston, 1976; Account Books, 5, p. 509.

landless laborer to a position of substantial wealth. When he died in 1683, Dorchester left an estate valued at £436, a not uncommon sum for an early American miller.[31] He negotiated the first of his many mill contracts with the Pynchon family in the early 1650s. On February 10, 1653, John Pynchon and his brother-in-law Elizur Holyoke "agreed with Anthony Dorchester for the Tole of the Mill for a yeare . . . He is to allow us Thirteene Pounds for our Share of the Tole of the Mill, the which Thirteene Pounds he is to pay us in such Corne as he grinds: quarterly he is to pay it: he is to maintaine all Coggs and Rounds fit for grinding and to leave the Mill in as good repaire as he found it." Because the grain Pynchon intended to export downriver constituted such a large proportion of the total amount ground, Dorchester's contract included a proviso for rating the cost of grinding it: "This thirteen Pound he is to pay us besides in valuation to what Corne the Plantation grinds: what percent corne I may grind into meale to Send out of Towne: he is to allow us half the Tole of that besides, and so Hee [is] to have half the profit of such corne according as I may agree with him for grinding it." The provisions evidently were satisfactory to Dorchester, as he took the initiative in renewing the contract the next year. Pynchon wrote in his account book that "Anthony Dorchester desires we would accept of £13 10s. for our share of the Toll of the Mill for this yeare 1654 which we yeilded to." During the early 1660s, the gristmill rent was raised to £18, where it remained until the destruction of the mill during the 1675 Indian attack. Dorchester also paid twenty-five shillings yearly for the land on which the mill was situated.[32]

The skills of an experienced miller were as considerable as they were varied. He monitored the density of his grinding, and likewise judged the density and content of the grain, which varied according to the wetness of the harvest and the manner in which it was threshed and winnowed. Moreover, Pynchon's requirement that Dorchester "maintaine all Coggs and Rounds fit for grinding" meant that he had to master the complicated mechanisms of the water-powered mill. Like all colonial gristmills, Pynchon's was built next to a small tributary stream and included that traditional nexus of dam, head- and tailrace, wheelpit, shafting, and gearing. The dam was constructed by piling up boulders, stumps, earth, and planks in the streambed. An undershot waterwheel powered the large wooden cranks that rotated the grinding stones. The horizontal shaft of the

[31] HCPC Rec., 2, pp. 17–18.
[32] Account Books, 1, pp. 128–129, 296–297; 3, pp. 105, 252; 5, pp. 132, 352–353.

wheel intersected with a bevel gear inside the mill that transmitted its power to the millstones. Grinding surfaces were of stone, whether the substance to be ground was grain, malt, bark, or flaxseed. Mills in the Connecticut Valley used red sandstone, generally from quarries on Mount Tom (ten miles north of Springfield center). The gears and all other working parts of the mill were lubricated by applications of sheep's tallow. The mill's wooden wheels were protected from ice and the elements by being enclosed in a small one-story building. Operations could be interrupted by flooding, drought, ice, or a collapsed dam, as well as by mechanical malfunction. When things went well, Dorchester could count on producing as many as twenty barrels of flour each week.[33]

Because the peak demand periods for gristmills came in the fall and those on sawmills in the spring, Dorchester also occasionally leased one of John Pynchon's sawmills. He paid £26 in 1673 to hold a gristmill and sawmill simultaneously.[34] The sawmill Dorchester rented was similar in appearance to the gristmill, but it was a good deal more complicated to operate. Seventeenth-century sawmills employed a reciprocating saw, in which the saw blade was fastened to a vertical, sash-like framework. The axle of the undershot waterwheel turned a crank attached to a connecting rod (the "pitman") that moved the saw frame up and down with each revolution. A connecting wheel powered the sliding carriage that pushed the log against the saw. (In more primitive sawmills, this was done by means of a large elastic pole.) In Springfield the races for sawmills and gristmills alike consisted of long trenches dug down from the dammed-up portion of the stream.[35] The tasks of keeping the races clear of debris and the dams in repair kept John Pynchon's day-laborers at work long hours in all kinds of weather. When things went smoothly, experienced tenders like Dorchester could saw five thousand feet of pine boards during an average

[33] Dorothy Hartley, *Lost Country Life*, New York, 1979, pp. 144, 188; Anthony F. C. Wallace, *Rockdale*, New York, 1980, pp. 14, 120, 131; Victor S. Clark, *History of Manufactures in the United States*, New York, 1929, 1, pp. 174–178; Account Books, 1, p. 128; 5, pp. 395, 518–519. When Anthony Dorchester finished grinding the grain into flour, he bagged it up in sacks made by John Barber. At various times in 1670, Pynchon paid Barber for "61 yards ½ yard which you allow in of Sacking at 2s. per yard which you have made into 20 sacks and allow the making into the Baragin [all is] £6 2s." and "By 77 yards of Sacking made into 25 bags [all is] £7 14s." In November 1676 Pynchon paid him 16 shillings 6 pence for "making 40 Baggs." Barber used part of his income from sackmaking to lease "5 acres at Cold Spring Bottom" at an annual rent of 30 shillings. Account Books, 3, p. 295; 5, pp. 43, 292–293.

[34] Account Books, 5, p. 352.

[35] Fox, Brooks, Tyrwitt, *The Mill*, pp. 44–48; Clark, *History of Manufactures*, 1, pp. 175–176; Account Books, 3, pp. 75, 107, 147, 160, 185.

week's work. The toll normally charged each customer was one-twelfth of the boards sawn.[36]

Throughout his association with Pynchon, Dorchester performed a myriad of timber-related activities. Account book entries during the early 1660s credit Dorchester for "your selfe and [son] John [10 days] Sawing . . . sawing for my Cider howse . . . 950 boards at 7s. . . . 400 of Boards." In 1666 he contracted to cart all the timber needed for a new sawmill being built by two of Pynchon's carpenters. The owner "Agreed with Goodman Dorchester . . . to cart the Timber for the Saw Mill; he is to cart al the Timber [that the carpenters] shall need . . . for all which I am to allow him £4 15s." And in January 1677, Pynchon paid Dorchester £7 for "sawing and getting Timber for my grist mill."[37]

The watermills utilized by Anthony Dorchester were constructed by one of the several millwrights periodically employed by John Pynchon. Millwrights were the prototypical mechanicians—those who alone carried and transmitted industrial skills until the separation of design from the manual arts in the mid-nineteenth century. Masters of the hydrologic cycle, they also combined the skills of carpenter, smith, mason, and surveyor.[38] Isaac Gleason was the most frequently utilized of Pynchon's millwrights. On April 2, 1684, Pynchon paid him for "the Running geare for my Mill [at] £10." Three years later, the owner "Agreed with Isack Gleason . . . that he is to Build me a house over my mill 25 foote long and 20 foote wide [for] £11 and some land." Gleason was also called in when the mill broke down. In 1683 Pynchon paid him 26 shillings for "worke at my Mill this Spring . . . mending the water wheele [and] 2 days worke about the Cog wheele." On other occasions, Pynchon credited the millwright for "25 days . . . at my Mill (at 3 shillings 6 pence daily) . . . 8 days at the mill at 4s. 6d." In one year, Gleason earned £9 7s. "for worke about my Saw Mill at Schoaungonick."[39] Another millwright, Zachariah Field of Northampton, was the man who supplied Pynchon with his millstones. After hewing the stones, the craftsman cut the radial flanges with a specially shaped stone adze. For a good pair of grinding stones, he earned between £20 and £25. Early in the 1670s, Pynchon paid Field for "making a pair of Millstones and delivering them at my mill for £21."[40]

After millers and millwrights, blacksmiths were the heavy artisans

[36] Account Books, 5, p. 352.

[37] *Ibid.*, 2, pp. 129–130, 137; 3, p. 85; 5, p. 353; William Pynchon Account Book, pp. 221, 272.

[38] Wallace, *Rockdale*, pp. 232–233.

[39] Account Books, 5, pp. 470–471, 518–519; 6, p. 221.

[40] *Ibid.*, 3, p. 223.

most highly prized in early New England communities. Springfield's first blacksmith, John Stewart, came to the town after he and his fellow Covenanter Scots were captured at the Battle of Dunbar in 1650.[41] The victorious Cromwellians sent the captives to Massachusetts as indentured servants and, as Stewart's contract identified him as a blacksmith, John Pynchon bought it soon thereafter. The two men struck a bargain for Stewart's eventual freedom but he failed to repay the £30 compensation according to schedule. Pynchon then consented to accept repayment in the form of a yearly work allocation: "I agreed with John Stewart to allow me yearly 12s. in smithy worke for three years which is for my staying so long for that £30 which is due to me for payment for releasing him from my service. And he . . . consented and promised to allow me for Three years, Twelve shillings per yeare in mending and making of Iron worke."[42]

No town could do without a blacksmith and, while Stewart may have grieved for the glens and moors of his native land, he found in Springfield a community eager for his services. A virtuoso among craftsmen, the blacksmith combined the talents of metallurgist and artist along with simple brute strength. As a nineteenth-century parents' directory to the professions asserts, "theirs is a laborious business, which chiefly consists in the management of the fire, the hammer, and the file." The blacksmith's tools, as this tripartite division suggests, were separated into three working areas. The first was the hearth, complete with bellows, water trough, shovels, tongs, rake, and poker. Second was the anvil, with its array of sledges, tongs, swages, cutters, hammers, and chisels. Third came the shoeing box, with its horseshoes, files, rasp, and knives.[43] Stewart rented most of his tools from Pynchon, including "1 greate Anvill, 1 great hand hammer . . . 1 left hand hammer . . . an Iron to imbritch guns . . . 3 great Tongs, 3 pair of Tongs, 1 chissell, 7 Punchers . . . a steele drill, one small chest with a good lockey there . . . a spring lock, and 21 pairs of horseshoes."[44] The smith worked with charcoal iron, named after the fuel used in the forging furnace. The quality of the charcoal iron depended upon the quality of the ore and the skillfulness with which the iron was extracted

[41] Maurice Ashley, *The Greatness of Oliver Cromwell*, London, 1962, pp. 246–258; Antonia Fraser, *Royal Charles: Charles II and the Restoration*, New York, 1979, pp. 93–94.

[42] Account Books, 1, p. 230.

[43] Henry J. Kauffman, *Early American Ironware, Cast and Wrought*, New York, 1966, pp. 51–79; quotation is found on p. 53.

[44] Account Books, 2, p. 283.

from the ore. Usually, ore was mined from soft surface deposits of bog iron (from areas adjacent to swamps) by means of pick and shovel. Even with the best ore, the limitations of the refining and rolling processes gave the iron an imperfect, fibrous texture. To compensate for this condition, the blacksmith heated the iron in the forge and then hammered it out on the anvil. This "drawing-out" process would then be repeated, increasing the iron bar's length or width by means of a cross-pein hammer. Additional tasks included upsetting (decreasing the length of a bar and hammering it flat) and punching (for decorative purposes or for joining together pieces of iron). The all-important plow chains were made by a process known as "collaring." This was done by wrapping a heated band of iron around two smaller pieces in order to join them together.[45]

The most common products made by seventeenth-century smiths like Stewart were plows, chains, harrows, horseshoes, pig rings, hearth utensils (andirons, trammels, tongs, cranes, skillets, pots, and skewers), door hinges, latches, and candlestands. One of Stewart's most frequent tasks in Springfield was to ring all swine above three months old in order to prevent them from rooting up crops. This duty involved a twice-weekly excursion through the community during the planting season in order to find any unrung pigs. Likewise, when the town needed "a lock 6s. and bolt 18d. and plate 6d. for the lock for the meeting house and keyes and cotters for the bell . . . hookes and hinges for the Meeting house windows," or "a branding iron" or "irony for the pound," it turned to Stewart.[46] The quality of his work must have pleased his fellow citizens, for in 1659 the town meeting voted that "The Smith's shop [shall be] given to John Stewart as his own forever."[47]

But, in comparison to the volume of work he performed for John Pynchon, Stewart's income for services done for the town remained secondary. Not until the mid-1660s did Stewart fully repay Pynchon the £30 owed for his release from service.[48] From the late 1650s onward, his credits for "smithy work" for the Springfield leader became progressively larger. In April 1654, Pynchon paid him £3 14s. for "Smithery worke and some few days about other worke and by smithery work for the mill." From earlier levels of between £3 and £6 annually (in addition to the work for his

[45] Kauffman, *Early American Ironware*, p. 55; *Springfield Town Recs.*, 2, pp. 347–348.

[46] *Springfield Town Recs.*, 1, pp. 216–217, 252–253, 366, 391, 408, 427.

[47] *Ibid.*, 1, p. 261.

[48] Account Books, 1, pp. 230–231.

freedom dues), Stewart's labor credits increased by 1664 to £11 for "Smithery worke for my mill and other work," and in 1667 Stewart earned £19 for "worke as in his booke." In 1671 he received £8 for smithery work for Pynchon as well as payments of £11 for labor performed for his son John and son-in-law Joseph Whiting. In 1677 Pynchon wrote in his account book that he had "Received by worke, all as in Goodman Stewart's Booke . . . the whole is £20 4s. 1d." Between 1680 and 1682 Stewart performed labor worth £13.[49]

Dependent on each other, Pynchon and Stewart forged patron-client ties that allowed the blacksmith to defer but not prevent forfeiture of his lands and housing. In November 1663 Stewart owed his former master £23 and "for the Payment . . . [Stewart] doth for my security formaly Ingage and make over to me his howse and orchard and lot . . . also a Lot of foure acres over the great River . . . which I am to have in case he pay me not this Sum of £23 2s. 4d. . . . within a yeare or Two."[50] As with other clients, Pynchon allowed Stewart an extension of the default date, but it was to no avail. In February 1670, five years after the original forfeiture date, he took formal possession of Stewart's "howse and all his land in Springfield . . . so I cross [out] his account." He allowed the blacksmith "Liberty to Live in the house till midsumer." Stewart thereupon secured a leasehold from Pynchon, after agreeing to "stub cleare and bring to Mowing about an acre and ½ or 2 acres of land . . . [part of which is] Routy high weeds and stubs, he to cleare it and bring it . . . to be mowing meddow and for so doing, he is to have the use of it 3 yeares now coming . . . and then to leave it."[51] Largely as a result of the volume of smithy work performed for Pynchon, Stewart was able to right himself financially. When he died in 1691, he left an estate valued at £225.[52] In an earlier petition to Governor Sir Edmund Andros seeking compensation for an impressed horse, the then bed-ridden Stewart emphasized that he had "a trade which might afford him a comfortable living." He told the governor that "God [had] bestowed some small estate [on him] . . . whilst he gave him ability to labor."[53]

After blacksmithing, the most recondite and technologically sophisticated of the heavy artisanal crafts was tanning. Making leather out of animal hides was an exceedingly laborious, time-consuming, and often unpredictable process and men experienced in this trade

[49] *Ibid.*, 1, p. 231; 3, p. 137; 5, pp. 91, 407.
[50] *Ibid.*, 2, p. 282.
[51] *Ibid.*, 3, p. 137.
[52] HCPC Rec., 1, p. 273.
[53] *Springfield Town Recs.*, 1, pp. 64–65.

were hard to come by. Communities, accordingly, spared few efforts in trying to attract tanners to settle in their midst, as a Springfield town meeting resolution of 1684 reveals. The inhabitants voted to give Thomas Sweatman a generous land grant "because they would accommodate themselves with such a tradesman as he is (viz. a dresser of leather)." The necessary equipment for tanning consisted of a number of wooden vats or boxes which were countersunk in the ground near a stream, and similar vats above ground for liming. A small lean-to or shed was used for a beam house. Bark was crushed at the rate of half a cord a day, usually by means of alternate wooden and stone wheels drawn around a fifteen-foot circular trough. Connecticut Valley tanners used sumac or the bark of hemlock as the main tanning agent, in contrast to the superior oak bark used in the southern colonies. As the Pynchon account books reveal, most of the leather produced by Springfield tanners was used to make shoes and breeches (the archetypal buckskin breeches of frontier lore).[54]

Springfield's first tanner, Griffith Jones, arrived in the town from his native Wales in the mid-1640s and immediately went to work for William Pynchon as a field hand. Presumably familiar with the tanner's craft from an earlier apprenticeship, he now worked to build up enough capital to establish his own tannery. By the early 1660s, this was accomplished and Jones began operation. The early income he derived from his craft suggests how well a skilled tanner could do in Springfield. In February of 1663 John Pynchon credited Jones £14 16s. for "Tanning 16 ox hides at 14s. and 9 Cow hides at 8s."[55] Needing leather both for local consumption and for export downriver, Pynchon could be counted upon to buy virtually all the hides Jones could tan.[56] The artisan's future appeared secure. The difficult days of field laboring were behind him, the tanning vats and sheds were fully operational, and he had mastered the rudiments of his craft. But Jones had neglected to build an equally important form of self-protection, patron-client ties with Pynchon, and this indiscretion eventually cost him the tannery.

In the early 1660s, Jones's indebtedness to Pynchon stood at £53 and Pynchon demanded immediate payment. The debtor could come up with only £18, and Pynchon refused to allow a further extension of the deadline. On April 8, 1663, he took "the howse and Lot and orchard all togither with the Tanhouse, Tan vats etc.,

[54] *Ibid.*, 2, pp. 263–264; Account Books, 2, p. 173; Clark, *History of Manufactures*, 1, p. 167; Russell, *A Long, Deep Furrow*, p. 175.
[55] Account Books, 2, p. 173; William Pynchon Account Book, pp. 110, 211–212.
[56] Account Books, 2, p. 173; 3, pp. 209, 219½.

that Lot as also a Lot of Three acres in the muxy meddow and also a woodlot of 4 acres and Likewise a Lot in the Plaine of 7 acres and ½. Togither with a yearling calfe I take all at £35 9s." Although he agreed to "promise that if I dispose not of it, I shall [allow Jones] the use of Tan vats if he please," Pynchon sold the house and homelot to Samuel Terry six weeks later, and in November he sold the tannery itself to Reice Bedortha for £15.[57] After the forfeiture of his house, land, and tannery, Jones reverted to his former status as a day-laborer for Pynchon, doing field work, mill work, and stringing wampum. In addition, he managed to purchase an £8 share in one of Pynchon's sawmills. Through these efforts he established a modicum of financial security. When he died in 1676, Jones's estate was valued at £119, and his outstanding debts to Pynchon were calculated at £24.[58]

Strikingly similar in technique to tanning was resin, tar, and turpentine manufacture. During the 1690s, John Pynchon decided to exploit Springfield's abundant supply of pine trees to produce naval stores. For those willing to go about the arduous and tedious processes needed to produce these substances, the work offered considerable profits. Tar kilns consisted of a pile of corded pitch pine knots, built on a clay-bottomed floor. The floor was built on an incline to drain off the tar into wooden barrels sunk into the ground. The pile was covered with either turf or dirt (as in making charcoal). Turpentine would then be distilled from the tar, and usually commanded a price twice as high as the parent material.[59]

The blacks Roco and Sue were among those most actively involved in naval stores production. Both workers came to Springfield as slaves. The date of their arrival in the community remains problematical. There were slaves in the Connecticut Valley as early as 1657, when John Pynchon paid John Leonard seven shillings, sixpence for "bringing up [the river] my Negroes."[60] In 1678 the town meeting paid a ten-shilling bounty for "one wolfe the Major's [Pynchon] black man killed."[61] This presumably was Roco, but subsequent events make it unlikely that he was one of the blacks who had come upriver in 1657. Possibly he was one of the offspring of the first black immigrants, or he may have been a later arrival.

[57] *Ibid.*, 2, pp. 173, 200, 316.

[58] *Ibid.*, 5, p. 45; HCPC Rec., 1, p. 192.

[59] *Ibid.*, 6, pp. 199, 267; Clark, *History of Manufactures*, 1, pp. 137–138, 165. In 1693, one of Pynchon's resin workers described his labors about the "Burning [of] Pine Trees at Rosin Hall . . . [as] such sore worke [that] he would not doe that for 3s. a day in money." Account Books, 6, p. 267.

[60] Account Books, 1, p. 98.

[61] *Springfield Town Recs.*, 1, p. 416.

Roco's initial appearance in the town records was not an auspicious one. Under examination by his master, Roco acknowledged "that he had (upon [Margaret] Riley's tempting him) the carnal knowledge of her body." Miscegenation was not viewed with disproportionate alarm in seventeenth-century Springfield, and Roco received the traditional punishment for convicted fornicators of a choice between fifteen lashes or a £3 fine.[62] The slave's next appearance in the records came on a more positive note. In 1687, he stood before the magistrate and married Sue, another Pynchon slave. Their master entered into the court records that "Roco and Sue, my Negroes [were] Joined in Marriage."[63]

Not long after their marriage, Roco and Sue moved from being slaves to being clients of John Pynchon. Roco secured a freedom contract from Pynchon for both himself and his wife, freedom that was eventually to be paid for in turpentine and tar. The first concrete expression of this agreement came in the town meeting on December 28, 1687. Pynchon rose up to request "a grant from the Town of four or five acres of Land at Skipmuck adjoining to that Land on the brooke which he bought of Charles Ferry, to be added to that where he is settling Roco his Negro."[64] Four years later, the two men signed a formal freedom agreement. Under its terms, Pynchon promised to release Roco and Sue from bondage and to lease them a farm at Skepnuck. The farm included broken-up land, meadow, a house, oxen, a mare, cow, plow, tackling, and "other Implements and household stuff (al which are mine and are to be returned to me when he shal dy or leave my farme)." The landlord also committed himself to build a 30-by-32-foot barn on the property. For rent, Roco was to pay £1 the first year with subsequent increments through the sixth year when the fee would level off at £10. He also agreed to "winter" (shelter and feed) three cattle for Pynchon.[65]

Anxious to pay off his freedom dues as soon as possible, Roco turned to both sawmilling and turpentine production within the next four years. In 1693 Pynchon leased to Roco and Joseph Thomas (a white) his sawmill at Pine Hall. Under the contract's provisions, Pynchon was to receive four hundred out of every thousand logs sawn. And in 1695, with part of the freedom dues still unpaid, Pynchon agreed with Roco "for his and his wife's freedom . . . He is to . . . pay me Twenty Five Barrels of good cleane pure Tur-

---

[62] *Pynchon Court Rec.*, p. 105.
[63] *Ibid.*, p. 105, n.9.
[64] *Springfield Town Recs.*, 2, p. 272.
[65] Account Books, 6, pp. 260–261.

pentine of 40 gallons to a Barrel and Twenty one barrels of Good merchantable Tarr."[66]

Light Artisans

The Pynchons' heavy demand for coats to exchange with the Indians for furs made tailors the most prosperous light artisans in Springfield. Thomas Stebbins, for one, began working for William Pynchon during the mid-1640s. Initially his labor was confined exclusively to agricultural tasks. In May of 1646 Pynchon paid Stebbins £4 for "worke in winter 60 days at 16d." and £3 for forty-four days of summer work. In a later entry for the same year, Stebbins took £6 for an additional eighty-two days of work. But doubtless recognizing the rising demands for coats at the Pynchon general store, he began to concentrate increasingly on tailoring. As with most of the town's artisans, Stebbins purchased the raw materials for his craft from the Pynchons. During the winter of 1647 William Pynchon "delivered to Tho. Stebbins . . . 59 yards ¼ and ½ red cotton," receiving later in payment from the tailor "4 dozen and ½ wastecotes . . . 6 wastecotes and 13 pair stockens . . . 2 dozen and 1 pair blue and white stockens."[67]

Every year Stebbins could be counted upon to supply the Pynchons with between seventy-five and one hundred waistcoats, caps, and pairs of stockings.[68] Four account book entries from January to October 1649 credit the tailor for "12 wastecoats . . . 12 Capps . . . 6 Caps more . . . 19 pair Stockens . . . 1 doz. and ½ of waste-coates . . . 12 Red wastecoates . . . 12 white wastecoates . . . in making stockens, wastecots, Caps, and Taylery worke . . . [2] dozen white wastecotes [19] capps . . . 1 dozen stockens . . . 6 white shag wastecotes."[69] Stebbins, doubtless with considerable help from his wife (and possibly apprentices as well), worked quickly. Between May and August of 1650, with the fur trade booming, he produced

---

[66] *Ibid.*

[67] William Pynchon Account Book, p. 54. Stebbins's tailoring evidently kept him out of his own fields, as in 1648 one of William Pynchon's workmen plowed "Tho. Stebbins's 5 acres and ½ and 2 acres of New ground." Pynchon and Stebbins had arranged beforehand for "the Ploughing done this yeare 1648 which [Stebbins] agreed should be paid halfe in worke . . . [and] halfe in wheate at 3s. 8d." But while Stebbins was too busy to do his own plowing he continued to perform occasional agricultural work for Pynchon. An earlier entry credited him for "Taylery worke, harvest work and carting £4 10s." And later in 1648, Stebbins was paid for "worke . . . for going with the plow . . . 7 days worked at 20d. . . . 9 days worke about hay," "6 days work at dung cast and some plowing," "and 2 days reaping." *Ibid.*, pp. 33, 139, 200.

[68] *Ibid.*, pp. 54, 137–139, 141, 199, 200, 201, 214, 249; Account Books, 1, pp. 91, 253–254.

[69] William Pynchon Account Book, pp. 199, 201, 249.

sixty-five coats of various colors. No less impressive is an account book entry for August 1652 crediting him for 197 coats, 120 caps, and twelve pairs of stockings, as well as three days' work mending harness.[70] During the subsequent ten months he produced an additional 95 coats and 264 caps.[71] In 1654 he again was paid for mending tack as well as tailoring: "[for] 10 days dressing Bever" and some "Taylery worke, mending Saddry." And at the same time, he received credits for 168 coats and 76 caps.[72] In later years, Pynchon simply allowed the tailor to keep his own books. In an account book entry two decades later, he paid for "worke of Serjeant Stebbins and else as in his Booke all from the years 1670, 71, 72, 73, 74, 75, and to this 26 Jan 76."[73]

Such productivity kept Stebbins and any assistants he had at work long hours. Sitting at his workbench next to the window, surrounded on the one side by stacked bolts of uncut cotton cloth, and discarded clippings on the other, the tailor's day had the kind of mechanical, predictable quality characteristic of most of the town's light artisans. These men could ply their craft come rain or shine, and the howling winds of winter demanded only more frequent banking of the fire. Productivity in Springfield did not cease with the onset of winter. Between December and March, when the frozen and often snow-covered landscape reduced outside tasks to gathering wood, carting dung from barn to field, and tending stock, light artisans continued to turn out their quota of coats, hats, shoes, and saddlery. While canoemen waited for the river to thaw and farmers waited for the ground to do the same, Thomas Stebbins continued to wield needle and thread, as well as the pair of "Taylre sheres" he bought from John Pynchon.

Stebbins's productivity as a tailor for the Pynchons made him a natural choice for patron-client ties, and he apparently made the most of it. Again, debt deferrals provide the most convincing evidence. In January 1677, Stebbins's overall debt to Pynchon stood at £57, of which £41 "hath bin due to [me] ever since the 22th of October, 1663."[74] But he lost no lands or housing for his debts, and Pynchon continued to ignore them until the tailor's death two decades after the original loan.[75]

[70] *Ibid.*, p. 214; Account Books, 1, p. 91.
[71] Account Books, 1, p. 91.
[72] *Ibid.*, 1, pp. 253–254.
[73] *Ibid.*, 5, p. 97.
[74] *Ibid.*, 5, p. 516.
[75] HCPC Rec., 1, p. 233. As Pynchon's allusions to Stebbins's military rank reveal, the tailor enjoyed the prestige of being an officer in the militia. By 1676 he had risen to the rank of lieutenant, an office that left him subordinate only to Pynchon.

Shoemakers, unlike tailors, worked under direct contract to John Pynchon. He provided the materials and the craftsmen made them into shoes. The contracts usually specified the rate-scale for various types of shoes. In June 1680, he agreed with John Norton "to make my leather into shoes." Pynchon agreed to "pay him for [sizes] 10s 11s and 12s Two shillings a Paire for Plaine shooe: and 2 shillings 6 pence a pair for french heeles." For his compensation, Norton was "to take his Pay out of the shoes and french heeles at 8 shillings 6 pence [a] pair and plain shooes from 10s to 12s at 6 shillings for woman's shoes [from size] 6 to 8 . . . at 6 shilling a pair." An account book entry for 1682 credited him £6 6s. for "shoes mending and etc." and an entry from 1684 allowed £2 17s. for "making 24 pair of shooes." By 1684 Norton no longer labored on a piecework basis, receiving instead weekly wages of seven shillings and sixpence. Weekly wages gave the shoemaker, in effect, the security of having a retainer.[76]

Shoemaking was a highly skilled craft that demanded the traditional five-to-seven-year period of apprenticeship. Unlike cobbling (shoe mending or repair), shoemaking was a well-paying, full-time occupation which could keep the craftsman's family sheltered and fed.[77] Colonial shoemakers worked out of a small kit that contained all the necessary tools: a lap-stone and a hammer, for beating the leather until it was pliable; a leather stirrup to tuck under the craftsman's heel in order to hold the shoe stock firmly in place; an awl for puncturing the leather; and a variety of pincers, scrapers, paring knives, heel knives, and waxed thread. Hammered-out soles were tacked to wooden lasts and then the uppers were sewn on. Upon completion, the shoe was soaked in water for tightening.[78]

High militia posts during the 17th century were invariably accorded to men of substance (in both meanings of that word). Individuals whose names were prefixed by Lieutenant, Major, or Colonel were recognized leaders, men the community could trust with the sometimes grave responsibilities attendant to militia service. The complexities of occupational status in early Springfield, therefore, are suggested by the inhabitants' decision to choose a tailor for such a position. An occupation that throughout the folklore and mythology of western culture has been synonymous with diffidence and humility proved no barrier to positions of social influence in early Springfield. Stereotypical assumptions are further confounded by Stebbins's agreement with the town in 1659 "about the setting up of the Towne pound." And in January 1679, the town meeting voted to allocate "Six pound . . . [to] Leifftenant Stibings for sweeping the meeting house the year 79 & 80." *Springfield Town Recs.*, 1, pp. 263, 422.

[76] Account Books, 5, p. 551; 6, Index, p. 12.

[77] *Ibid.*, 2, p. 157; 3, pp. 151, 161; 5, pp. 105, 267, 291, 551; 6, Index, p. 12.

[78] Alan Dawley, *Class and Community: The Industrial Revolution in Lynn*, Cambridge, Mass., 1976, p. 42; Clark, *History of Manufactures*, 1, pp. 443–445.

Building Trades

In the building trades, house carpenters were the craft aristocrats. With the demand for their services unrelenting throughout the seventeenth century, carpenters and joiners commanded the highest wages paid in early Springfield: from three shillings to five shillings per day. Homes, barns, and outbuildings needed to be built—and rebuilt—throughout the period and woodworkers were needed to do it.[79] As the career of Joseph Leonard shows, these craftsmen rarely experienced real poverty. When, after outliving five wives, he died at the age of seventy-five in 1719, Leonard left an estate valued at £640.[80] Apparently never formally apprenticed as a carpenter, Leonard began his work career in Springfield as an agricultural laborer. In June 1663, with the hay already heavy in the meadows, Pynchon "Agreed with Joseph Leonard well to mow and make and cart and rake . . . 10 acres of grass over Agawam for 6s. per acre."[81] His first woodworking contract came while Leonard was in his mid-twenties. In addition to "Mowing making and carting Hay at Agawam," Leonard received £9 for "shingling my Mill house" and "47 days worke about my Mill dam and hewing the Timber for the dam."[82]

Shingling commonly served as the first formal work for would-be carpenters. While not requiring the finished skills necessary for carpentry or joinery, shingling demanded the ability to lay the lathwork and fasten the yard-long shingles in a watertight fashion. To construct shingles (as well as clapboards, fence poles, or staves), suitable lengths were cut from the boles of straight-grained pine, ash, or oak. A hammer blow on a metal frow would split off a sheet of wood of the required thickness. The shingle would then be finished off with a drawing knife.[83] John Pynchon mandated that siding shingles be three feet in length; roof shingles were to be one and one-half feet.[84] The July 1667 contract for Pynchon's mill house spells out Leonard's obligations in detail. Pynchon "Agreed with Joseph Leanord to shingle my howse at the Mill with 3 foote shingles. I finding the shingles and laying them by the house . . . then Joseph is to lay them well and he is to get and lay all the Lath: he getting the lath which I am to cart . . . for every hundred of

---

[79] Account Books, 1, pp. 78, 176; 2, pp. 40, 353; 3, pp. 57, 115, 199, 295; 5, pp. 67, 171, 199, 383, 385, 441, 467, 527, 537; 6, p. 81.

[80] HCPC Rec., 4, pp. 14–15.

[81] Account Books, 2, p. 314.

[82] *Ibid.*, 3, pp. 57, 63.

[83] Russell, *A Long, Deep Furrow*, p. 84.

[84] Account Books, 2, pp. 145, 347.

shingle layd I am to allow him 12d. and to saw the lath at my saw mill."[85]

The relatively modest wages garnered for shingling contrast sharply with the payments for finished carpentry work. Seven years after the shingling contract, the now thirty-year-old Leonard signed an agreement to build Pynchon a house in Suffield. According to its provisions, Pynchon "Agreed with Jos. Leonard to Build me a house at Suffield . . . 29 foote long and 20 foote wide 10 foot standing: he to doe all the carpentry worke from falling [trees] to shingle: viz. dore, chimny, Runges, stairs, partition, windows, floares, and etc. all that is to be done by carpentry for closing and smithy all whatsoever." The contractor promised to "allow him the use of my Saw Mill to saw the Bords Into braces and struts." After all was "Compleated well . . . and substantial is all handsome and work-manlike I am to allow him £25 and 2 gallons of rum."[86] In a later contract for a sawmill in Springfield, Pynchon compensated Leon-ard equally well. For "the Sawmill over the River which is gon to Ruin But his worke he did before it was blown up Reckones to be about £40."[87] As we saw earlier, Sam Gaines earned £75 for building Pynchon's two mills in Suffield.[88] In 1694, for the relatively easy task of "Groundsilling my Barne," Pynchon paid Leonard £5.[89]

Oak and pine provided the primary materials for early New England carpenters like Joseph Leonard. Houseframes and clap-boards were of oak (or sometimes ash), siding was usually of pitch pine. Rough siding, floor planks, and fence rails were constructed by splitting small trees, followed by any necessary dressing with axe or adze. Tools needed for the production of lumber, fencing, or cordwood included the handaxe, adze, saw, and frow (used to split both shingles and clapboards). Lumber was cut by one of two meth-ods: up-and-down whipsaws located in trenches; and, in those towns lucky enough to have them, water-powered sawmills.[90]

The century-long boom in housing construction offered constant and remunerative employment for brickmakers as well as carpen-ters. Colonial communities need the brickmakers in order to free the inhabitants from reliance on either the notoriously combustible mud-and-thatch chimneys or cumbersome stone structures that

[85] *Ibid.*, 3, p. 57.
[86] *Ibid.*, 5, p. 67.
[87] *Ibid.*, 6, p. 63.
[88] *Ibid.*, 6, pp. 271, 273.
[89] *Ibid.*, 6, p. 63.
[90] *Ibid.*, 2, p. 34; 3, p. 57; 5, pp. 89, 459; Russell, *A Long, Deep Furrow*, pp. 83–84.

were the only alternatives to fired brick.[91] As always, John Pynchon was among the artisans' most eager customers. In December 1659, for example, Pynchon paid the brickmaker Francis Hacklington £28 for "a parsell of Bricks we guess in all 32 thousand and so many come to by the agreement." Hacklington also earned an additional five shillings for "making an oven over the River [and] mending my oven," as well as twenty-seven shillings for "200 Pavement at 13s." and "300 of bricks." On the same day, the two men signed a new contract for ten thousand more bricks. Pynchon "Agreed with Francis Hacklington for . . . Brickes to be delivered in the middle of May next for which Ten thousand I am to allow or pay him Nine Pounds."[92] In his zeal to fill the order, Hacklington neglected to observe the colony's strictures against work performed on Sunday. On September 24, 1661, he found himself again standing before Pynchon, this time as defendant rather than employee. According to the trial record, "Francis Hacklington beinge presented for breach of the Sabbath in working by carrying of bricks at his Kilne at Northampton on the Sabbath day, to the profaninge that holy tyme: The Corte judged him culpable."[93]

Early American brickmakers like Francis Hacklington performed their work by means of an iron-shod mold. After gathering the clay, molding it, and firing it in his kiln, the artisan stacked the finished products on pallets until an order was filled. A brick kiln, unlike an iron forge, could be kept in operation in subfreezing temperatures, so weather-related curtailments of his working periods were minimal. Accordingly, Hacklington signed his contracts in the fall for delivery the following spring or summer. Once the consignment was filled, the artisan was responsible for carting the finished brick to the customer (although hopefully not on the Sabbath).[94]

Housing construction also demanded the services of stonemasons, the human truckhorses of colonial America. Their task was to dig, cart, and lay the stones used to construct the cellars and foundations for the community's various dwellings. Their work was arguably the most backbreaking of any performed in Springfield. But, for those willing to accept its demands upon body and spirit, stonemasonry could offer substantial rewards. Unlike most forms of unskilled labor that paid the standard twenty pence daily rate, stonemasons earned between two shillings sixpence and four shil-

[91] Account Books, 2, pp. 212–213, 249; 3, pp. 26, 93; 5, p. 171.
[92] *Ibid.*, 2, p. 213.
[93] HCPC Rec., 1, pp. 7–9.
[94] Clark, *History of Manufactures*, 1, p. 166; Account Books, 2, p. 213.

lings daily. This high level of remuneration resulted not from the
skill level of the work, as in carpentry, but rather from its grueling
physical demands. For men like Rowland Thomas who were able
to meet these demands, stonemasonry offered a route from day-
laboring to freeholding. And, as with most work in early Springfield, this route began at the Pynchon general store.[95]

Thomas began and ended his career in Springfield as one of the
Pynchons' most valued employees. Soon after his arrival in the
community during the early 1640s, he began working as a field
laborer, sawyer, teamster, and stonemason. Various entries from
William Pynchon's account book credit him for "reaping . . . sawing
fetheredged bords . . . bringing up goods . . . 24 loads of stones
for my sellre at 20 pence . . . 910 foote boards, abating 10 foote
for cracks . . . [caulking] a boate 22 foot and ½ . . . keeping 10 cows
. . . fetching 3 load wheat . . . in fetching some stones from the
upper falls."[96] During the decade of the 1650s, Thomas increasingly
concentrated on stonemasonry and canoe work, being paid for
"putting stones under my cobhouse . . . Stones for Griffith Joanes
Tanning" and taking twelve shillings for "carrying down 35 bushels
of wheat and 6 hogsheads of goods."[97] By the 1660s, Thomas's
work for John Pynchon was confined almost exclusively to stonemasonry, sawing, and mill work.[98] A single account book entry in
1660 credits him for "falling Timber for my howse . . . 56 Trees
containe 133 foote at 3d. per foote . . . 7 days hewing Timber . . .
3 days ½ raising the howse . . . about underpinning and daubing
. . . By getting stones 100 load from the sixteene acres Stone at
12d. per load is £5, By 50 load of Stone from the hither stone place
at 15d. per load." Likewise, entries two years later credit Thomas
for "falling the Timber for the howse of correction . . . getting
chimney stones for the prison howse . . . By 10 load of stone."[99]

Springfield's midcentury population boom offered constant employment for the town's stonemasons. During the late 1660s, Pynchon paid Thomas for "working about stones . . . digging stones"
and "By worke at Westfield for my son[-in-law] Whiting 24 days
the first about getting stone and 20 days when stonning the celler
. . . 63 days worke in all at 65 days for loss in goeing and coming
at 2s. 6d. [is] £8 2s. 6d. . . . By 36 load of stone (besides) at 12d.

[95] William Pynchon Account Book, p. 155; Account Books, 3, pp. 35, 197.

[96] William Pynchon Account Book, pp. 124, 155–156, 218.

[97] Account Books, 1, pp. 73–74, 236.

[98] *Ibid.*, 2, pp. 159, 197.

[99] *Ibid.*, 2, p. 159.

. . . By allowing for your dyet there 10 weeke."[100] Thomas's digging skills could also be applied to less exalted tasks. In November of 1665 Pynchon paid him £5 10s. for "36 days at the Mill Trench [and] 4 days about the Dam." Two and one-half years later, the workman took £2 3s. for "20 days worke at the Mill Breech." In 1671, he earned £3 for "24 days worke at Quabaug Mill Trench . . . at 2s. 6d." Advancing age did not keep Thomas from his work, as his employment by Pynchon continued unabated through the decades of the 1670s and 1680s. Entries from the 1670s show "3 weekes at Stony River Saw mill . . . By underpinning my litle Room . . . By 5 days ½ underpinning Mr. Glover's house."[101] An entry from 1680, with Thomas nearing his sixties, credits him £19 for sixty days gathering stones, getting timber, and mill work.[102]

But despite the constancy of his work for John Pynchon, Rowland Thomas apparently failed to establish patron-client ties with the Springfield leader. Both his wage-rates and indebtedness records point to this conclusion. When Thomas built the foundation for Pynchon's son-in-law, Joseph Whiting in Westfield, he earned daily wages of two shillings sixpence for his efforts.[103] But two other stonemasons, Thomas Bascomb and his son, were also working on Whiting's cellar and the elder Bascomb's compensation was one shilling per day higher than Thomas's. Pynchon paid Bascomb £6 for "worke for Mr. Whiting about stoning his cellar and chimny . . . 35 days at 3s. 6d." Likewise, in 1675 Pynchon paid Bascomb £3 17s. for "worke in June . . . [getting] stone . . . 22 days at 3s. 6d."[104] Additional entries for "8 weekes worke and halfe is 51 days . . . 18 days . . . 24 days worke . . . 44 days worke at [stoning] my mill house" were made at the three shillings sixpence level.[105] On some projects, Pynchon paid Bascomb as much as four shillings per diem. For "worke hewing and Carying stone [for] my kitchin floore, hearth, and etc.," he credited the stonemason for "18 days himself at 4s. per day £4 12s. [and] 12 days his son at 2s. 6d. per day £1 10s."[106] Despite the fact that Thomas was an experienced, adult stonemason, he received the same wages as did Thomas Bascomb's son.

[100] *Ibid.*, 3, pp. 159, 197.
[101] *Ibid.*, 3, p. 159; 5, p. 15.
[102] *Ibid.*, 5, p. 509. In 1682 Thomas earned £5 9s. 6d. for "worke . . . about my Mill house and at the Trench."
[103] *Ibid.*, 3, p. 197.
[104] *Ibid.*, 3, p. 35.
[105] *Ibid.*, 2, pp. 148–149; 3, p. 35.
[106] *Ibid.*, 2, p. 149.

Rowland Thomas's pattern of indebtedness likewise indicates that he failed to establish cliency ties with John Pynchon. As with many of the town's residents, he found himself deeply indebted to Pynchon by the mid-1660s. In 1668 the figure stood at £48 and the creditor demanded payment. Thomas was not allowed an extension on the default, as on March 28 of that year Pynchon formally took possession of the debtor's "land at chikkuppy . . . all this land there being about 50 [acres] whereof 5 or 6 acres of meddow and 6 or 7 Plowed acres and house."[107]

While Thomas's judgment in not forming patron-client ties with Pynchon may be open to question, his tenacity is not. Not one to be broken by adversity, he quickly set about the ultimately successful task of reestablishing his freehold. As before, his principal employer was John Pynchon. By the time Thomas died in the 1690s, he had amassed a comfortable estate worth just under £200.[108]

Sea Trades

The Pynchons' extensive export operations usually gave coopers all the work they could handle. Everything William and John shipped out of Springfield, with the exception of grain, needed to be encased in barrels, and coopers were needed to build them. These craftsmen could also pick up additional income by constructing churns, butter tubs, cowls, clapboards, and shingles.[109]

Aware of the demand for their skills, coopers were among the most highly self-conscious craft societies in early America. Edward Johnson's *Wonder-Working Providence* in 1654 alluded to the successful organization of "coopers and shoemakers, who had either of them a corporation granted." Six years earlier, Massachusetts had organized both cooperage and shoemaking into formal craft societies with regulatory authority. The Court also mandated a five-year period of apprenticeship for those who wished to practice the craft. Like all craft societies, the coopers' motive in organizing were twofold: to ensure product quality and to restrict entry into the trade.[110]

Although requiring great skill, the actual process of barrel-making was characterized by "a functional simplicity little changed from Roman times." For their construction materials, coopers used oak plank for the staves and heads and strips of hickory for the hoops.

[107] *Ibid.*, 1, p. 236; 3, p. 159.
[108] HCPC Rec., 3, p. 46.
[109] William Pynchon Account Book, pp. 104–105; Account Books, 3, p. 87; 5, p. 119.
[110] Clark, *History of Manufactures*, 1, p. 162; Morris, *Government and Labor*, p. 141.

Staves had to be shaped according to the engineering principle of the arch. When each stave rested in a correctly listed position, bound at top and bottom by adequate external hoop pressure, the barrel would absorb any blow or external stress equally throughout every unit of material. This impressive functional utility inspires the foremost authority on early American barrels to rhapsodize that "When one considers the form of the chime, the opening in the center of the heading joints, the narrow and satisfactory croze [the small groove in either end of the stave in which the bead of the head fits], the arch construction of the body of the barrel, and the method of holding the whole together, making of it without doubt, the strongest possible container for any product, it makes one marvel at its simplicity and perfection, and any real improvement in its construction would be almost an impossibility."[111]

Tools for seventeenth-century coopers consisted of an axe for felling the necessary oak and hickory timber, a saw for cutting the timber into lengths, a drawing knife for shaping the staves, a "buckler" for fastening the stave, some clamps, and a windlass for closing the stave ends for hooping. Using these instruments, coopers turned out barrels (25 to 40 gallons capacity), kegs (40 to 60 gallons), and casks or hogsheads (60 gallons or more). Depending on the substance to be carried, the barrels were either "tight" or "slack." Tight barrels are used for liquids or liquid-packed meats (in Springfield, cider, rum, pork, beef, turpentine, or resin) and slack barrels carry solids (in Springfield, furs).[112]

John Mathews was Springfield's most highly skilled cooper. He arrived in the community during the mid-1640s and quickly established what would prove to be a thirty-five-year period of association with the Pynchon family. Various entries in William's account books during the period from 1646 to 1649 credit Mathews for "Coopering and other worke ... Copery worke and 2 days gardening and one reaping ... copery work, reaping and other worke."[113] In 1658 John Pynchon paid him £5 for "26 barrels for black lead ... a beere barrell ... a milking payle ... 200 Clapbord [and] one hogshead." Later account book entries reveal a similar diversity. They credit Mathews for "heading 3 barels ... a New Keeler ... a Cowle ... Changing a churn ... Hooping and Packing one hogshead Beaver [30] Barrels ... 1 Butter Tub ... 3 great Barells for Cider ... 9 hoops and burning Barells ... 33 barells at

[111] Franklin E. Coyne, *The Development of the Cooperage Industry in the United States, 1620–1940*, Chicago, 1940, pp. 7–8.

[112] *Ibid.*; Account Books, 1, p. 270; 3, p. 87, 5, pp. 119, 487.

[113] William Pynchon Account Book, pp. 104–105.

3s. 9d. per Barell," "38 barrells," "4 Beife Barrels," "51 Barrells for Porke [and] 64 barrells for cider and Porke." Pynchon, who leased six acres of meadow to Mathews, took "10 barrels received as rent" each year from 1664 to 1668.[114] Like other woodworkers, Mathews also supplied the Pynchons with shingles. In the late 1640s, William paid him for nineteen hundred shingles, and in 1658 John Pynchon "Agreed with John Mathews to get me Thirteen hundred and halfe good sound Three foote shingles." The following year, for the sum of £11 Mathews contracted to supply the younger Pynchon with twelve thousand shingles.[115]

But despite his considerable woodworking skills, John Mathews was stalked by indebtedness to the Pynchons throughout his stay in Springfield, and ultimately he ended up as a town charge. Before he was through, Mathews lost his house, lands, and child.[116] The explanation for this demise appears to have been a combination of personal irascibility and, rare in early Springfield, sloth.[117]

Mathews's craft skills enabled him to forge patron-client ties with John Pynchon; but the cooper's failure to keep up with Pynchon's production demands eventually severed the bond, and the employer then called in a number of longstanding debts. The process began in October 1656, when Pynchon "Accounted with Goodman Mathews and he owes me £19 12s. 7d."[118] Seven years later the balance stood at £20 17s. 10d. and the cooper promised to pay Pynchon "this winter in wheate."[119] But in February 1665, for debts of £10, Pynchon took two cows from him, observing "I should have had [them] long ago."[120] Mathews thereupon leased the animals. Two years later Pynchon admonished him to pay up or else. In addition to the old debt of £45, there was "besides the Bill of Laurence Bliss [which] is turned to me for John Matthews to pay me that £31 10s." The cooper was to "pay this sum of £45 or else to forfeite his land if he pay it not within 3 yeares." So "he mortgages his howse and land to me for the payment of it." The mortgaged property included virtually everything Mathews owned in Springfield—his house, homelot, orchard, woodlot, and wet meadow.[121] As before, Pynchon ignored the default deadline, but in December

---

[114] Account Books, 1, p. 270; 2, pp. 312–313; 3, p. 87; 5, pp. 119, 487.
[115] *Ibid.*, 2, p. 99.
[116] *Springfield Town Recs.*, 2, pp. 147–148.
[117] *Pynchon Court Rec.*, pp. 118–119, 243, 249.
[118] Account Books, 1, p. 269.
[119] *Ibid.*, 2, p. 312.
[120] *Ibid.*, 3, p. 86.
[121] *Ibid.*

1676, nine years after the mortgage was signed, he foreclosed.[122] Needing the property in order to live, Mathews immediately rented it back. In the January 1677 lease, Pynchon "Lett out to Rent to John Mathews the Homelot (and orchard) of four acres and better and wet meddow before it of almost two acres and halfe (all which I bought of him) which he is to hold and Injoy for Seven yeares he . . . paying to me . . . yearly the Rent or Sum of Three Pounds and one good thite Barrell for Porke yearly, and also he is [to] yearly repair and take care of the fencing which he is to leave in repair at the end of his time he being also to pay all the Rates on the said Land."[123] Renting from Pynchon did nothing to improve Mathew's financial well-being. By the time of his death, he had compounded his indebtedness problems by paying Pynchon £71 in rent for nineteen acres of meadow and plowland, an orchard, and two cows, in addition to a house and homelot.[124]

Town records suggest that Mathews helped bring on his own fall by poor work habits. His career reveals that the fact that a man's craft *could* provide a comfortable living was no guarantee that it *would* do so. Character was not destiny, but it counted. Highly skilled artisans who were slothful or truculent fared little better than did landless laborers. As we will see later, Mathews was one of a number of Springfield artisans who used the town's reliance on their skills to test the limits of social tolerance. In 1659 the commissioners ordered Francis Hacklington to serve a summons on the cooper. Mathews thereupon behaved with a "contemptuous and high carriage towards him that was sent with the Summons: commanding him off his ground and holding up his sickle at him and usinge other high words and unfitting carriage." The process-server beat a hasty retreat.[125] A year later Mathews was again fined by the court for "being found drunken and bereaved of his understanding which appeared both in his speech and behavior."[126] In 1669 he was brought before the court on the serious accusation of "abusing" the town's minister, Pelatiah Glover. Pynchon confronted Mathews with evidence of his "exceedinge contemptuous behavior" toward the Reverend Glover. After considering the evidence, the magistrate ruled that the cooper's conduct was "very odious and Shamefull . . . much after the custom of the Quakers,"

---

[122] Deed, John Mathews to John Pynchon, April 22, 1667, Hampden Co. Deeds, Volume A, p. 72.
[123] Account Books, 5, p. 487.
[124] *Ibid.*, 2, pp. 99, 312; 3, pp. 86–87, 283; 5, pp. 118–119, 486–487.
[125] *Pynchon Court Rec.*, p. 243.
[126] *Ibid.*, p. 249.

and sentenced that he be whipped and compelled to post a £10 bond for future good behavior.[127] Moreover, Mathews's neighbors, as well as the minister, were subject to his maledictions. In 1678, he was bound over by the Hampshire County grand jury for "his Scandoulous vile revileing of his Neighbor Jonathan Burt."[128]

John Mathews's wife was killed in the Indian attack on Springfield and he thereafter descended into the final indignity of his years in the town. Mrs. Mathews's death left the cooper with sole responsibility for the care of the family's infant son, a burden that the town meeting quickly decided he was incapable of bearing. On January 6, 1682, it was "Voted and Concluded by the Town that the Select men shall take Care for the setting out or providing for the Maintenance of John Mathews his child according as they shall Judge most fit." A month later, operating under the provisions of a colony law that "the Select men shal take care for and maintaine and dispose of such poor children whose Parents are either dead or so poor that they Cant nurse or provide for and maintaine such their children," the townsmen indentured young Mathews to Samuel Terry until "the said Child shal attaine the age of One and Twenty yeeres."[129]

The town meeting then addressed itself to what it saw as the critical point of issue—Mathews's indolence and lack of responsibility. Determined to make him use his time more productively, the meeting "voted and Agreed [that] the Select men shall take Care of John Mathews and have an inspection over him that hee follow his employment and make improvement of his time: and to setle him in a way that he may doe it."[130] The efforts of his fellow citizens to build a fire under Mathews came to naught and when he died his estate stood at but £8, with encumbrances five times that amount.[131]

After coopers had packed John Pynchon's barrels for export, canoemen such as Samuel Terry carried them down to Enfield falls or Hartford. Canoe-transport was among the easiest work to get in seventeenth-century Springfield. The canoe's most obvious advantage over the oxcart, of course, was speed. Even when their way was not impeded by mud or a deeply runneled roadway, oxcarts moved slower than a man walking, rarely more than three miles

---

[127] *Ibid.*, pp. 118–119.
[128] Green, *Springfield*, p. 137.
[129] *Springfield Town Recs.*, 2, pp. 147–148, 152–153.
[130] *Ibid.*, 2, pp. 147–148.
[131] HCPC Rec., 2, pp. 30–31.

an hour.[132] Virtually every able-bodied man in the town worked at one time or another as a canoeman. Over two dozen were active canoemen for most of their adult lives. Canoemen were the ones who carried the surplus grain, pork, beef, and naval stores down the river, to be exchanged for ironwares, textiles, medicine, salt, rum, or molasses. Early recognizing the canoe's importance for their commercial survival, the townsmen voted in February 1639 that "it shall be lawfull for any inhabitant to fell any Cannoe trees [growing on the common] and make them for his owne use or for the use of any inhabitant . . . but not to sell or any ways pass away any Cannoe out of the Plantation untill it be five years old." Indeed, the presence of so many canoes in Springfield was the most visible evidence of the town's deep involvement in the market economy.[133]

The experience of Samuel Terry reveals the extent of this market orientation. Beginning as a servant to William Pynchon during the 1640s, he became the most active of John Pynchon's canoemen a decade later. During seasonable weather, Terry took his birchbark canoe on as many as ten voyages monthly.[134] In July 1655 he received £2 for "carying down [to the falls] 84 bushels [of wheat and] . . . 70 bushels and bringing up 2 Tun of [goods]."[135] On a later journey, the canoeman earned a similar amount for "carying downe to the falls 71 bushels ½ of wheat 2 hogshead [and] bringing up 1 Tun ½ goods your halfe [and] 90 bushels, your halfe." In July 1656 he embarked on "six voyages to the Enfield falls." In a 1665 entry, Pynchon paid Terry for "Carying 76 bushels from the foote of the Falls at 2 pence ½ [per] bushel . . . Carying down 23 barrels of meate at 2s. [and] Bringing up 110 bushels of salt at 6d."[136]

The first nip of frost in the fall signaled the peak of the canoeing season when the town's agricultural surplus was shipped and portaged down to Enfield falls or Hartford. Pynchon's standard rate for the longer trips is suggested by an agreement signed with another canoeman "to Carry downe my Corne and Barrells to Hartford next Spring, my Corne he is to Carry for 4d. ½ per bushel and Barrells for 2s. a piece." The canoe trips usually demanded a two-man crew as Pynchon paid most of his canoemen for "your halfe." The companionship presumably made canoeing among the more attractive tasks available in early Springfield. Canoemen could,

---

[132] Hartley, *Lost Country Life*, p. 82.

[133] *Springfield Town Recs.*, 1, p. 164; Account Books, 1, pp. 147, 197, 291–292, 300, 316; 2, pp. 117, 245, 261, 360–361; 3, pp. 56, 64, 85, 105; 5, pp. 59, 165, 289.

[134] Account Books, 1, pp. 239–240; 3, pp. 144–145.

[135] *Ibid.*, 1, p. 239.

[136] *Ibid.*, 1, p. 240.

within reason, make their own schedules, and their work was not performed under the watchful eye of their employer. But perhaps most important for Terry and his fellow canoemen, the fifteen-mile round trip to the falls at Enfield was far from being unpleasant. While pushing the graceful birchbark canoe through the water, the two occupants were free to converse, joke, exchange gossip about their neighbors, and the like. And it is possible to imagine more onerous tasks than bringing a canoe into the wharves at Springfield as dusk fell on the Connecticut River.[137]

AGRICULTURAL WORKERS

Agricultural labor, like manufacturing, construction, and trans-portation work, was highly commercialized in early Springfield. The Pynchons' fields always demanded a labor force of between fifteen and forty men, with variations coming according to the rhythms of the crop cycle. For young men without skills or older men without prospects, field work was always available—weather permitting. The process of clearing new planting fields as well as cultivating established ones continued unabated until the Revolu-tion. There were always trees to be felled, stumps to be uprooted, ditches to be dug, rocks to be carted, and meadows to be bogged.

Of all the field tasks listed in the Pynchon account books, none

[137] *Ibid.*, 3, p. 207; John McPhee, *The Survival of the Bark Canoe*, New York, 1975, pp. 55–56. Terry also leased land from John Pynchon, and his career as a tenant began in the same fashion as did John Mathews's—after a forfeiture of land. On August 7, 1662, he lost "14 acres of land at Chikkupy" for debts of £13 10s. On the same day he signed a lease to take back the land in tenancy. Pynchon agreed to "Let out to Samuel Terry the 5 acres and ¼ of broken up land in the 14 acres above said in Chikkupy which I have bought." Less than a year later, Terry placed himself in Pynchon's debt for an additional £26 in order to buy a house, orchard, and lot that Pynchon had taken for debts from Griffith Jones a month earlier. The payment was to be "in wheat at 3s. 6d. per bushel and in merchantable Porke at 3d. per pound." According to the provisions of the contract, Terry was to "pay [Pynchon] £26 in 3 years. That is to say £9 michalstide coming 12 months which will be ano 1664 and £9 in michalstide 1665 and £8 in michalstide 1666." Unfor-tunately for Terry, the payment schedule was not kept, and he was forced to rent rather than buy the land and housing. In April 1680, after previously leasing "a horse of mine" and "those 2 oxen which I bought of Miles [Morgan]," Terry signed a contract for Pynchon's 80-acre "Tenement farme" across the river. On April 16, 1680, Pynchon "Delivered to Goodman Terry with my farme which he is to make good again when he delivers it up with my farme . . . a good new plow but 2 days agoe fetched from Thomas Dowey and with a good new share costs me now 16s. of John Stewart and coulter, plow chain 7½ feet long, new whipple and chain, draft yoak, clovis and pin, etc." Ultimately, Terry paid Pynchon £64 for his various lifetime rentals of land, housing, livestock, and tools. Account Books, 2, pp. 200–201; 3, pp. 144–145; 5, pp. 72–73, 447.

was more common than those for "stubbing and clearing." Stubbing involved removal by means of a grubhoe or mattock (and sometimes a team of oxen) of all the stumps and roots left in the ground after trees had been felled. The man John Pynchon usually called on first to do his stubbing was Increase Sikes. In a contract signed in July 1668, Pynchon "Agreed with Increase Sikes to Stub, Cleare and Plough up Sixe acres of Ground in my land comonly called Sheepes Pasture . . . for which well Stubbed and cleared and likewise well plowed and broken up I am to allow and pay him the sum of Eleven Pounds and one worsted pair of stockens . . . He is to doe this worke—wholy to finish the Stubbing and Ploughing of it all up by the 25th of Aprill next come 12 Months, and at least halfe of it is to be done and well plowed by the 25 of Aprill next, and all to be very well Plowed." A contract signed the following year is still more explicit regarding payments per acre. On April 22, 1669, Pynchon "Agreed with Increase Sikes to Stub cleare and plow up the rest of my ground at round hill next to that he was to doe by former bargaine. He is to cleare and Plow up all the remainder to the top of the hill where the cart way goes down to the plaine . . . for all which well stubbed and cleared and Plowed up, I am to allow and pay him Three and thirty shillings per acre and one stubbing hoe already delivered . . . he is to doe this worke by the 25th of . . . Aprill next come 12 Months: and 4 acres of it is to be done and well plowed by the 25th of Aprill next Spring." Payment levels were governed by the relative difficulty of the terrain. While the 1669 contract stipulated thirty-three shillings per cleared acre, one signed the following January included payments fourteen shillings per acre higher. The agreement bound "Increase to Stub that Plough Ground by my 3 corner meddow under the hill . . . all being well done by march come 2 yeare if not before [for which work] I am to allow and pay him 47s. per acre and 1 pair of Gloves of 4s. price already delivered him."[138] Regardless of the terrain, stubbing was a slow and painfully laborious process, and the two-year period allocated in 1668 to clear six acres was not atypical.[139]

[138] Account Books, 3, pp. 172–173.

[139] *Ibid.*, 3, pp. 14, 99, 122; 4, p. 87; 5, pp. 29, 123, 165, 185, 189, 287, 421, 547; 6, p. 71. For a recent study of the cycles of field preparation, cultivation, and harvesting, see Nicholas P. Hardeman, *Shucks, Shocks, and Hominy Blocks: Corn as a Way of Life in Pioneer America*, Baton Rouge, 1981, esp. pp. 20–137. Still invaluable are Paul W. Gates, *The Farmer's Age: Agriculture, 1815–1860*, New York, 1960, pp. 156–270; Percy Wells Bidwell and John I. Falconer, *History of Agriculture in the Northern United States, 1620–1860*, Washington, D.C., 1925; and especially Darrett B. Rutman, *Husbandmen of Plymouth: Farms and Villages in the Old Colony, 1620–1692*, Boston, 1967.

Contracts for stubbing were usually drawn up in the late winter or early spring. Work began with the first thaw. Some projects also involved ditching, filling, and leveling as well as stubbing the ground.[140] In a second contract signed in December 1669, Pynchon "Agreed with Increase Sikes that he shall fill in my ditch at the Round hill, all of it from one end to the other which he is to fill up, throwing in all the Bark to make it plaine fit for Plowing, he is also to stub up all the young Trees and stub in the Bank quite from the Ground plowed up . . . to the south side of the ditch and to doe all well fit and secure for plowing, all which he is to doe early in the Spring for which I am to pay him 20s."[141]

After preparing Pynchon's fields for planting in the early spring, with the arrival of June, Sikes turned to mowing his hay. Hay must be cut while it is still nourishing sap, but must be harvested dry to avoid spontaneous combustion.[142] The laborer passed the sultry Connecticut Valley summers amidst the sweet aroma of freshly cut English grasses. In a particularly detailed contract signed in January 1670, Pynchon "Agreed with Increase Sikes to mow and make into Hay next summer all my 10 acres of meddow over Agawam . . . he is to cut it all well and close and make it good hay and Rake it all up and cock it up . . . also to cart it and Rake after the carts and to set it on a Reeke by the River side fit for the Boate to fetch, and to Rake it well, to secure it from the Raine and all this to doe in season that I may have good hay, at least halfe of it to be done before Harvest if not all, for which I am to allow and pay him 5s. 6d. per acre." As this contract reveals, the mower cut the hay into swathes which were laid in lines to dry. He then raked the hay into small dollops, alternately spaced over the field, before cocking them up for cartage; and all this was to be accomplished before the time came to reap cereal grains. The continuities with English seasonal patterns bear emphasis here. The entry for July in Thomas Tusser's sixteenth-century planting calendar reads, "With tossing and raking, and setting on cocks, grass lately in swathes, is hay for an ox: That done, go and cart it, and have it away, the battle is fought, ye have gotten the day."[143]

[140] Account Books, 1, p. 282; 3, pp. 87, 140, 165, 171; 5, pp. 31, 77, 127, 183.
[141] *Ibid.*, 3, p. 173.
[142] Hartley, *Lost Country Life*, p. 153.
[143] *Ibid.*, pp. 151–153; Account Books, 3, pp. 172–173. Sikes also worked for Pynchon as a canoeman and a carpenter. On November 23, 1670, Pynchon "Agreed with Increase Sikes to Carry downe my Corne and Barrells to Hartford next Spring; my Corne he is to Carry for 4d. ½ per bushel and Barrells for 2s. [a] piece; when I have occasion to use but one Boate at a tyme I am to use him But If I have

After stubbing and clearing, ditching was the most common form of field work to be had at the Pynchon general store. Ditches were needed to keep hungry livestock out of the planting fields, or to serve as the races for John Pynchon's various mills. Because Springfield's soil, like that of most of New England, often appeared to be nine parts of rock for every one part of earth, ditching was an especially arduous task. Requiring a strong back and perseverance but little in the way of skills, it was difficult work and it paid poorly. In Springfield the closest equivalent to the proverbial ditch-digger was the Scot, William Hunter.[144] In 1666 Hunter received eight shillings nine pence for "8 Rod ¾ of ditching by the Indian Fort over the River" and £8 6s. for "scouring 34 Rod of ditching." In the fall of 1668, Pynchon "Agreed with William Hunter to make a parsell of ditching . . . for a stone horse of about 5 yeares old . . . [for which] he is to make 112 Rod of ditch." And "in payment of what he owes me he is to make 100 Rod of ditching more." The acquisition of a stonehorse, needless to say, would considerably facilitate the removal of boulders from the ditchway. In April 1669 Hunter received for "worke and severall things . . . [the sum of] £12 18s. 6d.," as well as for "your Plowing 5 acres for [Joseph Whiting] . . . your son, your horse and oxen £1 15s."[145] The following year Pynchon paid Hunter for the 168 rods of ditching already completed, while admonishing the laborer that "There is behind 44 Rod as you say your selfe to which I told you you should not faile to make me this summer."[146]

occasion to send more Boates than one at once I am to use who I se meete." On January 25, 1676, Pynchon contracted with Increase and his brother Victory to build him a barn with the dimensions of 52-by-24 feet for a fee of £14. Increase, in addition, rented bottom land and an apple orchard from his employer, paying Pynchon lifetime rents of £86. But although he had worked for and rented from Pynchon most of his adult life, Sikes managed to stay out of the landlord's debt; and while his work record shows that Sikes spent most of his days with his back to the wheel, he was spared the anxiety of wondering when he and his family might lose the roof over their heads. Account Books, 3, pp. 172–173, 207; 5, pp. 161, 417–418, 546–547.

[144] William Hunter arrived in Springfield with his family during the winter of 1663. He entered the community under the sponsorship of two other Scots. On February 23, 1663, "William Hunter was admitted an Inhabitant of this Town and John Riley and John Henrison doe bynd themselves . . . to the Town Treasurer and Select men . . . in a bond of Thirty pounds, to secure the Town from the said William Hunter or any of his family." The Scot community evidently hived together, as four years later the town granted "Liberty . . . to John Riley to build on his lott by William Hunter's." *Springfield Town Recs.*, 1, pp. 306, 361.

[145] Account Books, 3, p. 165; Hartley, *Lost Country Life*, pp. 245–251.

[146] Account Books, 5, p. 31. Hunter also rented land from his employer. In March

Digging ditches for others was not the way to get ahead in early Springfield, and when William Hunter was killed during King Philip's War, his estate included a Bible but not much else. His total wealth was valued at £37, including only sixteen acres of land.[147] Unfortunately for his widow, seven of these acres had been mortgaged to John Pynchon for an unpaid debt of £12, and in 1684 the land was forfeited to him.[148] However she may have felt about his seizure of her seven acres, Mrs. Hunter did not sever her family's ties with the creditor. Her daughter Sarah became a domestic servant in the Pynchon household for a brief period in 1679, and in October of 1690 Mrs. Hunter and Pynchon agreed that her son John would live as a servant with the Pynchon family for a yearly salary of £10.[149]

Some field hands boarded in the Pynchon household for virtually their entire adult lives. Francis Pepper, for one, worked for and lived with the Pynchons for over forty years. Without a wife to support or children in need of a patrimony, Pepper lived frugally but comfortably on his modest wages. When he died in 1686, his entire estate was valued at £155, of which £122 consisted of outstanding bills of credit. His debts totaled £3.[150]

1669 he leased broken-up acreage that Pynchon had taken for debts from Richard Sikes. For the rent, Hunter agreed to "allow and pay . . . Thirty Two shillings for the yeare and to repair the fence . . . formerly belonging to the whole 15 acres all the fence whatever in that field which belongs therto." In addition to tenant farming, he was also engaged in livestock husbandry. In November of 1670 he paid his bills at the general store with "119 pounds of Porke." Hunter's combined annual income from ditching and tenant farming rarely exceeded £35, and to raise additional money he put his daughter out to service—although evidently with some reluctance. On July 29, 1671, Hunter and his fourteen-year-old daughter Katherine stood before the magistrate, accused respectively of harboring a fugitive and desertion from service. John Pynchon examined the girl about "Departing from her Master's [Robert Ashley] service unlawfully." The deposition cited Katherine for disappearing "once last Tuesday and then Coming againe on Thirsday and yet goeing away againe on Friday Morning to her fathers: and for noe Cause that shee can relate her selfe but only that her dame once only and that some time before gave her a blow or 2 with her hand." After evaluating the testimony, Pynchon ruled that "there being nothing to justify her in her unlawfull departure I ordered her to the howse of correction, there to abide till I discharged her." The magistrate then turned to her father and declared "And William . . . for Harbouring his said daughter and not discharging her and sending her to her aforesaid Master (none Informing) [should be fined] 20s.," which Pynchon "respited . . . till some other tyme." Account Books, 3, p. 165; 5, p. 31; *Pynchon Court Rec.*, p. 275.

[147] HCPC Rec., 1, p. 182.

[148] Account Books, 5, p. 50.

[149] *Ibid.*, 5, p. 31; 6, pp. 240–241.

[150] *Ibid.*, 5, p. 159; HCPC Rec., 1, p. 259.

Throughout his stay in Springfield, Francis Pepper was the Pynchons' most reliable employee. He first began to serve the family in 1645, and the following spring he "Received . . . in wages to the first of April £4 1s." and "more due to him from the first of Aprill to the end of July which is 4 months at 20s. per month: [all] is £4." By 1647 Pepper was a salaried employee earning annual wages of £8 10s. An account book entry that year credits him for "¾ yeare's service," and in 1648 he "Received a yeare's wages . . . [of] £9."[151] In February of 1649, William Pynchon paid him forty-eight shillings for "4 months winter [work] at 12s. per month" and the following year the worker took forty-two shillings for "4 months service in winter." Soon after this time Pepper moved into the Pynchon household, taking his meals with the other servants in the mansion's kitchen. In October 1654, John Pynchon debited Pepper's account for "your dyet 30 weeks at 4s. per weeke" and the next July he made a similar entry for "36 weekes and ½ dyet at 4s. per weeke."[152] In November 1657 Pepper paid for "a yeares dyet at 4s. per weeke for 52 weeks is £10 8s."[153] This annual payment for bed and board remained constant unless unusual circumstances intervened. The year 1675 was such a time. The Indian attacks made normal field work impossibly harrowing. Resorting to what was more than a mild understatement, Pynchon abated Pepper's boarding charges £5, "it having bin a Troublesome yeare."[154]

For his method of compensation, Pepper alternated work as a wage laborer with work performed on a per diem basis. Those contracts that were signed typically fell within a three- to four-month range. In January 1654, Pynchon "Agreed with Francis Pepper to serve [me] to the end of March next for which tyme I am to allow him £2 5s." Soon thereafter, however, Pepper reverted to per diem compensation, receiving payments later that year for "44 days worke at 16d. [per day] [and] 56 days worke at 20d. . . . [and] more than 55 days worke at 16d. . . . 71 days at 20d." The following year he was credited for "100 days work at 20d. per day is £6 6s. 8d. . . . more 77 days work at 16d."[155] Per diem labor posed a risk because of the possibilities of weather-related curtailments on the number of available workdays. Its advantages were greater flexibility in task selection and the opportunity to work for other employers periodically. Weekly wages could offer the best of both

[151] William Pynchon Account Book, pp. 29–30.
[152] *Ibid.*, pp. 197–198; Account Books, 1, p. 203.
[153] Account Books, 1, p. 208.
[154] *Ibid.*, 5, p. 159.
[155] *Ibid.*, 1, p. 203.

worlds and tended to be favored by Pepper from the late 1650s onward. In 1657 Pynchon paid him £10 for "17 weeks winter worke . . . [and] 7 weeks 4 days Summer worke." In 1659 he received twenty-one shillings for "16 days worke . . . to the 9 December on which day he gave over working by the day."[156] This service contract, however, was short-lived and by 1660 Pepper was again being paid on a weekly basis, receiving credits for "33 weeks ½ worke at 10s. per week" and "6 weekes worke at 8s. . . . [and] 84 days."[157]

Workers like Pepper who labored on a per diem basis were required to be at their task literally from dawn to dusk. The 1563 Statute of Artificers mandated a working day from 5:00 A.M. to 7:00 or 8:00 P.M. from mid-March to mid-September, allowing two and one-half hours off for breakfast, dinner, and drinking. The work day during winter was to extend "from the spring of the day until night." Massachusetts statutes prescribed a ten-hour day for field workers, and a twelve-hour day for craftsmen.[158] A proposed bill in the General Court in 1670 calibrated field workers' wages on the assumption that they would labor "From the end of June to the end of September . . . 10 houres in the day besides repast."

---

[156] *Ibid.*, 1, pp. 208–209.

[157] *Ibid.*, 2, p. 227. As these figures reveal, Pepper's wages by the early 1660s had been raised significantly from their earlier levels. He now received 10 shillings weekly for summer work and 8 shillings for winter work rather than the original levels of between 16 and 20 pence per day. Whether this increment represents a genuine raise or reflects merely a change in the method of calibration is uncertain. In any case, it was not permanent. In the early 1660s, Pynchon compensated Pepper at a rate of 8 shillings weekly for winter work and 10 shillings for summer work; but these payments reverted to their normal levels of 20 pence and 16 pence daily by the middle of the decade. In 1661 Pynchon paid Pepper £2 15s. for "5 week and ½ . . . at 10 shillings per week"; and in 1662 Pepper received £16 5s. for "32 weeks worke and halfe (some days abated) at 10s. per weeke" and "8 weeks want one day at 8s. per week." In 1663, for "29 weekes to the 10 November," he received £14 10s. and another 13s. for "2 weeks almost . . . at 8s. per week." By 1665 Pepper's wages had returned to their earlier level. In January Pynchon paid him for "8 Months worke . . . at 20d. per day comes to £17 10s." And for "64 days work . . . at 16d. per day" he received £4 5s. For one final time, for "20 weekes sumer worke at 10s.," he was paid £10, and another £2 14s. for "7 weeks winter [work]." By 1666 Pepper's daily wages declined to the 18 to 20 pence level and there they remained. In the spring of that year for "worke . . . 6 weeks 2 days at 20d.," he was credited for £3 3s. 4d.; and for "46 days at the Mill at 20d.," he took £3 16s. 8d. And 30s. in pay compensated him for "18 days work this last summer at 20d. per day." In 1667 "44 days worke . . . winter days at 16d. per day" brought Pepper £2 18s. 8d.; for "89 days worke summer at 20d." he received £7 8s. 4d. Account Books, 2, pp. 227–229; 3, pp. 138–139.

[158] Thompson, "Time, Work-Discipline, and Industrial Capitalism," *Past and Present* (1967), p. 61, n. 16; Morris, *Government and Labor*, pp. 58–59, 65.

For "Master Taylors, and Such . . . one daye's worke [would be] 12 hours."[159]

How field workers were intended to spend their time during the day is suggested by a 1636 prescription for an English plowman's duties: " 'the Plowman shall rise before four of the clock in the morning, and after thanks given to God for his rest, and prayer for the success of his labours, he shall go into the stable.' After cleansing the stable, grooming his horses, feeding them, and preparing his tackle, he might breakfast (6–6:30 a.m.), he should plough until 2 p.m. or 3 p.m.; take half an hour for dinner; attend to his horses etc. until 6:30 p.m., when he might come in for supper."[160] While such a description probably tells as much about the author's desires to keep the workers occupied and out of trouble, it suggests the overall configuration of the day for most seventeenth-century laborers. A typical day for Francis Pepper when he was working on a per diem basis probably looked something like this:

4:30 A.M.	rise
4:30–5:00 A.M.	tend livestock
5:00–6:30 A.M.	field work
6:30–7:00 A.M.	breakfast
7:00–11:00 A.M.	field work
11:00–11:30 A.M.	cider or rum break
11:30 A.M.–2:00 P.M.	field work
2:00–3:00 P.M.	dinner
3:00–6:00 P.M.	field work, livestock maintenance, tool repair
6:00–7:00 P.M.	supper
8:30 P.M.	retire

Early American workers, unlike English field laborers, did not take a regular midday nap. They also relied on pork and cider for their dinner instead of the bread, cheese, onion, ale, and meat that were the standard fare of English workers.[161]

The yearly pattern of Pepper's work was governed by the rhythms of an agricultural society. The seventeenth-century calendar year began in late March, and appropriately so. First, fields needed to be drained and broken up by an ox-drawn plow. Plows were constructed out of ash or oak. Plowing techniques varied with the terrain and quality of soil. Typically, the most productive practice was to plow, crossplow, and harrow smooth. This procedure would

[159] Morris, *Government and Labor*, p. 65.

[160] Thompson, "Time, Work-Discipline, and Industrial Capitalism," *Past and Present* (1967), p. 77.

[161] *Ibid.*; Hartley, *Lost Country Life*, p. 152.

be followed by furrowing and crossfurrowing at three-to-four-foot intervals. Planting was then done at the intersections of the furrows. An experienced plowman like Pepper could turn over an acre or more a day of tilled land. Less assiduous husbandmen simply broke up the land—with a mattock if no plow was available—seeded by broadcast, and harrowed.[162] Plowing, even of soft bottom lands, was arduous work. Seventeenth-century plows, as Dorothy Hartley points out, needed to be "yanked out at the end of straight furrows, turned with a wide sweep, and started back again in a parallel line. Early ploughs could only work in one direction, and turn the furrow to one side. (The turn or 'wrest' plough, in which the ploughshare could be turned over to reverse the cut, was not invented till 1700.)" In addition to avoiding rocks and keeping the share and colter clean, the plowman had to monitor carefully the exertions of the draft animals. Again, from Hartley, "where oxen are used, a hundred and twenty feet is a fair length for a straight pull. The oxherd should always let his oxen stop and rest at the end of every furrow, so they go the whole length in the hope of this expected pause."[163] In addition to plowing Pynchon's fields, Pepper also broke up those of some of the family's tenants as well as those of other townsmen without plows. After the fields had been seeded, there was a two-month lull until haymaking season began, usually in late May. In Springfield the freshly cut hay from the rich bottom lands adjacent to the Agawam River was piled into ten-foot high ricks until it could be transferred to barns for storage until winter. The second crop of hay and the winter wheat were usually cut in early August. Harvesting of spring wheat, barley, oats, and peas (as well as any root crops) began in mid-September. As with the optimal times for sowing and cultivating, oral traditions provided guidance for reapers: "When barley hangs its head, and the oats begin to shed, and wheat stands stiff and begins to open." When these signs appeared, the time for the greatest labor requirements was at hand.[164]

Harvest time, more than any other period, revealed the importance of patron-client ties for Pynchon. He needed both laborers and labor discipline. A large and reliable force of reapers was essential if his extensive stands of grain were to be cut in time.

[162] James A. Henretta, *The Evolution of American Society, 1700–1815*, Lexington, Mass., 1973, pp. 18, 31–33; Russell, *A Long, Deep Furrow*, pp. 43, 81–84, 135, 176; William Pynchon Account Book, pp. 40, 72, 119, 192, 212; Account Books, 1, p. 328; 2, p. 63; 3, p. 97; 5, pp. 77, 115, 175, 345, 349.

[163] Hartley, *Lost Country Life*, pp. 78, 81–82.

[164] *Ibid.*, p. 174; William Pynchon Account Book, pp. 30, 136, 212, 216; Account Books, 1, p. 85; 2, pp. 171, 221, 314; 3, pp. 55, 171, 285; 5, p. 121; 6, p. 91.

Wheat and barley cannot be allowed to stand in the fields for more than two weeks after maturity, or the head breaks and the grain is lost; oats become moldy if not cut promptly. Working with a hand sickle, reapers could cut no more than one-half to three-quarters of an acre daily. As a result, John Pynchon could not have harvested his extensive fields without the assistance of Francis Pepper—and between twenty-five and forty of the other village men as well. Unwilling or unavailable laborers could have ruined him.

Once again, the employer's methods of securing adequate labor illustrate the conflation of capitalist and precapitalist relationships, as well as the role of the patron-client bond in mediating between the two and ensuring the dominance of the former. For non-clients, such as Jonathan Taylor, Pynchon guaranteed labor discipline by contractual means. As we saw earlier, Taylor's steer lease included a proviso that "he Ingages and promises me to reape and shock 2 acres of wheate and to cut one acre of pease when I call for it to be done next harvest and to doe it upon 2 days [notice]."[165] But a less cumbersome and equally reliable surety was the sense of personal obligation growing out of clientage. Come harvest time, Pynchon needed to know on whom he could count, and therefore he cultivated his clients in order that they would do the same to his fields.[166]

Once the crops were in, the remaining days of seasonable weather were devoted to sowing rye and winter wheat, gathering and processing fruit, and slaughtering animals. Because of John Pynchon's extensive pork exports, pigs made up the majority of animals slaughtered in early Springfield. Hog slaughtering always came in late fall and was followed by another month's to six weeks' work dressing carcasses, scraping hides, rendering lard, and salting and smoking hams, bacon slabs, and sides. Fall was also the time to cart apples to the cider-mill and dung to the planting fields.[167]

When winter's chill moved work indoors, Pepper began the time-consuming task of threshing and winnowing the grains he had helped plant and harvest. Each morning, his work day began with a trek to one of Pynchon's barns. As with most early American barns, Pynchon's were presumably built facing the wind to ensure a draft across the threshing floor sufficient for winnowing with

[165] Account Books, 1, p. 314.

[166] *Ibid.*, 2, p. 314; 3, pp. 104–105, 285; 5, p. 121; 6, p. 91; Henretta, *Evolution of American Society*, pp. 18, 22; Hartley, *Lost Country Life*, p. 174.

[167] William Pynchon Account Book, pp. 23, 26, 28, 302; Account Books, 1, pp. 78, 266; 2, pp. 227, 229; 3, pp. 241, 247; 5, pp. 81, 89, 423; Parker, "American Farmer," p. 183.

fans. There, working with a leather-and-wood flail, Pepper cleaned and sacked wheat, oats, barley, and peas. Wheat threshing earned Pepper five to six pence per bushel, oates and peas two and one-half pence. In the winter of 1660 Pynchon paid the workman for "threshing and cleaning 180 bushels of wheat at 5d. per bushel . . . threshing and cleaning bushels Pease . . . By 56 bushels ½ of oates and cleaning them at 2d. ½ per bushel." Later that winter, Pepper earned £4 for "threshing and cleaning 126 bushels of winter wheate at 6d. per bushel and 55 bushels of Summer wheate" and another thirty-three shillings for "threshing and cleaning oates and Pease." The following year, for "threshing and cleaning 50 bushels and ½ wheate at 5d. per bushel and 140 bushels of oates and Pease at 2d. ½" he was credited for £2 10s. 2d. With mechanical regularity, Pepper's winter days were consumed by the routine of flailing, separating, and bagging the various grains. He earned £5 in 1662 for "Threshing and cleaning 139 bushels of wheat at 5d. . . . By Threshing and cleaning 69 bushels of Pease, 110 bushels oates, 20 Barley . . . at 2d. ½ bushel." In January of 1665 Pynchon made an accounting and found that "I owe Frances for threshing and cleaning 229 bushels of wheat at 5d. per bushel £4 14s. [and] Threshing and cleaning oates and Pease 17 bushels oats at 2d. ½ per bushel £1 18s."[168] When not threshing, Pepper spent his winter days, like other men, making tools, shaving shingles, and mending tack.

Somewhat remarkably, given the multitude of his other tasks, Pepper also served as a shepherd for John Pynchon's flock of sheep. On October 6, 1656, Pynchon paid Pepper £5 2s. 6d. for "his keeping my Sheepe the yeare 1656," a figure that rose to £5 10s. the following year and by 1661 stood at £7 10s. Most shepherds, in the New World as in the Old, remained unmarried and, as we have seen, Pepper was no exception. Tending sheep meant staying with them twenty-four hours a day, and this left little time for normal familial obligations. Unlike in England and continental Europe, large-scale migratory sheep raising was not practiced in the colonies. Flocks typically remained within the environs of their owner's community, unless overgrazing or inadequate rainfall made brief periods of transhumance necessary. In a second departure from English practices, Springfield did not pasture its sheep in a common flock under the supervision of a town-supported shepherd. The privately hired shepherds such as Pepper stayed with the flocks in the outpastures, rather than returning to the town center to fold them for the night. Springfield likewise made no use

---

[168] Account Books, 2, pp. 227, 229.

of "stinting"—the practice of assigning the number of each kind of beast entitled to common pasturage under open field farming. Pepper's task was to keep the sheep away from the sown planting fields from March to November, usually by making resort to uncultivated outlying land grants. The early spring movement away from the town center signaled the beginning of an unchanging annual cycle for sheep cultivators.[169] Shearing time came in May, followed in Springfield by the sale of the wool at the Pynchon general store. June and July were devoted to cheese making, although this food was never the staple in American diets that it was in Europe. November brought a return to the planting fields as well as any slaughtering that there was to be done. Lambing time came in midwinter, often around Christmas, and with the onset of warm weather in March the whole process began anew.[170]

FEMALE LABOR

Francis Pepper may have been tempted to take a wife from the continuous stream of female domestics who passed a term of service in the Pynchon household, although by the young women's preference or his, he remained single.[171] In early Springfield the Pynchon mansion was the most available place of employment for young females, and over thirty girls worked in the household for a year or more.[172] In 1684 the mother of twelve-year-old Hannah Jefferys asked John Pynchon to take her daughter as a servant for six years. He entered in his account book that "Goodwife Jefferys being here and proffering her daughter Hanah to come to us: I

---

[169] *Ibid.*, 1, p. 208; 2, p. 227; *Springfield Town Recs.*, 1, p. 61; Russell, *A Long, Deep Furrow*, pp. 154–158. For a comparison with European practices, see Emmanuel Le Roy Ladurie, *Montaillou: The Promised Land of Error*, New York, 1978, pp. 69–119; Hartley, *Lost Country Life*, pp. 129–141.

[170] Account Books, 1, p. 282; 2, pp. 23, 61, 109, 273, 305; 3, p. 95; 5, pp. 127, 413; Le Roy Ladurie, *Montaillou*, pp. 69–119. Despite his sheep-tending and generally heavy reliance on employment by Pynchon for his subsistence, Pepper may have at least briefly aspired to be a freehold farmer. In February 1667 Pynchon "Sold to Francis Pepper That Alotment which I bought of William Brooks [for debts] in Chikkupy Plaine (a few days ago) being about 32 acres . . . for which Francis allows me £18." Pepper's motives for this land purchase remain conjectural. Perhaps he wanted to strike out on his own; or possibly be bought it for purely speculative purposes. In either case, the transaction availed him nothing, as the tract eventually reverted to Pynchon. Account Books, 3, p. 138.

[171] HCPC Rec., 1, p. 259.

[172] Account Books, 1, p. 224; 2, p. 243; 3, pp. 55, 69, 81; 5, pp. 4–5, 19, 25, 31, 61, 75, 183, 218–219, 249, 298, 461, 489, 512–513, 543; 6, pp. 22–23, 208–209, 248–249, 250.

treated with her and shee yielded to our having her (whom she says is 12 years old and since August last) till shee be 18 yeares old." After listening to Mrs. Jefferys's proposal, Pynchon consented to take the girl. He agreed to provide "her cloathes which shee now needs to wear" and to give her a pair of shoes. Both he and Mrs. Jefferys set their hand to the contract that "shee is to live with us till shee be 18 yeares of age, and [Pynchon] cloathing her and providing well for her." As his offer immediately to provide wearing apparel for Hannah suggests, the Jefferys were in difficult financial straits. For this reason, they had also put out a second daughter (apparently older) to service in the Pynchon household. In June of the preceding year, Pynchon "agreed with Goodman Jeffery for his daughter Sarah to live with us a yeare." Presumably because of his eroding economic fortunes, Jefferys was unusually adamant about the wages Sarah would receive. Pynchon "propounded her wage to be £5 10s. but he said it must be £6." To this demand, the magistrate consented, and "Shee came to us on Thursday afternoon 5th day of July 1683."[173] Abigail Dibble received the same wages as did Sarah Jefferys. Pynchon wrote in his account book that "Abigail Dibble came to us the 1st day of October 1678 and we are to give her £6 for a yeare service."[174] Likewise Hannah Morgan, whose father Miles in 1673 agreed with Pynchon "for his Daughter Hannah . . . [to] Live with us a yeare to begin [the] 1st of May which day shee is to come to us [for] £6 for the yeare."[175] These rates remained constant throughout the seventeenth century, as in 1691 we find that Susannah Ponder "Received by 2 yeares Service at £6 is £12."[176] And Hannah Holeman in 1692 came to the Pynchon household, "as a Servant faithfully and dilligently ought to doe," for annual wages of £6.[177] Finally, in 1699 Alice Beamont joined the Pynchon household at annual wages of £6.[178] The only exception to the £6 wage level, possibly because she was unusually skilled, was Priscilla Warner. On September 7, 1695, Pynchon wrote that "Priscilla Warner came to dwel with us for a yeare and for her yeares service I am to allow her £7 10s. in pay [goods or services] or £5 in money [specie]."[179]

The domestic's typical work-day of baking, brewing, cleaning,

---

[173] *Ibid.*, 5, p. 461.
[174] *Ibid.*, 5, p. 398.
[175] *Ibid.*, 5, pp. 4–5.
[176] *Ibid.*, 5, p. 219.
[177] *Ibid.*, 6, pp. 248–249.
[178] *Ibid.*, 6, p. 250.
[179] *Ibid.*, 6, p. 23.

and milking is suggested by John Pynchon's confrontation with his insouciant (and misnamed) maid, Mindwell Old. Wearied over her penchant for disappearing from the household for extended periods, thereby leaving his wife Amy to scramble to find hired substitutes, Pynchon upbraided Old and eventually docked a portion of her salary. In a revealing account book entry (one that divertingly illuminates the limits of a patron's power, even in towns like Springfield), he observed that, "Mindwel Old besides her many vagarys and often being gone part of a day into Towne, absented her selfe one whole Night and part of a day in June: again about the End of June shee went away and told the folk she would be home; however, we Saw her not next day, at least she did nothing, and often went out in an hour and neglect Milking [so] that my wife was forced to get others to Milk. On July first, or thereabouts, she went away with her Cloaths to Goody Parsons, though [she] Came again; [she also] neglected Brewing one day ... But went to and fro, sometimes to Morgan's, sometimes to Lamb's, sometimes to [Gilbert's?] [and so often to] Cousin Holyoke that he complained of her being there. [On] July 3d, [she] did something, but only part of the day. [On] July 4th In the Morning she went out and came not neere Milking so that my wife got others, though we ... saw her [going] to and fro yet came not to my house. In truth shee went from us in June before the end of it though shee was to and fro here to vex us til July 4th." Having had enough of this vexation, Pynchon decided that it was time pointedly to remind Old of her domestic responsibilities. "[A]bout noon, I lit out and told her shee should act like a Maid and right up things and Bake and Brew and [only then] take her liberty." His admonitions, however, had little effect, as "she went away the same day and came all and went out the house and then went unknon to us. She would be so many times gone for a whole Month and more that my wife was often forced to hire others to do the worke."[180]

A woman's contribution to her family's income was not, of course, limited to her wages as a servant. Mindwell Old notwithstanding, all women in early Springfield—unmarried and married alike—worked as long and as hard as did the men, and without constant female labor few households could have escaped privation.

In Springfield, as in all preindustrial societies, the domestic system of production rested on an explicit division of labor according to gender. Men looked after the fields, woods, and flocks. Women were responsible for preparing meals, housekeeping, making and

---

[180] *Ibid.*, 6, Index, p. 19.

repairing clothes, gardening, putting up preserves, making soap, milking cows, churning butter, pressing cheese, and making candles. The weekly round of a woman's work was as unrelenting as it was necessary. While men might daddle about the barn during winter months or after the first hay cutting, women confronted a year-round regimen of seemingly endless spinning, washing, mending, churning, cleaning, and baking. Moreover, come autumn, women also lent a hand with harvest, as the frequent allusions to "work of your wife's" in the Pynchon account books attest. And of course, women were charged with the task of bearing, nursing, and educating the children.

Emphasizing the potential sense of drudgery brought by such a routine, Mary Beth Norton notes that "The sameness was the quality that differentiated farm women's work from that performed by their husbands. No less physically demanding or difficult, men's tasks varied considerably from day to day and month to month. At most—during planting or harvest time, for example—men would spend two or three weeks at one job. But then they would move on to another. For a farmer, in other words, the basic cycle was yearly; for his wife, it was daily and weekly, with additional obligations superimposed seasonally. Moreover, men were able to break their work routine by making frequent trips to town or the local mill on business, or by going hunting or fishing, whereas their wives, especially if they had small children, were tied to the home."[181]

Because of the wide array of jobs assigned to her, a girl needed to start her domestic education early. Beginning around her seventh birthday, a female would be given instruction from her mother and older sisters on the variety of skills she would need. At age twelve, if the opportunity was available, she would be hired out as a domestic servant. In so doing she would continue her education in household economics and, not incidentally, bring in badly needed income for the family. Typically, as we have seen, a year's service as a domestic was worth £6.

Once married, the only way a woman could usually earn additional money for the household was by spinning wool into yarn. Few households were without a spinning wheel, and in Springfield both flax and wool were used as fibers. Because the labor of flax preparation was particularly long and tedious, the presence of so many sheep in the community helped ease the women's work load. Experienced spinners produced four skeins daily when working

[181] Mary Beth Norton, *Liberty's Daughters: The Revolutionary Experience of American Women, 1750–1800*, Boston, 1980, pp. 3–39.

alone, six if an assistant carded the wool.[182] As with their male counterparts, women workers usually found John Pynchon to be the one most eager for their services. In 1678 he wrote that "Goodwife Parsons had cotton made for my wife to Spin and brought hom the yarne this July . . . which I weighed and it was 8 pounds of yarne; for the spinning whereoff I paid her 10 pounds of cotton woole." The next month he "delivered her more cotton woole to spin for us . . . 16 pounds." And in January of the following year, he paid Mrs. Parsons nineteen shillings eight pence for "Spinning yarne for us 15 pounds at 20d. per pound." After men such as Samuel Marshfield sheared the fleece, it was given to women workers who dexterously pulled out, rolled, and bundled the fleece. After women like Mrs. Parsons had spun the wool into yarn, they returned it to male weavers such as Charles Ferry. When the weaving was finished, women again entered the productive process to "full" the cloth under water and stretch it out on "tents" to dry.[183]

Literate women were also able to earn income as private tutors. In November 1653, Pentecost Mathews (wife of the cooper) was credited by John Pynchon for "worke schooling my child . . . as in John Mathews booke [the sum of] £8 2s. 9d."[184] Again, on October 12, 1656, Pynchon wrote that "John Mathews came to me to set things straite about the schooling of my children and he ordered and agreed that I should allow him 40s. for all that is due to him."[185] Three years later, Pynchon credited "John Mathews Wife . . . By schooling Elizur [Holyoke] 2 yeers and Hannah till this November 1659 in all 35s." In addition to her schoolteaching, Mrs. Mathews received payment for "keeping of Marriage Bans."[186]

CHILD LABOR

Children were likewise vital to the labor force, especially for those families without sufficient resources to hire day-laborers. As Mikiso Hane has pointed out, "Farmers must have children. Three children are not enough. There must be at least five. If a farmer has too few children, the world will close in on him. If he has too many, he will have trouble supporting them, but there must be at least

---

[182] *Ibid.*, p. 17.
[183] Account Books, 5, p. 347; Hartley, *Lost Country Life*, pp. 133–138; Russell, *A Long, Deep Furrow*, pp. 139–141.
[184] Account Books, 1, p. 127.
[185] *Ibid.*, 1, p. 269.
[186] *Ibid.*, 2, p. 99.

five working hands in the family."[187] Accordingly, children's duties began at a tender age. Boys as young as five gathered wood, took pork and cider to field workers, and chased crows out of the newly sown planting grounds. They also began the ten- to fifteen-year-long process of learning how to farm by following their father and elder brothers about their respective rounds of chores. In communities such as Springfield where pork export was important, preteenage boys acted as swineherds, rounding up pigs with the aid of a dog and driving them out to grub for roots and acorns in order to fatten them for the winter slaughter. Young girls worked over the hearth or out in the garden, and as dairymaids they also helped to care for the town's large herds of livestock. Dairymaids, in addition to milking, skimming, and churning, looked after suckling calves and saw to it that after a sow farrowed, the piglets were cosseted, warmed, and fed on milk. Girls and boys together shared the onerous task of weeding, work that occupied much of the spring months. To quote again from Thomas Tusser's farming calendar: "In May get a weed-hook, a crotch and a glove and weed out such weeds, as the corn do not love. For weeding of winter corn, now it is best: but June is the better for weeding the rest."[188]

Work in seventeenth-century Springfield was a family—not a community—affair. Among the most striking omissions from the tasks listed in the local records are any references to communal labor projects: barn raisings, log rollings, fence buildings, or corn huskings. As the Pynchon account books plainly show, large projects in Springfield were accomplished by private contract, not public cooperation. Working to get ahead left little time for working for others, and the result was a settlement where conflict, not communalism, was the rule.

---

[187] *Peasants, Rebels, and Outcasts: The Underside of Modern Japan*, New York, 1982, p. 81. Hane is here quoting from a 20th-century Japanese informant, described as an "old farm woman." This citation was brought to my attention by E. J. Hobsbawm, "The Lowest Depths," *The New York Review of Books* (April 15, 1982), pp. 15–16.

[188] Hartley, *Lost Country Life*, pp. 103–104, 125.

• Chapter 5 •

Community

"Man is incapable of self-completion, and therefore never wholly predictable: a fallible, a complex combination of opposites, some reconcilable, others incapable of being resolved or harmonized; unable to cease from his search for truth, happiness, novelty, freedom, but with no guarantee, theological or logical or scientific of being able to attain them: a free, imperfect being, capable of determining his own destiny in circumstances favorable to the development of his reason and his gifts."
Sir Isaiah Berlin, *Four Essays on Liberty*
(New York 1969), p. 205

IN SEVENTEENTH-CENTURY SPRINGFIELD communal obligations were subordinated to individual needs. The town's inhabitants, far from reifying the concept of community, accepted the primacy of the individual family household as their dominant public value. The residents would cooperate with their neighbors when they had to, work in concert when it was necessary, or band together against outsiders when attacks came, but otherwise they concentrated on securing exclusively individual goals. These goals were, first, to earn their daily bread and, second, to provide a patrimony for their children. And in both of these pursuits they relied not on corporate solidarity, but on the maintenance of successful personal ties with the town's patron, John Pynchon. Non-familial relationships within the community tended to be vertical, between patron and client, rather than horizontal, among neighbors of equal status. When someone needed work, land, credit, or adjudication of a conflict, he turned to Pynchon, not the town meeting.

Rather than being an end in itself, community was the means to another end—personal advancement. Although the inhabitants publicly embraced the doctrine of the covenant, their central goals were rooted in the private acquisition of wealth. The "Articles of

Agreement" founding the town in 1636 reflect these priorities. The settlers began by professing their fealty to God and to each other: "We whose names are underwritten, being by God's providence engaged together to make a plantation at and over against Agawam upon Connecticut, do mutually agree to certain articles and orders to be observed and kept by us and by our successors." Their first resolution was that "We Intend by God's grace, as soon as we can, with all convenient speed, to procure some Godly and faithful minister with whom we purpose to join in church covenant to walk in all the ways of Christ." But the remaining fifteen resolutions of the articles pertain not to the moral ordering of a godly community, but rather to sundry formulae for allocating homelots, upland, and pasture. The second resolution asserted that "We intend that our town shall be composed of forty families, or, if we think meet after[ward] to alter our purpose, yet not to exceed the number of fifty families, rich and poor." The expectation that the town would be composed of both "rich and poor," as we have seen, was prophetic. The remaining resolutions divided up the shares of the town center (for homelots), the "cow pasture," the "Hassokey Marsh," as well as the various planting fields on the periphery of the center.[1]

As the pragmatic nature of its founding articles suggests, early Springfield bore little resemblance to the subsistence-oriented covenanted communities. It was not a "peasant utopia" or a "Christian Utopian Closed Corporate Community." Nor was it a "peaceable kingdom," a "one-class society," a "homogeneous communal unit" or a "nucleated, open-field village."[2] The inhabitants of early Springfield would have looked with wonder on such characterizations of their society. Their community was founded not as a peasant utopia, but as a fur-trading post. Although comprised of believing Christians, Springfield failed to make rigorous efforts to distinguish the unregenerate from the Visible Saints.[3] Significantly, the townsmen built a house of correction, as well as a church, to help promote an always precarious domestic tranquility. The community's inequitable land distribution patterns made tenancy and

---

[1] "Articles of Agreement, Springfield, Massachusetts," in John Demos, ed., *Remarkable Providences, 1600–1760*, New York, 1972, pp. 53–56.

[2] Lockridge, *A New England Town*, pp. 13, 16–17, 20, 167; Zuckerman, *Peaceable Kingdoms*, pp. 54, 143.

[3] The town's early church records have not survived, but the high rate of antisocial behavior among freemen (those during the first charter period who were fully admitted church members) suggests that the requirements for church membership were not excessively rigid. For an examination of religious discord in the Connecticut Valley generally, see Paul R. Lucas, *Valley of Discord: Church and Society along the Connecticut River, 1636–1725*, Hanover, N. H., 1976.

day-laboring commonplace. And no sooner had Springfield been founded than it began to fragment into four separate communities.

Nucleated settlement patterns, we have been told, were one of the principal reasons for widespread social conformity. These concentrated settlements engendered an atmosphere of continuous "neighborly scrutiny" of each other's actions. As Kai Erikson puts it in his influential study of deviance in early New England: "The towns were small and compact, the congregations watchful; every person was tuned in to the movements of his neighbor."[4] It has become axiomatic that the subsequent fragmentation of these nucleated communities signified a falling away from the first settlers' high ideals. Springfield, however, was almost from the beginning a dispersed settlement. Because of the Indians' refusal to decamp, the early inhabitants built their town on the east bank of the Connecticut River but established their planting fields on the considerably more promising west side. Some of the town's residents quickly wearied of the tiresome and dangerous trek across the river to tend their fields and, despite the Indians' protestations, built homes on the west bank. Others moved to more propitious locations north and south of the town center for the same reasons. By the late 1640s, three separate communities had emerged, and the town meeting appointed individual fence viewers for each section.[5]

By the mid-1660s, four discrete villages existed within Springfield, separated by either the Connecticut River or a minimum of three miles of forest. [See Springfield map.] These included: the town center on the east side of the river; Long Meadow, four miles south of the center; the west bank settlement (including Chicopee plain); and Skepnuck, three miles northeast of the center. In several letters to Boston, John Pynchon provided detailed presentations of this diffused settlement pattern. Writing to Governor John Leverett to dramatize Springfield's vulnerability to Indian attack, Pynchon asserted that "our People of this Towne [are] extreamely scattered."[6] In 1688, while seeking increased military aid from the governor's council, he stated that "this Towne . . . consists much of out farms and a few houses together . . . above half our people are abroad and at a distance from the Towne 3 or 4 miles each way."[7] Shortly thereafter, Pynchon presented a still more specific

[4] Kai Erikson, *Wayward Puritans: A Study in the Sociology of Deviance*, New York, 1970, p. 170.

[5] *Springfield Town Recs.*, 1, p. 195.

[6] John Pynchon to John Leverett, August 4, 1675, Rare Book Room, Boston Public Library, typescript copy, CVHM.

[7] John Pynchon to the Governor's Council, August 21, 1688, London, C.O. 1/65 51, typescript copy, CVHM.

description of the town's settlement pattern: "Springfield [contains] about 120 [households] But much scattered, and the men are in 4 parts, remote one from the other like so many smale villages." He then proceeded to give his reader a breakdown of the population distribution of the four settlements: "at the Long meddow about 4 miles Southward from the Towne 20 men, on the west side of the great River 28, at Skeepmuck ful 4 Miles North 12 other farms ... in the Towne [center] about 60 men."[8]

Sectional rivalries developed in the town meeting within a generation of settlement. Initially these conflicts involved relatively inconsequential matters, but eventually the issues separating one community from another assumed greater import. In 1667 the inhabitants on the west side of the river received abatement of one day's work on the county road on the east side in order to "make and repair their own highwayes."[9] Five years later the "Neighbors on the West side of the great River" received fifty acres from the town meeting on which to construct their own sawmill.[10] The west siders' request for a boat for crossing the river sparked a particularly nettlesome controversy, one that eventually required outside arbitration. In May of 1674 the west siders petitioned the town meeting "that a Boate might be made at the charge of the whole Towne" by reason of "their great trouble in getting over the river to come to the Publique worship of God and for other publique Meetings." The east siders resisted this proposal and "after Some Arguing about the matter," the meeting voted that "the question shalbe comitted to be decided and determined by three indifferent men that are not of this Town."[11] Despite the inhabitants' agreement to seek and abide by outside arbitrators, the boat problem remained unresolved. Five years later, the town again considered "an old Question," as to "whether or no the making a boat for the conveighance of the Inhabitants on the West side of the River over to the publike worship of God, and to other publike meetings" was not "rationally Chargable to the whole Town." Still deadlocked, the townsmen voted to refer the matter to mediators from Northampton and Hadley yet another time.[12] Labor conscriptions for road maintenance fared no better. In 1672 "Diverse persons that dwell on the East side of the great River haveing land ... on the West side of the great River" publicly complained that they were "op-

---

[8] Mass. Archives, 36, p. 56.
[9] *Springfield Town Recs.*, 1, p. 360.
[10] *Ibid.*, 1, pp. 402–403.
[11] *Ibid.*, 2, p. 122.
[12] *Ibid.*, 2, p. 141.

pressed" because they made "little or noe use of that way [which] they should be called to repair." Those dwelling in the settlements north and south of the town made similar refusals.[13]

After 1670 the town's judicial and civil institutions routinely differentiated among the four communities in their deliberations. A discovery jury convened in 1674 to find out how Abel Wright's four-year-old son died, selected "but 6 persons" instead of the customary twelve "in regard of the remoteness of the Place from the Towne, over at Skepnuck."[14] When the grammar school opened in the town center in 1679, children living in Long Meadow, Skepnuck, and the west side were excused from compulsory attendance. Their remoteness from the center often deprived the outlying communities of important information relating to town affairs. In 1688 both Skepnuck and Long Meadow complained that fines levied on them for non-performance of highway work were unjust because they were "not warned" of these obligations.[15]

Neighborly cooperation within, as well as among, the four villages was often at a premium. As each of the four communities elevated autonomy over corporate obligations, so did individual inhabitants often scorn cooperation within the hamlet itself. The critical problem of fence maintenance is a case in point. With hungry livestock always eager to feast in the planting fields and vegetable gardens, secure fences were essential in order to protect the community's food supply. Both the common fences around the planting fields and the individually maintained homelot fences needed to be kept "hog tight and horse high." Because the common fences were only as secure as their weakest section, all stood to suffer by any one person's negligence. Violations of the community's fence ordinances were especially common in the southern half of the town center. On September 23, 1645, the town meeting recorded that "divers neighbors between Francis Ball his lott and Benjamin Cooly's lott have complayned that some of that Neighbor hood refuse to Joyne with them in makinge a fence to save theyr neighbors harmless." The meeting thereupon reiterated the mandate that "all the sayd Inhabitants shal Joyne together in a sufficient generall fence, every man brakinge a proportionable share accordinge to each man's quantity of acres." The meeting likewise reaffirmed the need to build and keep homelot fences in good repair, even at the price of coercion: "if any neighbor from Francis Ball's lott to Goodman Cooly's shall desire to Inclose his yard with a garden or an

---

[13] *Ibid.*, 1, p. 398.
[14] *Pynchon Court Rec.*, p. 282.
[15] *Springfield Town Recs.*, 2, p. 197.

orchard, If his next neighbor refuse to Joyne for the one halfe of the said fence, he may compell his neighbors on each side of his lott to beare the one halfe of his fence, provided he compell them not to Joyne for above 20 rodds in length."[16] The same story was true in Long Meadow. In April 1649 the town meeting observed that "there is notice taken of a disagreement amongst severall of the neighbours who have lands lyinge in the longe meddowe." The landowners there had originally agreed to complete all fencing by the fifteenth of April, but it soon became evident that this goal was unattainable. Livestock roamed and foraged through the unfenced lots "to the aparent damage of many in the said field." Therefore, "for the better settlinge of this difference" and "for avoydinge of all contentions that may arise about the settling or proportioninge of the said fence," the town adopted yet another maintenance scheme. In 1669 when "Severall persons" complained that "they cant get theire Neighbours, where theire fences is in particular, to make up theire fence sufficient," the selectmen attempted to give fence viewers new enforcement powers. Where "there are Complaints against Neighbours, that any one of them doth not make good fence . . . where either Neighbour desires," the viewers were to demand on-the-spot rectification.[17]

The reluctance of Springfield's inhabitants to behave in a "neighborly" and confraternal fashion is likewise reflected in both criminal proceedings and civil litigation. The incidence of physical assaults, slander, family feuds, fraud, and witchcraft accusations suggests that Springfield did not enjoy the strong communitarianism of Dedham and Andover. Social conflict, of course, is not itself a sign of communal ill-health. The function of conflict in a community could often be ameliorative. Verbal and physical assaults and similar confrontations provided outlets for pent-up aggressive feelings that might otherwise have worked in more insidious ways to undermine social harmony.[18] Likewise, as David T. Konig convincingly argues, we must be careful in equating rates of litigation with levels of conflict. The courts could, and did, play an integrative role in seventeenth-century Massachusetts. Yet these considerations notwithstanding, court records offer the best available portrayal of the prevailing system of values. The dramaturgical or symbolic function of court proceedings publicly established the boundaries of acceptable behavior. Court records suggest what kinds of antisocial activities were common in the community as well as the bounds

[16] *Ibid.*, 1, pp. 181–182.
[17] *Ibid.*, 1, pp. 197, 379–380.
[18] Stanley Coser, *The Function of Social Conflict*, London, 1956, Chapter 1.

beyond which certain actions could not be sanctioned. Because the official court records for seventeenth-century Springfield are incomplete, accurate per capita statistics for various crimes and civil offenses cannot be compiled. But even when used only as literary evidence, the community's judicial records can be illuminating. Using a tip-of-the-iceberg approach to crime and civil wrongs—the assumption that resort to court bespoke deeper-seated animosities not accommodable to informal or ecclesiastical resolution—court proceedings can tell much about the broader substream of social relations.[19]

These records suggest that contentious and generally non-Puritan behavior was common in early Springfield. If a resident found himself enraged at a fellow villager, he was not constrained from expressing this antipathy by an overriding need to maintain communal harmony. Self-assertion, not self-abnegation, was the rule. The town always contained a number of contumacious and mercurial inhabitants, and their actions call into question quietistic images of early Massachusetts.

Most troublesome were the artisans. Their skills, not their personal rectitude, brought them to the community and they often displayed a marked unwillingness to abide by Puritan ethical norms. Moreover, Springfield's tendency to judge men by standards of utility rather than godliness allowed some of the more highly skilled craftsmen to flout social mores with relative impunity. Their economic value to the town in general—and Pynchon in particular—allowed artisans more latitude in personal behavior than farmers and the unskilled enjoyed. The experiences of shoemaker John Norton, shingler Philip Matoone, blacksmith John Stewart, brickmaker Francis Hacklington, and canoeman Samuel Terry all point to this conclusion.[20]

John Norton originally came to Springfield as a soldier during King Philip's War and decided to remain in the community, possibly at the urging of militia leader John Pynchon.[21] Pynchon always kept a sharp eye out for skilled craftsmen, and in a frontier setting shoemakers were especially prized. But no sooner had Norton settled down than he began to run afoul of the law. He was convicted at various times of philandering, drunkenness, and aggravated as-

[19] Konig, *Law and Society*, pp. 88, 158–191; Nelson, *Dispute and Conflict Resolution*. For an argument that the 16th century witnessed the "surfacing of the litigious spirit" generally in Western society, see Richard L. Kagan, *Lawsuits and Litigants in Castile, 1500–1700*, Chapel Hill, 1981, pp. 3–162.

[20] *Pynchon Court Rec.*, pp. 247, 263, 289, 315; HCPC Rec., 1, pp. 7–9.

[21] Account Books, 5, p. 551.

sault. In June 1678 he was "Complained of by Mary Crowfoote
and Hanah Morgan for offering abuse to them especially to Mary
Crowfoote taking up her Coates and offering baseness to her, etc."
Norton pleaded intoxication as a defense, "he professing his not
knowing what he did And it appearing by the Testymonys and
otherwise that he was Drunk." For "his Drunkenness" as well as
"his wicked and Lacivious cariage," the shoemaker received a £2
fine.[22] Again in 1686 drunkenness brought Norton before the bench.
Springfield's tavernkeeper, Samuel Ely, entered an action of battery
in that "Norton strake, abused, and drew Blood from the said Ely,
cutting a great Gash Just above his eye and sorely bruising his
forehead." The court learned that the altercation was sparked by
Ely's denial of additional cider to Norton on the grounds that he
had "had enough." Livid, Norton "rose up from the Table's end
. . . and said By God I wil make you fetch me cider, and Coming
to [Ely] struck me in the forehead with his hand or Fist with something (I suppose a shilling which before I saw in his hand) which
Cut a great Gash."[23]

The shingler Philip Matoone behaved in an even more egre-
giously non-Puritan fashion. One of John Pynchon's most active
woodworkers, Matoone, during the construction boom following
King Philip's War, was paid for "6 days worke shaving shingles . . .
By worke shingling over my ox house . . . By sawing 5600 shingles
. . . By covering my share of the Mill" as well as "6 days worke
about the mill floore." On March 1, 1679, Matoone agreed to shingle Pynchon's 51-by-24-foot barn in Round Hill for £6 10s. and
"all the left over shingles."[24] He also periodically worked in one of
Pynchon's sawmills, receiving £2 in 1687 for "sawing 4000 of Bords."[25]
Matoone was a valuable and versatile member of the pool of woodworkers needed to forge a town out of a wilderness. And their
skills allowed these craftsmen continually to test the limits of acceptable behavior.

Shortly after his arrival in Springfield during the mid-1670s,
Matoone began to show signs that he could not always be counted
upon to act in an upright and brotherly fashion. Within the space
of little more than a year, he was called before the magistrate to
answer charges of breaking and entering, cardplaying, defecating
in another man's cellar, and aggravated assault. In March of 1678
the selectmen of the neighboring town of Hatfield informed mag-

[22] *Pynchon Court Rec.*, p. 290.

[23] *Ibid.*, p. 315.

[24] Account Books, 5, p. 537.

[25] *Ibid.*, 6, p. 199.

istrate Pynchon "of severall persons unseasonably Playing at Cards
in their Towne, and other Misdemeanors: one of whom they say
Lived in this Towne, viz: Philip Mattoone." Pynchon thereupon
"sent for him the said Philip Mattoone and examining him, thereabouts: He very readly and Ingeniously owned That Sometime in
February last, being at Hatfield he did at an unseasonable tyme of
the Night at William King's Cellar, being there till about 10 or 11
of the clock at Night Play at Cards." The cardplayers' offense was
compounded by the fact that they also "layd their Tailes on King's
Beame and Loome, etc. [defecation]." For "being at so Nasty a
busyness," Matoone received a fifteen-shilling fine.[26] A year later,
Matoone was again brought before the magistrate, this time on a
charge of assault and battery against the joiner John Pope. On July
18, 1679, Pope complained "against Philip Matoone for abusing
him by word, and striking him on the head yesterday, etc." Moreover, the joiner declared that "he goes in feare of [his] life for that
Philip formerly abused him 2 severall tymes and now came secretly
behind him and strooke him on the head and . . . displacing of his
Jawbone, disabling him from speech . . . and afterward profferring
his Hatchet towards him." John Pynchon, both as employer and
magistrate, wanted construction workers using their hatchets on
buildings, not each other, and he bound Matoone in the "sum of
Ten Pounds" to ensure his good behavior. Millwright Isaac Gleason
and smith John Stewart, like Matoone both from Scotland, posted
the "Suertys in five Pounds a peice." The relative mildness of his
punishments—Matoone was not whipped for any of these offenses
and Pynchon released him from the bond within three months—
suggests that he may have had established patron-client ties with
the magistrate. Such a possibility might also account for the fact
that he was not warned out of town.[27]

The blacksmith John Stewart likewise took advantage of the fact
that Springfield was a commercial enterprise, not a peasant utopia.
In the late 1670s he engaged in a heated quarrel with John Bliss
and ended up assaulting his adversary with a knife.[28] After a brief
jail term, he received his freedom, but was soon brought back
before the magistrate for "unseasonable night meetings" and to
answer charges that "he Commonly suffered the [illegal game of
cards] to be played at his house."[29] The blacksmith also may have
drunk too much. Account book entries from July 12 to August 20,

[26] *Pynchon Court Rec.*, pp. 289–290, 292.
[27] *Ibid.*, pp. 292–293.
[28] *Ibid.*, p. 112.
[29] *Ibid.*, p. 263.

1677, debit him for "1 Gallon Rum . . . ½ pint Rum sugard [and] 1 quart Rum."[30]

The brickmaker Francis Hacklington, as we saw earlier, was once fined for hauling bricks on the Sabbath. But he also violated other ordinances, as well as the sensibilities of his fellow villagers. On July 13, 1660, Hacklington complained against Mary Ely for "Slander for sayinge that he was seen at an unseasonable tyme of the night with Hester Bliss and that there were unseemely passages between them."[31] In September 1661 he entered suit against Alexander Edwards for "defamation in Saying that he runne away with his mare." On the same day, Hacklington likewise sought no less than £20 in damages from Henry Cunliffe in "an action of defamation, in Sayinge he is a man of noe good report."[32]

Samuel Terry was John Pynchon's most active canoeman, and this may have helped make amends for his various sexually related offenses.[33] These transgressions began in Terry's youth and continued on throughout adulthood.[34] On July 28, 1650, two witnesses told magistrate William Pynchon that "they saw Samuell Terry standing with his face to the meeting house . . . next the street chafing his yard to provoak lust [masturbating]." Terry's offense was compounded by the fact that it occurred on "the Sabbath day," even "in sermon tyme." Because the two witnesses assured the magistrate that "they had kept it private," Terry received "private Correction with a rod on his bare back, 6 lashes well set on."[35] Fornication was Terry's next offense, as on September 24, 1661, "Samuel Terry and his wife beinge presented for that they beinge marryed on the 3d of January last, they had a Son born [on] the 10th of the 5th month, beinge about 12 weekes short of the ordinary tyme of women's goinge with child." The court concluded "it manifest that they did abuse one another before marriage" and offered the Terrys the option of a £4 fine or a public whipping of "10 Lashes appiece."[36] In February 1673 Terry and eight other men stood before magistrate John Pynchon "concerning an uncivill play acted." After characterizing the play as "Immodest and beastly," the court levied fines ranging from five to twenty shillings on each of the participants.[37]

---

[30] Account Books, 5, p. 91.

[31] *Pynchon Court Rec.*, p. 247.

[32] *Ibid.*, pp. 250, 254.

[33] Account Books, 1, pp. 239–240; 2, p. 201; 3, pp. 144–145.

[34] *Pynchon Court Rec.*, pp. 224, 276–277; HCPC Rec., 1, pp. 7–9.

[35] *Pynchon Court Rec.*, p. 224.

[36] *Ibid.*, p. 255.

[37] *Ibid.*, pp. 276–277.

Avarice, as well as concupiscence, got Terry into hot water with the local authorities. In August 1681 he was accused by the selectmen of malfeasance while holding the office of constable. During a meeting "for Calling former Constables to an account for overpluss money . . . Samuel Terry Senr . . . did agree to pay six bushells of indean Corn (being overplus mony in his Country Rates when hee was Constable) to the town."[38]

These various transgressions did not make Terry an alienated outcast. As the court records make plain, this kind of behavior was not unusual in early Springfield, and the inhabitants were accustomed to taking it in stride—particularly from hardworking or highly skilled craftsmen. No one chose to ostracize Terry. He had been selected to wield the considerable power of the community's constable; and less than six months after his conviction for official malfeasance, the selectmen gave Terry custody of John Mathews's infant son.[39]

Artisans were not the only ones in Springfield to violate Puritan norms, as several instances of physical assault reveal vividly. Like humble people in most preindustrial societies, Springfield's residents protected their dignity with their fists when necessary, acting first and weighing the consequences later.[40] In one such encounter, an exchange of hot words between Daniel Beamon and Thomas Sweatman soon led to a hair-pulling, rib-kicking brawl in the dust. Testimony given before the magistrate the following day cited Beamon for "his abusing said Sweatman yesterday by Reprochful words, calling him Rogue and Theife: Threatning his life, and by striking him and breaking the Peace." Sweatman told the court that Beamon "gave him many Blows with his fist and kickt him when he was downe, Tore the haire off his head and tore his jacket."[41] Likewise, an argument between William Morgan and John Earle led one of the disputants to grab a wooden kitchen bowl and use it to pummel the other. In filing complaint against Earle, Morgan offered his mangled face as evidence. He asked damages from Earle "for stringe him . . . with a bowle uppon his face and nose." The attack "broke his nose, which also was evident, his nose beinge much bruised and bloody."[42] In July 1679 some of James Sexton's hogs escaped from their pen and were attempting to do violence to a neighbor's vegetable garden. Following accustomed procedure, John

[38] *Springfield Town Recs.*, 1, pp. 436–437.

[39] *Ibid.*, 2, pp. 152–153.

[40] Richard Critchfield, *Villages*, New York, 1981, p. 115; William B. Taylor, *Drinking, Homicide, and Rebellion in Colonial Mexican Villages*, Stanford, 1979.

[41] *Pynchon Court Rec.*, p. 323.

[42] *Ibid.*, p. 247.

Sackett's adolescent son attempted to put the errant swine into the town pound. Enraged, Sexton accosted the boy and "gave him 3 blows with his fist and tooke him by the Throat and hindered the putting the rest of the hogs into the Pound."[43]

Small things, such as the theft of a watermelon, could bring men to blows in early Springfield. On September 20, 1680, the mill-wright Isaac Gleason complained against Isaac Morgan, a field worker and tenant of John Pynchon, "for that Isack Morgan Beate his servant Josias Miller at Chikuppy last Friday, and tooke away his Gun and knife." Magistrate Pynchon thereupon "sent for him the said Isack Morgan who putts the beating of him on profe and saith that he tooke his gun and knife from him that he might doe him noe hurt, he accounting him a distracted fellow." Possibly moved by clientage ties with Morgan, Pynchon fined both defendant and complainant equally, citing Miller's provocation: "what [Morgan] did was because Josias Miller tooke away and was eating his water Million. I adjudge the said Isack Morgan for taking a Gun: and beating him to pay but five shillings because of his taking his water Million to the said Josias Miller, and also a fine of five shillings to the County for quarrelling and disturbing of Peace."[44]

But the most common kind of assault in seventeenth-century Springfield was verbal, not physical. Henry Gregory's resentment over a fine he received in 1640 for "Cheating" John Woodcock out of a pig suggests the frequency of slander in early Springfield. He told the court that "I marvill with what consi[derations] the Jury can give such damages: Seeinge in the case of John Searles I had of him but Twenty shillinges for three slanders."[45] At a court session three months earlier, "John Leonard complaines in an action of the Case against Henry Gregory for taking more recompense for driving home of certaine stray sowes than his share comes to," and "William Warrener complaines against Henry Gregory in an action of the case for layenge false imputations of money dealinge in taking of those pompions that Richard Everit gave to both of them." Four days after Gregory's protest over the slander fine, "John Woodcoke [came to William Pynchon] for a warrant to warne Henry Gregory to answer him in 2 actions of slander."[46]

Springfield's tendency to judge a man's contribution by economic instead of godly standards produced a more tolerant attitude toward sexual misconduct—and hence more opportunities for sex-

---

[43] *Ibid.*, p. 291.
[44] *Ibid.*, p. 294.
[45] *Ibid.*, p. 207.
[46] *Ibid.*, pp. 206–207.

ually related accusations of slander.[47] A telling example of the town's willingness to overlook sexual misdeeds to retain a productive worker is the relationship between Arthur Dudley and the widow Anna Petty. When her husband John, who had been renting thirty-five acres of town land in Chicopee, died in 1681, Mrs. Petty "covenant[ed] and promise[d] to and with the present Select men, that she wil fulfill the Conditions [of the lease] to the abovesaid terme of years." The widow Petty's confidence that she could fulfill the conditions of the lease rested on the knowledge that, despite her husband's death, she would have help with the farm work. Arthur Dudley was already living with her, a fact that came to the selectmen's attention three months later. On July 25, 1681, they "Agreed upon that a stranger that for some tyme hath had his Residence at the Widdow Petty's [is given] notice . . . to depart the Town." But Dudley did some fast talking (presumably both to Mrs. Petty and the selectmen), as four days later the town fathers retreated from their earlier order: "Whereas . . . at the former Meeting, Arthur Dudly was according to order warned out of the Town and now making his application to the Townsmen, they give him a month's liberty to answer his ingagement to the Widdow Petty."[48]

Springfield's tolerance of premarital sexual offenses apparently inspired Thomas Stebbins, Junior, to author a satiric poem on the suspect virtue of the town's maids. In 1671 magistrate John Pynchon examined Stebbins about "Publishing a mariage intended betweene Richard Barnard and Sarah Clarke" (already pregnant out of wedlock by Barnard) "which was set up on the Post in greate letters without order or knowledge of the partys or Parents." Moreover, the sign was "underwrit in smaler Letters with a foolish and reprochful Rime casting reproch upon the Towne and the Maides in [the] Towne."[49] Springfield's women did not always wait for the magistrate to protect their reputations. When Joseph Brown made sexual advances toward Lydia Morgan, she turned on him with "abusive carriage and Language towards him" using "reprochfull and Scandalous speeches . . . as calling him base Baudy Rouge and saying of him he was so mad he was ready to gore out her Gutts."[50] But more typically, it was the husband who brought suit to protect his wife's reputation. In 1686 Benjamin Knowlton accused Charles Ferry of "defaming the wife of [Knowlton] By false reports and aspersing her as being the Raiser of scandalous reports on Miriam

[47] *Ibid.*, pp. 209, 236, 272–273, 292.
[48] *Springfield Town Recs.*, 1, pp. 415, 436.
[49] *Pynchon Court Rec.*, p. 273.
[50] *Ibid.*, p. 287.

Mirrick, deceased."[51] John Stiles of Windsor complained against Springfield's John Bennet for "defaminge his wife, in saying shee was a light woman and that he could have a leape on her when he pleased."[52]

Springfield also experienced the most extreme form of slander—witchcraft accusations. During the late 1640s and early 1650s Goody Marshfield, Hugh Parsons, and Mary Parsons were all brought before the magistrate to answer charges of malefic witchcraft.[53] In May of 1649 William Pynchon ordered Mrs. Parsons to suffer twenty lashes or pay a fine of £3 for criminal defamation of Goody Marshfield. Mrs. Marshfield had "Complained against Mary . . . for reporting her to be suspected for a witch." The cooper John Mathews testified that Mary Parsons had told him that when Mrs. Marshfield lived in Windsor, "she was suspected to be a witch . . . and that it was publikely knowen that the divill followed her house." Mrs. Parsons also informed Mathews's wife Pentecost that "there were divers stronge lightes seene of late in the meddow that were never seene before the widdow Marshfield came to Towne, and that [Mrs. Marshfield] did grudge at other women that had Children because her daughter had none, and about that tyme (namely of her grudging) the child died and the cow died."[54] But while the witchcraft allegations against Mrs. Marshfield merely earned the accuser a public whipping, the charges against Mary Parsons herself and her husband Hugh brought a public inquisition.

The Parsons witchcraft controversy symbolized three of the most prominent themes in early Springfield—acquisitiveness, individu-

---

[51] *Ibid.*, pp. 311–312.

[52] *Ibid.*, p. 236.

[53] *Ibid.*, pp. 219–220; Samuel Drake, *Annals of Witchcraft in New England*, Boston, 1869, pp. 249–250. For studies of early New England witchcraft, see Boyer and Nissenbaum, *Salem Possessed*; John Demos, *Entertaining Satan: Witchcraft and the Culture of Early New England*, New York, 1982; and "Underlying Themes in the Witchcraft of Seventeenth-Century New England," in Stanley N. Katz, ed., *Colonial America*, Boston, 1976, pp. 99–118; for a discussion of the relationship between social alienation and witchcraft, see Demos, "John Godfrey and His Neighbors: Witchcraft and the Social Web in Colonial Massachusetts," *WMQ*, 33 (1976), pp. 242–265; Konig, *Law and Society*, pp. 158–185, examines the relationship between witchcraft and attitudes toward the courts. For a comparative perspective on witchcraft in various cultural settings, see Max Marwick, ed., *Witchcraft and Sorcery*, Baltimore, 1970; H. C. Erik Midelfort, *Witch Hunting in Southwestern Germany, 1562–1684*, Stanford, 1972, esp. pp. 164–192; E. E. Evans-Pritchard, *Witchcraft, Oracles and Magic among the Azande*, Oxford, 1976; Clyde Kluckhohn, *Navajo Witchcraft*, Boston, 1962; Michael T. Taussig, *The Devil and Commodity Fetishism in South America*, Chapel Hill, 1980.

[54] *Pynchon Court Rec.*, pp. 219–220.

alism, and tolerance of social deviance. The nature of the accusations against Hugh and Mary Parsons tells us as much about the
community as about the defendants. Several years before the witchcraft controversy began, there had been indications that the Parsons
would not conform to conventional norms of social behavior, even
by Springfield's tolerant standards. In 1645, while still married to
"one Lewis a papist," Mary fell into what William Pynchon characterized as "a league of amity" with brickmaker Hugh Parsons.
Confessing that she had not cohabited with her lawful husband
"above 7 years," Mrs. Lewis asked Pynchon to secure permission
from the General Court to marry Parsons.[55]

Four years later Mrs. Parsons began to accuse fellow inhabitants
of the crime of witchcraft, first Goody Marshfield and then her
own husband.[56] While the town rallied around Mrs. Marshfield,
they decided that Mary's suspicions about Hugh were well-founded.
Although she became her husband's "principal accuser," thirty-five
additional town members came forth to testify against the suspected
witch. The Springfield tax list of 1646 contained the names of only
thirty-nine householders, so Parsons apparently had managed to
alienate most of his fellow villagers.[57]

The most striking revelation from the witchcraft testimony is that
Hugh Parsons was a virtual parody of Springfield's self-image:
acquisitiveness become greed, individualism become vengefulness,
deviance become diabolical. Whether the accusers were simply pro-
jecting their own guilt for the town's generally non-Puritan ways
must remain conjectural, but the witness examinations invite such
a supposition. Moreover, they underscore the general relationship
between commercial opportunity and witchcraft throughout early
New England. All the major instances of seventeenth-century witchcraft occurred in highly commercialized communities: Windsor,
Salem, and Springfield. The parallels between the Parsons case and
Salem seem particularly revealing. Hugh Parsons embodied the
extreme economic individualism that was, in fact, tempting everyone else. And, as in Salem where Boyer and Nissenbaum found
that the most obvious targets of witchcraft accusations were *not*
directly charged (because of their political or psychological power
over the accusers), so in Springfield people may have deflected
their dissatisfactions with William Pynchon onto Parsons: the accusers couldn't really go after the magistrate, so they sought a

[55] William Pynchon to John Winthrop, September 15, 1645, *Winthrop Papers*, 5,
pp. 45–46.

[56] Drake, *Annals of Witchcraft*, pp. 224–240.

[57] *Ibid.*, pp. 219–256; *Springfield Town Recs.*, 1, pp. 190–191.

symbolic victim. The array of charges brought against Parsons lends credence to such an interpretation.[58]

One of the principal charges leveled at Parsons by his wife was that he was "egar after the World."[59] This greed led him to both abuse his wife for not doing enough field work and endanger the life of his ailing infant. Mary Parsons told the magistrate that "though my Child be so ill, and I have much to do with it, yet my Husband keepes adoe at me to help him about his Corne."[60] Because her husband "expected help from her, and . . . her Tyme was taken up about her Child," she "suspected that he was a Meanes to make an End of his Child quickly that she might be at Liberty to help him."[61] Anthony Dorchester, who with his wife resided in the Parsons household, told the examiner that Hugh "never feared eather to greeve or displease his Wife any Tyme." He declared that "I saw Nothing [Parsons] did to comfort his Wife, but he did often blame her that she did not throw in the Corne from the Dore." When Parsons denied mistreating Mary, Dorchester retorted that "he never knew him [to] blame her for doinge too much Worke, except (saith he) that she helped my Wife at any Tyme, which Worke did not bring in any profitt to him."[62]

Similar accusations of greed arose from Parsons's dealings as a brickmaker. He argued and threatened over prices and attempted to back out of unsatisfactory contracts. Blanche Bedortha told the examiner that she had earlier clashed with Parsons "about some Brickes." When she "spake Somethinge about the said Bricks that did much displease Hugh Parsons," he replied "Gammer, you neded not have said Anythinge. I spake not to you, but I shall remember you when you little think on it." Soon thereafter, in the latter stages of pregnancy, Mrs. Bedortha awoke from her sleep with "a Sorenesse about her Hart," which "increased more and more in three Places . . . the Paine was so tedious, that it was like the pricking of Knifes, so that I durst not lie downe, but was faint to be shored up with a Bagg of Cotton Wool, and with other Thinges." The mysterious pain persisted for three days and then abated as quickly as it began. Whereupon, Mrs. Bedortha informed the magistrate, "my Thoughtes were, that this Evill might come uppon me from

---

[58] Erikson, *Wayward Puritans*, pp. 185–205; Boyer and Nissenbaum, *Salem Possessed*; Demos, "John Godfrey," *WMQ* (1976).

[59] Drake, *Annals of Witchcraft*, p. 241.

[60] *Ibid.*, p. 236.

[61] *Ibid.*, p. 241.

[62] *Ibid.*, p. 237.

the said threatning Speech of Hugh Parsons."[63] In a similar dispute, Parsons unsuccessfully attempted to void a contract with no less an eminence than the town's minister, George Moxon. The Reverend Moxon apparently threatened suit for non-performance, provoking Parsons to confide to his wife that "if Mr. Moxon do force me to make Brickes according to Bargaine, I will be even with him." Soon thereafter, the minister's two young children developed epileptic seizures of considerable severity. Their sickness brought speculation that Hugh Parsons "be the Cause of all the Evill that is befallen to Mr. Moxon's Childerne."[64] The threat that material goals, the tendency to be "eager after the World," would be carried too far always posed a danger to highly commercialized towns like Springfield. And perhaps it was with a shudder of self-recognition that the townsmen decided that Hugh Parsons had done exactly that.

For the same reasons, Parsons's vows to seek vengeance on his fellows showed the threat posed by unrestrained individualism. Towns such as Springfield, where the binding powers of the church and town meeting were problematical, were especially susceptible to destructive forms of egotism such as vengeance vows.[65] Accordingly, as the case of Hugh Parsons shows, such behavior was often an invitation to witchcraft accusations. Of all the charges directed against the brickmaker, none was more common than accusations of promised vengeance. John Lumbard testified that "I have often herd [Parsons] say, when he hath been displeased with any Body, that he would be even with them for it." William Branch likewise asserted that "he hath often herd Hugh Parsons say when he is displeased with Anybody, I do not question but I shall be even with him at one Tyme or [an]other." The widow Marshfield told the examiner that when she had refused to abate twenty shillings of a judgment of slander against Parsons, he had replied "well, if you will not, it had bin as good you had—it will be but as wild Fier in your House, and as a Moth in your Garment, and it will doe you no Good, Ile warrent it."[66] When Parsons entered the Pynchon general store to purchase "as much Whitleather as to make a Cappe for a Flayle," William Pynchon's servant Symon Beamon "would not let him have any." Irate, Parsons returned home promising revenge. He told his wife that Beamon "shall get Nothing by it. I will be even with him." She asked him "Husband why do you threaten

[63] *Ibid.*, pp. 224–226.
[64] *Ibid.*, pp. 227–228.
[65] Boyer and Nissenbaum, *Salem Possessed*, pp. 108–109.
[66] Drake, *Annals of Witchcraft*, pp. 249–251, 254.

the fellow so, it is like[ly] he was busy." But Parsons brushed aside such explanations, asserting that the real reason behind the clerk's actions was personal animus: "he answered againe, if Goodman Cooly or any One else that he had liked had come he should have had it. But Ile remember him."[67]

Springfield's relative tolerance of social deviance, likewise, could be pushed into destructive realms, as the town's reaction to Parsons's mistreatment of his wife reveals. Deviance of abnormal proportions imperiled the town's always somewhat fragile social bonds, and Hugh's sadistic treatment of his wife posed just such a threat. On some occasions he would return home late at night in a melancholic and surly frame of mind to subject her to all manner of humiliations. Mary testified that her husband "used to be out a[t] Nights till Midnight" and "he used to come Home in a distempered Frame, so that I could not tell how to please him." She related that "sometymes he hath puld off the Bed Clothes and left me naked a Bed, and hath quenched the Fier; sometymes he hath thrown Pease about the howse and made me pick them up."[68] Equally objectionable was Parsons's failure to display remorse when, as Mary predicted, their infant son died. He abandoned his wife and child during the height of the illness and, after the child expired, affected a light, even jovial manner. Magistrate Pynchon queried the brickmaker "why he did not show more Respect to his Wife and Child, but went into the long Meddow and lay there all Night when his child lay at the Point of Death," and when "he herd of the Death of it the next Morning never showed any Sorrow for it." While lying in the meadow that night, he encountered George Colton, who later told the examiner that "Hugh Parsons came into the long Meddow when his Child lay at the Point of Death; and that having Word of the Death of it the next Morning, by Jonathan Burt, he was not affected with it, but he came, after a light Manner, rushing into my Howse, and said, I here my Child is dead; but I will cutt a Pipe of Tobacco first before I goe Home: and after he was gone my Wife and myself did much wonder at the lightness of his Carriage, because he showed no Affection of Sorrow for the death of his Child." This casual demeanor continued through the child's funeral and burial. Benjamin Cooley testified that when he spoke to Parsons at the internment, "he cannot remember any Sorrow that he showed, for he came to him taking a Pipe of Tobacco." By 1652 Springfield's residents had concluded that Par-

---

[67] *Ibid.*, p. 254.
[68] *Ibid.*, p. 240.

sons's failure to grieve for his deceased child, like his mistreatment of Mary, reflected not mere inhumanity, but diabolism.[69]

While less serious than witchcraft accusations, a series of vitriolic family feuds was also symptomatic of the weakness of communalism in seventeenth-century Springfield. Particularly disruptive were the Hunter-Petty and Brooks-Bedortha conflicts. By the early 1670s, the Hunters and Pettys had been engaged in a prolonged verbal war, but now fists and sticks were used as well as words. On October 24, 1673, William Hunter complained against John Petty "for abusing him by striking him etc.: as also against James the son of John Petty for that the youth called him names and gave him bad and Ill language." In response, Petty "owned the full and acknowledged that he being in a rage for Hunter's striking his Boy a Box under the Eare, that he Run to him with a stick he tooke up and struk him a Blow, which Blow having Lamed his arme at present and being scarse well now 2 or 3 days after." The magistrate accordingly ordered Petty "to pay Ten shillings to said William Hunter in way of sattisfaction and five shillings as fine to the County." But Hunter's "sattisfaction" presumably was diminished by the disposition of a second suit filed that day, this time against his termagant wife Priscilla. John Petty had brought suit "against Goodwife Hunter for offering to mischeife his wife and giving her Ill Language." This ill language involved "Railing, Scolding and other exorbitancys of the Toung." Several neighbors came before the court to testify to "her continuall Trade upon every occasion to be exorbitant with her Toung." Magistrate Pynchon held for the plaintiff and sentenced Mrs. Hunter "to be Gagged or else set in a ducking stoole and dipped in water as Law provides: Shee to choose which of them shee pleases within this halfe houre." After the half-hour interval had passed and "She not choosing either," Pynchon ordered her to be "Gagged and so to stand halfe an hour in the open street, which was done accordingly."[70]

William Brooks spent most of his life in Springfield battling his neighbors, as well as indebtedness to the Pynchons. Brooks was accused at various times of fraud, willful assault, and battery. He

---

[69] *Ibid.*, pp. 236–238. Hugh Parsons was indicted by a grand jury at the Court of Assistants in May 1652 and convicted in the subsequent jury trial, but the assistants did not consent to the jury verdict and called for the cause to come before the General Court. On May 31, 1652, this body judged the defendant not legally guilty of witchcraft. Parsons never returned to Springfield. Mary Parsons, after being convicted of murdering her child, apparently died in a Boston jail. *Pynchon Court Rec.*, pp. 22–23.

[70] *Pynchon Court Rec.*, pp. 277–278.

also informed on the illegal activities of his neighbors. His first conviction came in November 1653 for "defrauding sundry persons in witholding from them, and converting to his owne use the goods of severall persons." The defendant "was adjudged to make sattisfaction to the Sum of £18."[71] In September 1670 Brooks and his wife were accused of hurling both curses and sticks at young Joseph Bedortha. Reice Bedortha, the boy's father, made "Complaint against William Brookes and Mary his wife for theire abusing of his son Joseph Bedortha by Bad language, flinging a stick at him and using Reproachfull words, Threatening expreshons and Taunting speeches." The court thereupon ordered Brooks to pay a fine of twenty shillings to the county and twelve pence apiece to seven witnesses.[72]

Some family feuds were conducted internally, as was the case with Obadiah and Joanna Miller. As we saw earlier, over a period of three decades the Millers progressively lost all their land and housing to John Pynchon for debts, and this dolorous plight may have undermined domestic tranquility. In March of 1656, Obadiah complained against his wife "for abusing him with reproachfull tearmes or names as calling him foole, toad, and vermine and threatninge him." Joanna was one to make good on her threats as "yesterday shee fell uppon him indeavoringe to beat him at which tyme shee scratched his face and hands." John Lamb told the court that "he heard her say shee would knock him on the head: and that shee did often call him foole and other reproachfull tearmes." Obadiah's brother Thomas "testifyed that when . . . Obadiah and his wife lived with him, she did comonly call him foole and vermine: and he doth not remember he ever heard her call him husband: and that she said shee did not love him but hated him: yea shee here said shee did never love him and shee should never love him." For her "vile misbehaviour towards her husband," the court ordered Mrs. Miller whipped unless she would promise to mend her ways and treat Obadiah with the respect due him.[73] These efforts evidently came to naught, as in August of 1665 the Millers were again bound over to the county justices for "haveing had Sad bickering and Strife between themselves."[74] In other families, feuds were between generations, as with the relationship between John Stebbins and his apparently enfeebled father. In May of 1655 the commissioners took notice of young Stebbins "for misbehavinge

[71] *Ibid.*, p. 229.
[72] *Ibid.*, p. 270.
[73] *Ibid.*, pp. 235–236.
[74] *Ibid.*, p. 114.

himself towards his aged Father calling him Old foole and uttering other unseemly words towards him." Stebbins was forced to post a bond "in the summe of Forty pounds" for his appearance to answer the charges, but luckily for him, "there was not found full proofe of such evill carriage" and he was discharged from the bond. Similarly, Samuel Ball was ordered to be flogged for using abusive language toward his father-in-law, Benjamin Mun, asserting that he respected him "no more than an old Indian," and exclaiming, "A father! There's a father indeed!"[75]

Social harmony in Springfield was also endangered by ethnic antagonisms—particularly against the Scots. Although the number of Scots in the town never exceeded a dozen men, their impact on the community was considerable. Several, such as the blacksmith John Stewart, were highly skilled and valued artisans; and Edward Foster, Hugh Dudley, William Hunter, and John Riley were all important to the Pynchons either as tenants or field workers. But many of the Scots, unlike the Welshmen, Miles Morgan, Thomas Mirrick, and Alexander Edwards, had come to the community involuntarily—usually as war captives.[76] Hence their personal commitment to Puritan norms was minimal. Most of the Scots appear in the court records as worldly, contentious individuals, who were suffered to remain in the community because of their contributions to the local economy. All of them appeared before the magistrate at one time or another, on charges varying from assault and attempted murder to drunkenness, cardplaying, and slander.[77] The Scots tested the limits of social tolerance in early Springfield, and sometimes the equanimity of their fellow villagers as well. While court records fail to specify if ethnic antagonisms drove John Stewart to take a knife to John Bliss, such animosity clearly sparked a dispute between Thomas Miller and John Henryson in 1659. On November 30, Henryson, a Scot, complained "against Thomas Miller for detayning a cart from him which he sayth he had right unto." Miller compounded his offense by "using reproachfull speeches," one of which included a reference to Henryson as a "Scottish dogg." In his defense, Miller retorted that Henryson had "threatned [him] in Saying that eyther he or Thomas Miller should dy before he should have the cart." The court decided to fine both men ten shillings for "one of them strikinge and the other threatninge Slaughter."[78]

[75] *Ibid.*, p. 234; Green, *Springfield*, p. 142.
[76] *Pynchon Court Rec.*, pp. 224–227; *Springfield Town Recs.*, 1, p. 306.
[77] *Pynchon Court Rec.*, pp. 112, 216, 243, 254, 316–317, 320–321.
[78] *Ibid.*, p. 243.

While Miller and Henryson disputed over the custody of the oxcart, they shared a common fondness for the illegal game of cardplaying, an accusation often brought against the Scots. Henryson and his wife Martha flouted local ordinances by hosting card games on a regular basis and, despite his threats of mayhem three years earlier, Thomas Miller was among those invited to one such gathering in 1662. On March 20, William Brooks testified before the commissioners that "one Night at John Henryson's house he saw Edward Foster, Thomas Miller, John Bag, and John Scot all foure of them playing at Cards: and I staying in the house neere an houre they continued theire play at Cards all the while." In the subsequent testimony, the novices tried to separate themselves from the more committed players. Foster told the court that "It is true I did then Play, but I am but a beginner to play at cards." Defendants Scot, Bagg, and Miller made similar protestations. But Henryson was forced to admit that he and his wife habitually played the illegal game, although his justification for the practice was somewhat unusual. He explained his actions by declaring that "I did not so well know the Law against it and I was willing to have recreation for my wife to drive away melancholy." Mrs. Henryson's emotional well-being became a central element in her husband's defense. Apparently a manic-depressive, her more melancholic periods drove John nearly to distraction. During his trial, Henryson readily acknowledged "Playing at Cards severall tymes at his howse," but said "he was willing to [do] any thing when his wife was Ill to make her merry." Unmoved by Henryson's husbandly solicitude, the court fined him twenty shillings.[79]

While their ethnicity and penchant for cardplaying may have set the Scots off from their fellow villagers, their violence and litigiousness did not, as the careers of John Woodcock and Thomas Mirrick attest. Neither man was a Scot; Woodcock was English, Mirrick Welsh. Their disputatious and strife-ridden careers symbolize the casual frequency of social conflict in early Springfield.[80]

Unusually godly and other-directed images for the first generation of Puritan New Englanders fail to comprehend someone like John Woodcock. Throughout his stay in Springfield, he engaged in one confrontation after another with his fellow citizens. Not love and forbearance, but disdain and hostility characterized his social attitudes. He took people to court at the drop of a hat and showed respect for no one, including the town's minister. Dissatisfied with

[79] *Ibid.*, pp. 257–258.
[80] *Ibid.*, pp. 204, 205, 206, 207–208, 209–210, 230, 231–232, 246–247, 256–257, 317.

some carpentry work performed on his house by John Cable, in November 1639 he sued Cable in an action on the case "for certaine worke he did to a house that was built on Agawam." One month later Woodcock again stood before the magistrate, this time to answer an accusation of slander against the Reverend George Moxon. Apparently finding Moxon's exhortations from the pulpit less than uplifting, he was charged with "laughinge in Sermon tyme" as well as "his misdemenor [of] idlenesse." The minister sought damages of £9 19s. but the jury awarded him only £6 13s.—which was still an unusually high sum for slander. Uncowed, Woodcock replied that "he owed Mr. Moxon no money nor none he would pay him," and compounded this defiance by the assertion that "he had showed Mr. Moxon more respect and reverence than ever he would againe."[81]

Despite the jury's judgment against Woodcock, his truculent behavior continued unabated. On September 10, 1640, he complained against Henry Gregory for "Cheatinge [him out of a] Pigg" to the amount of £4 14s. Woodcock's litigation was initially unsuccessful, but magistrate William Pynchon allowed the plaintiff a new trial on a writ of error and eventually ruled in his behalf. Civil actions in early Massachusetts, unlike criminal proceedings, were usually tried before a jury, and they ruled that Woodcock's claims for damages were exorbitant and awarded him but twenty-four shillings.[82] Later that week, he returned before the magistrate to accuse Gregory of "2 actions of slander." Pynchon used this opportunity to query the plaintiff regarding the £6 13s. damages still owed to the Reverend Moxon. Informed by Woodcock that he had no intention of paying, Pynchon thereupon ordered the constable to "attach the body of John Woodcoke [and see that you] kepe his body in prison or irons untill he shall take some course to satisfie the said George Moxon." If incarceration failed to achieve this end, the constable was to "put him out to service and labor till he make satisfaction."[83] Out of jail four months later, Woodcock was sued by Robert Ashley for non-delivery of a gun Ashley had bought from him. Ashley demanded compensation for "a gunn that he bought of him and paid him 22s. 6d. for it, yet the said John Woodcoke did not deliver it to him accordinge to bargaine." Woodcock denied the charges and attempted to impeach the plaintiff's credibility. Ashley, he said, "was a pratinge fellow" for "he had set off his gunn and now he did not owe him past 7 or 8s." Woodcock

[81] *Ibid.*, pp. 204–205.
[82] *Ibid.*, pp. 206–207.
[83] *Ibid.*, pp. 207–208.

then attacked one of the plaintiff's witnesses, accusing Judith Gregory of slander for "swearing before God I would break her head."[84]

Thomas Mirrick, like John Woodcock, spent much of his time in litigation with his fellow inhabitants. During the period from 1639 to 1661, he appeared before the bench a total of sixteen times.[85] On November 14, 1639, William Pynchon complained against Mirrick "for not delivering back the Boards he lent him."[86] A month later, Mirrick had more problems with unreturned lumber. He entered suit against his neighbor Thomas Horton "for 3 boards that the said Thomas Mirrick wants."[87] Going to court over such seemingly inconsequential provocations was not unusual in seventeenth-century Springfield, and Horton accordingly retaliated in kind. He charged Mirrick with "not doinge a sufficient daye's worke for the wages of a day," "taking away certaine planks or boards," "felling of two trees in the lot of Thomas Horton," and "changing of 4 bushells of corne after it was delivered." That same day, Mirrick complained against John Woodcock in an action of debt for two shillings sixpence as well as for the unpaid price of four bushels of corn.[88] In January 1642 Richard Hull brought suit against Mirrick for purloining "a Rugg [and] certaine tooles."[89] On December 21, 1643, Mirrick disputed with another neighbor, Robert Ashley, over "keepinge a pig which Mr. Thomas Mericke saith is his."[90] And, as we have seen, Mirrick was also fined at least twice for nonperformance of contractual obligations.

Thomas Mirrick's inability to live harmoniously with his neighbors persisted for the next two decades, sometimes taking an uglier tone. In 1648 he broke up a fist fight between his son and young Samuel Edwards, with apparently something less than total impartiality. Samuel's father Alexander, like Mirrick a Welshman, brought Mirrick to court "for abusing his child named Samuell Edwards, being about 5 or 6 years ould the 14 of Aprill last." The court judged Mirrick guilty of "3 batteries besides vilifieing words, as hang him better kill him than he kill my child." The actions of his daughter Hannah likewise brought Mirrick into conflict with his neighbors. In 1673 she successfully accused Jonathan Morgan

[84] *Ibid.*, pp. 209–210.

[85] *Ibid.*, pp. 204, 205–206, 209, 211, 214, 215, 216, 230, 231–232, 246–247, 256–257, 317.

[86] *Ibid.*, p. 204.

[87] *Ibid.*, pp. 204–205.

[88] *Ibid.*, pp. 205–206.

[89] *Ibid.*, p. 211.

[90] *Ibid.*, p. 214.

of the paternity of her child, securing a court order that he pay
two shillings sixpence weekly in child-support for four years.[91] Finally, in October 1686 "Deacon Jonathan Burt [was] plaintiff against
Thomas Mirick Senior for saying of Deacon Burt that he lyed basely
and was a Lying man."[92] All these confrontations with his neighbors, however, did not make Thomas Mirrick a social pariah. He
served as sergeant of the militia, a post of some distinction, as well
as town constable. Moreover, he was a fully admitted member of
the church, who was described in the General Court's 1665 certif-
icate of freemanship as a "settled inhabitant . . . orthodox in religion
of pious and laudable conversation." The Court, therefore, "allowes
and approves of him to be a freeman of this jurisdiction."[93] Mirrick
was not an outcast because, as we have seen, in early Springfield
confrontational behavior was not unusual.

The General Court's formulary description of Thomas Mirrick
raises the pivotal question of the church's role in Springfield—a
question rendered especially difficult by the loss of all seventeenth-
century church records. What evidence does exist points to the
fragile and problematical nature of the minister's position and authority in the town, analogous in many ways to the role the Reverend Samuel Parris played in Boyer and Nissenbaum's study of
Salem. Springfielders lived without a meetinghouse for the settlement's first decade, and without a minister during most of the
1650s. The two ministers who spent prolonged periods in the town,
George Moxon and Pelatiah Glover, engaged in a variety of heated
confrontations with their parishioners, including slander suits, salary disputes, and appeals to the General Court over ownership of
ministerial lands. Moxon, as we have seen, saw his two children
"bewitched," was slandered and treated contemptuously by the day-
laborer John Woodcock, and cheated by the brickmason Hugh
Parsons. Possibly such remembrances contributed to his decision
to return to England with William Pynchon in 1652. The community's two succeeding ministers made similar decisions within
months, not years, of their arrival. The town recorder laconically
observed in March of 1656 that the Reverend Mr. Thompson had
"deserted this Plantation." Glover, in residence from 1661 until his
death in 1692, threatened in 1669 to quit Springfield because he
believed his salary inadequate. And from 1676 until his death, he
bitterly contested the town's decision to retract ownership of his
house and lands, a dispute not resolved by a General Court decision

[91] *Ibid.*, pp. 216–217; Green, *Springfield*, p. 140.
[92] *Pynchon Court Rec.*, p. 317.
[93] *Mass. Recs.*, 4, Part 2, p. 285.

in the minister's favor in 1681. Not until January 1696 did the town meeting vote to compensate Glover's son for the loss of his inheritance: "It was voted to give mr. Pelatiah Glover [Jr.] a deed to Secure to him the Land that the Town did give him in way of Compensation for the ministry Land." Somewhat belatedly, the inhabitants also "voted that the Town Treasurer should see to the getting the arrears of the rates payable to the Reverend mr. Glover, his father." As the elder Glover had doubtless discovered a good deal earlier, the trials of the faithful shepherd in communities as contentious as Springfield were many and the rewards few.[94]

That such contentiousness was acceptable, as well as common, is shown by the town's relatively low level of out-migration. While, as with all New England communities, the settler generation was characterized by an exceedingly high level of population movement, by 1660 most inhabitants had ended their peregrinations. Of the seventy-two inhabitants entered on the tax list of 1664, fifty-five, or 76.4 percent, would die in Springfield. In 1672, seventy-six male inhabitants lived in the town. Sixty-one, or 80.3 percent, of these men remained permanently in the community. Even during the troublesome and dangerous decades of the Indian wars after 1675, Springfield's population continued relatively stable. Of the 120 male inhabitants on the tax list of 1685, seventy-six, or 63.3 percent, remained in the town until they died.[95] We cannot automatically assume that those who stayed in Springfield did so willingly; those men inextricably indebted to John Pynchon were not free simply to pull up stakes and move on. Those who tried it rarely escaped eventual property attachments.[96] But it is likely that most of the town's inhabitants remained in Springfield on their own volition. Economic peril there was, but there was opportunity as well—the reason most of them had come in the first place. If they had been seeking quietude, corporate security, and communal harmony— and had been sufficiently well-to-do—Dedham or Andover would have been a more logical choice. Even in the parochial world of seventeenth-century New England, towns doubtless quickly developed reputations for certain modes of behavior and public ethos. Migrants resting by the wayside exchanged intelligence regarding what various settlements "were like." Men traveling without family and without capital assets, like many of Springfield's earliest arrivals, learned where to expect a welcome and where to expect a

[94] *Springfield Town Recs.*, 2, p. 341; Green, *Springfield*, pp. 128, 180–181.

[95] *Springfield Town Recs.*, 1, pp. 159–161, 171, 175, 190–191, 220–221; 2, pp. 77, 115–117; 1685 Tax List.

[96] "Records of Execution," CVHM.

warning-out. They found out which towns were looking for skilled artisans and which were looking for Visible Saints. What these first settlers needed most was work, short-term credit, and an eventual chance to become a husbandman or even a yeoman. These were prospects that the Pynchons could offer. Developmental towns, therefore, grew out of the decisions made by workers as well as merchant-entrepreneurs.[97]

Springfield's settlers were a motley lot, and the community they built reflected this diversity. What bound them together was a kind of primitive Christianity and the desire to work. They were united by opportunity, not affection, and accordingly behaved as individuals, not as a community. They were tolerant of everything except laziness, as John Mathews learned to his grief. This was not fertile ground for generating and nourishing a common and coherent system of values, and much of what did emerge was the rough agrarian justice timeless in the English countryside. Ronald Blythe's description of Victorian villages could well apply to Springfield: "They were leisure-less communities for most of their inhabitants, full of cruelty and injustice, greed and pride—and full of imagination and satisfactions and goodness."[98] There is no need to see the town's inhabitants as either better or worse than they were. They were not the antiacquisitive communalists memorialized by Rousseau, nor were they Maxim Gorky's "half-savage [men], stupid, heavy, . . . lazily, carelessly, incapably slumped" across the land. Most of Springfield's residents emerge as decent, hard-working, reliable, if somewhat prickly, individuals. The town also included its share of less attractive people—malicious, dishonest, apathetic, and mean-spirited. Whatever their character, however, the motivation of these inhabitants—although preindustrial—was probably not remarkably different from our own.[99] What kept the settlers of early Springfield going were the small joys, gratifications, and reveries that make life meaningful or bearable in any place or time. Bone-weary, weatherbeaten men and women surely found respite and solace—perhaps even a small epiphany—from the quotidian: luminous stars, flowering orchards, awakening songbirds, or the lapidary joy of fine craftsmanship. But among these pleasures and

[97] For emphasizing this point (and many others) to me, I am indebted to Fred V. Carstensen.

[98] Ronald Blythe, "The Way We Lived Then," *The New York Review of Books* (June 25, 1981), p. 37.

[99] Jonathan Lieberson, "The Silent Majority," *The New York Review of Books* (October 22, 1981), p. 36.

satisfactions, forming strong affective ties with one's neighbor was not prominent.

The ties that mattered most in Springfield were not with one's neighbor, but one's patron—a point doubtless appreciated by Thomas Mirrick, one of John Pynchon's most active canoemen. And because of the strength and scope of patron-client ties in seventeenth-century Springfield, the townsmen challenged one another instead of their social betters—even during the most tumultuous period in the colony's history.

- *Chapter 6* -

Decline of the Gentry, 1684–1703

"They lied when they told me I was everything."
William Shakespeare, *King Lear*

THE GLORIOUS REVOLUTION was the greatest test of John Pynchon's authority in Springfield. The wave of antiauthoritarianism unleashed by the overthrow of the Dominion of New England brought rocketing factionalism and conflict to virtually every community in Massachusetts, of which the hysteria at Salem was only the most spectacular example. But in Springfield, tranquility reigned. While selectmen, representatives, and militia officers who had served the Dominion were summarily removed from office elsewhere, in Springfield the old guard remained secure. This docility was largely the result of Pynchon's financial hold over so many of the town's inhabitants. With the livelihood of over half the community's citizens resting in his hands, Pynchon's political authority remained unimperiled. But the same was not true *elsewhere* in the Connecticut Valley. Despite his activities as plantation founder and his ownership of extensive acreage in every settlement, Pynchon relied on deference, not dependence, to implement his will in the valley. And while dependence did not decline as a consequence of the Dominion, deference did. Nothing better illustrates the dichotomy between financial dependence and personal deference than the events of the decade after 1689.

The Dominion of New England is the central divide in the history of colonial Massachusetts. Within five years, it swept away the conditions by which men like John Pynchon asserted such remarkable dominance over their communities. The two prerequisites for this ascendancy had been their status as mediators and the fealty of the general population. Its results had been land grants and economic power. The Dominion, however, deprived the gentry of both their mediator's role and the inhabitants' fealty. During the second charter period (1691–1774), the Pynchons of Springfield, the Otises of Barnstable, and the Willards of the Merrimack Valley would have to share their power with competing elites. And they would have to earn, not assume by right, the loyalties of the general populace.

This decline was a direct result of the gentry's identification with the authoritarian Dominion government. The Dominion of New England (1686–1689) grew out of the Stuart Kings' determination to curb smuggling and reassert royal control in the northern colonies. By the early 1680s, the Crown's investigator, Edward Randolph, persuaded the Lords of Trade to issue a writ of *quo warranto* against Massachusetts.[1] The writ served notice on Massachusetts to show cause why its disregard of the Navigation Acts should not result in abrogation of the 1629 charter. The colonists' protestations of innocence were of no avail, and in 1684 the Crown suspended the first Massachusetts charter. Soon thereafter, Massachusetts, Plymouth, and New Hampshire were consolidated into a unified Dominion of New England, later to be joined by Connecticut, Rhode Island, New York, and the Jerseys.[2]

Centralization of authority—political, judicial, and military—became the byword of the Dominion. A royally appointed governor and council replaced the popularly elected governor, House of Deputies, and council. Justices of the peace, appointed by the governor, replaced magistrates as custodians of the county courts. Militia officers were likewise appointed by the governor alone. Together, the governor and council held exclusive power to legislate, tax, regulate trade, and enforce a system of quitrents. Church membership ceased to be the basis of political participation; and county courts were replaced by Courts of Quarter Sessions and Courts of Common Pleas—both staffed by justices of the peace. All writs were to run in the name of the King. Finally, town meetings were to be limited to one a year. Authority now emanated from Boston instead of being shared among local and provincial leaders working in

---

[1] For an examination of Randolph's role in the suspension of the 1629 charter, see Michael Garibaldi Hall, *Edward Randolph and the American Colonies, 1676–1703*, New York, 1969, pp. 79–97.

[2] The best recent case study of the local impact of the Dominion period is found in Konig, *Law and Society*, pp. 158–185. For the overall impact of the Dominion throughout New England, see Richard R. Johnson, *Adjustment to Empire: The New England Colonies, 1675–1715*, New Brunswick, N. J., 1981, pp. 71–305. Although dated in some of its interpretations, Viola Barnes, *The Dominion of New England*, New Haven, 1923, remains indispensable. See also T. H. Breen, *The Character of the Good Ruler: Puritan Political Ideas in New England, 1630–1730*, New Haven, 1970, pp. 134–202; Breen, "War, Taxes, and Political Brokers: The Ordeal of Massachusetts Bay, 1675–1692," in Breen, *Puritans and Adventurers: Change and Persistence in Early America*, New York, 1980, pp. 81–105; and Kenneth A. Lockridge, *Settlement and Unsettlement in Early America: The Crisis of Political Legitimacy Before the Revolution*, Cambridge, Eng., 1981, pp. 31–36.

concert. Because the governor, councilors, justices, and militia officers were now all appointed by the imperial authorities, local influence over these officials sharply declined.

But while the Dominion centralized authority in Boston, it factionalized it in the countryside. For mediators like John Pynchon, the replacement of a single assistant in a locality by several justices of the peace ended the exclusivity of access to provincial authorities that the old gentry had previously enjoyed. In the Connecticut Valley, rather than having to deal only through Pynchon, men could now solicit any one of the near dozen justices that served the region.[3]

The suspension of the first charter in 1684 transfixed Pynchon on an insoluble dilemma. The preservation of his dominant position depended on support for and by the colonial leaders in Boston. His role as mediator, by definition, demanded that he retain links with both the valley residents and the provincial government. The erosion of one position threatened the vitality of the other. If Pynchon alienated valley inhabitants, or alternatively, estranged himself from the provincial leaders in Boston, he risked losing his mediator's role. And because it was through this role that Pynchon had achieved preeminence, he could not lightly countenance its destruction.

After some hesitation, Pynchon chose to cast his lot with the rulers of the new regime, despite the likelihood that their authoritarian designs would deeply antagonize most New Englanders. In September 1685 Edward Randolph submitted Pynchon's name to the Committee of Trade and Foreign Plantations as a person "well disposed and fit" for membership in the reorganized government. Randolph's confidence that Pynchon would be a loyal servant of the Dominion proved well placed. The former Springfield magistrate accepted appointment as councilor immediately after the arrival of interim president, Joseph Dudley.[4] During the hiatus of authority, he acted as an intermediary between the incoming and outgoing governments. He and William Stoughton were "sent to the Magistrates to acquaint them with the King's Commands being

[3] John M. Murrin traces the impact of the judicial reorganization under the Dominion and second charter period in "The Legal Transformation: The Bench and Bar of Eighteenth-Century Massachusetts," in Katz, ed., *Colonial America*, 1971 ed., pp. 415–448; see also Murrin, "Review Essay," *History and Theory*, 2 (1972), pp. 226–275; Murrin, "Colonial Political Development," in *Oxford Conference in American Colonial History*, New York, 1983; Richard S. Dunn, *Puritans and Yankees: The Winthrop Dynasty of New England, 1630–1717*, New York, 1971, pp. 225–227.

[4] *Pynchon Court Rec.*, p. 49.

come." At Dudley's initial meeting with the old rulers on May 17, the order of entrance into the General Court was "Major Dudley the President, Major Pynchon" followed by the remaining members of the council.[5] In the succeeding days Pynchon accepted a variety of positions within the new government, including membership on the committee assigned to audit the previous treasurer's accounts, the committee formed to recommend more efficient procedures for collecting duties on wines and liquors (a position not likely to endear Pynchon to his fellow merchants), and the committee responsible for overseeing the proprietors of Narragansett County.

These services, however, were subordinate to Pynchon's more critical charge of using his influence to gain general acceptance of the Dominion government. Repeatedly Dudley called on him to lobby reluctant New England leaders into supporting the new government. In addition, both Dudley and his imperious successor, Governor Sir Edmund Andros, asked Pynchon to identify potential appointees who would look favorably on the new regime. The identification of potential officers for the militia was particularly critical. On June 1, 1686, Dudley informed the Committee of Trade and Foreign Plantations that "Our next case was to Intrust the Militia in the hands of persons well affected to his Majesty, the Chiefest whereof being Members of the council."[6]

Pynchon also helped Dudley and Randolph effect the submission of Connecticut, perhaps the most pressing objective of the new government. In July 1686 Randolph arrived in Springfield to confer with Pynchon about strategies for achieving this end. Shortly thereafter the Dudley council decided that Pynchon and Wait Winthrop would be dispatched as emissaries to the recalcitrant colony. The president mandated that "a letter . . . be sent unto Governor Treat of Connecticut, and Major Pinchon and Wait Winthrop Esquire desired to undertake a visit to so many of the Councill of said colony as can be conveyned at Hartford by the 3d day of August next."[7] In December 1686, in a related letter to Pynchon, Randolph revealed both his contempt of those New Englanders who opposed the Dominion and his expectation of support from the Springfield leader. In reference to the leaders of Connecticut, Randolph observed: "I hear the little Quacks there are endeavouring to divert their coming under one government, but his Excellency [Andros] has his Majesty's commands to accept of

---

[5] M. Halsey Thomas, ed., *The Diary of Samuel Sewall*, New York, 1973, 1, pp. 112–113.

[6] "Dudley Records," *Proc. Mass. Hist. Soc.*, 2nd Ser., 13 (1899–1900), p. 240.

[7] *Ibid.*, p. 259.

their surrender, which they cannot avoid." Randolph urged Pynchon to haste and assured him of the governor's esteem: "Now I intreat you . . . to come as soon as you can . . . I am to tell you his Excellency has a great kindness for you." He also informed Pynchon of a forthcoming letter "in which is an order of the Governor in Council to be communicated through your whole county." Randolph assured the Springfield leader that "We have Road Island already, and I fear not Connecticutt." He closed with a final contemptuous reference to Connecticut's civic leaders: "A dutifull submission will well become them . . . His Excellency will propose greater advantages for their ease and happiness than their weak phancy's can project."[8]

The arrival of Governor Andros in December 1686 further solidified Pynchon's position in the government. The two men were not strangers to each other. In October 1680, as we have seen, the Springfield leader had received a commission from the Massachusetts General Court to travel to Fort Albany and seek the "advice and consent" of Andros (then governor of New York) in negotiations with the Mohawks.[9] In addition, Pynchon had also come into contact with Andros through his trading connections with Robert Livingston. Accordingly, Pynchon's appointments multiplied under the new governor. He was renominated to the council and received a commission as a justice of the peace for Hampshire County. He was also chosen to sit on the Quarterly Court of Sessions, the Inferior Court of Common Pleas, and the Prerogative Court of Hampshire. In recognition of his former fur-trading activities, Pynchon was appointed to a committee with Gershom Bulkeley and Jonathan Tyng "for setting and ordering the methods of the beaver trade with the Indians."[10] And last, he accepted commissions as lieutenant colonel and eventually colonel of the Hampshire County militia.

Andros then reaffirmed the importance of Randolph's goal of using Pynchon's influence to secure the capitulation of Connecticut. In late October 1687, the governor, accompanied by a cavalcade of seventy-six men, traveled to Hartford to gain the colony's formal recognition of his government's sovereignty. Seven councilors, including Pynchon, made the five-day journey.[11] Pynchon's task was

[8] "Pincheon Papers," *Coll. Mass. Hist. Soc.*, 2nd Ser., 8 (1819), pp. 237–238.

[9] *Pynchon Court Rec.*, pp. 44, 51.

[10] "Andros Records," *Proceedings of the American Antiquarian Society*, New Series, 13 (1899–1900), pp 237–268.

[11] Albert C. Bates, "Expedition of Sir Edmund Andros to Connecticut in 1687," *Proc. Amer. Antiquarian Soc.*, N.S., 48 (1938), pp. 279–280.

doubtless eased by the enthusiastic cooperation of his two powerful relatives, John Allyn and Samuel Willys. Earlier, Allyn had written Fitz John Winthrop, another Andros adherent, asking for suggestions for overcoming the opposition of his fellow leaders in the colony; and Willys, according to Richard S. Dunn, was "one of Andros' warmest admirers."[12] A year later, Governor Andros again traveled to the Connecticut Valley. This time his objective was to insure the support of all "principal officers and magistrates," and to conduct inquiries into any real or potential opposition to his government. The governor began his eyre at Hartford by consulting with Allyn and other Connecticut leaders. His next stop was Springfield, where he conferred with Pynchon. After similar visits to Hadley and Brookfield, he returned to Boston via Worcester and Marlborough. Andros's obvious attempt to intimidate his opponents by these draconian inquests only cast the Dominion deeper into public odium. And in the Connecticut Valley, as elsewhere, those supporting Andros came into increased disrepute.

Within a year of its creation, the Dominion utterly alienated most New Englanders. The very presence of Andros, the first royally appointed governor of Massachusetts, galled inhabitants long accustomed to running their affairs untrammeled by imperial controls. Moreover, his reforms hit at the very core of New England life. He increased taxes, undermined all existing land titles, reduced local control over judicial institutions, enforced the Navigation Acts, and actively fostered the Anglican Church, still repugnant to many New Englanders. And the governor's inability to check Indian attacks on outlying settlements earned him the wrath of all who lived in frontier communities.

The Massachusetts version of the Glorious Revolution in April 1689 drove Governor Andros from office and ended the Dominion's transitory and strife-filled existence. Not surprisingly, the governor's fall from power occasioned great rejoicing throughout New England. Those celebrating, however, did not include many of the long-standing colonial leaders, most of whom had served Andros and now saw their status imperiled by his political demise. And, as subsequent events revealed, they had good reason for these fears.

The Glorious Revolution in Massachusetts resulted in the most complete repudiation of the colony's leaders since its founding. At both the local and provincial levels, those who had served the Dominion were summarily removed from positions of authority. In Dedham the "hatred of the 'foreign' regime was so great . . . that

[12] Dunn, *Puritans and Yankees*, pp. 242–243.

the townsmen followed up Andros' fall by repudiating every selectman who had served during the years of his rule." Eight men
with cumulative service exceeding fifty years held office between
1687 and 1689. Only one of these was ever elected again.[13] Plymouth colony experienced a similar overthrow of the old order.[14]
In Barnstable on Cape Cod the period after the Glorious Revolution "witnessed the unseating of the old order on the one hand"
and on the other "a period of dynamic experimentation and social
mobility that brought with it the advent of a political and economic
nouveau riche."[15] At the provincial level, this repudiation of leadership was no less dramatic. These disruptions, according to John
M. Murrin, resulted in "sweeping political changes." He observes
that "Remarkably few members of the colonial House of Deputies
ever got into the new House of Representatives in the 1690s."
Excepting Plymouth colony towns, "only one out of eight representatives had seen legislative service under the old Charter." He
concludes that the "real problem of the decade appears to have
been a lack of acceptable leadership at all levels. The old gods had
fallen, and nobody was convincing enough to proclaim their successors."[16] Still another historian describes Massachusetts as "utterly
bereft of first-class leadership."[17]

This wholesale repudiation of leadership, in turn, initiated a
period of protracted chaos and factionalism. The rejection of the
old rulers left Massachusetts rudderless, for the first time without
a coherent sense of hierarchy. From the beginning a patriarchal
society where men expected their leaders to "order them" and exact
"due obedience," New Englanders now floundered about in efforts
to erect new political structures. With their former officers in disrepute, the colony's inhabitants looked in vain for someone to in-
terpret their vision. The result, in the words of an unsympathetic
English observer, was a "Labyrinth of Miserys," and a search for
scapegoats.[18] The most dramatic manifestation of this collective loss
of moral authority was the witchcraft controversy at Salem, which

[13] Lockridge, *A New England Town*, p. 88.

[14] George Langdon, Jr., *Pilgrim Colony*, New Haven, 1967, p. 234.

[15] John J. Waters, Jr., *The Otis Family in Provincial and Revolutionary Massachusetts*,
Chapel Hill, 1968, pp. 50–51; Richard R. Johnson denies that the Glorious Revolution dramatically affected patterns of officeholding at the town level; *Adjustment
to Empire*, p. 114. But much of his own carefully gathered data suggests otherwise;
see especially pp. 71, 102–103, 116.

[16] Murrin, "Review Essay," *History and Theory* (1972), pp. 259–260.

[17] Dunn, *Puritans and Yankees*, p. 192.

[18] Professor T. H. Breen offers a convincing interpretation of the changes effected
during and after the Andros regime; see *Character of the Good Ruler*, pp. 134–239.

grew out of a clash between two factions within the town.[19] And in the Connecticut Valley, John Pynchon, the dominant figure in western Massachusetts for over forty years, now found himself rebuffed and traduced by those who had always offered him deference and obedience.

At first it appeared that Pynchon would ride out the storm. After the Glorious Revolution he gradually but surely recaptured his former official positions. Although his support for Andros led to exclusion from the Council for the Safety of the People and Conservation of the Peace (created as an interim government after the fall of the Dominion), Pynchon did not long remain out of power. In September 1689 he was reconfirmed as an Associate for the County Court of Hampshire. He reverted to the rank of major in the militia but remained the highest officer in the Hampshire County regiment. In 1693 he was again elected to the council and retained this position until his death a decade later. Pynchon soon discovered, however, that the authority that these positions had once conferred had diminished sharply.

Part of the reason for this decline was structural. The second Massachusetts charter of 1691 retained many of the political and judicial changes instituted under the Dominion. In particular, the centralizing features of the earlier reorganization remained virtually intact, thus depriving Pynchon of his former status as a mediator. Under the second charter, the governor nominated and appointed judges, commissioners of oyer and terminer, justices of the peace, and other lower judicial officials, although he now needed consent from the council. Councilors were not directly appointed by the governor as under the Dominion, but neither were they popularly elected as under the first charter. Under the second charter, assistants were elected by members of the two houses immediately after the May elections for the House of Representatives.[20] Accordingly, Pynchon failed to reclaim his "gatekeeping" function between the locality and the province. The post-Dominion centralization and proliferation of justices, again, denied him exclusivity of access between local and provincial spheres.

Equally important as the structural curtailment of his mediator's role was John Pynchon's loss of moral authority within the valley. By associating himself with the odious Dominion government, he lost the fealty of the general populace. And without this deference, his effectiveness as an instrument of General Court policy was

[19] Boyer and Nissenbaum, *Salem Possessed.*
[20] Dunn, *Puritans and Yankees*, p. 238.

markedly diminished. Under the first charter, Pynchon received land grants, fur-trading monopolies, and other emoluments because he successfully implemented General Court directives in the Connecticut Valley. His mediating functions rested on a delicate equipoise between deference in the valley and influence in Boston. Whether it was town founding (or governing), adjudication of boundary disputes, maintenance of social order, or oversight of the county militia, Pynchon's word had been law in the first charter period. After the Glorious Revolution, however, this was no longer true—particularly regarding the militia. His inability properly to "order" the militiamen was the most palpable sign of his fall from grace among valley residents. And the trouble began within three months of the Glorious Revolution.

In July 1689 the Springfield leader informed the authorities in Boston of the rise of a "discontented party" within Hampshire County. The militiamen in Northampton had mutinied against the officers who had led them during the Dominion period. With what seemed to Pynchon astonishing boldness, the malcontents demanded the overthrow of the existing militia leadership. One Sergeant James King had taken it upon himself to lead a rebellion against the old officers, and his efforts had been enthusiastically supported by the militia's rank-and-file. As Pynchon described the situation to the council: "there is a Party at Northampton who fal in with Serjeant King, or rather that are stirred up by him, who doe so blow up discontents against their former officers as make it difficult [to restore order]."[21] In open defiance of Pynchon, King and his cohorts decided that they could now choose their own officers without the General Court's prior approval. The rebels "account they have now Liberty to do what they Please without Consulting." King, moreover, was not confining his activities to Northampton. "For that an order hath lately been Improved in some of the Townes (By Serjeant King) for a new choise where were officers standing and under most sufficient settlement who had their Comissions from the former Government." To Pynchon's chagrin, King's rabble-rousing was having its desired effect. It had "disquieted some others that were quiet before."[22]

Unlike a riot in Hadley in 1675 in which Pynchon swiftly and forcefully disciplined the malcontents (without seeking or expecting help from Boston), he now stood by helpless. In an uncharacteristically pusillanimous fashion, he confessed to the colonial

[21] Mass. Archives, 107, p. 239.
[22] *Ibid.*, 107, p. 178.

leadership that his authority was insufficient to pacify the "disorderly faction." Replying to the governor's injunction that he take more forceful measures to reimpose authority, Pynchon confessed the futility of his previous efforts in this regard: "Concerning the Disorders and Irregularitys of the Soldiers in this County which you mention, I have not been wanting to allay the same." In this contest between Pynchon and an obscure militia sergeant from Northampton, James King emerged triumphant.[23]

Sergeant King succeeded in his efforts to turn out the militia officers who had served under the Dominion and replace them with democratically elected leaders. And King's methods in achieving these ends repudiated time-honored notions of order, hierarchy, and authority. Rather than appealing for support for those "able men" whom the community recognized as its natural leaders, King forged his alliance with a naked appeal for political support from his friends and relatives. Power politics and personal ambition replaced diffidence and popular passivity. Commenting on King's self-aggrandizing tactics, Pynchon observed "I understand it was carried on in designe by himself that he might be Captaine, and it hath so far prevailed that he is Nominated for Lieutenant." Pynchon ascribed this success to King's extensive kinship ties. He attributed King's election as lieutenant to his "having so many Relations as I am Informed about 32 in that Towne by Marriage and Blood who have halpen it on and are the Faction in that Busyness." According to the Springfield leader, others likewise cast their support to Sergeant King in order to achieve political ascendancy themselves. Medad Pomery "join[ed] with them and being of them (which also helpt him to the place of Deputy)." Most distressing to Pynchon was the success of this self-serving and rebellious faction rather than the "most sober and considerate" men who were "otherwise disposed and would rest in and with their former officers who were Commissioned before May 1686." Largely as a result of the agitators' efforts, people were "questioning everything."[24]

Two weeks later Sergeant King's defiance of John Pynchon passed beyond repudiation of duly appointed militia officers into open refusal to obey military orders. In early August of 1689, the Springfield leader attempted to organize an expedition aimed at protecting the most northerly valley towns from impending Indian attack. Pynchon successfully filled Springfield's complement of volunteers, but when he sought a similar levy from Northampton, he ran into a roadblock. He wrote the governor's council that he "sent

---

[23] *Pynchon Court Rec.*, pp. 284–286; Mass. Archives, 107, p. 239.
[24] Mass. Archives, 107, p. 239.

away 15 men from Springfield who readyly attended." But the directive that the "upper Townes [contribute] for more to make up 50 at Northampton" fell on deaf ears. He told the council that "Serjeant King cavilled about my Power, hindered the Comittee of Militia, etc. told them Springfield men would not obey me (tho it proved otherwise)." Continuing, Pynchon related an affront from King that would have been unthinkable a decade earlier. Without mincing words, the sergeant described Pynchon as nothing less than a political nullity. King asserted that "I had noe Power and they mattered me [not at all]." And to add insult to injury, King declared that he "would not give 3 skips of a louse" for Pynchon's authority. He concluded his tirade with the observation that Pynchon was effectively a eunuch because "the [General] Court could act nothing." As Pynchon later summarized the unhappy situation for the council, "[King] and Pomrey bid defiance to the old Commission officers, such a height of Pride are matters come to [at Northampton] that nothing would or could be done by or from my orders and directions. But they said they would If any came from Springfield goe as volunteers."[25]

Faced with such brazen contempt for his authority, Pynchon capitulated. Under the first charter, outright defiance of his will invariably brought the offender under the lash. Now, however, Pynchon did nothing. Like Sergeant King, he recognized that in the post-Dominion political climate, he needed the direct and open support of both the General Court and the local populace. One without the other was not enough. King's taunt that the "Court could act nothing" doubtless rankled the more because it was true.

The militia rebellion soon engulfed the entire upper valley. In every town except Springfield soldiers defied their superiors and repudiated John Pynchon's officer appointments. In direct violation of the 1668 General Court law banning local trainband elections, the rank-and-file of every militia unit followed King's example and argued that they themselves and not their colonel or governor should choose company-level officers. Pynchon informed the council in May 1690 that the importunate militiamen had refused to serve under any officers but those of their own choosing. "Our Soldiers I know wil much desire and Insist upon it, to have Commission officers of their owne (I meane such as they know)."[26] Pynchon continued to emphasize in his correspondence to the council

[25] *Ibid.*, 107, p. 258.

[26] Mass. Archives, 36, p. 56. For an examination of the changing pattern of militia elections in the seventeenth century, see T. H. Breen, "English Origins and New World Development: The Case of the Covenanted Militia in Seventeenth-Century Massachusetts," *Past and Present*, 57 (1972), pp. 74–96.

that any officers selected would have to be acceptable to the soldiery. Now he routinely asked the troops beforehand if a candidate would be satisfactory to them. Regarding one such case, he told the council that "Our Soldiers also were something Trobled they had not a Commission officer of their owne: But I pacified them and apointed them a Sergeant."[27] In February 1692 the Springfield leader appointed Jonathan Wells lieutenant of the Deerfield militia company. Pynchon assured Governor Simon Bradstreet that Wells was both "the fittest to take charge" and, more important, he was "to their owne Sattisfaction."[28]

In the critical area of military strategy, the militia companies likewise demanded local autonomy. The transparent need for a coordinated policy against the Indians failed to inspire the companies to heed John Pynchon's commands. Beside himself with frustration, in February 1690 he told Samuel Willys and John Allyn: "we are extreme naked and open and cant agree upon fortification, some being for one way and some another So that I feare we shall ly to the mercy of the enemy."[29] In December 1694 he wrote Secretary Isaac Addington, again underscoring the grave peril created by the militia companies' unwillingness to abide by his directives. Most alarming to Pynchon was the failure adequately to fortify the various valley settlements. "I did hint something to you about Fortifications in these towns. We are not in any good posture: both Hatfield, Hadley etc. as wel as this Towne and al Rest are too open." He directly ascribed the shoddy efforts at fortification to the antiauthoritarianism occasioned by the Glorious Revolution. The "Fortifications [are] gone to decay [because] for repairing or making new [fortifications] the People a litle wilful, inclined to do what and how they please or not at all." In concluding his letter, Pynchon sounded a theme that appeared with increasing regularity in his correspondence after 1689—the need for direct intervention from Boston. He told Addington that "an order from authority is necessary to enforce to what is meete and will strengthen the hands of those here [who have tried to] have something done but find obstructions to their discouragmt and laying it aside."[30]

The most vivid manifestation of the new antiauthoritarianism was the collapse of the Hampshire County Horse Troop. John

[27] Mass. Archives, 35, p. 102.

[28] *Ibid.*, 37, p. 306A.

[29] John Pynchon to Samuel Willys and John Allyn, February 24, 1690, Edes Ms., Mass. Hist. Soc.

[30] John Pynchon to Isaac Addington, December 3, 1694, Pocumtuck Valley Memorial Association, Deerfield, Mass., typescript copy, CVHM.

Pynchon, as commander of the cavalry troop, watched in dismay as the unit, once the pride of the valley, disintegrated. Disgruntled over the loss of some of their perquisites under a military reorganization bill in 1691, and caught up in the general malaise of the period, the horse troopers effectively disbanded. Many of the cavalrymen declared that the only unit they would join was the less financially demanding foot regiment. The substantial eligibility requirements for membership in the horse troop, ownership of £100 in estate, a horse, saddle, bridle, holster, pistol, and sword, perforce limited its recruitment pool to the "better sort." The majority of citizens simply did not possess the resources necessary for service in the cavalry. Accordingly, because of their class origins, when the horse regiment mutinied their actions were an especially serious blow to social order.[31] In July 1690 Pynchon wrote to Major General Wait Winthrop to "lay the state of the Troope in this County before your judicious Consideration." So dispirited was the troop, he lamented, that the question now was "Whether it be meete wholy to give it up or to Continue and settle it, or a Troope here or noe: For we are almost Come to Noe Troope now." He described the precipitous decline of the unit. "I think some few yeares ago This for a Countrey Troope was in as good a Posture, and the Troopers suitably spirited for service, wel equipped and Generally as compleate in Armes, as most Troopers or Troops were." However, "of late some discouragemt have made some decline the service, and let their armes and furniture goe to Ruine."[32]

The obvious need for a combat-ready cavalry force in the face of the ever-present threat of Indian attack failed to prevent wholesale defections. Recognizing the troop's strategic importance, Pynchon spared no effort to keep it intact. But his exhortations, admonitions, and outright threats of legal reprisal failed to stem the tide. The defection to the foot regiment of the officers and most experienced veterans was particularly galling to the Springfield leader. Some men had even thrown away their weapons and equipment. He informed Winthrop that "many and Generally the best of the Troopers here have [en]listed in the Foote, dispose[d] of their armes and Furniture, some out of the Country: and have left the Troope: And besides the officers of the Troop are taken off . . . and Indeed it is a Question whether now the Troope hath any Commission officers or any others almost." As their actions implied,

[31] Jack S. Radabaugh, "The Militia of Colonial Massachusetts," *Military Affairs*, 18 (1954), pp. 3–4; Morrison Sharp, "Leadership and Democracy in the Early New England System of Defense," *American Historical Review*, 50 (1945), pp. 244–260.

[32] John Pynchon to Major General Wait Winthrop, July 17, 1690, Winthrop Mss.

the soldiers were "much disgusted" and irascible and in no mood to cooperate with anyone—least of all Pynchon. "[T]hus you se," he concluded, "how broke the Troope is."[33]

The disintegration of the Hampshire Horse Troop placed serious and occasionally insurmountable restrictions on John Pynchon's options as commander. Deprived of the tactical flexibility offered by the cavalry, he abandoned his former strategy of search-and-destroy. He ordered the upper valley towns garrisoned, but without the troopers he could not pursue attacking Indians into their forest encampments. He described these constraints on his actions in a letter to General Winthrop. "In June last I had thoughts to have called the Troope together which they have not been never since the [Glorious] Revolution [but] . . . we apprehended it might be meete to forbeare til I had writ to you and given you an account of matters." Increasingly, he was forced to place exclusive reliance on foot soldiers. But they too soon rebelled against his authority.[34]

Desertion from the foot, as with the cavalry, was the most troublesome problem. After 1689 its ranks were progressively depleted as more and more men simply laid down their arms and refused to serve. Pynchon, of course, was responsible for prosecuting and disciplining deserters. But, again, his efforts to punish offenders usually came to nothing. Men continued to leave the militia with impunity, to the consternation of those who remained. In December 1689 he described the overall loss of morale because of the rising rate of desertion. Most destructive was the example set by those who fled from military service and remained unpunished. "One man after he was Impressed and particularly ordered to be ready ran away, to the great discontent of some and to the Embolding of others So that some of the Soldiers told me If he were let escape (for what he did was with a high hand) they would also run away."[35]

John Pynchon's inability to reimpose order in the Connecticut Valley led him to turn increasingly to Boston for assistance. He urged Secretary Addington "for the settlement and strengthing the hands of any in Authority in this county, To send orders and Commissions to them."[36] He informed the council of his impotence in the absence of this outside help. "I recken I must cease unless you give further orders to approve of what I have done." He emphasized that this support was necessary "that I may not be ob-

---

[33] *Ibid.*
[34] *Ibid.*
[35] Mass. Archives, 35, p. 102.
[36] *Ibid.*

noxious (as the Comission officers at Northampton are) to the Derision of Mr. King and Mr. Pomrey and such others as Joine with them." He consoled himself by reflecting on the sufferings of Christ. "Al Peckt at the Captain of our Salvation who Indured the Contridiction of sinners."[37]

Petitions for assistance from the authorities in Boston reflected Pynchon's loss of local autonomy. Under the first charter, Pynchon, as magistrate, colonel of the militia regiment, and county court judge, had been accustomed to acting on his own to resolve local issues. During the period from 1655 to 1685, he rarely sought advice or assistance from the governor or General Court. Indeed, the Massachusetts Archives, the repository of all official correspondence between magistrates and the General Court, contains no request for guidance from Pynchon before 1684. When rioters took to the streets in Hadley, militia deployments were needed, or additional provisions required, he acted unilaterally and on his own authority. When he did communicate with Boston, it was to inform the Court of actions he *already* had taken. After the Glorious Revolution, however, this situation changed dramatically. Now Pynchon began increasingly to seek support and counsel from Boston before acting. In January 1692 he told Governor Bradstreet that "we are thoughtful for our own security and desire to be set in the right way thereunto," and "[I] have always thought it a difficult concerne and not meete for me to act without application to your Honors" that "accordingly we may Receive meete directions and orders."[38]

With the legitimacy of his authority openly questioned in the Connecticut Valley, Pynchon was reluctant to take any action without explicit orders from Boston for fear of local recriminations. In 1694, with the militia garrisons at Deerfield and Brookfield undermanned and underprovisioned, Pynchon faced the decision either to abandon the settlements or reinforce their defenders. After a dangerous period of vacillation, he wrote Secretary Addington to complain that his repeated requests for guidance had gone unanswered. "Very desirous I have been to have advice about continueing or quitting the Garrison at Dearefeild and Brookfeild and therefore have several times writ for directions thereabouts, both to his excellency before he went off, and (If I mistake not) to yourself also, But have not Received one line, nor heard any thing in the least concerning the same." The Springfield leader closed

[37] Mass. Archives, 107, p. 258.
[38] Mass. Archives, 37, pp. 223–224B.

his letter with the comment that "[I] am loath upon my owne head to discharge them, least If any thing fal out not well, I should deservedly be Blamed."[39] Eight months later, Pynchon informed Lieutenant Governor William Stoughton that he had contemplated raising militia quotas but "yet I am necessitated to leave off, partly upon the account of it being too much for me to undertake upon my owne head without orders," especially "If it should not succeed as I hope for."[40] The following month he reiterated to Stoughton that the "disquiets and exercises . . . proves hard for me to doe what belongs to me . . . [and] I shal be glad of any good directions from your Honor."[41]

The nature of John Pynchon's power, accordingly, was transformed from that of mediator to that of communicator. No longer able to act on his own authority throughout much of Hampshire County, Pynchon became instead a conduit for implementing the policies of the governor and council. This function, of course, had always been an important part of his influence. But this power had always been *discretionary*: the General Court delegated authority to Pynchon to use as he saw fit. The Court had originally granted Pynchon this mandate because it recognized that his power in the valley was unchallenged. After the Glorious Revolution, however, with his authority openly disputed and his institutional autonomy eroded by the recent centralization, John Pynchon sought his legitimacy not as a local gentry leader, but as a commissioned royal official.[42]

The loss of his local autonomy meant that persuasion replaced coercion as the method used to bring offenders in line. In December 1690, a year and a half after the outbreak of the Northampton mutiny, Pynchon wrote to the ringleaders and admonished them to mend their ways. He cited the need for their cooperation in the face of both impending Indian attacks and the continuing threat of civil disorder. "Considering the state and condition of your Company and the unsettledness thereof . . . I have thoughts of moveing you to be in a due use of meanes for your ful Settlement and Establishment as to Military or Commission officers . . . this time of Commotion and danger cals for a meete and due Settlement without delay." Pynchon also explicitly stated that he now saw his

[39] John Pynchon to Isaac Addington, December 3, 1694, Pocumtuck Valley Memorial Association, typescript copy CVHM.

[40] Mass. Archives, 30, p. 368B.

[41] Mass. Archives, 51, p. 48.

[42] John M. Murrin explores the wider ramifications of the "royalization" of provincial Massachusetts in "Anglicizing an American Colony."

role as exclusively advisory. No longer did he threaten retribution or invoke the authority of the state. "I thinke it my duty to stir you up thereunto, and doe advise you to cal your Company together, and to propose to them (to whom If you please you may Impart these lines) the Supply and setling of a Captain So far as in them lyes, by Nomination of the most fit persons among you for that End." As suggested by his choice of words in communicating these views to the militiamen—"please," "advise," and "propose"—Pynchon was reduced to cajoling low-ranking militia officials in Northampton, at one point simply to transmit his views to their fellow company members.[43]

In his admonition to the Northampton militia to select the "most fit persons," John Pynchon sounded a theme he would repeat endlessly for the next five years—the hazards of repudiating society's "natural" rulers. He believed that the rejection of the former officers represented a turning away from men of "sober," "moderate," and "sound judgment." Those who supplanted these leaders, in Pynchon's view, were factious, hotheaded, and misguided. They elevated personal advancement above the public good. Accordingly, he urged the Northampton malcontents to "lay . . . aside al headyness, prejudice, commotion of spirit or single respects and misguided affections" and "act Judiciously with respect to the Publike good and advantage." He counseled them to "lay aside al animositys, disatisfaction upon personal and frivolous accounts, and . . . consider the good of the whole." In an attempt to show the rebels the folly of laying the blame for the "troblus times" exclusively at the feet of their former leaders, he resorted to historical allusion. "[A]s once in Padua, when much discontent was and Intentions of election of New Persons to office, one advised them . . . before they rejected the old ones to consider wel where they might find better, which advice allayed the hot spirits so that al the former were continued." He concluded by reiterating the need for social order and a due submission to legitimate authority. He urged the company to "Consider the best and fittest persons upon al accounts, and make noe alteration but what may be safe and beneficial to the Company and Publike good." The paramount necessity for an orderly transition of power was heightened by the "unquiet some of your people have been (upon what good Grounds or Reasons I know not, and they would doe wel to Consider)."[44]

John Pynchon's hopes for a restoration of public order rested

[43] Mass. Archives, 36, p. 242.
[44] *Ibid.*

on the receipt of a more authoritarian royal charter. Increasingly he believed that only new and more draconian directives from the Crown would quell the discontented spirits in the valley. He applauded when Secretary Addington received the first such communication. He expressed confidence that things would begin to get better "Now that you have new orders and directions from England which wilbe more available and effectual than former orders." In December 1689 he informed the council of "The Great Incouragement we have, that we spedyly may have our charter." With an uncharacteristic lapse into sarcasm, Pynchon declared that a charter would "quiet and settle al moderate and well disposed spirits" and as "for others, might they goe off . . . for I persuade my selfe the Country could well Spare them."[45] In May 1692, again bewailing the chaotic conditions, he expressed hope that the newly appointed governor, Sir William Phips, would bring about a "tendency to a hopeful good Settlement" of what Pynchon later refered to as this "Pore low Country."[46] Five days later, Pynchon wrote that he trusted that "God wil Incline the king to send good Governors to us."[47] Deprived since 1689 of his mediating functions, the Springfield leader still hoped for a restoration of his old authority—but now under the mantle of royal legitimacy. However, as his subsequent treatment at the hands of the General Court revealed, a return to the old days was impossible.

A corollary to John Pynchon's declining authority in the Connecticut Valley was his decreasing influence in Boston. As he had achieved dominance largely because of the reciprocal nature of local and provincial power, the erosion of one threatened the credibility of the other. By the early 1690s, largely dependent on support from the governor and council for his influence, Pynchon no longer commanded automatic diffidence in Boston. Under the first charter, the General Court handsomely rewarded him for his services because it could count on him to deliver. But with his post-Revolution impotence in valley affairs (Springfield, of course, excepted), Pynchon's petitions for remuneration for his services usually elicited only a token payment.

The most dramatic evidence of John Pynchon's fall from political grace was the result of one such petition presented to the General Court in late 1696. In an elaborately detailed rendition of his many services as militia commander since 1692, he importuned the Court to make restitution for his time and expenditures. In requesting

[45] Mass. Archives, 35, p. 102.
[46] Mass. Archives, 51, p. 1.
[47] *Ibid.*, 51, p. 6.

compensation for his "Imploy as Commander of the Regiment of Militia" he told the court that "[your petitioner] Hath according to his ability unwearedly Served the Countrey Foure yeares and Halfe, ever since the arrival of Sir William Phips: In which service he hath laid out himselfe more than a litle for the Publike: This end of the Province Having in this time of War been Infested with the enymys several attempts upon our Townes, which hath occasioned your Petitioner to spend a greate part of his time every yeare in attending the Duty of his Place and Command, Besides much experience otherwise therein: For all which He never had any least Consideration or allowance for the same." These services included "Impress[ing] and sending out men, Besides the Inspecting of the Garrisons at Dearefeild and Brookfeild." He also underscored his fidelity of service and burden of command. "The Care and ordering of al, Having wholy layne upon your Petitioner . . . [a] ready attending his duty therein upon al occasions," but "especially in times of greatest Exigency for the Publike advantage." The scope of these services "Imboldens your Petitioner, From these Premises, to aske your Honors' meete grattification and ordering him such a due allowance as your Honorable selves, [as] This general Assembly Shal judge a meete compensation for his Past and already chearful service." And the Springfield leader openly implied that his future availability for assistance to the Court would hinge on a satisfactory response to the petition. Adequate compensation, he observed, "wil be an obligation upon him to persist in whatever further Service he is Capable of."[48]

Although Pynchon submitted his request to the Court in November 1696, it was not answered until almost a year later, an unprecedented delay by the standards of the first charter period. On October 15, 1697, the document was read aloud in the House of Representatives. Without debate, the legislators proceeded to a vote. The result of the balloting was to pay the man, who a decade earlier had received eight square miles of land for a similar request, "for his Extraordinary Service and charges, the Sum of . . . Ten pounds, no more."[49]

The eclipse of John Pynchon's mediator status, did not, of course, signal the loss of authority within Springfield itself. Although no longer able to exercise the traditional prerogatives of a gentry leader at the county or provincial levels, Pynchon's hold over his own community remained secure. He continued his role as the patron

[48] Mass. Archives, 70, p. 309.
[49] *Ibid.*

of a town that had been since its founding the virtual fiefdom of his family. With the new royalization of Massachusetts, however, the days of their dominance were numbered. The conditions that had brought the family to power were eliminated by the Glorious Revolution, and the next generation would have to adjust to a very different political world. They would do, not command, the bidding of others. Although John Pynchon left no record of his thoughts during these declining years, one of his sharpest disappointments doubtless was the personal and financial ineptitude of his only surviving son, John. When his father breathed his last in January 1703, the younger Pynchon inherited the family's wealth and business enterprises; but the days of the titans were over. Even if he had been a more able and charismatic figure, he was powerless to prevent the emergence of new competing elites, men who—unlike his father and grandfather—served their King rather than their community.

Springfield, John Pynchon, and New England Society

THE SALIENT CHARACTERISTICS of seventeenth-century Springfield chronicled herein—developmentalism, diversification, acquisitiveness, individualism, contentiousness, and stratification—were not unique to the Connecticut Valley settlement. All existing studies of coastal ports such as Boston and Salem have revealed similar societies. Paul Boyer and Stephen Nissenbaum, in particular, found the same combination of factiousness, market-orientation, and witchcraft in late seventeenth-century Salem. Several recent examinations of Plymouth show the tenuousness of communalism in that colony; and a study of Windsor, Connecticut finds a markedly high level of tolerance for socially deviant behavior. David T. Konig's *Law and Society in Puritan Massachusetts: Essex County, 1629–1692* reveals litigiousness, social conflict, and heterogeneity from the mid-seventeenth century onward throughout northeastern Massachusetts. Paul R. Lucas entitles his study of church and society in the Connecticut Valley from 1636 to 1725, *Valley of Discord*. David Grayson Allen's, *In English Ways*, published in 1981, speaks of the "remarkable" diversity of land usage and custom in early New England and ascribes it to the variety of regional differences in the mother country. Social diversity in seventeenth-century Massachusetts is—or should be—an established fact.[1]

What we don't know is the respective population breakdown for the developmental, coastal, and corporate communities. Only such information will provide a means to measure whether Dedham or Springfield more nearly typified the experience of most New Englanders. Given the disproportionate size of Boston and Salem (Boston's population in 1700 was 6,700, Salem's in 1683 was 2,489,

[1] Rutman, *Winthrop's Boston*; Boyer and Nissenbaum, *Salem Possessed*; Richard P. Gildrie, *Salem, Massachusetts, 1626–1683: A Covenant Community*, Charlottesville, Va., 1975; Young, *From 'Good Order' to Glorious Revolution*; Demos, *A Little Commonwealth*; Langdon, *Pilgrim Colony*; Linda A. Bissell, "Family, Friends, and Neighbors: Social Interaction in Seventeenth-Century Windsor, Connecticut," Ph.D. dissertation, Brandeis University, 1973.

while in 1710 some 980 souls lived in Dedham), and Springfield's example from western Massachusetts, continued exclusive reliance on the Dedham model seems untenable.[2] It appears that many, if not most, seventeenth-century New Englanders lived in acquisitive, market-oriented societies. But the verdict is still out. We need more comparative data on patterns of work, land tenure, bankruptcy, and economic dependency generally in a much wider cross section of communities. To do this, historians of early America must turn away from primary reliance on church and town records, and exploit more fully available account books, probate inventories, and court records. Only then can the gap between prescription and performance be measured. Only then will we be able to bring the mosaic of images that we now have for Puritan New England into sharper focus. Despite calls for a moratorium—not a mandate—regarding new research on colonial Massachusetts, much work remains to be done.[3]

Even at the current vantage point, some of the wider implications of the Springfield experience seem clear. First is the developmental role of the merchant-entrepreneurs in the settlement of early New England. There was something exceptional about this New World gentry. They were able to control land, command commercial enterprises (unlike the English gentry studied by Lawrence Stone and Hugh Trevor-Roper), and to implement a new form of informal but effective social control without any of the official marks of the old aristocracy. The principal reason for their success, it seems, was their role in capitalizing and directing the development of New World settlement. In contrast to Old World gentry who, as Joyce Appleby observes, "spent rather than invested their income," the landed rich in early Massachusetts constantly rechanneled their profits into new enterprises.[4] While the function of English landlords was essentially preservative—to protect the integrity of an estate ultimately to be bequeathed in tail to the eldest son—New World landlords were risk-taking entrepreneurs who supplied the capital and leadership needed to turn a wilderness into a settlement. Their acquisitive values found expression in a legal system geared toward growth, not stasis. As strict enforcement of contractual obligations between employer and employee promoted predictability

---

[2] Cook, *Fathers of the Towns*, pp. 194–195.

[3] Bruce C. Daniels, *The Connecticut Town: Growth and Development, 1635–1790*, Middletown, Conn., 1979.

[4] "Ideology and Theory," *American Historical Review* (1976), p. 500. I am obliged to Olivier Zunz and Edward L. Ayers for helping me to reformulate these observations. Professor Ayers also suggested the book's title.

and efficiency in the labor market, so too developmental leases guaranteed improvement of the landlord's acreage.

This entrepreneurial role was played by some two dozen men in seventeenth-century New England, of whom John Pynchon is but one example. Examinations of the Willard family in the Merrimack Valley, the Winthrops of Boston and elsewhere, and the Otises in Barnstable all underscore the importance of merchant-entrepreneurs in financing and orchestrating settlement throughout early New England. Without these men, colonial America would have remained resource rich but capital poor. Through trade, investments, credit, work, developmental leases, manufacturing enterprises, and the like, the merchant-entrepreneur opened up new regions for settlement and served as a magnet for additional migrants thereafter. The modest initial endowments of many of the first settlers and their willingness to work made it sensible to accept what the merchant-entrepreneur had to offer—even at the price of personal dependency.

The parallel between the merchant-entrepreneur careers of Simon Willard and John Pynchon, both fur traders who became land magnates, seems particularly striking. Willard founded, exclusively as fur-trading posts, Concord (1636) and Chelmsford (1655) before moving on to Lancaster to compete for furs with its founder, John Prescott. There, and later at Groton, he reaped the benefits of being a mediator, including large land grants from the General Court. In 1658 Willard successfully petitioned the Court for five hundred acres on the spurious grounds that he deserved recompense for a loan default by a Pawtucket Indian. At his death in 1676, Willard owned 1,521 acres of land and an overall estate estimated at £8,000. In the words of the foremost authority on the early New England fur trade, "The figure of the fur trader Simon Willard towers above all others in the early annals of [the Merrimack Valley]. Deputy from Concord to the General Court for fifteen years, Assistant of Massachusetts Bay 1654–1676, Captain, Major, and Sergeant Major of Middlesex County, Willard was the leading man in the successive towns in which he resided. Town builder, Indian agent, explorer, his services were most valuable to the people of Massachusetts Bay, and prepared the way for those who came to till the soil."[5]

Also strikingly similar to the career of John Pynchon was that of John Winthrop, Jr. Richard S. Dunn writes that Winthrop was

[5] Moloney, *Fur Trade in New England*, pp. 75–77; see also Bailyn, *New England Merchants*, p. 56.

"Founder of three towns, industrialist, scientist, doctor, governor, diplomat, farmer, [and] land speculator." As with Pynchon and Willard, Winthrop received land grants, monopolies, and special privileges and immunities for acting as a developer and mediator. In September 1650, soon after his arrival in the town of Pequot (New London), Connecticut, Winthrop and his heirs were granted the "priviledge and Right of ordering and disposing all publick Building and affairs of this towne, now and for the future." Dunn points out that Winthrop "was given a stone quarry, the town ferry, the right to build dams or watermills in any of the local streams, the right to hunt, fish, and cut wood anywhere within the town limits, and all of his land was made tax free. He was encouraged to manufacture glass, for which purpose the town gave him the 'great white sandy beach over against Bachelors Cove' and let him dig freely for clay. To manufacture saltpeter he was given Gull Island outside Pequot harbor. He built and operated the town gristmill as well as a sawmill outside the town, getting various timber rights for the latter."[6]

A third example of the successful merchant-entrepreneur is John Otis II (1621–1684) in Barnstable. According to John J. Waters, Jr., Otis "refused to be content with producing for a market controlled by others. Rather, John II took his father's land, capital lent by his in-laws, and money entrusted by neighbors and entered into trade, industrial activity, and long-term land speculation." Waters writes that "During his life the second Otis had been consumed by two objectives: the accumulation of property and the settlement of his family." After moving from Scituate to Barnstable, Otis became "the richest man in that small community of 145 householders" and left a patrimony of £1,500 for the next generation.[7]

Evidence is abundant that communities appreciated the importance of having a merchant-entrepreneur in their midst. Fearing, rightly, that John Winthrop, Jr. was contemplating leaving their town for Boston in 1637, fifty-seven inhabitants of Ipswich petitioned the General Court not to deprive "our Church and Towne of one whose presence is so gratefull and usefull to us." And, as Dunn observes, the townsmen also "bribed him with an additional grant of land on Castle Hill . . . if he would stay."[8] Moreover, Boston and Ipswich were not the only communities that vied for Winthrop's presence. In 1654 John Pynchon wrote his friend that "New

[6] Dunn, *Puritans and Yankees*, pp. 59, 75.

[7] Waters, *The Otis Family*, pp. 29, 36, 38–39.

[8] Dunn, *Puritans and Yankees*, p. 70.

Haven I heare have sent againe to you this weeke."[9] Likewise, in August 1675, Pynchon wrote to John Allyn at Hartford "Hast, Post Hast" that "They much desire the presence of some principall man at Hadley to direct, as need requires, and to expedite affairs."[10] When in 1706 the town of Enfield needed a spokesman at the General Court, as Edward M. Cook, Jr. notes, "the voters ignored their own leaders and attempted to persuade Joseph Parsons, Esq., of Springfield and Northampton to settle in their town and become their representative."[11]

The motives behind these desires for politically well-connected merchant-entrepreneurs are not difficult to fathom. Towns needed the political capital that flowed from the presence of a mediator, but, even more, they needed the financial capital of the entrepreneur. Pynchon, Willard, Winthrop, and Otis were all risk-takers, men who supplied the credit, technology, and leadership needed to turn a wilderness into a settlement. Through their trading activities, the merchant-entrepreneurs acted as corporate patrons for their regions, absorbing price variations and carrying charges in inventories of foodstuffs and soft goods to provide an economic cocoon for the townsfolk. John Pynchon, in Springfield, absorbed the costs and secured the benefits of price fluctuations, which he could do because of his wealth and profits from fur. He, like the other merchant-entrepreneurs, was an economic buffer to the outside world. And the benefits of this patrimonial world applied to (selected) workers as well as customers. For the skilled artisan, Pynchon could offer higher income, or higher security, or off-season employment (itself a form of security). Pynchon was also the employer of last (as well as first) resort—witness his taking as domestics the girls of particularly poor families. It is also likely that William and John's resources actually made it easier on the working people of Springfield in the early years when the general store was a place to turn to for work or provisions when hard times (or even starvation) threatened. The store, in times of financial distress, could function as a safety net.

It was not a zero-sum game. John Pynchon's presence meant that everyone was *potentially* better off. He supplied credit, employment, investment opportunities, and capital improvements such as mills that in his absence would not be available. Indeed, if one were so

[9] John Pynchon to John Winthrop, Jr., October 20, 1654, Winthrop Mss.

[10] John Pynchon to John Allyn, August 22, 1675, *Public Records of the Colony of Connecticut*, ed. J. Hammond Trumbull and Charles Hoadley, Hartford, 1850–1890, 2, p. 353.

[11] Cook, *Fathers of the Towns*, p. 180.

disposed, it would be possible to cast Pynchon's developmental activities in a near-heroic light. It was his assets, courage, and vision that released, amplified, and reinforced the energies of the hard-working, often skilled but propertyless New World settlers. We have encountered many men in these pages—Anthony Dorchester (the miller), Joseph Leonard (the carpenter), Rowland Thomas (the stonemason), and John Stewart (the blacksmith)—who profited handsomely from their association with the Pynchons. These were enterprising and determined individuals, men who recognized the possibilities offered by Pynchon and made the most of their chance.[12]

That their efforts—and his own ventures—enriched Pynchon even more, there can be no doubt. His £8,000 estate at death alone attests to that. But, like entrepreneurs in any age, Pynchon had the most to lose as well as the most to gain. In a time before the protection of investments offered by insurance, Pynchon's capital holdings were exceedingly vulnerable, particularly after the mid-1670s when the threat of Indian attack loomed continuously. It was *his* gristmill and sawmills, not the town's, that the Indians destroyed during the October 1675 attack. He was sorely tempted to retreat to the comfort and safety of Boston in that troublesome winter, perhaps for good. But, as he told the governor in a letter, such an action would have meant that "ale will fale here." Even during peaceful times, the entrepreneur stood to suffer financially if he didn't directly oversee his enterprises in order to ensure that all was being run efficiently. Rejecting a plea that he travel to Albany in the summer of 1666 to negotiate with the Indians, Pynchon told Connecticut Governor John Winthrop, Jr. that "myself having work men about a Mill [I] cannot well be absent without great loss at this tyme."[13]

Pynchon was a resource who could be used or abused. He offered his clients credit, access to outside markets, work, and leases for land, housing, livestock, and equipment. Those who availed themselves of his services thereby put themselves at risk. With luck—and pluck—they could translate these opportunities into genuine financial gains. But more failed than succeeded. These were the men who took the risk and ended up losing their gamble—and often their house and land as well. For them, a continuously mounting indebtedness ledger at the general store meant a life of no little anxiety and travail. For these individuals, the corporatist security offered by the less commercially oriented communities might have

[12] I am indebted to Fred V. Carstensen for helping to clarify these points.

[13] Mass. Archives, 68, p. 6; John Pynchon to John Winthrop, Jr., July 17, 1666, Winthrop Mss.

been appealing indeed. Fewer opportunities meant fewer risks, and a correspondingly higher level of psychic ease.[14]

It is reasonable to conclude, therefore, that a person's attitude toward John Pynchon was colored by his financial condition, and views probably ranged from willing fealty to grudging obeisance. Those men who enjoyed a modicum of success—or more—were presumably grateful for the opportunities offered by their affiliation with Pynchon. To these men, he was a benefactor. To the others, however, men done in by their circumstances or their character, Pynchon's influence must have seemed blighting and oppressive. One can readily imagine the corrosive effects on personal happiness, family harmony, and neighborly relationships posed by economic dependency. We can envision, although not document, the anxious (sometimes desperate) conversations between husband and wife once the children were safely bedded down for the evening. Likewise, we can imaginatively recreate the sense of despair over impending foreclosures that would negate the toil of a decade or more. The potential damage to neighborhood reciprocity and obligations towards coreligionists in the church seems equally obvious.[15]

To some men, accordingly, Pynchon doubtless appeared grasping and possibly tyrannical. His monopoly of just about everything of major value in the community must have been a source of periodic frustration for many, perhaps most, of the town's inhabitants. Entrepreneurs are not always popular and American history is littered with business tycoons fiercely traduced in their day.[16] But, judged by the tenor of his time, Pynchon does not come off badly. While not a particularly warm man, and occasionally given to rigidity, and bouts of extreme self-pity ("all peckt at the Captain of our Salvation," and the like), he overall emerges as a decent, determined, and forthright individual. His account books show no evidence of duplicity or double-dealing, and he surely had ample opportunity for both. Likewise, in his treatment of debtors and tenants he appears to have been no worse than even-handed. For non-clients he could be draconian in enforcing contractual obli-

[14] Robert Redfield, *The Little Community* and *Peasant Society and Culture*, Chicago, 1967, pp. 66–80.

[15] For a recent study of the relationship between economic change and religious sensibilities, see Patricia J. Tracy, *Jonathan Edwards, Pastor: Religion and Society in Eighteenth-Century Northampton*, New York, 1980, pp. 147–170; see also Richard L. Bushman, *From Puritan to Yankee: Character and the Social Order in Connecticut, 1690–1765*, New York, 1970, pp. 3–195.

[16] Richard Hofstadter, *Social Darwinism in American Thought*, New York, 1959, pp. 105–122.

gations, but he did not go *beyond* the law for his own advantage. And for clients, he modified contracts on their, not his, behalf. On several occasions he seized the encumbered estates of impoverished widows, but he followed this up by employing the family's children in his household. Compared to the landlords of East Anglia or the merchants on Fleet Street, Pynchon can be accused neither of rack-renting nor rapacity. The same is true for comparisons from later periods. While nineteenth-century rents usually amounted to from one-third to one-half of annual yield, his leases rarely exceeded ten percent of yield. Tenancy *was* dysfunctional in a frontier society because of the lost labor investment, but that responsibility cannot be laid exclusively at Pynchon's door. He did not force anyone to rent. By the same token, he was often exceedingly indulgent with client debtors, foregoing collection for extended periods or forgiving them entirely, and increasing the prices he paid to settle when he took the land. This solicitude, as we have seen, was partly motivated by his needs for skilled artisans and sufficient numbers of reapers. But, as Pynchon's frequent allusions to the hand of the Lord attest, he believed himself to be among the godly, and there is no reason to doubt that Christian restraint and charity ameliorated his economic dealings. That his commercial and speculative activities brought hardships (and even ruin) to some, there can be no question. We have seen too many sobering examples in these pages to believe otherwise. The texture of Pynchon's negotiations with his clients, however, suggests that, but for his restraint, things would have been a good deal worse.

Both Christian charity and economic self-interest argued for such restraint. The general store, like any paternalistic enterprise, functioned as a safety valve as well as a safety net. By deferring foreclosures, forgiving debts, ignoring unpaid rents, or hiring workers in the off-season, Pynchon blunted the force of any potential class discontent. There were, after all, no tenant rebellions in Springfield, in contrast to the Hudson Valley, which was riven with agrarian unrest throughout the eighteenth century.[17] Moreover, Springfield did not experience an atypically high level of out-migration during the seventeenth century. If the opportunities and conditions were discernibly better elsewhere, more would have left.

That more did not do so is a phenomenon worthy of note. Springfielders, even those experiencing genuine destitution, did not live lives of unrelieved desperation. They apparently believed that the future would bring better things. That for many this hope was

---

[17] Mark, *Agrarian Conflicts*, pp. 13–163; Lynd, *Dutchess County*, pp. 1–54.

chimerical we know, but they would not be the last Americans to see the hardships of the present as but the necessary prologue to eventual success.[18] The hope that the wheel of fortune will ultimately turn in one's favor is the most powerful damper on class discontent. It is only the abridgment of hope that brings the rumblings of rebellion.[19]

But, to turn to the second implication of this study, this meant that Springfield's inhabitants sacrificed political autonomy—as well as corporate solidarity—on the altar of economic opportunity. Pynchon's dominion over the economic activities of his dependents diminished their political independence at every turn. Whether they were filing into the meetinghouse for an important debate, choosing the church deacons for the coming year, or gathering on the green to elect new militia officers, these men were never wholly autonomous. The practice of voice voting at town meetings, of course, made anonymity impossible. With John Pynchon always wielding the moderator's gavel in the meeting, it would have taken unusual bravery for dependent men to defy his wishes. Outright intimidation, arm-twisting, or even veiled threats were all unnecessary in these situations. And, as the records reveal, these were not tactics likely to be favored by Pynchon. The most invidious dimension of economic dependency was that it was self-inhibiting. Pynchon needed to do nothing, save gaze impassively down from the dais. For men lacking the self-confidence offered by self-employment and a debt-free estate, acquiescence in the decisions of their social superiors was the better part of valor.[20]

Third, there is the question of personal ambition and its effect on the meaning of community in early Springfield. At first blush, it seems less than surprising that migrants to the New World were personally ambitious. The men and women who settled Springfield left home and hearth to brave the terrors of the trans-Atlantic voyage with only the foggiest idea what lay ahead. Once in America they endured famine, Indian attack, and bankruptcy in forging a town out of a wilderness. Their motives in taking on this formidable task were myriad. Some came voluntarily, others as war captives. Some were devoutly religious, others not, and given the complexity of human nature, it is probably fruitless to seek a precise spectrum of motivation. But, as Richard Hofstadter (among others) has pointed out, the migration apparently acted as a kind of sieve, drawing

[18] Stephan Thernstrom, *Poverty and Progress: Social Mobility in a Nineteenth Century City*, New York, 1975, pp. 138–165.

[19] Crane Brinton, *The Anatomy of Revolution*, New York, 1965, p. 30.

[20] Gilmore, *People of the Plain*, pp. 51–127.

from the Old World its most ambitious, daring, unillusioned, and tough-minded people.[21] These were not passive "peasants" given to accepting the concept of a "limited good."[22] If Europe was largely populated by such people in the seventeenth century, they were not the ones who left for America. The men and women who came to Springfield—as their patterns of work, land acquisition, and social behavior reveal—came to the New World to get ahead. That they were acquisitive is not to deny that they were religious. Springfielders would have had little trouble accepting Samuel Johnson's aphorism that "There are few ways in which a man can be more innocently employed than in making money." As Max Weber and many others have pointed out, godly people often expect to be successful. Working hard and long to gain a patrimony for their children was not sinful for Springfield's early settlers. It was only when material goals became all-consuming that they became destructive.[23]

This acquisitiveness helps explain the weakness of communalism in highly commercialized towns like Springfield. Because theirs was an acquisitive—not merely materialistic—society, it tolerated diversity and heterogeneity. Rather than warning out a skilled artisan who was also a lecher and a drunk, the villagers profited by his skills and tried to minimize his excesses. Hence the high level of social conflict. Holistic, homogeneous communities are intolerant because they judge a person by his totality. Status, birth, wealth, education, or kinship, as well as diligence, self-discipline, temperance, honesty, and the like are assessed in determining one's acceptability.[24] Behavior in one sphere of activity affects all others. The fact that a cooper was a philanderer made him ineligible to pack one's furs. But Springfield was not a holistic community, only an economic community, based on skill and willingness to work. The key here, of course, is that Springfield's was a wage labor, not a manorial, economy. As Robert L. Heilbroner puts it, the "wage labor system in which workers are hired for a given length of time

---

[21] *America at 1750*, pp. 64–65.

[22] Two valuable, and contrasting, evaluations of the putative "peasant mentality" are Samuel L. Popkin, *The Rational Peasant: The Political Economy of Rural Society in Vietnam*, Berkeley, 1981; and James C. Scott, *The Moral Economy of the Peasant: Rebellion and Subsistence in Southeast Asia*, New Haven, 1981.

[23] Even the migratory servants to the Chesapeake studied by James Horn, although apparently defeated at every turn in their travels from city to city in search of work, had the forbearance to push on rather than remain in England to become public charges; see Horn, "Servant Emigration to the Chesapeake," Tate and Ammerman, eds., *The Chesapeake*, pp. 94–95.

[24] Carstensen, personal communication.

and then released from their 'servant' status effectively creates an 'economy' distinct from a 'society.' "[25] Separate spheres of activity were judged independently of one another. The hiring criterion was degree of skill, not personal probity. John Pynchon was impersonal in hiring in that he based evaluations of people on utilitarian, not holistic criteria. Unlike Old World patronage, this was one-dimensional. It was an economic-political axis, not a social, cultural, and spiritual one. Pynchon hired and fired on the basis of skillfulness and diligence, and a man's behavior out of the workplace was his concern, not Pynchon's. Social conflict in Springfield, therefore, was the reverse side of Pynchon's one-dimensional patronage.

The Springfield experience, in the larger frame, shows that migration to the New World brought a critical step toward the separation of spheres of authority that Weber characterizes as the legal/rational society. It is a world of individuals, not a community. The town's development corresponds with what J. M. Cameron has described as "the moment of transition from the old view of man as finding his fulfillment in his social role to the new view of man 'as an individual prior to and apart from all roles'—the transition, as Sir Henry Maine put it, 'from status to contract.' " And this transition came first in the New, not the Old World, as "it is only with the late eighteenth and early nineteenth centuries in Europe that we arrive at the notion of man as having moral substance apart from and prior to *all* social roles, as, for example, in the work of James Mill."[26] Such individualistic relationships, as Springfield vividly reveals, invite a society that was both litigious and market-oriented.

This brings us back to the question, posed at the outset, of how patron-client ties formed the bridge from the world of the manor to the world of the market, from master-servant bonds to those of employer-employee. The answer is that merchant-entrepreneurs like John Pynchon were not patriarchs responsible for *all* members of the community, but patrons answerable only to those selected individuals who had something to offer to—and gain from—an association with him. Because these were face-to-face relationships, they harkened back to manorial practices, but because at heart they were contractual and impersonal they prefigured—if they did not announce—the triumph of the market economy.

[25] "The Demand for the Supply Side," *The New York Review of Books* (June 11, 1981), p. 38.

[26] J. M. Cameron, "Can We Live the Good Life?", *The New York Review of Books* (November 5, 1981), pp. 45–46.

When viewed in the larger historical setting, it was not Springfield's commercialism but rather Dedham's corporatism that appears anomalous. Springfield's settlement and development fits naturally within the overall expansion of capitalism and empire in sixteenth- and seventeenth-century England. John Pynchon's construction of elaborate patron-client relations and his use of political privilege to gain enormous economic power within a new society are part of the story of late Elizabethan and Stuart mercantile expansion. Similar patterns developed in both Virginia and Ireland. The parallels with Ireland seem particularly inviting. There, too, a few people gained disproportionate control over land and rented it out to tenants, whose labor was extorted through the exaction of rent. Historians of Ireland stress that landlord-tenant relationships were a major barrier to agricultural improvement, because the tenant's efforts redounded only to the benefit of the exploiting landlord. This parallel suggests that the cast of Springfield is a cautionary tale of how New England might not have become so "exceptional" after all, how it could have gone the way of Ireland or old England if the fur supply had not run out or if a staple crop had been found. The Pynchons clearly were responsive to the mercantilist currents of their time. William Pynchon's condemnation of fur monopolies suggests that he favored a world of freer trade. Such ideas were taking root in the seventeenth century, yet could also be conjoined with patron-client exploitation under the notion that "free" contract was the basis of economic relationships. The merchant-entrepreneurs of the New World were laying the economic foundations of a liberal tradition at the same time that they were looking back to a manorial past.[27]

Finally, there is the question of the Glorious Revolution and its impact on the subsequent direction of social change. The overthrow of the Dominion, it seems, both prevented the possibility for a genuine gentry class in eighteenth-century New England and served as a dress rehearsal for 1776.[28] The eclipse of the old elites and their replacement by royal appointees brought in its train demands by the "common sort" for self-government and self-determination. Militiamen like James King publicly demanded leaders of "their own choosing." To use Locke's phrasing, after 1689 men such as King had "Confidence to turn [their] wishes into *demands*." But as things became more democratic at the local level, they became less

[27] I am indebted to Robert A. Gross for his contribution to these observations.

[28] David S. Lovejoy reached the same conclusion in "Two American Revolutions, 1689 and 1776," in J.G.A. Pocock, ed., *Three British Revolutions: 1641, 1688, 1776*, Princeton, N. J., 1980, pp. 244–262.

so at the colony level with the radical centralization of the flow of authority under the second charter. The "new men" who attempted to replace the Pynchons as leaders found themselves having to serve two contradictory masters: the Crown and their constituents. All was fine so long as public policy at both the local and provincial levels was in accord. But when the royal officials tried to implement unpalatable legislation—as they did between 1765 and 1776—the fragility of the system would be starkly revealed. Those local leaders who remained loyal to the Crown saw their community support evaporate with astonishing rapidity. The midcentury counterpart to John Pynchon in Springfield, Colonel John Worthington, learned this to his dismay during the Revolutionary crisis. Although he had long held a number of important civil, judicial, and military positions in the community, Worthington's continued fealty to the King brought expulsion from all town affairs and a hooting mob to the door. Among those who supplanted Worthington in the town's new leadership elite were two of the fifth generation of Pynchons, Charles and William. Ending the eclipse in local affairs their family had experienced since the turn of the century, they reemerged as leaders on the committee of correspondence and the committee of safety. Once again Pynchons were at the helm of local government in Springfield—but now under the mantle of republicanism.

The process of social, as well as political, change from the seventeenth to the eighteenth century is, therefore, in need of recasting. The communal, egalitarian, and quietistic models of the seventeenth century *do* make the later period seem considerably more factious and stratified. But if two of the three settlement zones in early New England—the coastal ports and the highly commercialized towns like Springfield—behaved in an acquisitive, market-oriented, and contentious manner in the seventeenth century, we cannot explain the Revolution by the sudden appearance of such behavior after 1740. Central to most of the existing arguments is an emphasis on an apparently dramatic rise in both wealth and poverty in the generation after the Great Awakening. While this study does not include an assessment of the distribution of wealth during the pre-Revolutionary generation, we do know that no one after 1703 remotely compared to John Pynchon in either wealth or influence. When the Pynchons lost their preeminence after the turn of the century, eager claimants—the Parsons, Hitchcocks, Dwights, and Worthingtons—arose to bid for the fealty of the general populace.[29] Accordingly, it seems reasonable to argue that

---

[29] Christine Leigh Heyrman, in her forthcoming study of Gloucester and Mar-

access to both land and political power came easier for ordinary inhabitants in the eighteenth century than before. By the same token, while religious and political disputes and community fragmentation continued into the 1740s and beyond, dissenters could now channel their energies into new churches or new precincts, rather than fighting it out in the old meetinghouse. Indeed, it seems possible to believe that it was the strength and unity of the New Englanders, not their privation and factionalism, that allowed them to stand successfully against the British in 1776.

---

blehead during the eighteenth century, likewise finds these communities becoming more, not less, harmonious as the Revolution approached. *Commerce and Culture: The Maritime Communities of Colonial Massachusetts, 1690–1750*, New York, 1983. See also, Gregory H. Nobles, *'Divisions Throughout the Whole': Politics and Society in Hampshire County, Massachusetts, 1740–1775*, New York, 1982, Chapter 1; and William Pencak, *War, Politics, and Revolution in Provincial Massachusetts*, Boston, 1981.

Index

TABLES

Multiple Career Analysis
and Dependency Tables,
1646–1703

Abbreviations:

AB	John Pynchon's Account Books
Bush	Bushel
D.	Died
HCPCR	Hampshire County Probate Court Recs.
Hhd.	Hogshead
JP	John Pynchon
Li	Pound (weight)
Pt	Part
PCR	*Pynchon Court Rec.*
Sp.	Springfield
TR	*Springfield Town Recs.*
Val.	Valued
WP	William Pynchon
WPAB	William Pynchon Account Book
Wt	Wheat

TABLE I, 1646
MULTIPLE CAREER ANALYSIS
Source: 1646 Tax List

Name   *Career Patterns*

Robert Ashley   D. Sp. 1684; estate val. at £404; selectman 10 terms.
  Occupations: Farmer, sawyer, horse trader. On April 18, 1668, JP credited
  him for "all your land [at Westfield] and the sawing of 200 of board
  I am to allow him . . . £35"; also credited for "34 bush. of wheate . . .
  26 bush wt . . . 194 li porke at 3d. per li . . . 2 days worke at the Mill
  . . . Carting for the Saw Mill Planks . . . fetching 2 load Pease" and
  "50 bush of wheat at 3s. 10d."

Debtor: On November 12, 1663, Ashley indebted to JP for £11 for "his pt of the land [at Westfield]."
Citations: 1AB, 95; 2AB, 346; 3AB, 152–153, 170–171; 1HCPCR, 227.

Francis Ball   Drowned in Connecticut River, 1648.
Occupation: Blacksmith.

Reice Bedortha   D. Sp. 1684; estate val. at £213.
Occupations: Farmer, tanner, sawyer. In one AB entry received credit for "332 li porke at 3d. . . . 30 Bush wheate . . . By loading my canoe with corne 3 times," "By a yoake of oxen £11 10s. . . . 1 day worke raising my Barne," "By a yoak of oxen now at Nath Burts £10 15s."
Debtor: In 1654 promised to bring JP a "certaine Calfe" and "20 bush of good wheate" toward the debt "within a month." On June 26, 1663, JP sold him tanning house (earlier taken for debts from Griffith Jones) and the contiguous 3-acre lot for £15 within 3 years; purchase price to be paid in wheat at 3s. 6d.; November 1663, in debt to JP for £32 12s. 10d.; in 1667 lost "his Howse and home lot of 4 acres, the Tan howse . . . 3 acres of wet medow and 4 acres woodlot even all his land and housing on this side of the great River" for debts of £32; in 1681 lost share in sawmill at 3 mile brook for debt of £4 and additional £4 given by JP.
Renter: Leased pasture, lot in 3rd division.
Citations: 1AB, 65–66; 2AB, 316; 3AB, 146–147; 5AB, 26, 548–549; 1HCPCR, 226.

Nathaniel Bliss   D. Sp. 1655; estate val. at £54.
Citations: 4HCPCR, 232–233.

William Branch   D. Sp. 1683.
Occupations: Farmer, barber, laborer. AB entry of January 9, 1664/65, JP "agreed with Wm. Branch for filling in my ditch and laying it levell [for] 20s. both sides. And the ditch at the Northside which he set Cast and Stub it and cleare it and lay it plaine . . . and the Carting of the wood . . . He is to ditch in that I have bought of Goodm Morgan for wch I am to give him 15d. per Rod . . . This which he hath done is 32 Rod"; in late 1660s was paid for "Barbing my folks 5s. 5d. . . . Barbing 5 psons this yeare Past . . . doeing fence in the lot 2s. 6d.";
occasional renter.
Debtor: In 1665 Barber lost 8-acre meadow to JP for £30 "in setling of what he owes me."
Citations: 1AB, 298–299; 2AB, 71, 343; 3AB, 140–141, 319; 5AB, 83, 100.

James Bridgman   D. Northampton 1676; in Sp. 1643 to 1654; emigrated to Northampton thereafter.
Citations: 1HCPCR, 169.

Henry Burt   D. Sp. 1662; estate val. at £182, with £49 in debts payable; selectman for 10 terms.

Citations: 1HCPCR, 17; 1TR, 26–39.

Samuel Chapin   D. Sp. 1676; selectman for 11 terms; magistrate's commission; first deacon of the church; after William Pynchon, Henry Smith,
and Elizur Holyoke, fourth most powerful man in the town in 1646.
Occupation: Farmer.
Citations: PCR. 62; 1TR, 26–39.

John Clarke   D. Sp. 1684; estate val. at £315.
Occupations: Farmer, canoeman, agricultural laborer. In mid-1660s AB
    entry, Clark was paid for "reaping . . . Bringing up Salt [from Enfield
    falls] 8 firkins of Soap and other worke 18s. and Scouring the Ditch
    . . . worke at the Mill Trench this summer 1666: 35 days himself and
    45 days his son . . . at 2s."
Debtor: On November 6, 1663, JP "Acoted with John Clarke and he owes
    me . . . Twenty Pounds sterling wch he promises and ingages to pay
    me in some short tyme about £7 of it being for goods lately dlrd he
    engageth wheate this winter at 3s. 6d. bush . . . being old debt."
Renter: On April 3, 1667, JP "Let out to John Clarke the lot (which was
    Powells) . . . [for] 30s. for this yeare . . . [and] 35s. [thereafter] in such
    Corne as grows on it."
Citations: 2AB, 190; 3AB, 107; 2HCPCR, 34.

George Colton   D. Sp. 1690; estate val. at £847; lieutenant in militia;
deputy 3 terms; selectman 18 terms.
Occupation: Farmer.
Citations: 1AB, 140; 2AB, 246–247; 3AB, 60; 3HCPCR, 68–70; 1TR,
    26–39.

Benjamin Cooley   D. Sp. 1684; estate val. at £1,241; selectman 19 terms;
ensign in militia.
Occupations: Farmer, weaver.
Occasional Renter: On November 25, 1662, paid JP for rent of ground
    "you have in the Long meddow this last yeare . . . [and] 11s. goes for
    the Rent of the Land in Long meddow 2 yrs."
Citations: 2AB, 304–305; 2HCPCR, 25, 37; 1TR, 26–39.

Thomas Cooper   D. Sp. 1675; killed during Indian attack; estate val. at
£287; deputy 1 term; selectman 20 terms.
Occupations: Fur trader, carpenter, farmer.
JP's Fur Agent/Debtor: JP supplied him with trading cloth and wampum;
    Cooper repaid JP with furs received from the Indians; on June 27,
    1652, Cooper received credit for "348 skins of Bever weighing 452 li
    and ½ at 9s. 4d. per li is £211 3s. 4d. . . . 8 otters [at] £3 17s."; on
    April 26, 1653, Cooper was paid for "stringing 212 fad and ½ [of]
    wampam . . . for Reaping . . . Mill worke . . . helping to pack my hhds";
    on May 6, 1652, JP "Sold him the commoditys here following to be
    paid in Bever at current price or in good wampam sometime in the
    year . . . 107 yds of Red Shag Cotton at 3s. per yard £16 1s., 2 doz.

cotton stockens at 26s. per doz . . . 6 doz. knives . . . 4 doz. sissors at ⅜ . . . 107 fadam of white wampam at 5s. per fadam . . . 321 fadam of white wampam . . . Binding tape Needles Points & c:" on October 1, 1656, Cooper's outstanding debits to JP stood at £1,000; Cooper's purchases continued to exceed his returns and he remained indebted to JP for the remainder of his life.

Carpenter: On February 28, 1645, Cooper contracted with the town to construct the first meetinghouse, for a price of £80, to be paid in wheat, pork, peas, wampum, debts, or labor.

Renter: On February 26, 1665/66, JP "Let out to Ensigne Tho Cooper my meddow lot on the South side of Agawam river, only reserving Ten acres of it to my selfe for mowing . . . the rest of my land there, Ensigne Cooper is to have for the Terme of Seven Yeares, with Liberty for Plowing Sowing or mowing it provided he doe not breake up the meddow or mowing land" for rental payments graded from £6 to £8 annually; held land for 7 years; total payments, £50.

Citations: 1AB, 78–80, 221, 326; 3AB, 51, 100–101; 1HCPCR, 167; 1TR, 26–39.

Alexander Edwards   From Wales; emigrated to Northampton 1655; purchased goods and marketed produce at JP's general store, even after departure from Sp.; on October 19, 1663, JP "Acoted and rests due to mee from Alex Edwards the sum of Sixteene Pounds, three shillings," which Edwards agreed to pay in wheat or "good fine flower" by the next spring; in early 1670s he received credit for "keeping Capt Clarks horse 2 winters . . . [and] 55 bush of wheate . . . Porke 441 li at 2d. ¾."

Citations: 2AB, 274; 3AB, 207.

Richard Excell   D. Sp. 1714.

Occupations: Agricultural laborer, canoeman, farmer. Performed manual labor for JP on a regular basis, transporting goods to Enfield falls, mowing, reaping, ditching, sawing, fencing, etc.; early 1650s, JP paid him for "a voyadge downe the falls . . . mowing 8 acres ¾ . . . 2 days Mowing Barly . . . 1 day Reaping"; on April 5, 1665, JP "Agreed with Rich Exsell to doe 30 rod of ditching . . . for one 20 Rod of it I have already pd him 2 yds of Trading cloth."

Citations: 1AB, 85; 3AB, 171.

John Harmon   D. Sp. 1661; estate val. at £104, with debts payable of £15.

Occupations: Farmer, sawyer, laborer, carter. In 1646 WP paid him for "20 days reaping"; in October of 1656, JP paid him for "Plowing 7 acres . . . 5 acres [more] at 9s. per acre . . . 12 days of worke . . . by carting, two Journey to the falls . . . carting a load of pease . . . Hedging"; in November 1657, JP paid him £8 18s. for "Plowing, carting, reaping [as well as a] Beife and 2 oxhides"; in 1659 he took 13s. for "8 days worke reaping and haying" and in 1660 he earned 35s. for sawing "500 of boards at 7s."

Debtor: On September 20, 1663, JP and Harmon's widow agreed that "for wch debt of £15 10s. shee doth for my security make over and firmly ingage . . . betwixt 14 and 15 acres . . . wch land I am to have provided I am not pd this debt within a Twelve month or there abouts"; by 1669, £2 17s. remained to be paid on debt; land released to sons John and Joseph.

Citations: WPAB, 91; 1AB, 328; 2AB, 35, 292–293; 3AB, 98; 1HCPCR, 6.

Elizur Holyoke   D. Sp. 1676; estate val. at £1,271, including 535 acres in the town of Lynn, Massachusetts; deputy 6 terms, clerk of writs, and recorder for Hampshire County; selectman 10 terms; member of every significant town committee; his father described by John Eliot as "Mr. [William] Pynchon's ancient friend"; married William Pynchon's daughter Mary on November 20, 1640.

Occupations: Farmer, miller.

Debtor: On December 29, 1668, for debts of £121 18s. 8d., JP took Holyoke's interest in a cornmill.

Citations: 1AB, 59, 63; 3AB, 43–45; 5AB, 11, 501; 1HCPCR, 173; PCR, 60–64; 1TR, 26–39; 2TR, 22.

Griffith Jones   D. Sp. 1677; estate val. at £119 with debts payable of £34.

Occupations: Tanner, farmer.

Debtor: On November 21, 1661, Jones indebted to JP for £53; lost tannery for it; see chap. 3.

Renter: On January 22, 1672/73, JP "Lett out to Griffith Jones: a yoake of young Cattle that wch I bought of him" for 30s. yearly; on March 10, 1672/73, JP rented Jones bottom land in 3rd division for 4 days work mowing; on October 28, 1674, Jones leased 4 acres over the river at 6s. per acre.

Citations: 1AB, 71; 2AB, 173; 5AB, 44–45; 1HCPCR, 192.

John Leonard   D. Sp. 1676; estate val. at £190.

Occupations: Farmer, occasional laborer. AB entry in 1652, received credit for "20 bush of wheate . . . 3½ days (almost) Mowing . . . a little steer . . . 1 day himself and his boy in harvest."

Debtor: On December 15, 1657, JP wrote "John Leanord hath sold me his foure oxen . . . for the payment of the debt [of £22 14s.] only he desires and I consented to . . . that he should keepe the oxen till Aprill 1660, and then to deliver them to mee well and sound, then he is to dlr them or make the debt good"; on January 14, 1666, JP "Recd . . . the cattle per contra toward the debt the sum of £15 18s. so rests £8"; again on October 5, 1672, Leonard sold JP oxen valued at £11.

Citations: 1AB, 97–98; 3AB, 192; 5AB, 65; 1HCPCR, 174.

John Lumbard   D. Sp. 1672; estate val. at £133, including total of 34 acres of land.

Occupation: Livestock farmer. At death owned 2 oxen, 2 cows, 2 steers, and a calf.

Citations: 1HCPCR, 140.

John Mathews D. Sp. 1684; estate val. at £8; heavily indebted.

Occupations: Cooper, sawyer. Mathews constructed the barrels the Pynchons used to ship beaver hides and pork to Hartford, Boston, London, and the West Indies; paid a portion of rent for land he leased from JP in "10 good tight barrels"; see chap. 4.

Debtor: Lost all land and housing to JP for debts.

Renter: Paid £71 for 35 contract years; rental career extended from 1663 to 1679; leased 7½ acres of meadow in the neck (between Agawam and Connecticut Rivers), 5 acres of plowland, 2 cows, 4-acre homelot, house, orchard, and 2½ acres of wet meadow (bought from him).

Miscl: Fined for assault, drunkenness, slander; lost child to town and ended up as a public charge.

Citations: 2AB, 99, 312; 3AB, 86–87, 283; 5AB, 118–119, 486–487; PCR, 243, 249; 2TR, 147–148, 152–153; 2HCPCR, 30–31.

Thomas Mirrick From Wales; d. Sp. 1704.

Occupations: Canoeman, farmer, agricultural laborer. In 1664 and 1665, JP paid Mirrick for "carying down 89 bush wheat [to Enfield falls] . . . carying 180 bush from the foote of the falls . . . bringing up 1 Tun Goods . . . bringing up 12 bush of Salt at 6d. . . . By your Teame loading the canoes at the wharfe," "14 days worke at the Mill."

Miscl: Disputatious; see chap. 5.

Citations: 1AB, 100; 3AB, 111–113; 5AB, 111.

Miles Morgan From Wales; d. Sp. 1699; selectman 5 terms.

Occupations: Canoeman, farmer. Regularly employed by JP; in June 1661, received credit for "5 voyadges downe the falls with Ed Foster when you caryd wheat at 4d. per bush and brought up goods at 12s. per tun"; entries for "carriage of Corne downe the falls . . . carying downe Corne several voyadges . . . carting down a load of corne . . . goeing down [the] falls with Sam Terry . . . carying downe the falls 243 bush ½ wheat at 5d. . . . 142 Mooseskins at 4d. . . . 10 barrels of meat at 2s. . . . Bringing up 19 bush ½ Salt at 6d. . . . carting Timber for the Boards for the house of correction . . . for carying downe in May 1666, 100 bush wheat and bringing up 10 bush salt," "Carying down Corn 577 bushels."

Citations: 1AB, 76–77, 265–266; 2AB, 131, 335, 339; 3AB, 143, 240–241; 4AB, 79; 5AB, 81.

George Moxon Town's first minister; Cambridge graduate; ordained in 1626, censured as a Puritan by the Bishop of Chester while serving in a Lancastershire parish; returned to England with WP in 1652.

Citations: PCR, 12.

James Osborne   D. Hartford 1676; emigrated after 1672.
  Occupations: Farmer, laborer. During 1650s, JP paid him for "19 days
    worke . . . 23 days worke . . . 6 days threshing, and wintering sheep."
  Debtor/Renter: On April 25, 1663, JP "Let out to James Osborne that
    howse and land which I had of widow Burt, for the space and time
    of Two yeares" for £3 10s. annually; on November 16, 1663, JP and
    Osborne agreed that if Osborne could pay JP £10 yearly for four
    years, he could have the farm for his own at the end of that time; on
    November 7, 1665, Thomas Powell took over payments from Osborne
    who was credited with only £1 4s. 5d.; by the mid 1660s, Osborne was
    unable to cope with his indebtedness to JP and others; in February
    1666/67 the town meeting intervened, declaring that "it is . . . mutually
    aggreed by the Inhabitants that . . . James Osborne doth prejudice
    him self and his family by disadvantagious bargaynes. It is therefore
    voted and concluded that none of the Inhabitants of this Town shall
    or will make any bargayne with the said James Osborne without con-
    sent of 2 or 3 of the Select men that shall amount to above 10s. value."
  Citations: 1AB, 249; 2AB, 276–277; 3AB, 14, 100–101; 5AB, 121; 1TR,
    359.

Hugh Parsons   D. Watertown, Massachusetts 1675.
  Occupations: Bricklayer, sawyer. Accused of witchcraft in early 1650s;
    wife Mary, who was his principal accuser, also tried for witchcraft;
    Hugh Parsons left Springfield permanently after witchcraft contro-
    versy; see chap. 5.
  Citations: Drake, *Annals of Witchcraft*, 219–256.

Joseph Parsons   D. Sp. 1683; estate val. at £2,088; lived in Northampton
  1656–1679; cornet in militia.
  Occupation: Fur trader/merchant. JP's fur agent in Northampton; on
    August 24, 1657, JP "Agreed with Joseph Parsons for the trade at
    Nalwotag [Northampton] and from thence up the River, for which
    he is to allow for this year Ensuing the sum of Twelve Pounds to be
    paid in Bever. The winter bever at 8s. pr lb, the Spring at 9s., and I
    am to furnish him with Trading cloth at 7s. 6d. pr yd and with shag
    cotton at 3s. 7d. pr yd"; on February 4, 1657/58, Parsons indebted to
    JP for £613 17s. 2d.; on June 18, 1658, JP wrote "upon my motion
    Joseph Parsons hast surrendered up to me . . . 20 acres" for £6 10s.;
    on November 26, 1679, JP sold to Parsons for £150 "certaine psells
    of land Late Tim Coopers decd which said John Pynchon is Legally
    possessed [of by] Execution . . . ten acres homelot . . . and seven acres
    and half together with a woodlot of ten acres."
  Citations: 1AB, 330; 2AB, 4–5; 3AB, 215; Deed, JP to Parsons, November
    26, 1679, CVHM; 1HCPCR, 235.

Roger Pritchard   D. 1681 New Haven, Connecticut; emigrated to Milford,
  Connecticut some time after 1651.

William Pynchon   D. England 1662; the founder of Sp.; see chap. 1.

Thomas Reeve   D. Sp. 1650; served as town drummer.
Citations: 2TR, 631.

Richard Sikes   D. Sp. 1676; estate val. at £154, with debts payable of £27; selectman 2 terms.
Occupations: Farmer, carpenter, miller, laborer. Paid by WP in 1646 for "worke in summer 26 days and in winter 9 days at the mill at 20d. and for coggs and rungs at mill [and] Plowing 3 acres ¼ and 16 Rod"; in early 1650s, JP paid Sikes for "making a Plow . . . for making the Meetinghouse stairs . . . the window . . . ladder in the Bell Tower"; in 1656 credited for "grinding 280 bushels at 3d. . . . grinding 392 bushels"; in 1661 was paid for "60 days work . . . 42 days worke"; took £4 16s. in 1663 for "38 days ½ work"; on January 17, 1664/65, JP "Agreed with Rich Sikes to Tend my Mill."
Renter: In 1665, JP "Lett out to Rich Sikes my Plowed Land in the neck being 5 acres"; in addition, Sikes paid £2 15s. for the "hire of the oxen you had of me 1 year and 7 mo."
Citations: WPAB, 46–49; 1AB, 87, 329; 2AB, 28, 187; 3AB, 22, 82–83; 5AB, 135; 1HCPCR, 183.

Henry Smith   D. England 1681 or 1682; son-in-law to William Pynchon; his mother, twice widowed, married William; Sp.'s first town recorder, deputy 1 term; selectman 7 terms; General Court appointed Smith magistrate for Springfield as the successor to William Pynchon; returned to England shortly after Pynchon's departure.
Citations: 1TR, 26–39; 2TR, 637–638.

John Stebbins   D. Northampton 1679; emigrated to Northampton 1656.
Occupations: Farmer, fur trader, canoeman, carpenter, laborer. In 1646 WP paid him for "carying downe 30 bushels of wheate . . . his share of a Tun and ½ [of goods brought up from falls] . . . 13½ days [work] at 20d. . . . mowing 4 acres . . . making hay his wife 9 days"; credited in 1648 for "stringing 404 fadam of wampam . . . 14 days Summer work at 20d. . . . 4 days winter work at 16d"; on October 25, 1661, JP made agreement with him "for shingling the howse of correction"; in 1668 JP paid him £13 10s. for "shingling Mr. Whiting's house at Westfield with the back room."
Citations: WPAB, 55, 185; 2AB, 79; 3AB, 223.

Rowland Stebbins   D. 1671 Northampton; emigrated to Northampton after 1664.
Occupations: Farmer, laborer. In mid-1640s credited for "24 days worke," "33 days," "10 days in the Spring"; from 1653 to 1657 was paid, at various times, for "33 days ½ worke this summer . . . summer worke 18 days at 18d. and 30 days at 20d. . . . 24 days worke . . . 51 days work."
Citations: WPAB, 81–83; 1AB, 109–110.

Thomas Stebbins   D. Sp. 1683; estate val. at £294; selectman 3 terms, lieutenant in militia.

Occupations: Tailor, farmer, laborer. Stebbins indebted to JP for over £40 from 1663 to 1677; total debt in 1677 set at £57; leased 3¾-acre lot, oxen, and 2-acre meadow; used JP's bull as stud; see chap. 4.

Citations: 1AB, 90; 2AB, 299; 3AB, 130–131, 165; 5AB, 97; 1HCPCR, 233. 1TR, 26–39.

Rowland Thomas   D. Sp. 1697; estate val. at £199; selectman 3 terms.

Occupations: Stonemason, canoeman, laborer. AB entries in mid-1660s credit him for "63 days worke . . . 36 load of stone . . . 8 days and ½ about Levelling my ground," "for 8 days worke in the orchard and underpinning . . . goeing to Hadley . . . Triming my hedge . . . 36 days work at the Mill Trench . . . 4 days ditching"; see chap. 4.

Debtor: On March 1, 1667/68, for debts of £48, JP took Thomas's "land . . . about 50 [acres] whereof 5 or 6 acres of meddow and 6 or 7 Plowed acrs and house."

Citations: 1AB, 73–74; 3AB, 158–159, 197; 3HCPCR, 46.

Thomas Thompson   Emigrated in late 1640s.

William Vaughan   Emigrated in late 1640s.

William Warrinar   D. Sp. 1676; estate val. at £166; selectman 2 terms.

Occupations: Canoeman, farmer. In 1638 WP paid him £8 for "three quarters of yeere"; in 1645 credited for "34 days winter worke"; in 1664 paid by JP for "carying downe Corne and bringing up Goods with G. Morgan . . . 3 Journys your cart to the foote of the falls one Journy your Teame . . . Bringing up 50 bush salt from the wharfe . . . more 20 bush salt from the wharfe . . . carying 20 bush wt to the foote of the falls and bringing up Boards from fresh water River"; in 1667 credited for "falls worke . . . 216 bush of wheat at 5d. . . . 142 Moose at 4d. . . . 10 barels of wheat at 2s. . . . bringing up 19 bush ½ Salt at 6d."

Debtor: On November 2, 1663, Warrinar indebted to JP for £15 6s. 3d.; for which he gave as security to JP "Twelve acres of land . . . by the Great River" to ensure payment by next summer.

Citations: WPAB, 3, 50; 2AB, 344; 3AB, 133; 1HCPCR, 182; 1TR, 26–39.

Samuel Wright   D. Northampton 1665; emigrated in 1656.

Occupations: Laborer, cobbler, canoeman. In 1646 credited for "49 days ½ [at] 18d.," and in 1647 took £4 10s. for "15 days winter at 16d. [and] . . . 42 days summer [work] at 20d."; in 1648 was paid for "making 7 pair of shoos at 12d., 3 pair at 6d., 4 pair of heeles"; in 1653, credited for "carrying from my house to the foot of the falls 44 bush of wheate . . . 1 day at the mill . . . Reaping and carying Indian [Corne]."

Citations: WPAB, 84–86; 1AB, 111.

TABLE II, 1665
DEPENDENCY

Source: 1665 List of Springfield Inhabitants
Total Inhabitants: 72
Total Dependent: 40
Percent Dependent: 55.6%

Name   *Form of Dependency*

John Bagg

Worker: Logger, shinglemaker, laborer. On November 27, 1660, JP "Agreed with John Bagg to get and deliver me at the wharfe 5 hundred of good substantial Log Poles full 6 foote long . . . [for] 12s. per hundred"; in November 1663 JP agreed with him "to get me 2,000 of good 3 foote shingles at 40s. per 1000"; in 1666 credited for "18 days worke at 2s. 6d. per day."

Debtor: 1676, JP took 60 acres for debts of £44 2s.

Renter: Leased 20-acre lot, 24-acre lot, orchard; paid £21 for 10 contract years.

Citations: 2AB, 80–81, 347; 3AB, 160–161; 5AB, 25–28.

Jonathan Ball

Worker: Laborer, canoeman, ditcher. In 1665, JP wrote "Jonathan Ball came to me the 21 March . . . and he is to be with me 2 month for which I am to allow 20s. per Month"; following this agreement, entries for "carting dung 6 days . . . 2 months work in 1665 per agmt . . . a Journy to N. London and looking up cattle . . . 15 days worke . . . 11 days worke at the Mill . . . 2 days worke sawing . . . fencing at woronoke . . . (Rayls 25s. . . . ditching 9s. . . . Log fence 10s.)"; in early 1670s, was paid for "carying Corne downe the falls . . . bringing up wine, sugar, Cords, etc. . . . 50 Rod of ditch."

Renter: Leased, with Sam Taylor, JP's 80-acre "tenement farme" for £18 annually; also rented, at various times, 11 acres in the 3rd division for £3 8s. annually, 2 acres of meadow, a 1½-acre lot, and a yoke of oxen; rental career extended from 1667–1701; paid £145 for 25 contract years; owned 29 acres in 1685; see chap. 3.

Citations: 3AB, 128–129; 5AB, 40–41, 524–525; 6AB, 18–19; 1685 Tax List.

Thomas Bancroft

Worker: Miller, canoeman, laborer. In August 1654 was paid for "carying of Corne down the falls (3 voyages) . . . bringing up of goods 2 Tun ½"; during 1650s also credited for "mowing 8 days . . . 4 days ½ gardening . . . mowing 5 acres at home, 2 acres over river . . . mowing 5 acres ¾ at 2s. 9d."; was paid in 1665 for "400 of Clapbord . . . floaring my Milstones"; credited in 1680 for "9 days Mowing English grasses . . . floaring and laying my millstones."

Renter: In 1666 leased JP's "Mill and Mill howse for Seven yeares, hee

to Doe all the worke that belongs to it for the ready and well Grinding of the Corne of the Plantation" for annual rental payments of £8 the first year and £13 thereafter; JP's corn to be ground without charge; remainder of inhabitants pay toll directly to Bancroft; 1667, leased JP's 10-acre lot contiguous to mill; 1672, mill rental increased to £18.
Citations: 1AB, 147, 245–246; 2AB, 117; 3AB, 75; 5AB, 233.

Symon Beamon
> *Debtor*: Lost 10 acres to JP for debts in 1655; 1659, JP sold him cow for £4; Beamon unable to meet payment and was forced to rent the animal for 20s. yearly.
> *Renter*: Leased cow, 4½ acres of land, 1½ acres of upland.
> *Worker*: Canoeman, cobbler, laborer. Servant to Pynchons during early 1650s; JP paid him £7 1s. 6d.; in 1655 for "7 voyadges downe the falls"; received payments at various times for "mending shoes . . . 9 days ½ worke in harvest," "34 days worke . . . 19 days worke at 2s.," "worke mending shoos and Blooding horses."
> *Citations*: 1AB, 197, 290–292; 2AB, 88; 3AB, 120.

Reice Bedortha. See Table I.

William Branch. Table I.

William Brooks
> *Worker*: Logger, canoeman, laborer. In December 1660, agreed to deliver JP "500 of good broad and substantial Rayls 11 foote and ½ long . . . and 500 of good broad and substantial log rayls . . . full 6 foote long . . . [and] 500 good cut oak Posts 6 foote long"; in 1663 was paid for "44 Rod of fencing"; in 1675 credited for "carying down barrels . . . 5 weekes worke at Stony River Saw mill."
> *Debtor*: Lost cow to JP for debts, 1658; mortgaged and ultimately lost 10 acres for debt of £12 5s. in 1663; indebted to JP in 1667, Pynchon to "grant him one [more] yeares tyme longer to pay the debt per contra . . . [if not paid] the land to be mine"; 1668, lost two steers for debts, rented them back for 40s. per annum; 1675, "in settling what he owes me," JP took 153 acres from Brooks for debts of £83; 1686, Brooks at JP's house agreed he owed JP £7 6s. "above four years"; see chap. 2.
> *Renter*: Leased cow, steers, and 30 acres; paid for 12 contract years.
> *Citations*: 2AB, 34, 214–215; 3AB, 162–163; 5AB, 27, 308–309.

Thomas Cooper. Table I.

Joseph Crowfoot
> *Debtor/Renter*: 1663, indebted to JP for £6 1s. 3d.; gave him 4 acres over the river by Black Pond as security and "unless Joseph Crowfoote doe pay this Sum of £6.1.3 betwixt this and next Springs wheate at 3s. 6d. bush," land to be JP's; formally surrendered December 7, 1666; Crowfoot then rented 3 of the acres back: "rent of the 3 acres of land you had of me viz. of which I bought of you you having had it this 2 yeare

past"; in 1667, Crowfoot rented additional 10 acres—total annual
payment £4; 1669, leased "yoake of oxen" for one year; paid 40s. and
all rates.

Worker: Performed a variety of manual tasks for JP, "Scouring my ditch,"
"reaping," "mowing oates," "seting up fence," "rayling"; in mid-1660s
was paid for "18 Rod ditching . . . 12 days worke," "14 days about
stone," "15 days worke"; in early 1670s credited for "12 days ditching
and draining the meddow . . . 16 days at Stony River . . . 50 of Rayles."

Citations: 2AB, 170–171; 3AB, 186–187; 5AB, 21, 120.

Thomas Day, Sr.

Renter: Paid £41 for 18 contract years; rental period extended from
1668–1698; leased 5-acre lot on west side and lot of unspecified size
in 3rd division.

Worker: Cobbler, canoeman. Day purchased his leather from JP and
performed cobbling for the Pynchon family on a regular basis; in May
1666, JP paid him £12 1s. 6d. for "worke: making and mending shoes,
and wheate and else"; at same time, purchased 17 "Hides of sole
leather"; in May 1673, was paid for "carying downe Porke in all 57
barells at 21d."

Citations: 3AB, 150–151; 5AB, 107, 514–515; 6AB, 150–151.

Anthony Dorchester

Renter: Dorchester leased (at different times) JP's corn- and sawmills for
annual rents up to £18; on February 10, 1653, Dorchester leased a
cornmill owned jointly by JP and Elizur Holyoke for £13 annually; by
1669, the rental payment was £18; held lease until 1672, and possibly
after; also leased oxen and 5 acres of land; oxen formerly Dorchester's
which he lost to JP for debts; leased JP's sawmill in 1673.

Worker: Miller, canoeman, laborer. In 1664, received credit for "Carying
Corne . . . bringing up goods . . . carying Corne 681 bush from foote
of falls . . . 7 days ½ Sawing . . . ferying . . . scowering the ditch . . .
work about the Mill . . . carying corne to Hartford 390 bush at 4d.
. . . bringing up 60 bush of salt . . . 2 days 3 hands and your Boats
fetching hay"; see chap. 4.

Citations: 1AB, 129, 296; 2AB, 136–137; 3AB, 85, 105, 252; 5AB, 132,
352–353, 528.

Hugh Dudley

Debtor: From Scotland; William Pynchon purchased his indenture April
29, 1650; he and his wife both became servants to the Pynchon family;
termination of Dudley's indenture did not end his dependence on the
Pynchons; on November 16, 1663, "for this debt of Twelve Pounds
Seven shillings" Dudley "doth Ingage and make over to me for my
security his 3rd division Lot over the grt River containing Ten acres
. . . and also five acres . . . both wch parsell and Land are to stand
formaly mortgaged to me for this debt"; on December 14, 1666, JP

assumed formal ownership of the land: "I have Recd by land viz. Hugh Dudly's howse and Lot 7 acres and ½ over the grt River . . . and so cleare my Books"; in 1669, JP took 4 acres of Land at Westfield for what "Hugh Dudly owes me"; in 1670, for debts of £7 10s., JP took Dudley's 2 acres of land at Westfield.

Citations: 1AB, 224, 270–271; 2AB, 220; 3AB, 176, 268–269.

John Dumbleton
> *Renter*: Lifetime payments of £117 for 66 contract years; rental period extended from 1652–1692; leased at various times 6 acres in the neck, oxen, a bull, land in Chicopee plain, 10-acre meadow, lot in Chicopee, horse, 10 acres in 3rd division, 3¼ acres in 3rd division, 11 acres in 3rd division, 5½ acres in 3rd division, 3 acres in 3rd division.
>
> *Miscl*: Selectman for 16 terms, officer in militia.
>
> *Citations*: 1AB, 67–69; 2AB, 164–165; 3AB, 180–181; 5AB, 50–51, 182–183, 540; 6AB, 196.

Nathaniel Ely
> *Debtor*: On December 11, 1664, Ely's outstanding debt to JP stood at £132 19s. 4d.; Ely and JP agreed that Ely would pay interest at an annual rate of £5 per £100 on the unpaid debt.
>
> *Renter*: Leased house and lands from JP "till he can attaine to Buy it" for £75; lease signed April 2, 1667; purchase never completed; Ely paid £116 for 18 contract years, holding estate until his death in 1675; thereupon Ely's wife continued to hold the lease until 1685.
>
> *Worker*: Brickmaker, carpenter, surveyor. Credited in 1663 for "3000 of Bricks . . . 200 of Cutt Bricks . . . 200 of Clapboards"; in December 1664, JP paid him for "measuring 130 acres of land at freshwater brooke," and for "measuring land in Chik Plaine"; in April 1668, JP paid him for "1 day to measure land at Woronoak" and for "measuring land at Mill River"; in 1669, credited for the "stairs for the Prison house cellar" and "To get the Prison house finished"; Ely purchased the wine and rum needed for his ordinary in JP's general store.
>
> *Miscl*: Selectman for 6 terms.
>
> *Citations*: 2AB, 249; 3AB, 108–109, 199; 5AB, 112, 452.

Richard Excell. Table I.

Charles Ferry
> *Debtor*: June 3, 1668, JP took "30 acrs of land at Skeepnuck . . . which I take for the Debt."
>
> *Renter*: Leased 15 acres over the river, 2 acres in the pickle, and 6 acres over Agawam in early 1690s.
>
> *Worker*: Weaver, logger, canoeman. JP paid him, at various times, for "63 yards of weaving," "severall voyadges downe the falls . . . 150 logg Poles, 9 rayles"; purchased cloth from JP's general store, including "searge," "Silke," and cotton.
>
> *Miscl*: Selectman for 1 term.

Citations: 2AB, 261; 3AB, 126–127; 5AB, 109, 484–485; 6AB, 235.

Edward Foster
Worker: Miner, canoeman, laborer. From Scotland; Foster and his wife
  Mary Bliss one-time servants of Pynchon family. In 1659, credited for
  "his worke at the lead mines," "goeing downe the falls and carying
  77½ bushels wheat"; in 1662, was paid for "127 foote of boards"; in
  mid-1660s, credited for "11 days Mowing," and "26 days ½ at the Mill
  Trench."
Renter: paid £153 for 36 contract years; rental career extended from
  1667–1698; see chap. 3.
Citations: 1AB, 217; 2AB, 206–209; 3AB, 184–185; 5AB, 58–59, 474;
  6AB, 54–55.

William Hunter
Debtor: From Scotland, Hunter never achieved economic well-being in
  Springfield; at his death in 1675, Hunter was indebted to JP for £12
  4s. 6d.; total value of his estate at death £37; in 1684, the balance of
  the debt still unpaid, JP took 7 acres from Hunter's widow.
Renter: In 1669, leased 15 acres from JP.
Worker: Ditcher, sawyer, laborer. In March 1668, JP paid him for "sawing
  946 foote" of timber; in 1670 paid him for "ditching (besides the 112
  Rod for the horse . . .)"; see chap. 4.
Citations: 3AB, 164–165; 5AB, 31, 50; 1HCPCR, 182.

Griffith Jones. Table I.

Samuel Marshfield
Worker: Canoeman, tailor, sheep-shearer, laborer. In 1648–49, WP paid
  him for "25 days worke Taylering" and "11 days worke in Taylering";
  in 1653 JP paid him £4 4s. 4d. for "Taylery Work"; credited at other
  times for "carying 5 Barrels of beife to Hartford . . . sheep shearing,"
  "by 100 of Clapboards."
Debtor: April 2, 1667, to "Cleare the debt" of £53 14s., JP took Marshfield's "howse and land viz. all his howsing and all his land on this
  side of the grt River"; on September 13, 1686, Marshfield lost an
  additional 124 acres to JP for debts of £150 12s. 3d.
Renter: Marshfield paid £35 for 18 contract years; rental career extended
  from 1665–1691; leased 3½-acre lot, steers, 7½-acre lot, land in pickle,
  plowland over Agawam.
Miscl: Selectman for 13 terms, deputy 3 terms.
Citations: WPAB, 182; 1AB, 108; 2AB, 109; 3AB, 110–111; 5AB, 36–
  37, 471; 6AB, 188–189; PCR, 381.

John Mathews. Table I.

Obadiah Miller
Debtor: Lost over 95 acres for debts of £80; see chap. 3.

Renter: Paid £45 for 20 contract years; leased 5¼ acres in 3rd division, 9 acres, cattle, and 2½ acres.
Citations: 2AB, 134; 3AB, 178–179; 5AB, 47, 542–543.

Thomas Mirrick. Table I.

Miles Morgan. Table I.

Benjamin Mun
   Laborer: Worked extensively as an agricultural laborer for JP; in mid-1660s JP paid Mun £4 6s. for "worke 43 days all to about 6 or 7 days at the Mill worke," for "32 days worke," and "worke in the Mill Trench . . . 30 days"; at various times Mun credited for "reaping," "Smithery work," "mowing 4 acres and 8 acres over the River," and "carting corn to the wharfe"; at his death in 1676, Mun's estate valued at £41, including "10 acres of mean land valued at little."
   Citations: WPAB, 60; 1AB, 93; 2AB, 63; 3AB, 97, 128; 1HCPCR, 167.

Thomas Noble
   Debtor: January 3, 1667/68, indebted to JP for £24 17s. 7d.; JP "Recd this whole debt per land"; in addition "also he pays me what he owes on Bills and for Skeepnuck and for Broth Smith's debt all that is due to me upon the severall Bills which are dlrd up to him all is betwixt £61 or £62."
   Worker: Tailor. In 1656 credited £11 for "Taylering"; in 1658 was paid £10 11s. 2d. for "Taylery worke"; in 1662 for "worke Taylering" took £23; in 1669 credited £8 13s. 3d. for "worke Taylering."
   Citations: 1AB, 317; 2AB, 97, 333; 3AB, 134–137; 5AB, 21.

James Osborne. Table I.

Francis Pepper
   Laborer: Pepper began working for and boarding with JP during the early 1650s and continued to do so until his death in 1685; see chap. 4.
   Citations: 1AB, 202–203, 208; 2AB, 227–229; 3AB, 138–139; 5AB, 159; 1HCPCR, 259.

John Petty
   Renter: One of JP's farmers; paid £160 for 21 contract years; in 1667 he leased JP's 80-acre "Tenement Farme" complete with oxen on the west side of the river; see chap. 3.
   Worker: Laborer. Frequently performed agricultural labor for JP; on January 26, 1666/67, JP paid Petty for "5 days Mowing," "6 days at the Mill . . . carting timber for the barn Ano 1666, 6 days and more ¾ day . . . By Carting Timber for the Barne Ano 1667, 12 days at 6s. per day," annual payments for "wintering 3 cattle."
   Citations: 3AB, 154–155; 5AB, 62–63, 424–425.

John Scot

> *Renter/Debtor*: June 1668, Scot's debt to JP set at £64 18s.; leased one of
> JP's farms; on March 25, 1670, apparently gave up lease on farm;
> also leased 2½-acre meadow at 24s.; held land until 1681, possibly
> until 1686.

> *Worker*: Carter, logger, sawyer, fence builder. In March 1658, JP paid
> him £7 14s. 6d. for "carting Timber, Clay, hay, thatch, Stones, rayls,
> and Posts"; in April 1660, credited for "29 rod of log Poles [and] . . .
> setting up 107 rod of fence"; in 1663, was paid £4 for "fencing in the
> Common feild"; frequent entries for "carting dung," "falling timber,"
> "making cyder," "plowing up" new ground, and "keeping a yoake of
> cattle."

> *Citations*: 2AB, 24–25, 268–269; 3AB, 189; 5AB, 56–57.

Richard Sikes. Table I.

Thomas Stebbins. Table I.

John Stewart

> *Worker/Debtor/Renter*: Scot blacksmith. Came to Sp. as servant to JP; per-
> formed extensive smithery work for JP until his death in 1690; lost
> all housing and land in Sp. to JP for debts of £25 in 1670; eventually
> reestablished himself; see chap. 4.

> *Citations*: 1AB, 230–231; 2AB, 46–47, 282–283; 3AB, 26, 136–137; 5AB,
> 90–91, 407; 1HCPCR, 273; 1TR, 261.

Peter Swinck

> *Renter*: Swinck, a black, began career in Springfield as servant to Pynchon
> family; after release from service, he leased land from JP; on February
> 24, 1664/65, JP "Lett out to Peter Swink for this yeare coming the lot
> over the River . . . for which he is to allow and pay me the sum of
> 25s. and he to looke after and repr the fencing"; also "Let out to him
> all the Land which was Bagg's for this yeare at 30s."; held lease until
> 1670, possibly longer; on October 8, 1670, JP "Agreed with Peter to
> have the use of my ground in the 3rd Division from Jonath Ball's
> Land . . . 7 [acres] in all which he is to have for 3 or 4 year"; in April
> 1683, Swinck leased 8 acres in the 3rd division free of costs; Swinck
> only to pay rates and maintain fencing.

> *Worker*: Field worker, stable hand. Credited at various times for "Stub-
> bing and clearing 5 acres at 16s. per acre," "milking my Cows," "6
> days helping to make Cider," "1 weeke Haymaking," "mending fence
> for me."

> *Citations*: 3AB, 166–167; 5AB, 39.

James Taylor

> *Renter*: Paid £84 for 54 contract years; rental career extended from
> 1667–1698; leased, at various times, lot of undetermined size, 4 acres
> of plowland, oxen, cow, house, 4 acres of meadow, 12 acres, 9 acres,
> sheep, 3½-acre lot; principal lease signed on February 10, 1674/75;

in it JP leased to Taylor "12 acre in 3d div. . . . 13 acr in 2d div. or homelots" and "2 lots in the Neck being about 7 acres" for 7 years; total rent of £5 14s. due on 10th of February yearly; Taylor, a freeman by 1664 and married by 1667, landless in 1685.

Worker: Field worker, stable hand. Between 1659 and 1664 paid by JP for "8 months service . . . 30 days work," "30 weeks worke . . . at 7s. per weeke . . . 7 weeks . . . 6 weeks," "4 weeks work last winter . . . 24 weeks . . . 10 days getting Timber and carting . . . 10 [days] Sawing," "8 Months and a weeke," "2 days ½ looking in horses . . . a Journey to [the] Bay . . . 9 days goeing with my teame . . . 16 days worke in Hay tyme and Harvest . . . a Journey to New London your selfe and horse being gon 18 days."

Citations: 1AB, 250; 2AB, 121, 337; 3AB, 72–73, 121; 5AB, 456–457; 6AB, 240–241; 6AB Index, 4; 1685 Tax List.

Jonathan Taylor

Debtor: Perennially indebted to JP; lost extensive tracts of land as well as livestock; died in 1682 with an estate of £47 and debts of £40; see chap. 3.

Renter: Paid £37 for 19 contract years; on March 10, 1667/68, JP "let out to Jonath Taylor my house (on the west side of the River) and 7 acr ½ of Ground [which JP had taken earlier from Hugh Dudley for debts] he is to repr the house by thatching it (else he should have given 40s. if noe more) and he is to repr all the fencing"; Taylor held lease for house and land until his death sixteen years later; also rented "2 black steers."

Worker: Field worker. Credited at various times for "21 days worke," "7 days in carting dung," "10 days worke," "10 days at the Mill . . . milking my Cows last year . . . milking my Cows this yeare 6 weekes," "6 days ½ Haymaking, 2 days reaping."

Citations: 1AB, 125–126, 314; 2AB, 228–229; 3AB, 174–175; 5AB, 52–53, 368–369; 2HCPCR, 39.

Samuel Terry

Renter/Debtor: Paid £64 for 40 contract years; began career in Springfield as indentured servant to William Pynchon; thereafter, on October 15, 1650, apprenticed to Benjamin Cooley to learn the art of weaving; on August 7, 1662, Terry lost "14 acrs of land at chikkupy" to JP for debts of £13 10s.; on the same day, Terry leased the land back from JP: "Let out to Saml Terry the 5 acrs and ¼ of broken up land in the 14 acrs abovsd in Chikkupy wch I have bought"; on May 19, 1663, JP sold Terry the house, orchard, and lot he had taken for debts from Griffith Jones a month earlier; purchase price of £26 to be paid in 3 years; on October 17, 1666, Terry's debt to JP stood at £31 12s.; Terry returned briefly to England during mid-1660s; JP paid his crossing fare: "To paymt of your Passadge to England" £7; on March 22, 1668/69, Terry leased "2 oxen . . . which Sam Terry is to have a yeare to use them well and keep them well next winter and to pay the Rates and allow and pay for the hire of them 40s. in wheat and Indian [corn] and a weeke plowing"; on April 16, 1680, JP "Dlrd to [Sam] Terry with my farme . . . a good new plow . . . with a good new share . . . and coulter, plow chain 7½ ft long, new whipple and chain, draft yoak, clovis and pin etc."

Worker: Canoeman, field worker. Worked extensively as a canoeman and field laborer for JP; see chap. 4.

Citations: 2AB, 200–201; 3AB, 144–145; 5AB, 72–73, 447; PCR, 226–227.

Rowland Thomas. Table I.

James Warrinar

  Renter: Paid £33 for 16 contract years; leased "good mowing land in 3d div"; on March 24, 1693/94, leased "11 acr of broken up land" in 3rd division for £3 10s. annually; held lease jointly with his son; in February 1666/67 purchased land in Skepnuck from JP for £18.

  Worker: Logger, sawyer, stable hand, carter, canoeman. On July 20, 1669, JP "Agreed with James Warrinar and John Hitchcock to cart all the Loggs to the Sawmill which James Warrinar is to get all that psell of 123 loggs they are to cart them all to my Saw Mill and Lay them fit for sawing which they are to cart to the mill . . . by the begining of June next: For which I am to allow and pay them 22d. per Log"; credited at various times for "Boards 600 foote . . . cowkeeping," "14 days ½ Sawing . . . 300 of boards . . . carying wheate downe the falls."

  Miscl: Selectman 7 terms.

  Citations: 2AB, 32, 143; 3AB, 119; 6AB, 20–21.

Abel Wright

  Renter/Debtor: Paid £56 for 31 contract years; rental career extended from 1668–1686; on March 25, 1668, Wright leased "yoake of cattle" for £2 annually, plus rates; five days later JP "Let out to hire to Abel Wright for 3 yeares That land at Skeepnuck which I lately (viz. 2 days agoe) took of Goodm Dorchester, namly the 4 acrs of Plowed up ground within the fence and also the meddow without the fence" for 38s. annually for three years; also leased bullock, 5½-acr lot, lot of undetermined size, and 1¾ acres near Round Hill; in 1668, Wright sold JP 40 acres of land at Ashkannunsuck for £3; land's distance from town center presumably reduced its value; Wright indebted to JP for £93 5s. 7d. in late 1680s.

  Worker: Field worker. Credited at various times for "worke about the ditch . . . carting . . . reaping . . . worke in harvest . . . Mowing . . . digging stones," "By a Journey yourselfe and horse to Paratuck with Mary Pynchon," "the Mill viz. 3 days worke."

  Miscl: Selectman 2 terms, militia lieutenant, and deputy to General Court.

  Citations: 2AB, 38–39, 233; 3AB, 116–117; 5AB, 102–103; 6AB, 174; 6AB, Index, 4.

TABLE III, 1672
DEPENDENCY

Source: 1672 List of Springfield Town Meeting Voters
Total Voters: 76
Total Dependent: 32
Percent Dependent: 42%

| *Name* | *Form of Dependency* |

John Bagg. See Table II.

John Barber
Renter/Debtor: Paid £88 for 27 contract years; leased 5 acres in Cold Spring bottom, 12 acres in 3rd division, 11 acres in 3rd division, and meadowland; rental career extended from 1671–1697, with interruptions; on March 3, 1678/79, Barber lost "12 acres of land in the 3d Division" for debts of £15.
Worker: Sackmaker, stable hand, tailor, fence builder. In 1669 JP paid him £6 2s. for "61 and ½ yd which you allow in of Sacking at 2s. per yd which you have made into 20 sacks . . . By 77 yds of Sacking made into 25 bags"; in 1676 credited for "blooding of horses . . . Rounding cattle . . . stringing wampam 10 days ½ . . . making 40 Baggs . . . Rounding up horses"; in 1680s was paid for "fence . . . 15 rod at 4d.," "stubbing to enlarge land . . . worke Tayloring . . . carting fencing . . . mending my natural fence."
Miscl.: Selectman for 3 terms.
Citations: 3AB, 295; 5AB, 42–43, 292–293; 6AB, 222–223.

Reice Bedortha. Table I.

William Branch. Table I.

William Brooks. Table II.

Thomas Cooper. Table I.

Joseph Crowfoot. Table II.

Thomas Day, Sr. Table II.

Anthony Dorchester. Table II.

John Dumbleton. Table II.

Nathaniel Ely. Table II.

Charles Ferry. Table II.

Edward Foster. Table II.

Griffith Jones. Table I.

Joseph Leonard
Renter/Debtor: Paid £95 for 14 contract years; on December 19, 1671,

leased 5 or 6 acres in 3rd division; JP agreed to pay for plowing each spring; on October 2, 1673, leased JP's rich meadow and plowland over Agawam for 7 years at annual rent of £10 10s.; on October 3, 1677, JP sold Leonard 5½ acres over river for £32; three years later, purchase price unpaid, JP required him to pay rent on property; in 1687 Leonard's outstanding debt to JP £116 6s. 5d.; on February 18, 1688/89, Leonard owed £79 13s. 6d. "of old acot wch hath bene long due"; on October 21, 1689, Leonard sold yoke of oxen to JP for £10 10s.

Worker: Carpenter, field worker. Performed extensive field work and carpentry for JP; see chap. 4.

Citations: 2AB, 314–315; 3AB, 57, 63; 5AB, 66–67, 532–533; 6AB, 62–63.

Samuel Marshfield. Table II.

John Mathews. Table I.

Obadiah Miller. Table II.

Thomas Mirrick. Table I.

Miles Morgan. Table I.

Benjamin Mun. Table II.

James Osborne. Table I.

John Riley

Renter: Scot; leased cows and land; on March 25, 1668, JP "let out to hire to John Riley the 2 cows which I have bought of him for which he is to allow me 40s. . . . He is carefully to keepe the cows and water them well next winter as if they were his owne and pay the Rates on them"; also leased land for £3 10s. for 3 years, possibly longer.

Worker: Field worker, fence builder, hedger. Took payments for "hedging my ditch over the River and 46 rod at 6d. . . . 5 days worke last summer mending fence," "fencing over the River . . . 9 days worke and ½ this year and last yeare mowing, reaping and etc."

Citations: 2AB, 245; 3AB, 182–183; 5AB, 32–33.

Increase Sikes

Renter: Paid £86 for 22 contract years; rental career extended from 1669–1696, with interruptions; principal lease signed November 15, 1681; in it Sikes rented land in the neck, for £4 annually; held lease until 1696, last three years in joint tenancy with Jonathan Burt; also leased at various times steers, 2 acres near Round Hill, and a 4-acre lot near the wharf.

Worker: Field worker, carpenter, logger. Performed carpentry, logging, and agricultural labor for JP on a regular basis; Sikes also agreed to tend JP's saw mill for £12 annually; held at least one year; see chap. 4.

Citations: 3AB, 83, 172–173; 5AB, 417–418, 546–547.

Victory Sikes
> *Worker*: Carpenter, field worker, millwright. Performed occasional agricultural labor and carpentry for JP; took payments for "work about Cogs, rounds, and mending the water wheele for my Corne Mill," "22 days ½ about my corne mill . . . worke at the Sawmill making the carriage," "the frame of my Barne," "your halfe of the Barn Building."
> *Renter*: Leased mill lot in joint tenancy with John Warner early 1680s; later on October 13, 1684, Sikes and George Granger leased half of JP's "middle meddow over Agawam" for £5 12s. annually; held lease until 1691, possibly longer; see chap. 4.
> *Citations*: 5AB, 357, 482; 6AB, 106.

Thomas Stebbins. Table I.

Jonathan Taylor. Table II.

Samuel Terry. Table II.

Rowland Thomas. Table I.

John Warner
> *Renter/Debtor*: Described by JP as "my Miller"; paid £120 for 20 contract years; on November 15, 1676, JP and Warner agreed that Warner would tend JP's cornmill at Quabaug: "he to tend it well and grind all the Corne that comes to it, and allowing me one-half of the Tole"; paid JP £33 6s. 6d. for 1677, and £24 for 1678; on April 5, 1680, JP sold Warner a 4-acre homelot and 2½ acres of meadow for "wch he is to pay me Ninety Pounds"; JP subsequently reduced the purchase price to £80 if promptly paid; in 1682, Warner having paid only £18, JP asked him to pay rent for the land "for the use or rent of £72 (being but about £18 pd) . . . £5 1s."; paid rent (interest) on unpaid principal until 1699; also leased land in neck in joint tenancy 1674–1677.
> *Citations*: 5AB, 335–337.

James Warrinar. Table II.

Abel Wright. Table II.

TABLE IV, 1685
DEPENDENCY

Source: 1685 Tax List
Total Inhabitants: 120
Total Dependent: 56
Percent Dependent: 46.7%

Name   *Form of Dependency*

Jonathan Ball. See Table II.

John Barber. See Table III.

James Barker

> *Renter*: On March 31, 1688, Barker leased 32 acres in Chicopee plain for 10 years; 3 or 4 acres broken up; Barker agreed to pay rates, repair fences, and pay 20s. annual rent; held lease until 1699; on December 20, 1684, JP and Barker agreed to a land exchange; JP took Barker's land and housing at Suffield; Barker received 25 acres on the west side; agreed to pay JP additional £15 in peas or Indian corn within three years.
>
> *Citations*: 6AB, 114–115.

Joseph Bedortha

> *Renter*: Leased, at various times, 8¾ acre lot in Chicopee, 5½ acres in 3rd division, 3 acres, 10 acres, 5 acres at Cold Spring bottom, 1½ acres near Connecticut River, land in pickle, land in 3rd division; paid £25 for 25 contract years; rental career extended from 1673–1696; on February 20, 1681/82, JP bought Bedortha's ⅕ share in Joseph Leonard's saw mill for 12 acres over the river that JP had taken for debts from Obadiah Miller.
>
> *Worker*: Field worker, stable hand. In December 1673 JP "Agreed with Joseph Bedortha to Stubb, cleare, and Plough up Three acres of New ground . . . [for] foure Pounds"; later was paid for "bringing a horse, breaking, and keeping him till Spring . . . fetching in horses from Westfield."
>
> *Citations*: 5AB, 29, 186–187; 6AB, 22–23.

Thomas Day, Sr. Table II.

Thomas Day, Jr.

> *Renter*: One of JP's "Farmers"; paid £115 for 24 contract years; rental career extended from 1684 to 1702; after leasing 5 acres in 3rd division in joint tenancy with his father, 5 acres in Chicopee field, and 16 acres near Black Pond, Day rented a farm on April 11, 1691, in joint tenancy with John Mirrick; farm contained barn, 2 cows, housing and 50 acres of land (35 acres of planting ground and 15 acres of meadow), annual rent graded from £15 to £19 and all applicable rates; Day held lease until 1700, his brother Samuel replacing Mirrick as cotenant in 1698; on May 10, 1697, Thomas and Samuel Day also leased JP's ½ interest in the sawmill at Sixteen Acres, for "£3 in money and sawing"; Day to pay for ordinary, JP for extraordinary, repairs.
>
> *Worker*: Field worker, carter, logger, cobbler. Credited in 1680s for "Loggs for my Saw mill . . . 525 feet at 15s. per 100 feet . . . by 10 days worke at my mill dam . . . 1 pair of shoes . . . mending Hannah's shooes"; in 1693 received labor credits amounting to £20 13s. 9d.
>
> *Citations*: 5AB, 266–267; 6AB, 151, 168–169, 216–217, 254–255.

John Dumbleton. Table II.

Charles Ferry. Table II.

Edward Foster. Table II.

James Gerald

Renter: On February 20, 1688/89, Gerald leased 30 acres in Chicopee field for 4 years at annual rent graduated from £3 to £3 10s; on the same day, leased additional 20 acres in Chicopee field for 7 years for rent graduated from 35s. to £3 10s. annually; on February 2, 1696/97, leased JP's 14-acre lot in Chicopee for 9 years at £3 10s.; Gerald also agreed to clear 2½ acres of swamp land, maintain fencing, and pay all rates; in 1699, leased 5 acres in Nonesuch at 5s.; payment record incomplete; entries for £31 for 11 contract years; owned 20 acres in 1685; left estate of £84 and debts of £23 at death in 1700.

Worker: Field worker, ditcher, drover, boarder. Between 1688 and 1692 was paid for "worke about fencing . . . mil dam, Haymaking . . . 20 Rod ditch in the Boggy Meddow"; one entry credits him £10 15s. 9d. for "worke as per James account"; was paid 12s. for "driving a yoake of cattle to Boston"; he paid JP £9 12s. for "48 weeks dyet" in 1691.

Citations: 6AB, 108, 200–201; 3HCPCR, 75.

Thomas Gilbert

Indigent: Although the grandson of Deacon Samuel Chapin, Gilbert began his career as indentured servant; worked as a laborer and occasionally rented land from JP; landless in 1685, although 26 years old and married; left estate of £47 and £13 in debts at death in 1698.

Citations: 6AB, 126; 3HCPCR, 48, 52.

Symon Gowin

Worker/Debtor: Worked as a field laborer for JP; died, unmarried, in 1693 with estate valued at £69 and £49 in debts.

Citations: 3HCPCR, 9.

John Humphreys

Renter: On July 1, 1686, Humphreys leased land in Chicopee field for £3 10s. and one day of work annually; held lease until 1691.

Worker: Field worker, boarder. Paid by JP at various times for "16 rod of New ditch," "ditching of old 40 rod," "3 days spreading dung . . . 38 rod ditching"; in December 1685, JP wrote that "John Humphrey came to my House to Board with me"; in 1687, paid JP £5 for "25 weeks dyet"; in 1688 paid JP £7 6s. for "36 weeks dyet"; on March 24, 1692/93, Humphreys agreed to become a fulltime servant of JP; his salary set at £11 in country pay (grains, etc.) and £4 in specie.

Citations: 6AB, 14–15, 71.

Ebenezer Jones

Renter: One of JP's "Farmers"; paid £74 for 28 contract years; on August 22, 1684, Jones and Thomas Taylor leased JP's 80-acre farm over the river for 7 years; included house, barn, orchard, pasture, and cattle; rent set at £16 annually and all town rates; lessees agreed to break up 5 acres of new ground before end of term and winter two cows for JP; Jones replaced by James Petty in 1690; Jones also leased, at various

times, 6 acres of broken up land in Chicopee, 5 acres in Cold Spring bottom, a mare, 2 steers, and a lot of undetermined size in 3rd division.
Worker: Field worker. Received credit for labor worth £34 16s. in 1690.
Citations: 5AB, 456; 6AB, 102–103, 118–119.

Samuel Jones
    Renter: Paid £40 for 28 contract years; rental career extended from 1674–1691; leased, at various times, "plow land," mare, 7½ acres in 3rd division, "Bottom in 3d div. wch Jones's father had," and 2 steers; principal lease signed February 15, 1685/86; it provided for Jones to rent 15 or 16 acres in Chicopee field for £2 6s. annually and all rates up to 5s.; Jones agreed to clear all but 1 acre of meadow; held lease for full 6-year term.
    Debtor: In late 1670s, JP took 43 acres from Jones over Agawam for debts of £52 14s. 4d.; Jones, born in 1650, owned 28 acres by 1685; emigrated to Deerfield, where he was killed in an Indian attack in 1704, leaving an estate valued at £46.
    Worker: Fence builder. Signed agreements with JP in late 1670s for "22 Rod of 5 Raile fence . . . 40 rod of good 5 Raile fence . . . 100 good white oake Posts . . . 24 Rod of 5 Rale fence . . . mending fence over Agawam."
    Citations: 5AB, 45, 458–459; 6AB, 118–119; 3HCPCR, 117.

John Kilum, residing in Springfield by late 1680s.
    Renter: Paid £66 for 16 contract years; rental career extended from 1689–1697; principal lease signed on January 24, 1688/89; under its provisions, Kilum leased 45 acres over Agawam for 15 years; he agreed to clear and improve at least 15 acres, build house (23' × 18'), and plant an orchard; rent to include labor and payment of sum graded from £3 10s. to £7 10s.; also leased 6 acres in the plain, a house, plowland of undetermined dimensions, 1½ acres of meadow, 11 acres at further end of 3rd division (for £3 8s. annually, joint tenancy with Pelatiah Jones), and 7½ acres in 3rd division at £2 5s.; see chap. 3.
    Worker: Field worker, boarder. Paid by JP for "40 rod of posts . . . clearing 3 Acres of Land . . . at 26s. per acre . . . filling the walls of Joseph Leonard's house . . . threshing and fanning"; in 1692 JP wrote "Goodman Kilum came to my House May 12th 1692 . . . By 37 days worke . . . By making my well."
    Citations: 4AB, 87; 6AB, 92–93, 228–229.

Benjamin Knowlton
    Renter: Prison house keeper who also leased land from JP; leased a 7½-acre lot in 3rd division in joint tenancy with John Mirrick in 1687–1688; thereafter leased 11-acre lot, at first in joint tenancy with George Remmington and then at thirds with John Burt and Thomas Mirrick; married to Hannah Mirrick in 1676, Knowlton owned 21 acres in 1685; at death in 1690, estate valued at £72.
    Worker: Field worker, flax breaker, sawyer. On December 26, 1681, JP

"Agreed with B. Knowlton well to Brake and swingle 60 pounds of flax at 3d. per yard"; later paid him for "9 days worke at the Mill," and for additional work cutting logs, reaping, and mowing.

Citations: 5AB, 415; 6AB, 192–193; 2HCPCR, 61.

Joseph Leonard. Table III.

Josias Leonard
> *Renter*: Paid £50 for 19 contract years; on February 12, 1676/77, leased 3¼ acres at further end of 3rd division for 22s. annually; held land for 8 years; on March 24, 1680/81, leased half of JP's middle meadow over Agawam (which his brother Joseph had held until that time) for £5 10s.; paid rent for 9 years; also leased "yoak of steers."
> *Citations*: 5AB, 506–507; 6AB, 62–63.

Josiah Marshfield
> *Debtor*: Son of Samuel Marshfield, he inherited father's debt obligations to JP; on Dec. 30, 1695, balance of £22 16s. 10d. due to JP, Josiah having paid £42 of original debt of £72; JP agreed to abate balance to £18 if paid within 10 or 20 days; on January 13, 1695/96, for remainder of debt, Marshfield gave JP 13 acres of land at further end of 3rd division; on April 18, 1702, Marshfield, again indebted to JP, lost all his commons land on the east side of river to "clear up" his debts.
> *Renter*: In October 1689, Marshfield leased JP's ⅛ share of the ketch "Northern Venture"; rent set at £5 10s. yearly.
> *Citations*: 6AB, 230–231.

Samuel Marshfield. Table II.

Lazarus Miller
> *Renter*: On March 22, 1679/80, leased 10–12 acres, orchard, and house at "hither end Chic Feild" for £3 10s., and all town rates; rental term set at 5 years; payments due on first day of March in "good and well dressed grain"; on April 16, 1684, leased 24-acre lot in Chicopee field for 30s. and rates; in 1686 and 1688 respectively, leased 2 black steers and 4–6 acres in Chicopee plain for 5 years; on February 28, 1693/94, leased 30-acre lot in Chicopee for 35s. and rates; Miller also agreed to build a shelter and clear land; paid £34 for 22 contract years; see chap. 3.
> *Debtor*: On November 2, 1682, Miller sold 6 acres and 3 swine to discount debt of £7 3s.; after Miller's death (at age 42) in 1697, his brothers approached JP and asked him to abate a portion of widow's debt; Miller's estate at death valued at £38.
> *Citations*: 5AB, 490–491; 6AB, 190–191; 3HCPCR, 38.

Obadiah Miller. Table II.

John Mirrick
> *Renter*: One of JP's "Farmers"; paid £120 for 12 contract years; after

leasing 7½ acres in 3rd division in 1689/90, Mirrick signed lease for farm in 1691; on April 11, 1691, he and Thomas Day agreed to rent JP's 50-acre farm over the river for payments graded from £15 to £19; held lease until 1698, when replaced by Samuel Day.
Citations: 6AB, 164, 254–255.

Thomas Mirrick. Table I.

David Morgan
Renter: Leased middle meadow over Agawam in joint tenancy with James Warrinar at £2 18s. yearly from 1695–1701; also leased pasture which he unsuccessfully attempted to purchase in 1697; paid 30s. for next four years.
Worker: Carpenter, canoeman, field worker. In January 1677/78, JP agreed with David and Jonathan Morgan for them to build him a house of 24' × 18' for £14, JP responsible for sawing; also paid Morgan for "10 days worke at our lodging Room and closset for my wife," "5 days Mowing," "fetching my hay," "bringing up goods" from Enfield falls and "3 days worke at the sawmill at stony brook."
Citations: 5AB, 385; 6AB, 78, 146.

Isaac Morgan
Renter: One of JP's "Farmers"; paid £63 for 16 contract years; after leasing 9 acres at Chicopee in 1672, Morgan signed a contract to rent a farm on December 25, 1673; contract provided for Morgan to lease 42-acre farm for 11 years at rental payments graduated from £14 to £22; see chap. 3.
Worker: Field worker, canoeman, factotum; see chap. 3.
Citations: 5AB, 189, 420–423.

Jonathan Morgan
Renter/Debtor: On August 7, 1674, for debts, Morgan sold JP a "yoak of oxen" for £11 10s; on November 16, 1677, leased "2 steers (5 or 6 yre old) for 3 yrs"; from 1680 to 1683, Morgan leased a house for £2 annually; on December 4, 1689, he leased JP's sawmill for three months.
Worker: Carpenter, canoeman, surveyor, carter, field worker. On January 18, 1677/78, he and his brother, David, contracted to build JP a house (24' × 18') for £14; twenty-two years later, Morgan still performing carpentry for JP; agreed to build barn with dimensions of 48' × 24' × 14'; also credited at various times for "shingling my house at the Round hill and laying the Bords . . . 20 days your selfe and horse at 4s. per day . . . to Albany about Running the Line," "bringing up 20 bushels of salt," "24 days worke framing the Mill," "11 days ½ worke," "14 days carting for the fort," "6 days ½ your teame carting Dung at 5s.," "Plowing my Lot, mending Cart"; in 1685, at age of 40, Morgan owned 34 acres in Springfield.
Citations: 3AB, 12; 5AB, 149, 383–385; 6AB, 81; 1685 Tax List.

Miles Morgan. Table I.

Pelatiah Morgan
> *Renter/Debtor*: On March 12, 1671/72, Morgan leased 20-acre lot in Chic-
> opee field for 6 years; agreed to break up at least 5 acres of new
> ground and pay rent graduated up to £3 10s.; on March 6, 1673/74,
> lost a yoke of steers to JP for debts of £9.
> *Worker*: Field worker. Paid by JP in 1673 for "26 rod of fence"; on
> November 22, 1673, JP agreed with Morgan "to stub and cleare and
> throw in of ditch of my land at 3 corner meddow."
> *Citations*: 5AB, 184–185.

Benjamin Mun. Table II.

James Mun
> *Renter*: Leased 4-acre lot over river from 1688 to 1699 at rental payments
> graduated from 20s. to 25s.; in 1685, owned 19 acres.
> *Worker*: Field worker, canoeman, carter. Mun paid by JP at various times
> for "1 weekes worke," "6 days worke finding dung," "a Journey to
> Boston," "goeing downe the falls for Salt," "bringing up Sugar, Rum,
> Salt," "4 days worke. . . . carting Timber."
> *Citations*: 5AB, 99; 6AB, 86–87; 1685 Tax List.

Thomas Noble. Table II.

John Norton
> *Worker*: Shoemaker who worked for JP on a contractual basis; see chap.
> 4.

James Osborne. Table I.

Francis Pepper. Table II.

James Petty
> *Renter*: One of JP's "Farmers"; leased 80-acre farm in joint tenancy with
> Thomas Taylor, 1685–1690; also leased, at various times, 6½ acres of
> plowland, 30 acres at Chicopee, 4 acres of meadow, and a yoke of
> oxen; payment record incomplete; paid at least £59 for 10 contract
> years; emigrated to Brookfield by 1700.
> *Citations*: 5AB, 425; 6AB, 100–101.

Roco
> *Servant/Renter*: JP's slave; see chap. 4.

Henry Rogers
> *Renter/Debtor*: Paid £53 for 37 contract years; rental career extended
> from 1675–1699; leased, at various times, 12-acre lot, 6½ acres in the
> 3rd division, meadow in 3rd division, 2½ acres of meadow in 3rd
> division, 4 acres in homelots; two principal contracts; on February 28,
> 1675/76, leased 6½ acres in 3rd division for 5 years; held land for
> next 13 years; on May 3, 1684, Rogers agreed to purchase the lease-
> hold for £15; 4 years later, however, Rogers still paying rent for the
> land; on September 10, 1681, Rogers leased 2½ acres of "mowing

ground" in rich 3rd division meadow for 30s. annually; held land for next 18 years; on February 3, 1681/82, Rogers sold JP 14 acres in 3rd division and 2 cows to offset debts of £22 1s. 3d.

Citations: 5AB, 464–465; 6AB, 88.

Nicholas Rust

Renter: A Dutch immigrant, Rust lived as a boarder in the Pynchon household for extended periods during the 1670s; on February 1, 1678/79, Rust agreed to purchase 3½-acre lot at the wharf for £30, payable in three annual installments of £10; Rust failed to meet the terms of the contract and paid rent of 30s. for the next 21 years; also leased, at various times, 2-acre lot, 1-acre lot, and a yoke of oxen; rental career extended from 1676–1699.

Worker: Cobbler, naval stores worker. Paid £9 8s. by JP in 1676 for "shooes" and another £6 for "shooes delivered the soldiers and others"; credited £7 for "10 barrels of Tar."

Citations: 5AB, 502–503, 548–549; 6AB, 24.

John Scot. Table II.

Increase Sikes. Table III.

James Sikes

Renter: On April 15, 1693, Sikes leased 4 acres in the pickle and swampland in the neck; held lease until JP's death in 1703; also leased 5½ acres in plain in 1696; Sikes, in his mid-thirties in 1685, owned 32 acres; at his death in 1714, his estate was valued at £75, with outstanding debts of £33.

Citations: 6AB, 194–195; 2HCPCR, 104; 1685 Tax List.

Victory Sikes. Table III.

Edward Stebbins

Renter: Paid £45 for 22 contract years; leased, at various times, a yoke of oxen, meadow at Round Hill, 9 acres of meadow over Agawam, lot in Chicopee field, and 14 acres in Chicopee plain; principal lease signed on April 13, 1685; under its provisions, Stebbins rented 9 acres in the middle meadow over Agawam for £2 10s. annually; held lease for next 14 years; Stebbins's rental career extended from 1681–1698; born in 1656; owned 35 acres in 1685.

Worker: Cooper. Paid by JP in 1678 for "10 Barrels . . . hooping and etc. . . . 4 Barrels, 3 Cider Barrels . . . 4 Barrels," as well as "shingles for the Meetinghouse."

Citations: 5AB, 494–495; 6AB, 142–143, 148; 1685 Tax List.

Peter Swinck. Table II.

James Taylor. Table II.

Jonathan Taylor. Table II.

Samuel Taylor, Jr.

Renter/Debtor: One of JP's "Farmers"; paid £59 for 11 contract years; on February 8, 1676/77, Taylor and Jonathan Ball leased JP's 80-acre farm over the river for 7 years at an annual rent of £18; renters agreed to maintain fences, dig a ditch around the orchard, and winter two of JP's cattle; held lease for duration of contract; in early 1680s, JP presented Taylor with "His Father's debt [of] £31 18s. 3d."; however, "he meddles not with his father's debt"; lost yoke of cattle for debts of £10 15s. in 1689.

Worker: Blacksmith. Paid by JP at various times for "shoeing a horse. shoeing [another] horse," "mending the warming pan," "3 days drawing Timber to Suffield Mill," and "1 day ½ Raising my Mills."

Citations: 5AB, 41, 239, 272–273.

Thomas Taylor

Renter: One of JP's "Farmers"; paid £130 for 14 contract years; in 1685, after leasing 5½ acres in 3rd division, 2 acres of meadow, and a 4½-year-old mare, Taylor leased 80-acre farm from JP for £16 annually; held farm until 1691, possibly longer.

Citations: 5AB, 368–369; 6AB, 102–103.

Samuel Terry. Table II.

Rowland Thomas. Table I.

David Throw

Debtor: In 1677, lost 6-acre lot to JP for debts of £3 10s.; on May 10, 1699, JP "Recd this by his Right in the Commons devided viz. his 3d devision on the East side of the River and 2nd dev on the west side wch I allow him this £13 8s. and this debt is thereby pd me and discounted."

Citations: 5AB, 39, 530.

John Warner. Table III.

James Warrinar. Table II.

Abel Wright. Table II.

Wage Tables Contents

Wage Tables, 1638–1703

BARBING

Date	Name	Service	Rate
1664	William Branch	"By Triming Peter 0. 1. 6" 2AB, 343	18d. per haircut
22 Sep. 1665		"By Barbing [2 persons] 0. 2. 0"	1s. per haircut
30 Jun. 1666		"By Barbing [2 persons] 0. 2. 6" 3AB, 141	15d. per haircut
2 Nov. 1667		"By Barbing my folks 5s. 5d."	5s. 5d. for servants' haircuts
25 Jan. 1668/69		"By Barbing 5 persons this year Past viz. whole year and Joseph Pynchon 3 tymes"	Payment for 8 haircuts
6 Dec. 1669		"By Barbing Joseph 1s." 3AB, 319	1s. per haircut

BLACKSMITHING

Date	Name	Service	Rate
1645–1649	Thomas Reeves	"Recd in smithy work making and mending as much as comes 1. 10. 3"	£1 10s. 3d. for smithery
		"Recd in smithy worke and 1 day reaping at 20d. [is] 1. 8. 7" WPAB, 44	£1 6s. 11d. for smithery

BLACKSMITHING, *cont.*

Date	*Name*	*Service*	*Rate*
30 May 1649		"25 pounds of Iron at 3d. [is] 0. 6. 3"	3d. per pound of iron
8 Jan. 1650/51		"Recd by his Smithy worke . . . 3. 10. 4" WPAB, 213	£3 10s. 4d. for smithery
22 Apr. 1654	John Stewart	"Recd by Smithery worke and some few days about other worke and by smithy work for the mill . . . 3. 14. 8" 1AB, 231	£3 14s. 8d. for smithery
27 May 1654	Thomas Bancroft	"Recd 1 day smithery 0. 2. 0" 1AB, 147	2s. per diem for smithery
3 Apr. 1655	Tahan Grant	*Dr.* "To a parcell of Seacoale my Cousin Allyn Sold him 10. 0. 0" 1AB, 161	Pays £10 for pit coal
Nov. 1658	Miles Morgan	"Recd by 7 pitchfork steale . . . 0. 3. 6" 1AB, 266	6d. per pitchfork handle
10 Jan. 1658/59	John Stewart	"The Smiths shop is given to John Stewart as his own forever" 1TR, 261	Blacksmith shop given to Stewart
1660		"By shoeing up horses to fort Aurenia 0. 10. 0" "By Smithery work . . . 24s. 6d. of it was Iron for my cider press" "By 8 Rings for 8 swine 0. 2. 0" 2AB, 46–47	10s. for shoeing 24s. 6d. for iron for cider press 3d. per swine ring
May/Jun. 1661	Miles Morgan	"By 2 Pitchfork steale 0. 1. 4"	8d. per pitchfork handle

BLACKSMITHING, *cont.*

Date	Name	Service	Rate
17 Jul. 1661		"By 2 Pitchfork steale 0. 0. 8" 2AB, 131	4d. per pitchfork handle
2 Nov. 1663	Jeremy Horton	"By harrow teeth for Goodman Thomas 0. 2. 8" "By shutting a ring 4d." "Mending a flagon and pot 0. 1. 0" 2AB, 359	2s. 8d. for harrow teeth 4d. for closing ring 1s. for mending flagon and pot
Nov. 1663	John Stewart	"By Smithery worke . . . 6. 19. 8" 2AB, 47	£6 19s. 8d. for smithery
30 Mar. 1665		Stewart, from March to November, to go through town twice a week and ring any unrung swine at 3d. per hog 1TR, 216–217	3d. per hog for ringing
Jun. 1665		"By Smithery worke for my mill and other work all is 11. 6. 4" "By Mr. Andrews for your shoeing his horse . . . 0. 2. 0" 3AB, 137	£11 6s. 4d. for smithery 1s. per horseshoe for shoeing
9 Feb. 1665/66	Jeremy Horton	"By shooeing 2 horses 2s., mending a bridle 3d., a Band for a wheele 3s. 8d., sharpe share and Colter 8d., mending chaine and like 2s. 8d. [all is] 0. 7. 0," "sharpening share 4d., shoeing 3 horses 3s., churns 12d., forke tines, and funell 17d., shoeing a horse 12d., Shoeing 2 horses 2s., mending a flagon 20d., laying a share	1s. per horseshoe for shoeing 3d. for mending bridle 3s. 8d. per wheelband 8d. for sharpening share and colter 2s. 8d. for mending chains, etc. 4d. for sharpening share 1s. per churn

BLACKSMITHING, *cont.*

Date	Name	Service	Rate
		and Colter, mending kettles and Pewtar" 3AB, 124–125	17d. for fork, tines, and funnel
7 May 1667	Tahan Grant	"By 2 pair hooks and hinges 0. 7. 6"	3s. 9d. per pair of hooks and hinges
		"By 2 new axes 0. 11. 0"	5s. 6d. per [broad?] axe
2 Oct. 1668		"By 1 pair fetters last yeare 0. 4. 0"	4s. per pair of fetters
		"By 1 pair fetters now 0. 4. 0"	4s. per pair of fetters
		"By 1 stubbing hoe and now a 2nd stubbing hoe 0. 14. 0"	7s. per stubbing hoe
		"By 2 Croes of Iron 1. 4. 0"	12s. per crowbar
		"By 2 horse shoes 12d."	6d. per horseshoe
		"60 horse nayls 18d." 3AB, 287	1s. per 40 horse nails
Jan. 1668/69	John Stewart	"For a branding iron 0. 4. 0" 1TR, 366	4s. per branding iron
26 Aug. 1669		"To 49 pounds of iron at 3d. ½ [all is] 0. 14. 4" 3AB, 137	3½d. per pound of iron
Aug.– Nov.1669		"2 pounds steele Goodman Aires had for Web, more 4 pounds steele Goodman Aire had Nov. 8 1669,"	
		"Iron delivered John Stewart for Quabaug worke weighs 312 pounds, Recd back againe 23 pounds, So the Iron they had was 290 pounds at 3 and ½d. per pound comes to 4. 4. 8"	3½d. per pound of iron
		"And they had my old 8/2 gudgeons weigh 27 lb. at 5d. [all is] 0. 14. 3"	5d. per pound of iron

BLACKSMITHING, *cont.*

Date	Name	Service	Rate
		"Paid Goodman Stewart for working up this Iron 6. 6. 0"	4s. 8d. per pound for working up iron
		"1 Bar Steele 16¾ pounds at 16d. [all is] 1. 2. 4"	16d. per pound of steel
		"20 pounds Hoopes at 12d. [all is] 1. 5. 0"	1s. per pound for barrel hoops
		"6 pounds Steele for Webb as above 0. 8. 0" 3AB, 26	16d. per pound of steel
1 Jan. 1669/70		"To 10 pounds of iron 1. 0. 6" 3AB, 137	2s. ⅔d. per pound of iron
1670		"Iron for John Stewart to make for Quabaug, 2 hoops for a Trundle head, 2 hoops for the shaft, 2 gudgeons, 4 Bolts and keys, 20 little wedges for the gudgeons, 250 Spikes or Brads, Sledge and Pick, Croe, The 2 Hoopes they had to Quabaug weighed 20 pounds weight" 3AB, 26	Iron to be made into hoops, gudgeons, bolts, keys, wedges, spikes, brads, sledge, pick, and crowbar
Dec. 1670		"For a lock 6s., and bolt 18d., and plate 6d. for the lock for the meeting house doore and keyes and cotters for the bell is 0. 11. 0"	6s. per lock 18d. per bolt 6d. per plate
		"hookes and hinges for the Meeting house window 0. 6. 0" 1TR, 391	6s. for window hooks and hinges
29 Apr. 1671	Tahan Grant	"By a Stone hammer 4s. 6d., for Thomas" "An ax 5s. 6d." "By a hoe 0. 7. 0" 3AB, 287	4s. 6d. per stonehammer 5s. 6d. per [broad?] axe 7s. per hoe

BLACKSMITHING, *cont.*

Date	Name	Service	Rate
16 Jan. 1671/72	Jeremy Horton	"By shooeing 2 horses 1s. 8d., sharpening share and coulter 8d. [all is] 0. 2. 4" "By shoeing 2 horses 2s., making 120 brads 3s., wedge for Saw mill 1s." "By burning colts . . . 1. 16. 0" 5AB, 17	10d. per horseshoe for shoeing 8d. for sharpening share and colter 1s. per horseshoe for shoeing 1s. per 40 brads 36s. for branding colts
1 Feb. 1672/73	Samuel Taylor	"Shoeing a horse 0. 2. 0" "Shoeing a horse 0. 4. 0" 5AB, 239	1s. per horseshoe for shoeing 1s. per horseshoe for shoeing
22 Jan. 1673/74	Tahan Grant	"Nayles . . . saws . . . guages . . . hooks . . . Timber chaine . . . 6. 17. 0" "600 of Nails for to cover my Saw mill 0. 12. 0" More blacksmith work 6. 6. 0 5AB, 365	£6 17s. for tools and supplies 1s. per 50 roofing nails £6 6s. for smithery
29 Dec. 1674	John Stewart	"For irony for the pound 0. 5. 3" 1TR, 408	5s. 3d. for ironwork for town pound
21 Jun. 1677	Tahan Grant	Blacksmith work 5. 16. 0	£5 16s. for smithery
1677		"By worke Spindle and Ryne and crowne for the Corn Mill at Stony Brooke and etc. . . . 14. 10. 0" 5AB, 365	£14 10s. for spindle, ring, and crown for gristmill
29 Dec. 1679	John Stewart	"Eye for the gate 0. 1. 0" 1TR, 427	1s. per gate eye

BLACKSMITHING, *cont.*

Date	Name	Service	Rate
1680	Tahan Grant	Smithery work for "Leonard's sawmill" etc., 9. 18. 0 5AB, 365	£9 18s. for smithery for sawmill
9 Nov. 1681	Samuel Taylor	"By 2 days about my Mill . . . and mending the warming pan 0. 7. 0" 5AB, 239	7s. for smithery
1687	Obadiah Miller, Jr.	"By worke . . . old Booke the Sum off 4. 14. 0" "By smithy work 7. 0. 10" 6AB, 181	£4 14s. for smithery £7 10d. for smithery
1690		*Dr.* Rent for use of JP's tools, anvil, vices, etc., 5. 0. 0 6AB, 180	£5 per annum for rent for smith's tools
1690s?		"I found iron [By making a hook for the wall [By seting on 2 horse shoes"	Payment for making a hook and horseshoeing
1690–		"By shoeing horses 0. 5. 0," "making a hook for the wall, By seting on 4 horse shoes, By mending the Tongs, By making a hook and hinges" 4AB, 99	5s. for shoeing horses Payment for smithery
17 Jun. 1690	Thomas Dyett	"A note of Tooles Lent Thomas Dyett the Smith as followeth: 3 pair of Tongs, 1 hand hammer, 1 left hand hammer, 1 nayle toole, 1 Bolster, 1 Square bolster, 3 chisels, 6 Punches . . . 1 hand vice, 1 steel drill, 1 Iron to imbritch guns, 1 Paring Iron, an Iron to make an ax . . .	List of tools rented from JP

BLACKSMITHING, *cont.*

Date	Name	Service	Rate
		1 Screw Plate with 3 taps, 1 Beckhorne" 6AB, 236	
1694	Obadiah Miller, Jr.	Smithery work: 7. 2. 3	£7 2s. 3d. for smithery
1695		9. 5. 0	£9 5s. for smithery
1696		8. 19. 0 6AB, 181	£8 19s. for smithery

BOARDING

Date	Name	Service	Rate
Aug.–Oct. 1654	Francis Pepper	"Due to mee for your dyet 30 weeks at 4s. per weeke to the 28th of October 6. 0. 0"	4s. per week for meat and drink
Dec. 1654– Jul. 1655		"To 36 weekes and ½ dyet at 4s. per weeke, to this 9th of July 1655 [is] 7. 6. 0"	4s. per week for meat and drink
Feb. 1655/56		"For [his] dyet 30 weeks to this 9th Feb. 1655/56" 1AB, 203	Debit for meat and drink for 30 weeks
2 Nov. 1657		"To a yeares dyet at 4s. per weeke for 52 week is 10. 8. 0" 1AB, 208	4s. per week for meat and drink
23 Dec. 1657	Thomas Barber and son	"To 3 weekes dyet of himself and his son want 3 days 0. 19. 0" "To 1 weekes dyet of himself and son, To 2 weeks dyet of himself and son at 7s. per weeke 1. 1. 0" 2AB, 40	7s. per week for meat and drink for father and son 7s. per week for meat and drink for father and son

BOARDING, *cont.*

Date	Name	Service	Rate
Nov. 1658	Francis Pepper	"Francis owes me for dyet . . . from the 14th of November 1658 to this 26[?]th March 1659, being all 19 weekes at 4s. per weeke 3. 16. 0" 1AB, 209	4s. per week for meat and drink
19 Feb. 1659/60		"To 14 weekes and ½ dyet from the 21st November 1659 to this 15 day of March 1659/60 at 4s. per weeke is 2. 18. 0" 2AB, 226	4s. per week for meat and drink
20 Jun. 1660	Edward Griswald of Windsor	"To 3 weekes dyet of Goodman Bascomb 0. 12. 0" 2AB, 237	4s. per week for meat and drink
1660–1661	Francis Pepper	"To a yeares dyet from the 1st March last to this 1st March 1660, 52 weekes at 4s. per weeke is 10. 8. 0"	4s. per week for meat and drink
Apr. 1661		"To a yeares dyet from the 1st March 1660 to this 1st of March 1661, 52 weekes at 4s. per weeke 10. 8. 0" 2AB, 226	4s. per week for meat and drink
Apr. 1661	Samuel Grant	"To 2 weeks dyet 0. 16. 0" "To 1 weeks dyet 0. 8. 0" 2AB, 122	8s. per week for meat and drink [for father and son?]
Mar. 1663	Francis Pepper	"To a yeares dyet from 1st March (61) To the 2nd March 1662/63, 52 weeks at 4s. [is] 10. 8. 0" 2AB, 226	4s. per week for meat and drink

BOARDING, cont.

Date	Name	Service	Rate
20 Jan. 1664/65		"Paid him by his dyeting . . . from the 20th of November 1663, to this 20th of Jan. 1664 [65] is 61 weekes at 4s. per weeke comes to 12. 4. 11" 2AB, 229	4s. per week for meat and drink
1666	Rowland Thomas	"By allowance for your dyet [at Westfield while stoning Joseph Whiting's cellar] 10 weeke ½ [is] 2. 2. 0" 3AB, 197	4s. per week for meat and drink
1671	Corporal Richard Coy	"By 5 weeke and 3 day Goodman Thomas, his dyet 1. 5. 6" 5AB, 327	4s. 7d. per week for meat and drink
28 Aug. 1675	Nicholas Rawlings of Suffield	Began dieting with JP for 4s. per week 5AB, 209	4s. per week for meat and drink
1676	Francis Pepper	"Francis Pepper began Boarding at my house about the 10th or 11th of March 1675/6"	Boarding schedule
11 Dec. 1676		"Agreed with Francis Pepper That for his worke this summer past till now (it having bin a Troublesome yeare) I should allow five Pounds and his dyet in also" 5AB, 159	Abatement of £5 and meat and drink
19 Jan. 1683/84	Richard Waite	"To 13 weekes and ½ dyet to this 30 of Aprill 1684 [is] 2. 14. 0" 6AB, 74	4s. per week for meat and drink

BOARDING, *cont.*

Date	Name	Service	Rate
2 Dec. 1685	John Humphreys	"John Humphrey came to my House to Board with me"	Boarding schedule
1686		"36 week dyet 7. 6. 0"	4s. ½d. per week for meat and drink
10 Dec. 1687		25 weeks "dyet" £5 6AB, 15	4s. per week for meat and drink
17 Feb. 1695/96	Thomas Parsons	"Thomas Parsons came to Board at my House and is to pay me 3s. per week in Money" 6AB, 171	3s. per week in specie for meat and drink
1698	Jedediah Bartlet	"Dyet for 48 weeks 10. 16. 0" 6AB, 258	4s. 6d. per week for meat and drink

BOATING

Date	Name	Service	Rate
5 Aug. 1658	John Bagg	"1 day boating hay 0. 2. 0" 2AB, 81	2s. per diem for boating hay
4 Apr. 1661	John Henryson	"By boating over the Rayles 0. 3. 0" 2AB, 205	3s. for boating rails
24 Jan. 1661/62	Lawrence Bliss	"By 4 days your cannoe fetching hay 0. 4. 0" 2AB, 207	1s. per diem for leasing canoe
1666	William Warrinar	"By Hadley Boate, 5 days [is] 5s.; halfe of it to John, and your halfe 0. 2. 6" 3AB, 133	1s. per diem for boating to Hadley
Jan. 1679/80	Thomas Miller	"By Boating to Hartford 4. 15. 11" 5AB, 289	£4 15s. 11d. for boating to Hartford

BRICKMAKING

Date	Name	Service	Rate
19 Feb. 1645/46	William Vaughan	"Recd 15 Pavements and a few Bricks 0. 2. 8" WPAB, 113	2s. 8d. for 15 pavements and several bricks
Dec. 1659	Francis Hacklington	"By a parsell of Bricks we guess in all 32 thousand and so many come to the agreement we made the sum of 28. 0. 0" "By 300 of bricks for over here and over the River," "By Pavement . . . in all 200 Pavement at 13s. per 100 [all is] 1. 7. 0"	17s. 6d. per 1000 bricks

13s. per 100 pavements |
| 1660 | | "Recd 5025 of Bricks 5. 2. ½," "Recd more 6. 7. 0," "All is 32,500 [bricks] . . . 27. 10. 0," 100 of good Pavement at 7d. [is] 2. 9. ½" "500 of Pavements at 3. 10. 0," "27 Pavements," "1000 bricks" 2AB, 213 | 20s. per 1000 bricks 7d. per pavement

14s. per 100 pavements |
1660	Samuel Marshfield	"Recd by Bricks from Samuel Marshfield 1. 4. 0" 2AB, 213	24s. for bricks
20 Aug. 1663	Nathaniel Ely	"By 3000 of Bricks 3. 0. 0," "By 200 of Cutt Bricks 0. 8. 0" 2AB, 249	20s. per 1000 bricks 4s. per 100 cut bricks
Mid-1660s	Sam Ball	"For 5000 Bricks 5. 0. 0" 3AB, 26	20s. per 1000 bricks
2 Mar. 1667/68		"Agreed with Sam Ball for 5000 or 6000 of good bricks at least ⅔d Weather	20s. per 1000 bricks

BRICKMAKING, *cont.*

Date	Name	Service	Rate
		Bricks, which he is to dlr into the Boate at Chickuppy by midsumer next, and I to allow him 20s. per 1000 unless he can afford them cheap to pay for the Cariage of them to my worke."	
		"By 5000 Bricks for Mr. Glover's house 5. 0. 0," "By 1000 Bricks to Mr. Whiting 20s."	20s. per 1000 bricks
1668		"By 6000 of Brick 6. 0. 0"	20s. per 1000 bricks
8 Apr. 1669		"Agreed with Sam Ball for 6000 of bricks for Mr --- chimmeys at 20s. per 1000, is £6 but if there need but 5000, I am to have them at £5 and he is to allow me over 250 of Bricks, which I am to have on to the Bargaine" 3AB, 93	20s. per 1000 bricks
9 Dec. 1678		"By 3300 bricks . . . [and supporting logs for prison house chimney] 3. 6. 0"	20s. per 1000 bricks
		"By 1 dozen pavements for my . . . house [bricks, chimneymaking] 3. 0. 0"	£3 for bricks, pavements, chimneymaking
		"By 100 of bricks and 8 Pavements to my house over the River" 5AB, 171	Payment for 100 bricks and 8 pavements

BRICKMASONRY

Date	Name	Service	Rate
28 Nov. 1655	Rowland Thomas	"By building an oven 0. 4. 0" 1AB, 234	4s. for building oven

BRICKMASONRY, *cont.*

Date	Name	Service	Rate
Dec. 1659	Francis Hacklington	"By making an oven over the River 2s. 6d.," "mending my oven 6d." 2AB, 213	2s. 6d. for building oven 6d. for mending oven
1661	Edward Griswald of Windsor	"To 26 weeks at 4s. [for construction work] 5. 4. 0," "By Building my Newhouse with Stone and brick 40. 0. 0," "By making the chimneys . . . 7. 0. 0" 2AB, 237	4s. per week for construction work £40 for stonemasonary and brickmasonary for JP's new house £7 for building chimney
9 Jan. 1670/71	Rowland Thomas	"By mending oven and hearth 0. 1. 0" 5AB, 15	1s. for mending oven and hearth
1672	Edward Griswald	"By making Mr. Glover's chimney 5. 0. 0" 5AB, 363	£5 for building brick chimney
9 Dec. 1678	Sam Ball	"By building the Prison House Chimney 3. 0. 0" "By building the chimney for Round hill 1. 17. 0" 5AB, 171	£3 for building prison house chimney 37s. for building chimney

CANDLEMAKING

Date	Name	Service	Rate
8 Apr. 1663	Deacon Samuel Chapin	"By making 43 pounds of candles 1661 [is] 0. 7. 2" "By making candles 1662 [is] 0. 8. 4"	2d. per pound of candles 8s. 4d. for making candles
29 Oct. 1664		"By making candles 0. 4. 6" 2AB, 266	4s. 6d. for making candles

CANDLEMAKING, *cont.*

Date	Name	Service	Rate
25 Nov. 1665		"By making of candles 0. 7. 6"	7s. 6d. for making candles
8 Nov. 1666		"By making 114 pounds of candles last year 0. 19. 0" 3AB, 107B of Supplement	2d. per pound of candles
Jan. 1669/70		"By making Candles 1. 5. 7, By making Candles againe 0. 14. 5" 3AB, 107C of Supplement	£2 for making candles
Feb. 1671/72		"By making 4 pounds of candles 0. 0. 8"	2d. per pound of candles
		"By making 34 pounds candles 0. 5. 8"	2d. per pound of candles
		"45 pounds candles 0. 7. 6"	2d. per pound of candles
		"By 40 pounds ½ candle making 0. 6. 9"	2d. per pound of candles
		"20 pounds 0. 3. 4"	2d. per pound of candles
		"By 51 pounds candlemaking 0. 8. 6"	2d. per pound of candles
		"By 32 [pounds] 0. 5. 4"	2d. per pound of candles
		"44 pounds ½ [is] 0. 7. 1"	2d. per pound of candles
		"By 53½ [pounds candles] 0. 8. 11"	2d. per pound of candles
10 Dec. 1675		"By making 61 pounds ½ candles 0. 10. 3" 5AB, 87	2d. per pound of candles

CANOEING

Date	Name	Service	Rate
Nov. 1645	Thomas Mirrick	"3 Tun [of goods brought up from Enfield falls]"	Payment for carrying 3 tuns of goods from the falls [tun = 4 hogsheads]

CANOEING, *cont.*

Date	Name	Service	Rate
		"Freight down 3 hogsheads 0. 7. 6, 80 bushels wheate at 4d.; more 57½ [bushels] at 4d." WPAB, 64–65	4d. per bushel for carrying wheat to warehouse at head of Enfield falls 2s. 6d. per hogshead carried to the falls [hogshead = 51 gallons]
1645–1646	Thomas Cooper	"His share of 1 Tun and hogshead up the falls at 12s." "His share of 1 Tun, 3 hogsheads at 12s. per Tun is 0. 10. 0" WPAB, 20	12s. per tun for carrying goods from the falls 12s. per tun for carrying goods from the falls
1645–1646	Abraham Mundyne	"Bringing up the goods at 12s. per Tun" WPAB, 27	12s. per tun for carrying goods from the falls
1646	Thomas Mirrick	"Recd bringing up 1 hogshead . . . 0. 3. 6" "Bringing up 1 Tun goods 0. 12. 0" WPAB, 67	3s 6d. per hogshead carried from the falls 12s. per tun for carrying goods from the falls
1646	John Stebbins	"Recd carying downe 30 bushels of wheate, his share is and for . . . 0. 7. 6" "His share of a Tun and ½ [is] 0. 7. 6" "His share of 1 Tun and 3 hogsheads and . . . at 12s. per Tun is 0. 10. 0" WPAB, 55	7s. 6d. for falls work 10s. per tun for carrying goods from the falls 12s. per tun for carrying goods from the falls
6 Apr. 1647	Thomas Sewell	"Recd freight of corne downe and goods up the falls 0. 16. 4"	16s. 4d. per man for round trip to the falls

CANOEING, *cont.*

Date	Name	Service	Rate
3 Jul. 1647		"Recd in fraight: carying downe 37 bushels and ½ at 3d. and 2 hogsheads Bever at 2s. 6d., his half is 0. 7. 2"	3d. per bushel for carrying corn to the falls 2s. 6d. per hogshead for carrying beaver to the falls
		"Bringing up 2 Tun his halfe is 0. 12. 0" WPAB, 134	12s. per tun for carrying goods from the falls
5 Aug. 1647	Thomas Mirrick	"Sent to Trumbull on August 5, 1647 by Goodman Mirick 37 bushels ½ of wheate, 2 hogsheads of Bever and 1 little bundle of canvas"	Payment for carrying wheat, beaver, and canvas
	Thomas Sewell	"In Thomas Sewell's Canoe is 30 bushels and ½ of wheate, 7 bushels of pease and 2 hogsheads of Bever"	Payment for carrying wheat, peas, and beaver
	Hugh Parsons	"In Hugh Parsons's canoe is 35 bushels of wheate and 9 bushels Pease"	Payment for carrying wheat and peas
	Thomas Mirrick	"Goodman Mirick brought up 12 roles of cloth, 1 hogshead, 1 box candles, 2 box pipes"	Payment for carrying cloth, goods, candles, and pipes
	Thomas Sewell	"2 Tun ½ hogshead, 13 Roules of cloth, 2 hogsheads"	Payment for carrying goods and cloth
	Hugh Parsons	"1 Tun ¾ want a firkin, 10 Rouls, 1 Pack of cloth, 1 barrell Raisons, 1 quart Cask wine" WPAB, 147	Payment for carrying goods, cloth, raisins, and wine

CANOEING, *cont.*

Date	Name	Service	Rate
Oct. 1647	Thomas Mirrick	"Bringing up 1 Tun of goods 0. 12. 0"	12s. per tun for carrying goods from the falls
		"Recd bringing up Tun and ½ [is] 0. 18. 0" WPAB, 67	12s. per tun for carrying goods from the falls
7 Jun. 1648	Thomas Sewell	"Recd in bringing up 4 barrels . . . knives . . . 0. 4. 8" WPAB, 168	4s. 8d. for falls work
12 Jun. 1648	Thomas Miller	"Made up the reckning with Thomas Sewell and William Brooks about bringing up the Raisons, hogshead of Salt, Wheels and etc. and the whole is 14s. so Thomas Miller's share is 0. 4. 8" WPAB, 230	4s. 8d. for carrying raisins, salt, and wheels from the falls
1648	Thomas Mirrick	"Recd in carying downe 27 bushels wheat at 3d. and 1 hogshead of Bever to [falls] 0. 9. 3"	3d. per bushel for carrying wheat to the falls
		"Bringing up a Tun and ½ hogshead of goods . . . 0. 13. 6"	12s. per tun for carrying goods from the falls
		"Carrying downe 2 hogsheads and a Pack 6d. [is] 0. 5. 6" WPAB, 68	5s. 6d. for falls work
1652	Thomas Miller	"Recd by carrying downe Corne and other goods and bringing up Goods from May last to the 7th of September 1652 [is] 3. 7. 10"	£3 7s. 10d. for carrying wheat and other goods to and from the falls
		"Recd by carying downe and hogsheads in September with Rowland	12s. for falls work

CANOEING, *cont.*

Date	Name	Service	Rate
		[Thomas] . . . 0. 12. 0" 1AB, 63	
1652	Rowland Thomas	"Recd by carying down 35 bushels of wheat and 6 hogsheads of goods . . . is 0. 12. 0"	12s. for carrying goods to the falls
		"Bringing up 5 hogsheads and ½ of goods, your part 0. 8. 3"	3s. per hogshead for carrying goods from the falls
		"Recd by carying downe Corne meale and Bever to John Gallop your part is 0. 12. 0"	12s. for falls work
22 Dec. 1652		"Recd by bringing up goods from Goodman Wilton's house . . . your part is 0. 2. 3" 1AB, 73	2s. 3d. for carrying goods from Woronoco [Westfield]
12 Apr. 1653	Thomas Mirrick	"Recd by a voyadge downe the falls with Anthony [Dorchester] 0. 11. 9"	11s. 9d. per man for voyage to the falls
		"Recd by carrying downe Tarr before winter 0. 5. 0" 1AB, 99	5s. for carrying tar to the falls
24 May 1653	Deacon Samuel Wright	"Recd by carrying from my house to the foot of the falls 44 bushels of wheate . . . 0. 13. 0" 1AB, 111	3⅔d. per bushel for carrying wheat to the falls
1653	Miles Morgan	"Recd by a voyage downe the falls 0. 13. 6" 1AB, 76	13s. 6d. per man for voyage to the falls
6 Jan. 1653/54	Rowland Thomas	"Recd by the use of your canoe . . . fetching hay at 16d. . . . 0. 9. 4" 1AB, 74	16d. for renting canoe

CANOEING, *cont.*

Date	Name	Service	Rate
5 Aug. 1654	Thomas Ban- croft	"Recd by carying of Corne down the falls (3 voyages) . . . bringing up of goods 2 Tun ½ your pt is 15s. [is] 2. 15. 6" 1AB, 147	£2 15s. 6d. for falls work
2 Dec. 1654	Samuel Terry	"Recd by bringing up heavy hogsheads 0. 7. 0" "Bringing up a hide of leather 0. 0. 6" 1AB, 239	7s. for carrying heavy hogsheads from the falls 6d. for carrying a hide of leather from the falls
13 Dec. 1654	Symon Beamon	"Recd by 7 voyages downe the falls with Rowland your part of them is 5. 0. 6½" 1AB, 197	14s. 4d. per man for voyage to the falls
1655	Miles Morgan	"Recd by a voyadge downe with Sam Terry 0. 16. 4" 1AB, 265	16s. 4d. per man for voyage to the falls
12 Jul. 1655	Samuel Terry	"Recd by carying downe 84 bushels, your halfe [with canoe abated] 0. 12. 6" "Recd by carying downe 70 bushels and bringing up 2 Tun of [goods] your part is 1. 2. 5" 1AB, 239	3½d. per bushel for carrying wheat to the falls 22s. 5d. per man for round trip to the falls
8 Nov. 1655		"Recd by carying downe to falls 71 bushels ½ of wheat, 2 hogsheads, bring- ing up 1 Tun ½ goods, your halfe is 9s. [abate for canoe] 1. 11. 11" "Recd by carying corne to the warehouse with Symon Beamon 90 bushels, your halfe [canoe abated] 0. 6. 9"	31s. 11d. for falls work 6s. 9d. per man for carrying corn to warehouse at Enfield

CANOEING, *cont.*

Date	Name	Service	Rate
		"Recd by another voyage with Goodman Miller with cannoe abated 0. 11. 0"	11s. per man for voyage to the falls
		"Bringing up a Dram ½ Salt, another of Liquor 0. 4. 0"	19d. per dram for carrying salt and liquor from the falls
		"Recd by a voyage with Goodman Morgan the 17th October 1655 your halfe, canoe abated is 0. 7. 4" 1AB, 240	7s. 4d. per man for voyage to the falls
14 Dec. 1655	Symon Beamon	"Recd by 7 voyadges downe the falls (cannoe abated) all comes to 7. 1. 6"	20s. 2½d. per voyage to the falls
		"Recd by 3 voyadges to Pequot [New London] 1. 5. 0" 1AB, 291	8s. 4d. for voyage to New London
19 Mar. 1655/56	William Brooks	"Recd by a voyadge downe the falls with John Clark your half is 0. 13. 6"	13s. 6d. per man for voyage to the falls
		"Recd by a voyadge with John Clark to Wethersfield . . . your half is 1. 11. 0"	31s. per man for voyage to Wethersfield
		"Recd by another voyadge canoe abated 1. 11. 0"	31s. per man for voyage to Wethersfield
		"Recd by a voyadge with G. Lamb 0. 17. 7" 1AB, 300	17s. 7d. per man for voyage to the falls
12 May 1656	Thomas Mirrick	"Recd by carying downe 81 bushels and bringing up a bayle of cloth and a kettle 1. 13. 6"	33s. 6d. for carrying 81 bushels [of wheat, corn?] to the falls and carrying up cloth and a kettle
20 May 1656		"By carying downe 53 bushels 0. 17. 8"	4d. per bushel for carrying wheat to the falls

CANOEING, *cont.*

Date	Name	Service	Rate
Jul. 1656		"Recd by allowance to one of the voyadges that went to Wethesfield 0. 6. 0" 1AB, 316	6s. per voyage to Wethersfield
1656	Thomas Miller	"Recd by voyadge to the falls with Terry 1. 2. 0"	22s. per man for voyage to the falls
		"By another voyadge with Sam Terry 1. 1. 0"	21s. per man for voyage to the falls
		"Recd by a voyadge downe the falls with Sam Terry June 5 [1656] your halfe, canoe abated is but 0. 14. 0"	14s. per man for voyage to the falls
		"Recd by a voyadge with Terry in July, your halfe, cannoe abated is 0. 16. 0" 1AB, 300–301	16s. per man for voyage to the falls
6 Jul. 1656	Samuel Terry	"Recd by a voyage downe with John Lamb 28 Aprill 1656, your halfe cannoe abated is 1. 6. 0"	26s. per man for voyage to the falls
		"Recd by bringing up a bayle of cloth with Goodman Morgan your part is 0. 2. 6"	2s. 6d. per man for carrying a bolt of cloth from the falls
		"Recd by a voyage down with Rich cannoe abated 0. 13. 0"	13s. per man for voyage to the falls
		"Recd by a voyage with Goodman Morgan canoe abated 0. 12. 6"	12s. 6d. per man for voyage to the falls
		"Recd by a voyage with Miller 5 June (56) [is] 0. 13. 6"	13s. 6d. per man for voyage to the falls
		"Recd by a voyage with Miller July (56) [is] 0. 15. 11"	15s. 11d. per man for voyage to the falls
30 Sep. 1656		"Recd by a voyadge downe the falls with Miller [canoe abated] 1. 2. 2"	22s. 2d. per man for voyage to the falls

CANOEING, *cont.*

Date	Name	Service	Rate
		"Recd by another voyage with Miller [canoe abated] 1. 1. 8" 1AB, 240	21s. 8d. per man for voyage to the falls
2 Oct. 1656	William Warrinar	"Recd 3 voyadges downe to the foote of the falls 1. 7. 0" 1AB, 268	9s. per voyage to the foot of the falls
14 Oct. 1656	Thomas Mirrick	"Recd by a voyadge down the falls with Joseph Parsons in June 1653, you caryed 71 bushels of [winter] wheate your part is 0. 13. 4"	13s. 4d. per man for carrying 71 bushels of wheat to the falls
		"Recd by your carying downe in May 1654, 75 bushels 1. 5. 0"	4d. per bushel for carrying wheat to the falls
		"Recd by a voyadge in July 1654 carying 54 bushels 0. 18. 0"	4d. per bushel for carrying wheat to the falls
		"Recd by the use of your cannoe to fetch hay 0. 5. 0" 1AB, 316	5s. for rent of canoe
1657		"Bringing up 1 Tun ½ goods, when I was in England 0. 16. 6"	11s. per tun for carrying goods from the falls
1658		Credited for voyages in: April, 2 May, 15 May, 24 May, 29 May, 5 June, 11 June, 18? June, 30 June 2AB, 61	Payments for falls work
Aug. 1658		"By severall voyages to Hartford this summer to August 1658, all amounting to 13. 16. 4"	£13 16s. 4d. for several voyages to Hartford
		"By bringing up salt, oatmeale, and ankin Liquor 0. 1. 6"	1s. 6d. for carrying salt, oatmeal, and liquor from the falls

CANOEING, *cont.*

Date	Name	Service	Rate
17 Aug. 1658		"Bringing up one Tun of goods and 6 bushels of Salt all comes to 21s."	21s. for carrying 1 tun of goods and 6 bushels of salt from the falls
Dec. 1658		"By bringing up goods from Hartford and carting them from Windsor 0. 3. 6" 2AB, 87	3s. 6d. for carrying goods from Hartford via Windsor
1659	Symon Beamon	"1 voyadge this summer 0. 15. 0" 1AB, 292	15s. for voyage to the falls
1660	Symon Lobdell	"By bringing up 2 Tun ½ goods 0. 18. 0"	7s. 3d. per tun for carrying goods from the falls
		"By carying down 4 barrels beife 0. 6. 0"	18d. per barrel for carrying beef to the falls
		"By bringing up 30 bushels malt, 1 barrel of ale 0. 16. 6" 2AB, 195	16s. 6d. for carrying 30 bushels of malt and one barrel of ale from the falls
19 Oct. 1660	Charles Ferry	"By severall voyadges downe the falls this summer 1660 with Goodman Mirick, your half of bringing downe the corne and bringing up goods 3. 15. 0" 2AB, 261	£3 15s. for several voyages to the falls
2 Feb. 1660/61	Thomas Bancroft	"By a voyadge downe the falls in (59) your part 0. 13. 6" 2AB, 117	13s. 6d. per man for voyage to the falls
4 Apr. 1661	John Henryson	"By a voyadge downe the falls with Miles 0. 12. 0" "By bringing up 18 bushels	12s. per man for voyage to the falls 4d. per bushel for

CANOEING, *cont.*

Date	Name	Service	Rate
		of salt with Goodman Mirick . . . your halfe is 0. 6. 0"	carrying salt from the falls
		"By a Journey to Hartford 0. 2. 3"	2s. 3d. for journey to Hartford
		"By bringing up 15 bushels of malt at 6d. your half is 0. 3. 9"	6d. per bushel for carrying malt from the falls
		"By carying downe 10 bushels of wheat your halfe is 0. 1. 8" 2AB, 205	4d. per bushel for carrying wheat to the falls
May–Jun. 1661	Miles Morgan	"By 5 voyadges downe the falls with Edw. Foster . . . and brought up goods at 12s. per Tun [£10, abate £5 for canoe] 5. 0. 0"	12s. per tun for carrying goods from the falls
		"By carying downe 101 bushels of wheate at 4d. with John Henryson your part is 0. 18. 0" 2AB, 131	4d. per bushel for carrying wheat to the falls
1661	Charles Ferry	"By 2 voyages downe the falls in May (61) . . . 1. 13. 0" 2AB, 261	16s. 6d. per man for voyage to the falls
2 Feb. 1662/63	Miles Morgan	"By carying downe the falls 243 bushels ½ of Corne at 5d. per bushel because you put it in the warehouse most of it otherwise . . . 4d."	5d. per bushel for carrying corn to the falls and putting it in the warehouse, 4d. per bushel if not placed in warehouse (overpayment)
		"By carying 261 [bushels] from the foote of the falls at 3d. because into warehouse 8. 6. 0" 2AB, 335	3d. per bushel for carrying wheat from the foot of the falls to the warehouse

CANOEING, *cont.*

Date	Name	Service	Rate
12 Nov. 1663	Nathaniel Burt	"By carying down 33 bush-els of wheat at 4d. [is] 0. 11. 0" "By bringing up hogshead of Sugar 0. 4. 0" 2AB, 360–361	4d. per bushel for carrying wheat to the falls 4s. per hogshead for carrying sugar from the falls
1664	Samuel Terry	"By worke carying Corne and bringing up goods in the yeare 1664 with Good-man Morgan and David Ashley your part 1. 7. 0" 3AB, 145	27s. per man for round trip to the falls
1664	Thomas Mir-rick	"By carying down 89 bush-els of wheate Anno 1664 [is] 1. 17. 1" "By carying 180 bushels from the foote of the falls 1664 [is] 2. 5. 0" "Bringing up 1 Tun Goods 1664 to the foote of the falls 0. 6. 0" 3AB, 113	5d. per bushel for carrying wheat to the falls 3d. per bushel for carrying wheat from the foot of falls to the warehouse 6s. per tun for carry-ing goods from the warehouse to the foot of the falls
1664	William Warri-nar	"By carying downe Corne and bringing up Goods with Goodman Morgan Ano 1664 your halfe 2. 0. 4" 3AB, 133	40s. 4d. per man for round trip to the falls
9 Jan. 1664/65	Thomas Miller	"By carying downe hides to Windsor 0. 4. 0" 3AB, 191	4s. for carrying hides to Windsor
10 Jan. 1664/65	Jedediah Strong	"By Carying downe 6 Bar-rells at 5s. [is] 1. 10. 0"	5s. per barrel carried to the falls

CANOEING, *cont.*

Date	Name	Service	Rate
1665		"By carying downe 6 barells October 65 [is] 1. 10. 0" 3AB, 205	5s. per barrel carried to the falls
1665	Captain Aaron Cooke	"By carying down 12 barrels of flowre to Windsor before winter in Ano 1665 [is] 3. 0. 0" 3AB, 199	5s. per barrel for carrying flour to Windsor
1665	Thomas Mirrick	"By falls worke this yeare 1665 your share of all to this 10th July 1665 is £4 5s." "By bringing up 12 bushels of Salt at 6d. [is] 0. 6. 0" "By your Teame loading the canoes at the wharfe 0. 1. 6" 3AB, 113	£4 5s. for falls work 6d. per bushel for carrying salt from the falls 18d. for rent of team of oxen to load canoes at wharf
1665	Samuel Terry	"By carying downe Corne this yeare with Goodman Warinar from May to the end of June for 938 bushels at 5d. per bushel 19. 10. 0, your part is 9. 15. 0" "Carying 76 bushels from the foote of the Falls at 2d. ½ per bushel is 15s. 10d., youre part of it is 0. 7. 11" "Carying down 23 barrels of meate at 2s., your halfe is 1. 3. 0" "By bringing up 110 bushels of salt at 6d. per bushel, your halfe 1. 7. 6" "By bringing up 1 Tun and ½ of Goods 18s. your halfe 0. 9. 0" 3AB, 145	5d. per bushel for carrying corn to the falls 2½d. per bushel carried from the foot of the falls to the warehouse 2s. per barrel for carrying meat to the falls 6d. per bushel for carrying salt from the falls 12s. per tun for carrying goods from the falls

CANOEING, *cont.*

Date	Name	Service	Rate
1665	Anthony Dorchester	"By carying 681 bushels [of corn] from foote of falls and part from home 10. 13. 0" 3AB, 85	£10 13s. for falls work
1665	William Warrinar	"By goeing down with Sam Terry: carying downe Corne at 5d. per bushel and 2d. ½ from the foote of the falls and carying barrels at 2s. a peice: bringing up Salt at 6d. per bushel and goods at 12s. per Tun: In all you have earned together £26 2s. 10d., for your half of it is £13 2s. 5d. . . . abate for the Boate which I am to allow to 13. 2. 5" 3AB, 133	5d. per bushel for carrying corn to the foot of the falls 2½d. per bushel for carrying corn from the foot of the falls to the warehouse 2s. per barrel carried to the falls 6d. per bushel for carrying salt from the falls 12s. per tun for carrying goods from the falls
21 Sep. 1665	Anthony Dorchester	"By carying corne to Hartford, 390 bushels at 5d. [is] 8. 2. 6" 3AB, 85	5d. per bushel for carrying corn to Hartford
Oct. 1665	Jedediah Strong	"By carrying downe 6 Barrells at 5s. [is] 1. 10. 0" "By carying downe 6 barells October 1665 [is] 1. 10. 0" 3AB, 205	5s. per barrel carried to the falls 5s. per barrel carried to the falls
15 Dec. 1665	Nathaniel Burt	"By bringing up 3 hogsheads of sugar from Hartford 0. 10. 0" 3AB, 65	3s. 4d. per hogshead for carrying sugar from Hartford
2 Jun. 1666	Captain Aaron Cooke	"By carying downe 2 barrells of flowr 0. 10. 0" 3AB, 199	5s. per barrel for carrying flour to the falls

CANOEING, *cont.*

Date	Name	Service	Rate
1666	William Warrinar	"By goeing downe the falls with Sam Terry your part 5. 5. 0" 3AB, 133	£5 5s. for falls work
Jul. 1666	Samuel Terry	"Recd by worke downe the falls and etc. all to this 14 July 1666 comes to as in day booke 11. 14. 0" 3AB, 144	£11 14s. for falls work
1667	William Warrinar	"By falls worke with Goodman Morgan carying down: 216 bushels of wheat at 5d. [is] 4. 10. 0" "142 Moose [skins] at 4d. [is] 2. 7. 4" "10 barels of wheate at 2s. [is] 1. 0. 0" "bringing up 19 bushels ½ Salt at 6d. [is] 0. 9. 9" 3AB, 133	5d. per bushel for carrying wheat to the falls 4d. per moose skin carried to the falls 2s. per barrel for carrying wheat to the falls 6d. per bushel for carrying salt from the falls
17 Jun. 1667	Samuel Porter	"By bringing up a Bale of Linnen your halfe 0. 2. 6" 3AB, 271	5s. for carrying a bolt of linen from the falls
Dec. 1667– May 1668	Miles Morgan	"By Carrying downe 7 barells pork at 2s. [is] 0. 14. 0" 4AB, 49	2s. per barrel for carrying pork to the falls
1667–1668	William Warrinar	"By Carrying downe 22 bushels wheat 0. 9. 0" "By Carrying downe 3 barrels of Porke 0. 6. 0" 4AB, 51	5d. per bushel for carrying wheat to the falls 2s. per barrel for carrying pork to the falls
28 Mar. 1668	Anthony Dorchester	"By bringing up 20 bushels of Salt 1667 [is] 0. 10. 0" 3AB, 105	6d. per bushel for carrying salt from the falls

CANOEING, cont.

Date	Name	Service	Rate
23 May 1668	Thomas Day	"By 25 bushels wheat delivered at Hartford and put on board Marke Keeler 5. 0. 0"	4s. per bushel for carrying wheat to Hartford and placing it aboard ship
Jun. 1669		"By bringing up 25 bushels of Salt at 8d." 3AB, 151	8d. per bushel for carrying salt from the falls
17 Jun. 1669	John Field	"By 20 bushels wheate to Jonathan Gilbert's warehouse 4. 0. 0" "By 112 bushels wheat delivered Goodman Hulburd at 3s. [is] 16. 16. 0" 3AB, 245	4s. per bushel for carrying wheat to Hartford 3s. per bushel for carrying wheat to Northampton
22 Jun. 1669	Miles Morgan	"By Carying down Corn 577 bushels, also barrels and other things and bringing up 2 Puncheons and 25 bushels salt . . . 16. 10. 2" 3AB, 241	£16 10s. 2d. for falls work [puncheon = 72 gallons for beer, 120 gallons for liquor]
20 Dec 1669	Henry Chapin	"Bringing the Barrells last tyme from Chickopee 0. 4. 6" 3AB, 157	4s. 6d. for carrying barrels from Chicopee
30 Sep. 1670	Jonathan Morgan	"By bringing up 20 bushels of salt 0. 13. 4" 5AB, 175	8d. per bushel for carrying salt from the falls
23 Nov. 1670	Increase Sikes	"Agreed with Increase Sikes to Carry downe my Corne and Barrells to Hartford next Spring; my Corne he is to Carry for 4d. ½ per bushel and Barrells for 2s. a piece; when I have occasion to use but	4½d. per bushel for carrying corn to Hartford 2s. per barrel carried to Hartford

CANOEING, *cont.*

Date	Name	Service	Rate
		one Boate at a tyme I am to use him; But If I have occasion to send more Boates than one at once I am to use who I se meete" 3AB, 207	
22 May 1671		"By carrying Corne downe and Porke to this 22th May 1671 all is 4. 1. 0 and bringing up lead is 4. 2. 0" 5AB, 161	£4 1s. for carrying corn and pork to the falls £4 2s. for carrying lead from the falls
25 May 1671	Thomas Mir-rick	"By a voyadge to Hadley for Barrells 0. 15. 0"	15s. for voyage to Hadley for barrels
		"By carying down 10,000 of Planks and Bords to Middletown at 10s. per 1000 is £5 . . . halfe . . . 3. 0. 0" 5AB, 111	10s. per 1000 board feet carried to Mid-dletown
1671	Samuel Har-mon	"By bringing up Salt from Hartford 0. 11. 0" 5AB, 165	11s. for carrying salt from Hartford
15 Mar. 1672/73	James Warrinar	"By carying corne and etc. downe the falls 3. 6. 0" 5AB, 93	£3 6s. for carrying corn to the falls
20 Mar. 1672/73	Victory Sikes	"By bringing up 1 hogs-head Sugar 0. 5. 0" 5AB, 357	5s. per hogshead for carrying sugar from the falls
28 Apr. 1673	Increase Sikes	"By bringing up 16 bushels Salt to the foote of the falls 0. 8. 0" 5AB, 161	6d. per bushel for carrying salt from warehouse to foot of falls
1673	Rowland Thomas	"By bringing up 2 hogs-head Sugar 0. 9. 0" 5AB, 15	4s. 6d. per hogshead for carrying sugar from the falls

CANOEING, *cont.*

Date	Name	Service	Rate
1674–1675	Joseph Stebbins	"By a voyadge downe the falls with Goodman Dorchester 0. 10. 0"	10s. per man for voyage to the falls
		"By carying downe 7 barrels, your ½ [is] 0. 7. 0"	2s. per barrel carried to the falls
		"By your part of a voyadge for Salt 0. 10. 0"	10s. for carrying salt from the falls
		"By 2 days voyadge about salt and etc."	
		Canoe work: 1676 "4. 13. 0"	£4 13s. for falls work
		1677 "6. 5. 0"	£6 5s. for falls work
		1678 "2. 7. 0" 5AB, 427	£2 7s. for falls work
Nov. 1675	Increase Sikes	"By a voyadge downe the falls Nov. 1675 [is] 0. 12. 0" 5AB, 417	12s. for voyage to the falls
14 Jan. 1675/76	Samuel Stebbins	"By your voyadge for Salt 0. 10. 0" 5AB, 173	10s. for voyage to the falls to get salt
Feb. 1675/76	Edward Foster	"By a voyadge downe the falls for Salt 0. 12. 0" 5AB, 59	12s. for voyage to the falls to get salt
1675–1676	Thomas Miller	"By voyadges downe the falls last Summer, May and June 1675, Carying downe in all 554 bushels of Corne at 4d. is 9. 4. 4"	4d. per bushel for carrying corn to the falls
		"And Porke 30 barrels at 21d. [is] 2. 12. 0"	21d. per barrel for carrying pork to the falls

CANOEING, *cont.*

Date	Name	Service	Rate
		"Bringing up Salt at 8d. [is] 0. 16. 0"	8d. per bushel for carrying salt from the falls
		"Bringing up 18 firkins of sope 0. 9. 0" 5AB, 289	6d. per firkin for carrying soap from the falls
Jun. 1677	James Mun	"By bringing up Sugar, Rum, Salt, with Joseph Stebbins your share 0. 9. 8" 5AB, 99	9s. 8d. per man for carrying sugar, rum, and salt from the falls
20 Apr. 1680	James Warrinar	"By carrying downe 40 bushels of Pease from chikuppy to Hartford at 21d. per bushel 3. 10. 0" 5AB, 93	21d. per bushel for carrying peas from Chicopee to Hartford
1701–1702	John Lumbard	"Bringing up goods at 21d. per pound 29 and ¼ [is] 2. 9. 1¼"	21d. per pound for carrying goods from the falls
28 Apr. 1702		"By a parsell of goods in Boston 31. 0. 3" "Bringing up said Goods at 2s. [is] 13. 3. ¼"	2s. per pound for carrying goods from the falls
28 May 1702		"By bringing up said goods at 21d. per pound 0. 8. 7"	21d. per pound for carrying goods from the falls
Jul. 1702		"By Bringing up said Goods at 21d. per pound 0. 9. 4¼" 4AB, 73	21d. per pound for carrying goods from the falls

CARPENTRY

Date	Name	Service	Rate
1652	Richard Sikes	"Recd by making a Plow 0. 5. 0"	5s. for building plow

CARPENTRY, *cont.*

Date	Name	Service	Rate
		"Recd by what I am to allow for making the Meeting House stairs 25s., for the window 16s."	25s. for building stairs for meeting-house 16s. for building window for meeting-house
		"Recd by your making [?] the frame of the Bell 2. 0. 0"	40s. for building bell frame
		"Recd by a ladder in the Bell Tower . . . 0. 10. 0" 1AB, 87	10s. for building bell tower ladder
26 Apr. 1653	Thomas Cooper	"Recd by your Removing my Cowhouse to the Barne 10. 0. 0" 1AB, 78	£10 for moving cowhouse
2 Dec. 1657	Thomas Barber	"Agreed with Tho Barber to Build me a Barne over the grt River, 50 foote long and 24 [or 34?] foote wide with a leanetoe all along the back side, to be good substantial timber well braced and strong with Barne doors and also lean-toe doors, all to be compleated agt Harvest next, for wch I am to allow him £21 and to find Goodm Thomas one day to seeke out the Timber and 3 days worke . . . more when he falls the Timber, also I am to find the boards for the Barne dores and nails and promise [?] help at raising" "Wish Goodm Barber to make the rafters feete good and long that I may have large and deepe eves" 1AB, 176	£21 for building 50 × 24-foot barn

CARPENTRY, *cont.*

Date	Name	Service	Rate
		Oct. 1658, £21 paid 2AB, 40	
23 Oct. 1658	Thomas Barber and son	"Recd by worke about my house [wainscoating?] and [finishing?] 17 days your self and Thomas, more 2 day worke you self and Thomas, making the doors and etc. all is 19 days at 5s. [is] 4. 15. 0" 2AB, 40	5s. per diem for fin- ishing work
25 Jun. 1659	Thomas Barber	"Recd by making my Cider press 5. 0. 0" 2AB, 40	£5 for building cider press
14 Dec. 1659	Richard Sikes	"Recd making Plough and mending 0. 10. 0" 2AB, 27	10s. for building and mending plow
23 Oct. 1660	Samuel Bewell	"By 12 days worke the first tyme, By 48 days worke at two tyme more: all is 60 days . . . 8. 12. 0" 2AB, 279	2s. 10⁴/₁₀d. per diem for carpentry
27 Oct. 1660	Thomas Barber and son	"Recd by himself and Son each 29 days at 5s. 6d . . . [in all] 58 days worke . . . 7. 19. 6" "Recd by 14 days more himself . . . 2. 2. 0" 2AB, 40	5s. 6d. per diem for carpentry, father and son 3s. per diem for car- pentry
17 Jan. 1660/61	Richard Sikes	"Recd by worke about my New house 16. 0. 0" "And 14 days [his son] In- crease 0. 14. 0" 2AB, 27	£16 for carpentry on JP's house 1s. per diem for ap- prentice work as car- penter

CARPENTRY, *cont.*

Date	Name	Service	Rate
26 Oct. 1661	Samuel Bewell	"By 27 days worke and ½ to this 26 October 1661 and I allow you for day goeing downe" 2AB, 279	Payment for 28½ days of carpentry
14 Nov. 1661	William Clark of Hartford	"Agreed with him to groundsill my Barne and also to groundsill my lathe howse by it, sometime in March or Aprill next, for which being compleate and fully done well and sub-stantial, I am to allow him £5 and one weeks dyet; the Timber for it to bee all of good sound white oake which he setting out and shaping, only I am to fall and bring them home" 2AB, 327	£5 and one week board for groundsill-ing barn and lath-house, JP responsible for felling and cart-ing timber
22 Feb. 1661/62	David Shippey [stepson or ap-prentice of Samuel Pearly?]	"By 4 weekes worke of David Shippy 2. 0. 0"	10s. per week for carpentry
	Samuel Pearly	"By Samuel Pearly's worke 10 days 1. 5. 0" "Agreed with Sam Pearly for 4 months at Au-saltnnig[?] to begin some-time in Aprill; he is to tend my worke . . . of carpen-try[?] or otherwise and to find tools for 2 men be-sides himself, and to repair .[?] his horse 2 voyadges thither, and in case of hindrance and disappoint-ment by weather or things not setting well . . . for	2s. 6d. per diem for carpentry £4 and meat and drink per month for carpentry

CARPENTRY, *cont.*

Date	Name	Service	Rate
		worke: he promises to last on for a week worke: for all which . . . I am to find him dyet and give him £4 per month beginning one week in the middle of . . . and it was agreed (at the conclusion when I yielded to allow him £4 [a] Month) That if he came to towne in the tyme he allow for it" 2AB, 259	
1 May 1662	William Clark and Nicholas Clark of Hart-ford	"Agreed with Nicholas and William Clarke to Build me a Barne over the River 46 foote long and 21 or 22 foote wide, eleven foote high between, Join with a Leantoe on the Back side, to make doors, all to be finished substantial well and workmanlike, fit to lay the shingle by a month of early Michalsmas next for which I am to allow them £18 and a fortnight's dyet of them two, and what Timber is gotten towards it already, what is wanting more they are to get and provide ready; I only cart-ing it and I am to find boards for dores" 2AB, 327	£18 and 2 weeks board for building 46 × 21 × 11-foot barn, JP to provide bulk of materials
14 Dec. 1662	Nicholas Clark of Hartford	"Recd by Building the House of Correction £20 being to be allowed for not finishing it is 6. 0. 0" 2AB, 326	£14 abatement for not completing con-struction of house of correction

CARPENTRY, *cont.*

Date	Name	Service	Rate
5 Nov. 1663	John Lamb	"John Lamb is to Ground-sill my Barne and Granery for which worke well done I am to allow him 6d. per foote and I to fetch him the groundsils"	6d. per foot for groundsilling barn
		"228 foote at 6d. [is] 5. 14. 0" 2AB, 353	Payment for ground-silling barn
Mar. 1666	David Ashley	"8 days ½ at the mill dam, carpenter at 2s. 6d." 3AB, 115	2s. 6d. per diem for carpentry
1667	Cornelius Williams	"By worke at the house of Corection laying the floares, partitions, and etc., all agreed at 62. 12. 3" 3AB, 313	£62 12s. 3d. for laying floors and building partitions for house of correction
1668	John Baker	"By 48 days carpentering at 3s. [is] 7. 4. 0"	3s. per diem for carpentry
17 Jul. 1668		"By my Barne over the River when wholy finished 35. 0. 0"	£35 for building barn
		"Acoted with John Baker and have Reckned for his Building of my Mill howse and my Barne over the River and so will be due to him when finished 20. 11. 9" 3AB, 57	£20 11s. 9d. for building millhouse and barn
21 May 1669	Aaron Cooke	"Recd per the frame of . . . my son Whiting house . . . and per timber and other additions 41. 10. 0" 3AB, 12	£41 10s. for building houseframe, timber, etc.
1669	Nathaniel Ely	"By stairs for the Prison house cellar and etc, and	£10 7s. 10d. for building stairs for

CARPENTRY, *cont.*

Date	Name	Service	Rate
		40s. allowed for your tyme and care . . . 10. 7. 10" 3AB, 199	prison house cellar
6 Jan. 1669/70	Cornelius Williams	"By worke mending and fasoning the Bell 0. 2. 0" 3AB, 313	2s. for mending and reseating bell
1670 [?]	Goodman Billing	"By worke with John Mossly about my son Whiting's frame, that part which I allow you is 13. 0. 0" 3AB, 267	£13 for carpentry on house frame
1670 [?]	Thomas Barber	"By 2 days worke laying my floare 0. 5. 0" 3AB, 295	2s. 6d. per diem for laying floors
8 Mar. 1671/72	Richard Sikes (and Victory)	"By Victory a day Raising son Whiting's house 0. 2. 0"	2s. per diem for house raising
		"By so much due to you for making mr. Glover's howse out of the Town Rates which I take 3. 0. 0"	£3 for carpentry work on minister's house
		"By making my little Roome and groundsilling the old Parlour 4. 10. 0" 5AB, 135	£4 10s. for building small room and groundsilling parlor
Sep. 1672	David Morgan	"By 10 days worke at our lodging Room and closset for my wife 1. 10. 0" 5AB, 385	3s. per diem for carpentry
10 Feb. 1672/73	Benjamin Dunnidge	"Making Raft for Stony River and goeing down with it 0. 7. 0" 5AB, 193	7s. for building and delivering raft for Stony River
20 Mar. 1672/73	Victory Sikes	"By your halfe of Building and Covering my Barne at	£20 for building and shingling 46 × 24-

CARPENTRY, *cont.*

Date	Name	Service	Rate
		the Round hill, the other halfe to you Brother Increase 10. 0. 0" 5AB, 357	foot barn
24 Nov. 1674	Increase Sikes	"By Building my Barne at the Round hill 46 feet long 24 [feet wide] and covering it your halfe is 10. 0. 0" 5AB, 417	£20 for building and shingling 46 × 24-foot barn
1674	David Morgan	"By the house at the Round hil (for Isack) 5. 0. 0" 5AB, 385	£5 for building house at Round Hill
3 Dec. 1674	Thomas Copley	"By the floares for my Son Whiting 8. 10. 0" 5AB, 171	£8 10s. for building floors for house
8 Dec. 1674	Joseph Leonard	"Agreed with Joseph Leonard to Build me a house at Suffield on my land on feather streete, of 29 foote long, and 20 feet wide, 10 feet standing: he to doe all the carpentry worke from falling to shingle, viz. dor, chimney, Runges, staires, partition, windows, floares, and etc., all that is to be done by carpentry, for closing and smithy all whatsoever I am to allow him the use of my Saw mill to saw the Bords Into braces and struts, he also to doe all the carpentry for all which Compleated well . . . and substantial in all handsome and workmanlike, I am to allow him £25 and 2 gallon of rum . . . " 5AB, 67	£25 and 2 gallons of rum for building 29 × 20 × 10-foot house

CARPENTRY, *cont.*

Date	Name	Service	Rate
1675	Victory Sikes	"By your halfe of the leanto on stable . . . 0. 8. 6" "By the frame of my Barne, £14 10s. . . . you halfe is 7. 5. 0" 5AB, 357	17s. for building lean-to on stable £14 10s. for building barn frame
Nov. 1675	Increase Sikes	"By worke in mending my Saw Mill 0. 14. 6" 5AB, 417	14s. 6d. for mending sawmill
18 Nov. 1675	Jonathan Morgan	"By 24 days worke framing the Mill" 5AB, 383	Payment for 24 days work framing mill
29 Feb. 1675/76	Increase Sikes	JP agrees with Increase and Victory Sikes to build him a barn with the dimensions 52 × 24 feet for £14 5AB, 417	£14 for building 52 × 24-foot barn
26 Mar. 1676	Benjamin Dunnidge	"Agreed with Benjamin Dunnidge to [build] us a Raft well and stronge built [for] 45s." 5AB, 193	45s. for building raft
8 Dec. 1676	Thomas Stebbins, Jr.	"By the Prison House [£44] whereoff Isack Gleason hath 7. 9. 6 [Stebbins's part is] 36. 10. 6" 5AB, 515	£44 for building house of correction
20 Dec. 1676– 3 Jan. 1676/77	John Allys	"By allowing you for Building the Meetinghouse" £130 "[and] the gallery £10" 5AB, 271	£140 for building meetinghouse with gallery
1677	Philip Matoone	"By 6 days worke about the mill floor 0. 12. 0" 5AB, 537	2s. per diem for installing mill floor

CARPENTRY, *cont.*

Date	Name	Service	Rate
1677	John Pope	"By making the Pulpit Canopee, Deacon's seate, and stairs 5. 10. 0"	£5 10s. for building pulpit canopy, deacon's seat, and stairs for meetinghouse
		"By my Pew 4. 10. 0"	£4 10s. for building JP's pew
		"By a Table in my Pew 1. 0. 3"	£1 3d. for building table in JP's pew
		"By my wife's Pew 3. 10. 0"	£3 10s. for building Amy Pynchon's pew
		"By the court seate 2. 15. 0" 5AB, 527	£2 15s. for building court seat
Nov. 1677	Increase Sikes	"By the frame of my Barne £14 10s. your halfe is 7. 5. 0"	£14 10s. for building frame for barn, 2 men
		"By making the stable on end Barne . . . 0. 8. 6" 5AB, 417	8s. 6d. for building lean-to on barn
18 Jan. 1677/78	David Morgan	JP agreed with Jonathan and David Morgan for them to build him a log house 24 × 18 feet, everything except the sawing for £14 1680 "By your halfe Building house . . . 7. 0. 0" 5AB, 385	£14 for building 24 × 18-foot log house
	Jonathan Morgan	3 Dec. 1684 "By Building my little house with your Brother David, your half of it is £7" 5AB, 199	
1678	Increase Sikes	"By work about my Sawmill mending and etc. all is 1. 5. 0"	£1 5s. for mending sawmill

CARPENTRY, *cont.*

Date	*Name*	*Service*	*Rate*
		"By the frame of the Barne as a house, your halfe is 6. 5. 0" 5AB, 417–418	£13 for building barn frame, 2 men
1678	Jonathan Bush	"Agreed with Jonath Bush to Build me a house about the Round hill of 28 feet Long, 20 feet wide betwixt 9 × 10 feet Stand . . . [for] £20" 5AB, 513	£20 for building 28 × 20 × 10-foot house
24 Apr. 1683		"By Building my House at Round hill 20. 0. 0" 5AB, 441 "By Building my long roome . . . 3. 0. 0" "Laying Barne floare 1. 0. 0" 5AB, 513	Payment for building house at Round Hill £3 for building long room £1 for laying barn floor
12 Dec. 1678	Victory Sikes	"By your halfe of the Barne Building 6. 5. 0" 5AB, 357	£12 10s. for building barn, 2 men
2 Jun. 1679	Thomas Stebbins, Jr.	"It haveing been formerly at a Town meeting propounded to the Town, that they would set up a school house for the Town, they concluded that such a house should be erected, and appointed the Select men to bargain with any meet person to build such an house for such use: accordingly they have bargained with Thomas Stebbin Junr to get timber for such a building, and frame it, whose length is to be 22	£14 for building 22 × 17 × 8-foot schoolhouse

CARPENTRY, *cont.*

Date	Name	Service	Rate
		foot: and breadth 17 foot: and stand 8 foot and halfe and he the said Thomas Stebbin is to carry the frame to place and to naile the clap boards close on both sides and ends, and to Lath and shingle the roofe, and to make three light spaces on one side and two lights on one end, and to set up a mantletree, and set up a rung Chimney, and to daub it, and the said Thomas is to have for his work so done fourteen pounds paid to him by the Towne, and in case it so prove that the said Thomas Stebbin have had an hard bargaine, it is hereby agreed that he shal have 10s. more of the Town" 1TR, 413	
4 Sep. 1679	Nicholas and William Clark of Hartford	"I say Recd all and consideration for the damadges done me by not Building my Barne . . . whereby I had much damadge [to] my Timber, Bords, and Planks and etc. But we have agreed upon Receiving the oxen this 4th Sept. 1679 to Ballance and Quit all accounts" 2AB, 326–327	Oxen for damages for breach of contract
2 Feb. 1679/80	Jonathan Morgan	"By 1 day Boring my Barn 0. 2. 0" 5AB, 199	2s. per diem for boring barn

CARPENTRY, *cont.*

Date	Name	Service	Rate
9 Jul. 1685	Henry Stiles	JP agrees with Stiles to make JP a wharf at the foot of the falls, for £40 5AB, 282	£40 for building wharf at foot of falls
14 Apr. 1686	Jonathan Morgan	"Making Ladder for my cart 0. 3. 0" 5AB, 199	3s. for building cart ladder
Aug. or Sep. 1686	John Hawkes	"John Hawkes being at my house discoursing [?] about the 16 Commons . . . I called on him to Build my Barne . . . at Enfeild" 5AB, 467	Agreement for building JP a barn at Enfield
4 Jan. 1686/87	James Petty and Thomas Taylor (farmers)	JP agreed with Petty and Taylor that they would build a water fence over the river next spring or summer for £24? 6AB, 100	£24? for building water fence
18 Feb. 1688/89	Joseph Leonard	"Joseph Lenord urging for some allowance about the Sawmill over the River which is gone to Ruin, But his worke he did before it was blown up he Reckns to be about £40"	£40 for partial completion of sawmill
1693–1694		"By groundsilling my Barne 4. 15. 0" 6AB, 63	£4 15s. for groundsilling barn
28 Dec. 1700	Jonathan Morgan	Morgan to build JP a 48 × 24 × 14-foot barn 6AB, 81	Contract for 48 × 24 × 14-foot barn

CARTAGE

Date	*Name*	*Service*	*Rate*
15 May 1655	Thomas Gilbert	"Recd by carting load of wheat to the warehouse 0. 9. 0" 1AB, 120	9s. for carting wheat to warehouse at Enfield falls [team normally 4 cattle]
28 Nov. 1655	Rowland Thomas	"Recd by carting 4 baggs of wheate from the 3 Corner medow 0. 4. 0" "By the use of your oxen 4 days 0. 8. 0" 1AB, 234	1s. per bag of wheat carted from Three Corner meadow 2s. per diem for use of yoke of oxen
19 Mar. 1655/56	Benjamin Cooley	"Recd last year 44 bushels ¼ ½ wheate at 3s. 8d. [is] 8. 2. 0" "Recd by carting 30 bushels of it the falls 0. 9. 0" 1AB, 273	3⅗d. per bushel of wheat carted to the falls
30 Sep. 1656	Samuel Terry	"Recd 2 days fetching hay 0. 4. 0" "Recd 1 day Carting 0. 2. 0" 1AB, 240	2s. per diem for fetching hay 2s. per diem for carting [using JP's team?]
1 Oct. 1656	John Harmon	"Recd by carting, two Journey to the falls 0. 18. 0" 1AB, 328	9s. for carting to the falls
2 Oct. 1656	Symon Beamon	"Recd by goeing to the falls with your cart 0. 6. 0" 1AB, 291	6s. for carting to the falls
20 Oct. 1657–26 Jan. 1657/58	John Scot and Joseph Crowfoot	"Recd by carting dung and etc. to my 3 corner meddow 0. 18. 0" "Recd 7 days and ½ carting Timber for my house over the river at 6s. [is] 2. 5. 0" 2AB, 24	18s. for carting dung 6s. per diem for carting

CARTAGE, *cont.*

Date	Name	Service	Rate
2 Mar. 1657/58	John Scot	"By carting Timber, Clay, hay, thatch, Stones, rayls, and Posts all is 7. 14. 6" 2AB, 25	£7 14s. 6d. for carting building materials
1658	Thomas Mirrick	"By carting to Hartford 12 bushels of wheate at 6d. [each]" 2AB, 61	6d. per bushel of wheat carted to Hartford
1660	Robert Ashley	"By carting 5 days 1. 10. 0" 2AB, 113	6s. per diem for carting
18 Feb. 1660/61	John Clark	"By a voyadge downe with your Teame to the foote of the falls 0. 11. 0" 2AB, 191	11s. for carting to the falls
Oct. 1661	James Warrinar	"By carting hay from the wharfe . . . 0. 6. 0" "By 3 days carting stones 0. 18. 0" "By 1 day carting with 2 bullock 0. 4. 0" 2AB, 143	6s. for carting hay from the wharf 6s. per diem for carting stones 4s. per diem for carting with two bullocks [instead of customary 4]
8 Jan. 1661/62	William Warrinar	"Recd by wheate, Indian [corn] carting above 20 days and a Journey to the foote of the falls: days worke and all by Mr. Payne . . . 15. 14. 6" 2AB, 32	£15 14s. 6d. for grains and carting
24 Jan. 1661/62	Lawrence Bliss	"By 2 days carting 0. 10. -" "By 1 voyadge your Teame to the falls, your cattle and cart 0. 7. 0" "By 1 day carting stones 0. 6. 0"	5s. per diem for carting 7s. for carting to the falls 6s. per diem for carting stones

CARTAGE, *cont.*

Date	Name	Service	Rate
		"By 3 days carting hay over the River 0. 18. 0" "By 1 load from the wharfe 0. 1. 6" 2AB, 207	6s. per diem for carting hay 1s. 6d. per load carted from wharf
May 1662	George Colton	"By his Teame a Journey to the foote of the falls 0. 11. 0" "By carting a load to the falls and bringing a load from the falls 1. 0. 0" 2AB, 247	11s. for carting to the foot of the falls £1 for carting to and from the falls
Sep. 1662	Lawrence Bliss	"By a voyadge your Teame downe to the warehouse 0. 12.0" "By 1 day carting stones 0. 6. 0"	12s. for carting to warehouse 6s. per diem for carting stones
5 Jan. 1662/63		"By 1 day carting stones 0. 6. 0" 2AB, 207	6s. per diem for carting stones
2 Feb. 1662/63	Miles Morgan	"By carting downe of Corne to the foote of the falls your teame twice caryed 30 bushels each tyme 0. 18. 0" 2AB, 335	9s. for carting 30 bushels of corn to the foot of the falls
16 Sep. 1663	Lawrence Bliss	"By 1 voyadge down to the foote of the falls with your Cart 0. 10. 0" 2AB, 207	10s. for carting to the foot of the falls
22 Oct. 1663		"By a voyadge downe to the foote of the falls with your Team 0. 10. 0" 2AB, 309	10s. for carting to the foot of the falls
6 Nov. 1663	John Clark	"By 3 days carting 0. 18. 0" 2AB, 191	6s. per diem for carting

CARTAGE, *cont.*

Date	Name	Service	Rate
20 Nov. 1663	Thomas Mirrick	"By 1 Journey your Teame to the foote of the falls 0. 10. 0"	10s. for carting to the foot of the falls
		"By 1 Journey your Teame to Hartford 1. 13. 0" 2AB, 323	33s. for carting to Hartford
26 Feb. 1663/64	Thomas Cooper	"By 9 days carting dung 2. 9. 6"	5s. 6d. per diem for carting dung
		"By 1 day carting hay over Agawam 0. 6. 0" 2AB, 321	6s. per diem for carting hay
1664	William Warrinar	"By 3 Journy your cart to the foote of the falls 1. 7. 0"	9s. for carting to the foot of the falls
		"One Journy your Teame 0. 10. 0" 3AB, 133	10s. for carting to the falls
1 Aug. 1664	Jonathan Ball	"By carting dung 6 days 0. 12. 0" 3AB, 129	2s. per diem for carting dung [using JP's team?]
1664–1665	James Taylor	"By a Journey to Hartford with Goodman Marshfield's Teame, which you are to have the pay of, carying downe corne and bringing up goods 1. 13. 0"	33s. for carting to Hartford with another man's team
		"1 Day carting this sumar 0. 6. 0"	6s. per diem for carting
		"By 9 days going with my teame at the falls 1. 0. 0" 3AB, 121	2s. 4d. per diem for carting with JP's team
1665	William Warrinar	"By carting 2 load of Wheate to the wharfe 0. 2. 0"	1s. per load of wheat carted to wharf
		"3 load to the wharf 0. 3. 0"	1s. per load of wheat carted to wharf
		"1 Load wheate to the wharfe 0. 1. 0"	1s. per load of wheat carted to wharf

CARTAGE, *cont.*

Date	Name	Service	Rate
		"Bringing up 50 bushels salt from the wharfe 0. 2. 0"	½d. per bushel of salt carted from wharf
		"More 20 bushels salt from the wharfe 0. 1. 2"	7/10d. per bushel of salt carted from wharf
		"Carying 20 bushels wheat to the foote of the falls and bringing up Boards from fresh water River 0. 9. 0"	9s. for carting to and from Freshwater River
Nov. 1665		"Carting to the foote of the falls 0. 3. 6" 3AB, 133	3s. 6d. for carting to the foot of the falls
5 Dec. 1665	Thomas Stebbins	"A cart went 5 tymes to the falls, with Corne and he takes 9s. a tyme: and when he brought up goods, also then 12s. [is] 10. 9. 0" 3AB, 131	9s. for carting to the falls 12s. for carting to the falls when also bringing up goods
1666–1667	John Petty	"By carting timber for the barne Ano 1666, 6 days and more ¾ day 2. 0. 0" 3AB, 155	6s. per diem for carting timber
1666	Richard Sikes	"By 1 day carting for this New Mill and more Carting 12d. [is] 0. 7. 0" 3AB, 83	6s. per diem for carting
6 Apr. 1667	Lawrence Bliss	"By 3 days Carting for my Barne 0. 18. 0" "By 1 day Carting shingle 0. 6. 0" 3AB, 103	6s. per diem for carting timber 6s. per diem for carting shingles
1667	Robert Ashley	"By carting over the River for my Barke, 9 days 2. 14. 0" 3AB, 153	6s. per diem for carting

CARTAGE, *cont.*

Date	Name	Service	Rate
1667	John Petty	"By Carting Timber for the Barne Ano 1667, 12 days at 6s. per day 3. 12. 0" 3AB, 155	6s. per diem for carting timber
19 Apr. 1668	Lawrence Bliss	"By 9 Load of Stones from Wachuit, which he is to bring to my Mill and I am to cleare his acot for said 9 Load of Said Stones and . . . they are 2. 5. 2" 3AB, 103	5s. per load of stones carted
25 Dec. 1668	Robert Ashley	"By 2 day carting stones 12s." 3AB, 249	6s. per diem for carting stones
Jan. 1668/69	David Ashley	"4 days Carting Timber for son Whiting 1. 4. 0" 3AB, 115	6s. per diem for carting timber
2 Mar. 1668/69	Timothy Cooper	"Agreed with Timothy Cooper to cart all the 120 loggs above which he is to cart to my saw mill fit to be sawne: such as he carts only to the top of the Hill he is to Rowle downe and to take care of them when they are rowld downe so to order you that they may ly convenient and handy for one hand to get them to the saw; for which loggs I am to give him 20d. per log for the carting of them and laying them fit to saw" 3AB, 55	20d. per log carted to sawmill

CARTAGE, *cont.*

Date	Name	Service	Rate
2 Mar. 1668/69	Lawrence Bliss	"By carting a load of wheate to the Boate 0. 1. 0" 3AB, 103	1s. per load of wheat carted to wharf
20 Jul. 1669	James Warrinar and John Hitchcock	"Agreed with James Warrinar and John Hitchcock to cart all the Loggs to the Sawmill which James Warrinar is to get all that parcel of 123 loggs; they are to cart them all to my Saw Mill and Lay them fit for sawing, which they are to cart to the mill and lay fit for one hand to take to the Saw by the beginning of June next: For which I am to allow and pay them 22d. per Logg" "By carting 123 logs your halfe 5. 10. 0" 3AB, 119; 5AB, 93	22d. per log carted to sawmill
29 Jul. 1669	Increase Sikes	"Agreed with Increase Sikes to Cart 50 of those logs he gets for my Saw mill: 50 logs of those which ly betwixt Timothy Cooper's and James Wariner's, which he is to lay at the saw mill ready and fit for one hand to take to the Saw, for which I am to allow him for which is already delivered him accounted 30 of these loggs" 3AB, 173	30 logs for carting 50 logs to sawmill
3 Aug. 1669	Richard Sikes	"By worke carting loggs . . . cutting joine loggs, a plow, carting stones, and some	£8 4s. for cartage and general work

CARTAGE, *cont.*

Date	*Name*	*Service*	*Rate*
		help about the Mill . . . 8. 4. 0" 3AB, 89	
15 Dec. 1669	Abel Wright	"You are to cart the 50 loggs that Thomas is to get me: to the Saw Mill for £4 15s." 3AB, 117	22d. per log carted to sawmill
20 Dec. 1669	Henry Chapin	"By your cart to Hadley fetching 20 barells at 8d. pce [is] 0. 13. 4" 3AB, 157	8d. per barrel carted from Hadley
1670	Increase Sikes	"By Carting 30 loggs at 20d. per log 2. 10. 0" 5AB, 161	20d. per log carted to sawmill
22 May 1671	Lawrence Bliss	"By carting a load of Barrels to the wharfe 0. 1. 0" 5AB, 117	1s. per load of barrels carted to wharf
25 May 1671	Thomas Mirrick	"By carting 2 load bushes 2s.; 2 load wood 2s. [is] 0. 4. 0"	1s. per load of bushes carted 2s. per load of wood carted
		"By carying downe of 6 load to the wharfe to load the Boates 0. 6. 0" 5AB, 111	1s. per load carted to wharf
1671	Increase Sikes	"By Carting 20 logs at 20d. [is] 1. 13. 4" 5AB, 161	20d. per log carted to sawmill
14 Jul. 1671	John Hitchcock	"By carting 123 loggs at 22d. per log comes to £11, your halfe 5. 10. 0" "By fetching goods from the wharf 0. 1. 0" "Carting 1 load pease 0. 2. 0"	22d. per log carted to sawmill 1s. per load of goods carted from wharf 2s. per load of peas carted

CARTAGE, cont.

Date	Name	Service	Rate
		"By carying corne, 2 load to the Boate at the wharfe 0. 2. 0" 5AB, 89	1s. per load of corn carted to wharf
26 Jan. 1671/72	Jonathan Ash-ley	"Carting 3 load Hay from wharfe 0. 3. 0" "Carting 6 load of corne for the Indians 0. 6. 0" 5AB, 79	1s. per load of hay carted from wharf 1s. per load of corn carted
8 Mar. 1671/72	Richard Sikes	"By worke carting Loggs and etc. 10. 0. 0" 5AB, 135	£10 for carting logs
15 Jun. 1672	Samuel Steb-bins	"4 days ½ carting wood 0. 9. 0" 5AB, 173	2s. per diem for cart-ing wood [using JP's team?]
1672	John Stebbins, Jr.	"By carting hay 0. 2. 6" 5AB, 279	2s. 6d. for carting hay
14 Jan. 1672/73	John Taylor of Northampton	"By carting Barrels to Windsor 0. 5. 0" 5AB, 249	5s. for carting barrels to Windsor
1673	John Terry of Windsor	"By carting logs before the Bargaine, 3 days 0. 16. 0" "By carting 34 loggs in Spring . . . 3. 12. 6" 5AB, 401	5s. 4d. per diem for carting logs 25½d. per log carted to sawmill
27 Nov. 1673	Robert Ashley	"By 4 day carting Timber for my Barne 1. 0. 0" 5AB, 77	5s. per diem for cart-ing timber
29 Nov. 1673	John Terry of Windsor	"Agreed with John Terry to doe all my carting of Loggs for my Sawmill at Stony River; he to cart logs seasonably and beforehand as they shall be needed to	16d. per log carted to Stony River sawmill

CARTAGE, *cont.*

Date	Name	Service	Rate
		saw so that the Mill may not stand still for want of loggs to saw, and to cart all for the supply of the Mill till May next: for which I am to allow and pay him 16d. per logg for all that he can deliver under his cart" 5AB, 401	
8 Dec. 1673	John Clark	"By 8 days ½ carting dung . . . 2. 2. 6" 5AB, 115	5s. per diem for carting dung
Dec. 1673– Jan. 1673/74	Jonathan Ashley	"By 5 days carting loggs 1. 8. 0" 5AB, 79	5s. 7d. per diem for carting logs
Jun. 1674	Richard Waite	"By 1 day carting wood 0. 2. 0" 5AB, 391	2s. per diem for carting [using JP's team?]
26 Jun. 1674	John Terry	"By 23 logs carted . . . 1. 8. 0"	15d. per log carted to sawmill
1674		"By 53 logs carted this winter 3. 6. 0" 5AB, 401	15d. per log carted to sawmill
30 Dec. 1674	Samuel Stebbins	"By 1 day carting to the wharfe 0. 10. 0" 5AB, 173	10s. per diem for carting to wharf
10 Mar. 1674/75	George Colton	"By your Teame to the foote of the falls 0. 10. 0" 5AB, 147	10s. for carting to the foot of the falls
1676	Judah Trumble	"By carting loggs at 15d. per log 0. 12. 6" 5AB, 343	15d. per log carted to sawmill

CARTAGE, *cont.*

Date	Name	Service	Rate
Jun. 1677	James Mun	"By 4 days your selfe Carting dung with 2 cattle at 4s. 6d. [is] 0. 18. 0" 5AB, 99	4s. 6d. per diem for carting dung with 2 cattle
9 Feb. 1677/78	Joseph Trumble	"By carting of Loggs at 15d. per Log 0. 18. 0"	15d. per log carted to sawmill
1678		"By 2 days carting fence which Barker is to set up 0. 10. 0" 5AB, 343	5s. per diem for carting fence
1678	Benjamin Parsons	"By carting 1 load stones for Mr. Denton 5s." "By 20 load of Stones to my Mill from Smale Brooke 3. 15. 0" 5AB, 413	5s. per load of stones carted 3s. 9d. per load of stones carted
6 Dec. 1678	John Bissell	"By 9 days ½ carting logs at my Saw Mill at Suffeild 2. 10. 0" 5AB, 369	5s. 3d. per diem for carting logs
3 Feb. 1678/79	Nathaniel Bliss, Jr.	"By 1 day carting loggs for me 0. 6. 0" 5AB, 35	6s. per diem for carting logs
1679	Obadiah Cooley	"By 3 days carting dung Oct 1670 [is] 0. 15. 0" 5AB, 195	5s. per diem for carting dung [Fields dunged in October]
Apr. 1679	John Bissell	"By 5 days carting at Stony Brooke . . . 1. 10. 0" 5AB, 369	6s. per diem for carting
3 Jan. 1679/80	John Taylor of Northampton	"By carying downe to Windsor 2 Barrels of floure 0. 10. 0" 5AB, 249	5s. per barrel of flour carted to Windsor

CARTAGE, *cont.*

Date	Name	Service	Rate
1680	John Terry	"By 11 days ½ carting loggs 3. 9. 0" 5AB, 401	6s. per diem for carting logs
1680	Hugh Roe of Suffield	"By 2 days carting about Mill 0. 11. 0" 5AB, 483	5s. 6d. per diem for carting
13 Dec. 1681	Samuel Bliss, Jr.	"By 1 day carting Bords 0. 6. 0" 5AB, 145	6s. per diem for carting boards
14 Aug. 1682	Judah Trumble	"By 2 days carting dung 0. 10. 0" "By 20 Loggs and etc. to the Sawmill 0. 14. 6"	5s. per diem for carting dung 14s. 6d. for carting 20 logs and additional materials to the sawmill
		"By 1 day and ½ your Teame . . . 0. 10. 0" 5AB, 343	6s. 8d. per diem for carting
Oct. 1685	Benjamin Parsons, Jr., of Enfield	"By Carting 7 days, 35 Load Stones with your cattle at 15d. ½ a load 2. 5. 0" 6AB, 65	15½d. per load of stones carted
1686	John Osborne	"By 1 day carting clay at Fall Harbour 0. 5. 0" 5AB, 207	5s. per diem for carting clay
6 Apr. 1688	Thomas Remmington of Suffield	"By sledging Timber to the Mill . . . 0. 16. 0" 5AB, 201	16s. for sledging timber to the sawmill
8 Jun. 1689	Samuel Taylor	"By 3 days drawing Timber to Suffield Mill 1. 3. 0" 5AB, 273	7s. 8d. per diem for carting timber

CIDER MAKING

Date	Name	Service	Rate
1657–1658	John Scot and Joseph Crow-foot	"2 days making Cyder 0. 3. 0" 2AB, 24	18d. per diem for making cider
1672	John Barber, Jr.	"By making 15 barrels of cider . . . 1. 10. 0" "By making 9 barrels of water cider 0. 17. 0"	2s. per barrel of cider 22⅔d. per barrel of water cider
Oct. 1674		"By making 19 Barrells of Cider at . . . 1. 10. 0" "By making 15 barrels of Cider at 18d. [is] 1. 2. 0"	19d. per barrel of cider 18d. per barrel of cider
Nov. 1676		"By making 19 barrels of Cider and water cider 1. 14. 0"	21d. per barrel of cider
25 Nov. 1677		"By making Cider . . . 36 barrells at 21d. [is] 3. 3. 0"	21d. per barrel of cider
23 Nov. 1678		"By making a barl of Cider and 8 of water cider 1. 12. 0" 5AB, 191	3s. 7d. per barrel of cider
12 Jan. 1681/82	John Clark	"By John Clark, 9 days making Cider 18s." 5AB, 197	2s. per diem for making cider
Sep. 1686	Richard Waite	"By making Cider in Sept 1686 [is] 0. 2. 0" "By 2 days gathering apples . . . 1 day making cider 0. 6. 0" 6AB, 75	2s. [per diem?] for making cider 2s. per diem for making cider and gathering apples

COOPERAGE

Date	Name	Service	Rate
10 Oct. 1646	John Mathews	"Recd in Coopering and other worke 0. 19. 5" WPAB, 104	19s. 5d. for cooperage
19 Dec. 1648		"Recd in Copery worke and 2 days gardening and one reaping, in all 1. 2. 0"	22s. for cooperage and gardening
24 Oct. 1649		"Recd in coperying work, reaping, and other worke 0. 17. 8" WPAB, 105	17s. 8d. for cooperage and field work
10 Aug. 1654		"Recd by Cooping work 1. 6. 6" 1AB, 127	26s. 6d. for cooperage
Sep. 1658		"Recd by 26 barrels for black lead 3. 14. 0" "Recd by a beere barrell 4s., a milking payle 18d. [is] 0. 5. 6" "One hogshead 0. 5. 6" 1AB, 270	2s. 10d. per lead barrel 4s. per beer barrel 18d. per milking pail 5s. 6d. per hogshead
1659		"By a new cowle . . . milking Payle 0. 1. 10" "4 Barrels 0. 18. 0" "A Cover for a Tub 0. 2. 6" "1 Barrell 0. 4. 6"	22d. for cowl and milking pail 4s. 6d. per barrel [32 gallon?] 2s. 6d. per tub cover 4s. 6d. per barrel
25 Aug. 1663		"By Coopery Worke, and also in John Mathews's booke to this 25 August 1663, all is 4. 9. 0" 2AB, 99	£4 9s. for cooperage
5 Nov. 1663		"By 4 great Barrells at 5s. 6d. [is] 1. 2. 0"	5s. 6d. per "great Barrell" [48-gallon?]

COOPERAGE, *cont.*

Date	Name	Service	Rate
		"By 8 Barrells at 4s. 6d. [is] 1. 16. 0"	4s. 6d. per barrel
		"By heading up of 4 Beife Barrels 0. 1. 0" 2AB, 313	3d. for heading a beef barrel
1664		"One great barel 0. 5. 6"	5s. 6d. per "great barrel"
		"By heading 3 barels: one beere barell 4s. 6d., one Pail 1s. 6d. [is] 0. 6. 0"	4s. 6d. per beer barrel 1s. 6d. per pail
		"Hooping a barrel 0. 1. 0"	1s. for hooping a barrel
		"A New Keeler 4s. 6d., a Cowle 4s. 6d. [is] 0. 9. 0"	4s. 6d. per keeler 4s. 6d. per cowl
		"By 2 Porke Barrels 0. 8. 0"	4s. per pork barrel
		"Changing a churn 12d., a great Cowle 9s. [is] 0. 10. 0"	12d. for refiting a churn 9s. per "great Cowle"
		"Hooping and Packing one hogshead Beaver 0. 1. 6"	1s. 6d. for hooping and packing a hogshead of beaver
		"By 7 Barel . . . "	Payment for 7 barrels
		"These 3 Barrels are to be taken out now for rent of land, and 1 more"	Payment for 3 barrels
		"20 Barrels at 4s. is £4 but I give but 3. 16. 0"	4s. per barrel
		"Hooping and packing 1 hogshead Bever 0. 2. 0"	2s. for hooping and packing a hogshead of beaver
		"1 Butter Tub 0. 3. 6"	3s. 6d. per butter tub
		"3 great Barells for Cider at 5s. 6d. [is] 0. 16. 0"	5s. 6d. per cider barrel
		"By 6 hoopes for a Barell 0. 1. 0"	2⅓d. per barrel hoop
		"By 5 hoopes more 0. 1. 0"	2⁴⁄₁₀d. per barrel hoop
		"By 9 hoops, and burning Barells 0. 3. 6"	3s. 6d. for cooperage
		"By 33 barells at 3s. 9d. per Barell: so I agreed with you for more Barrells 6. 3. 9"	3s. 9d. per barrel

COOPERAGE, *cont.*

Date	Name	Service	Rate
16 May 1666		"Recd the 10 barrels for Goodman Wilton's debt, and Recd 10 barrels for Rent, In all 30 Barrels"	Payment for 30 barrels
		"Recd more 10 barells at 3s. 9d. per barrel 1. 17. 6"	3s. 9d. per barrel
		"more 1 barell which I had last yeare after the reckning 0. 3. 9"	3s. 9d. per barrel
		"By 1 Paile 0. 1. 10"	22d. per pail
		"By Riming a Seive 8d., a hoop for Cowle 3d., [is] 0. 0. 11"	8d. for rimming a sieve 3d. per cowl hoop
28 Feb. 1666/67		"By one barell which you say I shall have Tomorrow 0. 3. 9"	3s. 9d. per barrel
		"In all I have paid John Mathews for 38 barrells" 3AB, 86–87	Payment for 38 barrels
28 Dec. 1668–Aug. 1669		"By 12 barells for meate, the rest you have allowed viz. 20 towards Rent of the meddow land in the neck: So that there is but 12 to Reckne for to this tyme: at 3s. 9d. per barrell 2. 5. 0"	3s. 9d. per barrel
		"By Worke Copery, and etc. all to this August 1669 as in John Mathews his Booke is 2. 17. 0" 3AB, 283	£2 17s. for cooperage
1669–1673	Richard Weller	"By 6 barrells I had in 1669 as per your note 0. 15. 0"	2s. 6d. per barrel
		"By 4 barrells in 1672 [is] 0. 10. 0"	2s. 6d. per barrel
		"By 2 barrells in 1673 [is] 0. 5. 0" 3AB, 197	2s. 6d. per barrel

COOPERAGE, *cont.*

Date	Name	Service	Rate
13 Jan. 1670/71	Sam Ely	"By 4000 of staves and heading to Goodman Mathews 7. 4. 0" 5AB, 151	1s. per 27 staves and heading
29 Jun. 1671	Samuel Partrigg	"By 60 barrells 11. 5. 0" "By 8 Barrells 1. 12. 0" 3AB, 223	3s. 9d. per barrel 4s. per barrel
18 Jul. 1672	John Mathews	"By 51 Barrells for Porke at 3s. 9d. peice 9. 11. 3"	3s. 9d. per pork barrel
11 Mar. 1672/73		"By 9 hoopes for hogsheads at 4d. . . . 0. 3. 0" "By 12 hoopes for barrels at 3d. [is] 0. 3. 0" "By 64 barrells for cider and Porke at 3s. 9d. [is] 12. 0. 0"	4d. per hogshead hoop 3d. per barrel hoop 3s. 9d. per cider or pork barrel
23 Jul. 1674		"By 15 hogshead hoopes 0. 5. 0" "By 16 barrell hopes 0. 4. 0" "By a Cowle 8s. 8d., a milk keel 2s. 6d." "a great Powdering Tub 0. 9. 0" "By 25 barells for Porke 4. 2. 6"	4d. per hogshead hoop 3d. per barrel hoop 8s. 8d. per cowl 2s. 6d. per milk keel [tub] 9s. per "great Powdering Tub" 3s. 4d. per pork barrel
Jan. 1675/76		"By worke in Goodman Mathews his Booke, his account is to this Jan. 1675 [is] 4. 10. 4" 5AB, 119	£4 10s. 4d. for cooperage
27 Jun. 1678	Edward Stebbins	"By 10 Barrels . . . 1. 15. 0" "By hooping and etc. 0. 2. 0"	3s. 6d. per barrel 2s. for hooping

COOPERAGE, *cont.*

Date	Name	Service	Rate
12 Dec. 1678		"By 4 Barrels 0. 14. 0" "More 4 Barrels 0. 14. 0" "3 Cider Barrels 0. 12. 0" 5AB, 495	3s. 6d. per barrel 3s. 6d. per barrel 4s. per cider barrel
12 Nov. 1679	John Mathews	"By worke as in John Mathews his Booke, Barrells and other worke to this 12 November 1679 [is] 4. 7. 4" 5AB, 487	£4 7s. 4d. for cooperage
1680	Edward Stebbins	"By 4 Barrels now this winter 1680 [is] 0. 14. 0" 5AB, 495	3s. 6d. per barrel
1681	John Mathews	"By Packing my Porke barrels 0. 2. 0" 5AB, 487	2s. for packing pork barrels
29 Jan. 1684/85	Daniel Cooley	"By 14 hogsheads . . . to carry to sea 5. 5. 0" "By 25 Barrels at 3s. 9d. [is] 4. 15. 0" 5AB, 227	7s. 6d. per hogshead 3s. 9d. per barrel
1695	Symon Smith	"By 15 Barrels . . . 3. 16. 6" "By 6 cider Barrels . . . 1. 5. 0" Pail, mending tub, churn, butter tub, 0. 12. 6 6AB, 233	5s. 1d. per barrel 4s. 2d. per cider barrel 12s. 6d. for cooperage

DAUBING AND PLASTERING

Date	Name	Service	Rate
17 Feb. 1657/58	Reice Bedortha	"Recd by 1 day daubing my chimny 2s." 2AB, 43	2s. per diem for daubing chimney

DAUBING AND PLASTERING, *cont.*

Date	Name	Service	Rate
20 Oct. 1658	Thomas Bancroft	"1 day daubing the chimney over the River 0. 2. 6" 1AB, 246	2s. 6d. per diem for daubing chimney
Apr. 1663	Edward Griswald of Windsor	"By 12 days worke Plastering 1. 16. 0" 2AB, 237	3s. per diem for plastering
20 Dec. 1671	Thomas Miller's sons	"For your sons daubing my Lodging Room 0. 8. 0"	8s. for daubing JP's lodging room
4 Feb. 1673/74		"By 2 days daubing chambers 0. 4. 0" 5AB, 61	2s. per diem for daubing

DITCHING AND HEDGING

Date	Name	Service	Rate
Oct. 1656	Benjamin Parsons	"Recd by ditching in my sheepe pasture, all the ditching in the Plaine being 52 rod at 12d. [is] 2. 12. 0"	1s. per rod for ditching
		"and 7 rod ditched upon the hill 0. 8. 0"	13½d. per rod for ditching
		"Recd by hedging 50 rod and 2 rod ditching 0. 1. 8"	20d. for ditching and hedging
		"6 days worke at ditching 0. 15. 0" 1AB, 282	2s. 6d. per diem for ditching
20 Nov. 1658	William Branch	"Agreed with William Branch to ditch and hedge and make a fence sufficient in my meddow betwixt him and me for the streete-fence to his part of the fence sufficient; I am to allow him 8d. per rod, only I am to cart the hedging stuff, also he is to do my fencing at the end of his meddow"	8d. per rod for ditching and hedging [JP responsible for carting]

DITCHING AND HEDGING, *cont.*

Date	Name	Service	Rate
		"By 25 rod (clensing) the ditch and ½ [is] 0. 19. 1 ½" 2AB, 71	9d. per rod for ditching and cleaning
1658–1659	Benjamin Parsons	"By ditching over the great river 90 rod 4. 17. 0" "By ditching betweene me and Goodman Ashley 42 rod ½ [is] 2. 2. -" 2AB, 61	13d. per rod for ditching 1s. per rod for ditching
16 Sep. 1663	Lawrence Bliss	"By ditching over Agawam 9 acres ½ [is] 0. 9. 6" 2AB, 207	1s. per acre for ditching
12 Nov. 1663	Benjamin Parsons	"By 10 Rod ditching 0. 10. 0" 2AB, 273	1s. per rod for ditching
20 Nov. 1663	Richard Excell	"By 26 Rod and ½ ditching at 14d. [is] 1. 10. 10" 2AB, 329	14d. per rod for ditching
9 Jan. 1664/65	William Branch	"Agreed with William Branch for filling in my ditch and laying it level, I am to give him for that ditch about the meddow I bought of him 20s. for both sides; And the ditch at the Northside which he set, Cast and Stub it and cleare it and lay it plaine, for all the ditch from the west end to the east: I am to give him 15s. and the Carting of the wood on it which he is to have; He is to ditch in that I bought of Goodman Morgan for what I am to give him 15d. per Rod, he making a good	15d. per rod for ditching 4½ × 3½-foot ditch [Dimensions of ditch]

DITCHING AND HEDGING, *cont.*

Date	Name	Service	Rate
		bank and the ditch 3 or 4 Inches above, 4 foote and ½ wide and 3 fote ½ deepe; This which he hath done is 32 Rod is 2. 0. 0" 3AB, 141	
2 Mar. 1664/65	John Riley	"By hedging my ditch over the River and 46 rod at 6d. [is] 1. 3. 0" 3AB, 183	6d. per rod for hedging
5 Apr. 1665	Richard Excell	"Agreed with Richard Exsell to doe 30 rod of ditching . . . , for one 20 Rod of it I already paid him 2 yards of Trading cloth, and for the other 10 Rod I am to pay him 10s., and in case I can get this last 10 Rod done by then In season, I am to free him, or otherwise he is to do it as aforesaid for 18s." 3AB, 171	1s. per rod for ditching [Work incentive]
15 Apr. 1665	Joseph Crowfoot	"By ditching on the Long Meddow 0. 4. 0" "By 2 days ½ clearing the ditch to the Mill" "By 1 day Scouring my ditch at the Brooke 0. 2. 0"	4s. for ditching Payment for 2½ days ditching 2s. per diem for scouring ditch
May 1665		"By 18 Rod ditching 18s., 3 Rod ½ log fence 3s. 6d." 3AB, 187	1s. per rod for ditching
16 May 1666	John Mathews	"Agreed with Goodman Mathew to doe 4 Rod of Trench for the Mill water (which is set out by Goodman Thomas) for depth he	12 lbs. 10 ozs. of sugar for digging 4 rods of 2 × 8-foot ditch [Dimensions of mill ditch]

DITCHING AND HEDGING, *cont.*

Date	*Name*	*Service*	*Rate*
		is to dig it 2 foote and 3 or 4 Inches deeper than the top of the dam, and the bredth is to be 8 fote on the bottom at the end next the dam, and he is to save all the Stone he can which are fit for all my building; I to give him 12 and 10 pounds of sugar: all to be finished by the 1 Sept next" 3AB, 87	
1666	William Hunter	"By 8 Rod ¾ of ditching by the Indian Fort over the River 0. 8. 0" "By scouring 34 Rod of ditching Skeepnuck at 3s. per Rod is 8. 6. 0" 3AB, 165	11d. per rod for ditching 3s. per rod for scouring ditches
1667	Joseph Crow-foot	"By 8 Rod ditching, you are to make a good Hedge on the ditch for the pole you had 0. 8. 0" 3AB, 187	1s. per rod for ditching
21 Feb. 1666/67	Benjamin Parsons	"By 48 Rod ½ of ditching at 12d. rod in the wet meddow sides 2. 8. 6" 3AB, 95	1s. per rod for ditching
1 Mar. 1667/68	Rowland Thomas	"By 4 days ditching and clearing my Brooke at 2s. 4d. and etc. 0. 9. 0" 3AB, 159	2s. 4d. per diem for ditching and clearing brook, pays 2s. 3d.
28 Sep. 1668	William Hunter	"Agreed with William Hunter to make a parsell of ditching for me as follouth, viz. for a stone	Contract for 212 rods of ditching

DITCHING AND HEDGING, cont.

Date	Name	Service	Rate
		horse of about 5 years old . . . he is to make 112 Rod of ditch, and in paymt of what he owes me he is to make 100 Rod of ditching more, only I am to let him have kersey for a Jacket and for a wastecott for his wife, and something for a bed blanket weight of payer All" 3AB, 165	
2 Dec. 1669	Increase Sikes	"Agreed with Increase Sikes that he shall fill in my ditch at the Round hill, all of it from one end to the other, which he is to fill up throwing in all the Bark to make it plaine fit for Plowing; he is also to stub up all the young Trees, and stub in the Bank quite from the Ground plowed up and sprung [?] to the south side of the ditch, and to doe all well fit and secure for plowing, all which he is to doe early in the Spring for which I am to pay him 20s." 3AB, 173	20s. for filling ditch
1670		"By filling in my ditch at round hill 1. 0. 0" 5AB, 161	Payment for filling ditch
18 Nov. 1670	William Hunter	"By ditching (besides the 112 Rod for the horse) more as you say 56 Rod you have done already at 12d. per rod 2. 16. 0" 5AB, 31	1s. per rod for ditching

DITCHING AND HEDGING, *cont.*

Date	Name	Service	Rate
25 Aug. 1671	Benjamin Parsons	"Agreed with Benjamin Parsons to make the ditch to bring the Brooke in, which he is to take where I showd him and to bring . . . ; I marked another; he is to make the ditch 4 feet and 9 inches broad at top and 3 feet 3 inches in the Bottom, to dig it deepe enough to carry the water and lay the Bank 6 Inches only of the edge of the ditch; he to doe all the worke excepting making the dam; and if he can to doe all before Winter . . . which I am to allow and pay him Three Pounds, Ten shillings"	£3 10s. for digging 4¾ × 3¼-foot ditch
		"By ditching over the meddow about 28 Rods . . . 2. 15. 0" 5AB, 127	£2 15s. for ditching [Dimensions of ditch]
Jun. 1672	William Hunter	"By 45 Rod of ditching at 12d. per Rod" 5AB, 31	1s. per rod for ditching
5 Nov. 1672	Isaac Morgan	"By 58 Rod ditching 2. 18. 0" 5AB, 189	1s. per rod for ditching
24 Feb. 1672/73	Robert Ashley	"By throwing in the ditch over the meddow 20 Rod at 9d. per Rod is 15s." 5AB, 77	9d. per rod for filling ditch
Apr. 1673	William Hunter	"By 5 days worke scouring ditch 0. 12. 0" "By 16 Rod ditching orchard 0. 16. 0" 5AB, 31	2s. 5d. per diem for scouring ditch 1s. per rod for ditching in orchard

DITCHING AND HEDGING, cont.

Date	Name	Service	Rate
1673	Isaac Morgan	"For 35 Rod of ditching 1. 15. 0" 5AB, 189	1s. per rod for ditching
1674	Daniel Alexander	"10 Rod ditching 10s., 10 Rod of hedge 5s." 5AB, 201	1s. per rod for ditching 6d. per rod for hedging
1688	James Gerald	"By 20 Rod ditching in the Boggy Meddow 1. 0. 0" 6AB, 201	1s. per rod for ditching

DROVING

Date	Name	Service	Rate
15 Jan. 1655/56	Benjamin Parsons	"Recd by bringing up my sheepes 0. 6. 0" 1AB, 146	6s. for driving sheep from Enfield falls
19 Mar. 1655/56	Benjamin Cooley	"Recd by what I am to allow you for driving my cattle and bringing my sheepe from the Bay 2. 2. 10" 1AB, 273	£2 2s. 10d. for driving cattle to Boston and returning with sheep
1658–1659	Samuel Marshfield	"By bringing up sheep from Windsor 0. 4. 0" 2AB, 109	4s. for driving sheep from Windsor
30 Nov. 1660	Symon Beamon	JP gives him boots worth 10s. for bringing mare to James Rogers at New London 2AB, 288	10s. for driving mare to New London
Jan. 1660/61	Thomas Cooper (son Timothy)	"By Timothy driving my swine to freshwater Brooke 0. 3. 0" 2AB, 49	3s. for driving swine to Freshwater brook

DROVING, *cont.*

Date	Name	Service	Rate
30 Mar. 1661	Symon Beamon	"By your last Journy to New London 0. 14. 0"	14s. for journey to New London [droving]
		"By 2 days looking up the mares last weeke 0. 4. 0" 2AB, 289	2s. per diem for rounding up mares
15 Jan. 1668/69	John Keepe	"By bringing up a Colt from Windsor 0. 1. 6" 3AB, 67	18d. for driving a colt from Windsor
13 Jan. 1669/70	John Stebbins	"By carying mare and colt to Pacomtuck 0. 3. 6" 3AB, 223	3s. 6d. for driving mare and colt to Deerfield
5 Apr. 1671	Symon Beamon	"Agreed with Symon to allow him for his Journey to the Bay now with my cattle 15s. besides the Bootes, Stockes, and Shoeing his horse"	15s., boots, stockings, and horseshoeing for driving cattle to Boston
Nov. 1671		"By bringing up horses with Jonath Ashley, he Reckns I should allow you 2s. besides your bringing" 5AB, 19	2s. for driving horses from the falls
1675	Edward Messenger	"By carying all my cattle from Brother Wyllys down to me and etc. . . . 0. 1. 10"	22d. for driving cattle from Hartford to Springfield
		"By driving my fat cattle to Boston 0. 15. 0"	15s. for driving cattle to Boston
		"By driving downe all my cattle in October 1675 to Hartford (for wintering) and bringing up last summer a Cow and Calfe and heifer, also another cow 1. 5. 0"	25s. for driving 4 head of cattle to and from Hartford
		"Agreed with him to drive my fat cattle to the Bay next March 0. 6. 6"	6s. 6d. for driving 2 cattle to Boston

DROVING, *cont.*

Date	Name	Service	Rate
		"Bringing up 8 cattle 2. 0. 0" 5AB, 415	£2 for driving 8 cattle [from Hartford?]
30 Dec. 1680	Joseph Bedortha	"By fetching in horses from Westfield 0. 3. 0" 5AB, 187	3s. for fetching horses from Westfield
13 Mar. 1681/82	Obadiah Cooley	"By driving my oxen to the bay in Spring 0. 15. 0" 5AB, 277	15s. for driving oxen to Boston
1682	Joseph Thomas	"By looking in Horses 1 day this summer 1682 [is] 0. 3. 0" 5AB, 449	3s. per diem for rounding up horses
2 Feb. 1691/92	James Gerald	"By driving a yoake of cattle to Boston 0. 12. 0" 6AB, 201	12s. for driving a yoke of cattle to Boston

FEMALE LABOR, GENERAL

Date	Name	Service	Rate
19 Nov. 1645–1648	Katherine Johns	"6 Pullets . . . 20 eggs 6d.; above is due to Katherine 3s. [all is] 3s. 6d." "So rests Due to my father from Katherine this 29 April 1647 [is] 0. 6. 11 . . . more for 3 fowls Recd the 6 Sept 1648 at 10d. apiece 0. 2. 6" WPAB, 79	3s. 6d. for poultry and eggs 10d. per chicken [Poultry maid]
1645–1646	Abraham Mundyne's wife	"His wife 1 day ½ weeding 0. – 6" WPAB, 27	Payment for female's weeding
1646	John Stebbins's wife	"Making hay his wife 9 days 0. 9. 0" WPAB, 55	1s. per diem for female's making hay [raking into windrows?]

FEMALE LABOR, GENERAL, *cont.*

Date	Name	Service	Rate
2 Oct. 1656	William Warrinar	"Recd by little Mary her board besides what your wife allowed 6. 0. 0" 1AB, 268	Payment for servant's board
Nov. 1658– Feb. 1661/62	Joanna Branch	"By your wife's help in summer and at the beginning of winter 7 weeks 1. 8. 0"	4s. per week for domestic work
1 Feb. 1661/62		"By Goody Branch tendance of my wife in Lying in 7 weeks at 5s. per week 1. 15. 0" 2AB, 71	5s. per week for lying in
Apr. 1663	Henry Chapin's wife	"By spinning 8 pounds of hemp 0. 3. 4" 2AB, 243	5d. per pound for spinning hemp
16 Feb. 1667/68	Nathaniel Pritchard's wife	"By your wife's knitting gloves and ½ day goeing with Goodman Bascomb 0. 4. 0" 3AB, 97	4s. for knitting gloves and ½ day assisting stonemason's family
10 Jun. 1668	Timothy Cooper's wife	"Timothy Coopers wife took up for Edward Church and wife now at their house, and promised me . . . 1 yard blew linen at 3s. and 1 yard of blew linnen at 2s. 6d. [is] 0. 5. 6" 3AB, 55	2s. 6d. and 3s. per yard for blue linen
19 Apr. 1669	Rowland Thomas's wife	"By sowing worke of his wives 0. 5. 2" 3AB, 159	5s. 2d. for female's sowing
1669	William Warrinar	"Your wifes help 4 days 0. 4. 0" 3AB, 133	1s. per diem for female's work

FEMALE LABOR, GENERAL, *cont.*

Date	Name	Service	Rate
30 Mar. 1674	Thomas Miller's wife	"By your wifes Tendance and help when my son's wedding 1. 0. 0" 5AB, 61	20s. for helping with wedding
Jul. 1678	Goodwife Parsons	"Goodwife Parsons had cotton made of my wife to Spin and brought home the yarne this July 1678 which I weighed and it was 8 pounds of yarne; for the spinning whereof I paid her 10 pounds of cotton woole and . . . "	10 pounds of cotton wool for 8 pounds of yarn
8 Aug. 1678		"Delivered her more cotton woole to spin for us [16 pounds]"	Delivery of 16 pounds of cotton for spinning
30 Jan. 1678/79		"By Spinning yarne for us 15 pounds at 20d. per pound 0. 19. 8" 5AB, 347	20d. per pound for spinning yarn

FENCING

Date	Name	Service	Rate
31 Jan. 1645/46	William Vaughan	"7 days Samuel houlding Railes at 15d. [is] 0. 8. 9" WPAB, 112	15d. per diem for youth's holding fence rails
9 Dec. 1649	Henry Chapin	"Recd 20 Rod of fencing for Brother Holyoke 2. 13. 4" WPAB, 40	2s. 8d. per rod for fencing
1653	Thomas Miller	"Recd by fencing and wharfe work, it appears 3. 10. 0" "Recd by fencing 9 rod ½ of log rale, 11 pale [?]	£3 10s. for fencing and wharf work 23s. for fencing

FENCING, *cont.*

Date	Name	Service	Rate
		posts 25s., but I [delivered] a load [some abated] so is but 1. 3. 0" 1AB, 64	
Apr. 1660	John Scot	"By setting up 107 rod of fence about the Pasture . . . 1. 2. 0" "By 29 rod of log Poles . . . 3. 12. 6" 2AB, 269	payment for fencing 2s. 6d. per rod for log poles
19 Jan. 1662/63	John Riley	"By fencing over the River 3s. 6d." 2AB, 245	3s. 6d. for fencing
5 Nov. 1663	William Brooks	"By 44 Rod of fencing at fresh water at 2s. 6d. [per rod] 2. 15. 0" 2AB, 215	2s. 6d. per rod for fencing (half)
Late 1660s	John Kilum	"For seting up 40 rod of posts . . . at 18d. per rod 3. 0. 0" 4AB, 87	18d. per rod for setting up fence posts
5 Feb. 1672/73	Josiah Carter	Agreement for Carter to fence and ditch in JP's commons in Deerfield: 18 "Cow Commons" and 4 sheep commons, and 9 "Commons" and "likewise my farme lot." Ditches to be 4 foot wide. 12d. a rod for ditching, 2s. a rod for fencing 5AB, 261	1s. per rod for ditching 2s. per rod for fencing
1673	Aaron Cooke	"By 3 days worke mending fence 6s. . . . 2 days a Teame mending fence 12s. [is] 0. 18. 0" 5AB, 197	2s. per diem for mending fence 6s. per diem for team

FENCING, *cont.*

Date	Name	Service	Rate
1673?	Sampson Frary	"By 38 Rod of fence, 5 Raile fence at 2s. per Rod 3. 16. 0" 5AB, 387	2s. per rod for 5-rail fencing
Oct. 1673	Thomas Copley and Jonathan Ball	"By 37 Rod of logs fence at 8d. per Rod 1. 4. 8" 3AB, 14	8d. per rod for log fencing, JP's tenants
Nov. 1673	Pelatiah Morgan	"By 1 day ½ worke setting up fence 0. 3. 0" "By 26 rod of fence 3. 5. 0" 5AB, 185	2s. per diem for fencing 2s. 6d. per rod for fencing
27 Nov. 1673	Moses Cooke	"By 80 Rod of fence at Westfield for son John, 5 Raile fence 9. 0. 0" 5AB, 199	2s. 3d. per rod for 5-rail fencing
Feb. 1673/74	Edward Foster	"By making 8 rod of fence against the River or street which is the front of the lot I had to Crowfoote 0. 15. 0" 5AB, 59	22½d. per rod for fencing
1674	Daniel Alexander	"59 Rod fence at Westfield for Son John, Posts and 5 Railes at 2s. 3d. per Rod" "2 day mending up fence there, 0. 4. 0" 5AB, 201	2s. 3d. per rod for 5-rail fencing 2s. per diem for mending fence
5 Mar. 1674/75	Samuel Stebbins	"By 5 Rod of five Raile fence to fence in the New Meetinghouse yard 0. 12. 0" 5AB, 173	2s. 5d. per rod for 5-rail fencing
30 Jan. 1677/78	Jonathan Taylor, Jr.	"Agreed with Jonathan Taylor, [Jr.] to Set me up	2s. 6d. per rod for 5-rail fencing

FENCING, *cont.*

Date	Name	Service	Rate
		Twenty rod of good fence with Posts and 5 Railes, the Posts to be good Thick and substantial [at 2s. 6d. per] Rod is 2. 14. 6" 5AB, 167	
10 Apr. 1678	Samuel Kent	"By 60 Rod of 5 Raile fence in the lot betwixt you and me, whereoff you accounted 30 Rod to be mine"	Payment for 60 rods of 5-rail fencing
		"By fencing . . . 2. 10. 0" "4 Rod ½ Raile fence 0. 9. 0" 5AB, 345	£2 10s. for fencing 2s. per rod for rail fencing
22 Nov. 1678	Samuel Roe of Suffield	"Agreed with Sam Roe to set me up good 5 Rayle fence on the front of my Lot in high street: viz. 40 rod he is to doe of" 5AB, 301	Contract for 40 rods of 5-rail fencing in Suffield
30 Nov. 1678	Samuel Jones	"Agreed with Sam Joanes to set me up at my farme 22 Rod of 5 Raile fence . . . [at] 2s. 5d. per Rod"	2s. 5d. per rod for 5-rail fencing
16 Jan. 1678/79		"Agreed with Sam Joanes to get and set up 40 rod of good 5 Raile fence, in good white oak Posts . . . [at] 2s. 6d. per Rod"	2s. 6d. per rod for 5-rail fencing
		"Agreed with him also for 100 of good white oake Posts . . . delivered at my house by March next for which . . . 4d. per Post, well holed for 5 Rayle [fence]"	4d. per mortised white oak post
		"By 24 Rod of 5 Rale fence at Round hill 3. 0. 0" 5AB, 459	2s. 6d. per rod for 5-rail fencing

FENCING, *cont.*

Date	Name	Service	Rate
1680	Hugh Roe of Suffield	"By 41 Rod ½ fence 4. 3. 0" 5AB, 483	2s. per rod for fencing
1680	John Burbank	"By fencing 17 Rod of log fence 0. 17. 0" "By 1 rod of 5 raile fence 0. 3. 0" 5AB, 287	1s. per rod for log fencing 3s. per rod for 5-rail fencing
9 Sep. 1681		"Agreed with Goodman Burbank to set me up 60 rod of good 4 Rayle fence [oak] £5" 5AB, 287	20d. per rod for 4-rail fencing
15 Mar. 1681/82	Jonathan Taylor, Jr.	"By 55 rod of 5 Raile fence about my orchard 6. 17. 6" "By 7 Rod and ¼ over the River at my farme 0. 17. 6" 5AB, 167	2s. 6d. per rod for 5-rail fencing 2s. 5d. per rod for fencing
6 Dec. 1682	Isaac Morgan	"Agreed with Isack Morgan to do 20 rod of good 5 Raile fence at fresh water . . . 37s." 5AB, 421	22d. per rod for 5-rail fencing
1 Jan. 1686/87	John Crowfoot	"By worke 5 days he says he did for me about rayl fence 0. 10. 0" 6AB, 123	2s. per diem for rail fencing
May 1687	James Stevenson	"By 40 rod of 2 Rayles fence upon my New ditch over Agawam River (I did the carting) at 9d. per rod 1. 10. 0" 5AB, 321	9d. per rod for 2-rail fencing [JP responsible for carting]

FERRYING

Date	Name	Service	Rate
1667	Joseph Crow-foot	"By feridge 0. 2. 0" 3AB, 187	2s. for ferrying
14 Mar. 1667/68		"Recd by feridge 6 days 0. 6. 6" 3AB, 186	13d. per diem for ferrying

FIELD WORK

Date	Name	Service	Rate
1645	Henry Chapin	"Recd 46 days at 20d. [is] 3. 16. 8" "9 days and ½ at 20d. [is] 0. 17[?] 5., 11 days at 16d. [is] 1. 2. 8" WPAB, 39	20d. per diem for field work 16d. and 20d. per diem for field work
1645	James Bridge-man	"5 days worke and ½ at 2s. [is] 0. 11. 0" "Recd 5 days worke at 2s. [is] 0. 10. 0" WPAB, 69	2s. per diem for field work 2s. per diem for field work
12 Sep. 1645	William Warri-nar	"Recd 2 days worke at 20d. [is] 0. 3. 4" "34 days winter worke 2. 5. 0" "6 days worke at 20d. [is] 0. 10. 0" WPAB, 50	20d. per diem for field work 16d. per diem for winter work 20d. per diem for summer work
10 Feb. 1645/46	William Vaughan	"Recd 2 days [one day at 20d.] and ½ worke at 2s. [is] 0. 4. 8" WPAB, 113	20d. and 2s. per diem for field work
14 Apr. 1646	James Osborne	"Recd 5 days of worke at 18d., and 1 day at haying at 20d. [is] 0. 8. 4"	18d. per diem for field work 20d. per diem for haymaking

FIELD WORK, *cont.*

Date	Name	Service	Rate
		"Recd in 4 days winter at 16d. [is] 0. 5. 4" WPAB, 32	16d. per diem for winter work
Apr. 1646	Richard Sikes	"Recd worke in summer 26 days 2. 12. 0" WPAB, 46	2s. per diem for summer work
1 May 1646	Henry Burt (sons)	"Recd 14 days work Jonathan at 16d. [is] 0. 18. 8" "9 days David at 12d. [is] 0. 9. 0" " . . . day David in Sumer at 16d. [is] 0. 1. 4" "Jonathan 14 days at 20d. [is] 1. 3.[?] 4" WPAB, 88	16d. per diem for youth's field work 1s. per diem for youth's field work 16d. per diem for youth's summer work 20d. per diem for youth's field work
12 May 1646	Thomas Stebbins	"Recd worke in winter 60 days at 16d. [is] 4. 0. 0" "Recd in Sumer 42 days at 20d., 2 days at 18d." "Recd 30 days at . . . 2. 10. 0" "and 22 [days] at . . . 1. 14. 0" "Recd 30 days at 20d. [is] 2. 10. 0" WPAB, 54	16d. per diem for winter work 18d. and 20d. per diem for summer work 20d. per diem for field work 18½d. per diem for field work 20d. per diem for field work
1646	Rowland Stebbins	"Recd 10 days in the Spring, Recd first 33 dayes 3. 9. 8" WPAB, 83	25d. per diem for field work
1646	John Stebbins	"Recd 5 days worke at 2s. [is] 0. 10. 0" "13 and ½ [days] at 20d. [is] 1. 11. 6" WPAB, 55	2s. per diem for field work 20d. per diem for field work (pays 2s. 4d.)

FIELD WORK, *cont.*

Date	Name	Service	Rate
1646	John Leonard	"2 days reaping at 2s. [is] 0. 4. 0"	2s. per diem for reaping
		"5 days at 20d. [is] 0. 8. 4"	20d. per diem for field work
		"Recd 10 days worke at 16d. [is] 0. 13. 4"	16d. per diem for field work
		"Recd 12 days worke at 16d. [is] 0. 16. 0" WPAB, 63	16d. per diem for field work
1646	James Bridge-man	"3 dayes and ½ worke 0. 5. 10"	20d. per diem for field work
		"10 day [and other work] 3. 9. 8"	£3 9s. 8d. for un-specified work
		"4 days and ½ about . . . 0. 7. 6"	20d. per diem for field work
		"5 days . . . 0. 10. 0"	2s. per diem for field work
		"6 days and half" WPAB, 70	Payment for 6½ days of field work
4 Sep. 1646	Rowland Thomas	"1 days ½ at 20d. [is] 0. 2. 6" WPAB, 124 (first of two p. 124s)	20d. per diem for field work
16 Oct. 1646	Rowland Steb-bins	"Recd 24 days worke 2. 0. 0" WPAB, 81	20d. per diem for field work
28 Oct. 1646	Roger Prit-chard	"Recd 4 days and a little more at weeding 0. 5. 0" WPAB, 92	14d. per diem for weeding
30 Oct. 1646	William Vaughan and sons Sam and Josiah	"[26½ days] 0. 17. 6" WPAB, 112	8d. per diem for youth's field work
7 Nov. 1646	Samuel Wright	"Recd Samuel work, 9 days at 14d. [is] 0. 10. 6"	14d. per diem for field work

FIELD WORK, *cont.*

Date	Name	Service	Rate
		"Recd 49 days ½ [at] 18d. [is] 3. 14. 3" WPAB, 84	18d. per diem for field work
22 Feb. 1646/47	Richard Sikes	"Recd 14 days ½ Summer work . . . 1. 9. 0" WPAB, 47–49	2s. per diem for summer work
13 Jun. 1647	William Brooks	"Recd 9 days worke at 16d. [is] 0. 12. 0" "1 days and ½ in harvest at 22d. [is] 0. 2. 9" "1 day haymaking 0. 1. 8" WPAB, 148	16d. per diem for field work 22d. per diem for reaping 20d. per diem for haymaking
15 Jul. 1647	Henry Burt	"Recd in worke 3 days at 16d. [is] 0. 4. 0" "Recd 17 days at 20d. [is] 1. 8. 4" WPAB, 90	16d. per diem for field work 20d. per diem for field work
9 Oct. 1647	Henry Chapin	"Recd 14 days ½ Goodman Chapen himself at 20d. [is] 1. 4. 2" "6 days and ½ winter worke at 16d. [is] 0. 8. 8" WPAB, 41	20d. per diem for field work 16d. per diem for winter work
9 Oct. 1647	David Chapin (Henry's son)	"Recd 24 days David at . . . 20d. [is] 2. 0. 0" "Recd 4 days David about the sellar at 20d. [is] 0. 6. 8" "Recd 10 days worke at 18d. [is] 0. 15. 0" WPAB, 41	20d. per diem for field work 20d. per diem for cellar work 18d. per diem for field work
12 Oct. 1647	Samuel Wright	"Recd by 15 days winter at 16d. [is] 1. 0. 0" "Recd 42 days summer at 20d. [is] 3. 10. 0" WPAB, 85	16d. per diem for winter work 20d. per diem for summer work

FIELD WORK, *cont.*

Date	Name	Service	Rate
Mar. 1648	Henry Burt	"Recd 22 days worke at 20d. [is] 1. 16. 8" "6 days at harvest at 2s. [is] 0. 12. 0" WPAB, 188	20d. per diem for field work 2s. per diem for reaping'
19 Apr. 1648		"Recd 23 and ½ days worke at 16d. [is] 1. 31. 4" "17 days worke at 20d. [is] 1. 8. 4" WPAB, 159	16d. per diem for field work 20d. per diem for field work
1648	James Bridge-man	"Recd 44½ days work summer 4. 9. 0" "15 days in the Winter 1. 5. 0" "Recd 60 days worke in su-mer 6. 8. 0" "Recd 13 days winter 1. 1. 8" WPAB, 71–72	2s. per diem for summer work 20d. per diem for winter work 25⅗d. per diem for summer work 20d. per diem for winter work
1648	John Stebbins	"Recd 14 days Summer work at 20d., 4 days winter work at 16d. [is] 1. 8. 0" WPAB, 185	20d. per diem for summer work 16d. per diem for winter work
1 Nov. 1648	Thomas Steb-bins	"Recd more 7 days worke at 20d. [is] 0. 11. 8" "6 days work at dung cast-ing, and some plowing 0. 10. 0" WPAB, 200	20d. per diem for field work 20d. per diem for dung-casting and plowing
29 Dec. 1648	Samuel Wright	"Recd Sam 18 days and ½ at 20d., only 2 of them were reaping at 25d." WPAB, 86	20d. per diem for field work 25d. per diem for reaping
5 Feb. 1648/49	William Brooks	"Recd 1 day worke harvest 0. 1. 10" WPAB, 192	22d. per diem for reaping

FIELD WORK, *cont.*

Date	Name	Service	Rate
22 Feb. 1648/49	John Stebbins	"Recd 8 days winter work at 16d. [is] 0. 10. 0"	16d. per diem for winter work (pays 15d.)
		"5 days last summer at 20d. [is] 0. 8. 4" WPAB, 186	20d. per diem for summer work
11 Oct. 1649	Thomas Cooper	"Recd 5 days work and ½ last winter at 20d., 53 days ½ Sumer at 2s. [is] 5. 7. 0" WPAB, 203	20d. per diem for winter work 2s. per diem for summer work
9 Dec. 1649	Henry Chapin	"Recd 10 days at 22d. and a pce of a day at 18d. [is] 0. 19. 0"	18d. and 22d. per diem for field work
		"9 days at 18d. per day 0. 13. 6"	18d. per diem for field work
		"4 days harvest at 2s. [is] 0. 8. 0"	2s. per diem for reaping
		"1 day work at 16d. [is] 0. 1. 4" WPAB, 40	16d. per diem for field work
12 Dec. 1649	Henry Burt (sons)	"Recd Jonathan 4 days winter work - 5. 4"	16d. per diem for winter work
		"2 days harvest 0. 4. 0"	2s. per diem for reaping
		"2 [?] days work 0. 3. 4" WPAB, 193	20d. per diem for field work
Mar. 1652	James Bridgeman	"Recd 9 days . . . worke 16d. [is] 0. 18. 4, 30¼, 24, 29½ . . . [is all] 144¼ [days work]" 1AB, 101	16d. per diem for field work (pays 2s.)
20 Aug. 1652	John Lamb	"Recd 24 days ¼ at 2s. per day is 2. 10. 2" 1AB, 148	2s. per diem for field work
24 Dec. 1652	Jonathan Taylor	"Recd 21 days worke 1. 15. 0" 1AB, 125	20d. per diem for field work

FIELD WORK, *cont.*

Date	Name	Service	Rate
1653	Rowland Stebbins	"Resting due to Goodman Stebbins more due to him for 33 days ½ worke this summer 1653 at 20d. [is] 2. 14. 10"	20d. per diem for summer work
1654		"Recd by this summer worke 18 days work at 18d. and 30 days at 20d. [is] 3. 14. 0" 1AB, 109	18d. and 20d. per diem for summer work
1654	Francis Pepper	"By 56 days worke at 20d. [is] 4. 13. 4" 1AB, 203	20d. per diem for field work
24 Oct. 1654	James Bridgeman	"Recd by 20 days worke 2. 0. 0" 1AB, 102	2s. per diem for field work
28 Oct. 1654	Francis Pepper	"Accounted with Francis and I owe him more for 55 days worke at 16d. [is] 3. 13. 4" "By 71 days at 20d. [is] 5. 18. 4" 1AB, 203	16d. per diem for winter work 20d. per diem for summer work
31 Jan. 1654/55	James Osborne	"Recd by 19 days worke at 18d . . . 1. 10. 2" 1AB, 249	18d. per diem for field work (pays 19d.)
14 Dec. 1655	Symon Beamon	"Recd by 34 days worke 2. 14. 0" "More 19 days worke at 2s. [is] 1. 10. 0" 1AB, 291	20d. per diem for field work (pays 19d.) 2s. per diem for field work (pays 18d.)
Dec. 1655	Rowland Stebbins	"Recd 24 days worke this summer and last winter at 16d." 1AB, 109	16d. per diem for both summer and winter work

FIELD WORK, *cont.*

Date	Name	Service	Rate
1656	Francis Pepper	"By what I owe to Francis for worke done for me this summer 100 days work at 20d. per day is 6. 6. 8" "Recd more 77 days work at 16d. [is] 5. 2. 8" 1AB, 203	20d. per diem for summer work (underpayment) 16d. per diem for winter work
1656	Samuel Terry	"Recd by 2 days worke at 20d. [is] 0. 3. 4" "4 days ½ pitching cart [dung?] 0. 9. 0" 1AB, 240	20d. per diem for field work 2s. per diem for pitching [dung?]
30 Sep. 1656	James Osborne	"Recd 23 days worke haymaking, carting dung, and some in harvest 1. 15. 0" 1AB, 249	18¼d. per diem for field work
Oct. 1656	James Taylor	"Recd 10 days worke . . . abate for his 2 weeks dyet 0. 10. 0" 1AB, 250	1s. and meat and drink per diem for field work
21 Apr. 1657	Francis Pepper	"Recd by worke from November unto April 21, 1657: in all 17 weeks winter work 6. 16. 0" "Recd 7 weeks 4 days Summer worke 3. 12. 8" 1AB, 208	8s. per week for winter work 9s. 6d. per week for summer work
1657	Rowland Stebbins	"13 days worke 0. 19. 6" 1AB, 262	18d. per diem for field work
1657?	Thomas Salmon of Northampton	"Recd by 29 days worke at 2s. 4d. . . . 3. 7. 6" 2AB, Index	2s. 4d. per diem for field work
16 Nov. 1657	Thomas Bancroft	"Recd by 4 days ½ gardening 0. 9. 0" 1AB, 245	2s. per diem for gardening

FIELD WORK, *cont.*

Date	Name	Service	Rate
26 May 1658	David Chapin	"Recd by 36 days worke about my house over the River 4. 10. 0" 1AB, 294	2s. 6d. per diem for work
5 Jul. 1658	James Warrinar	"Recd by 4 days worke at 20d. [is] 0. 6. 8" 2AB, 32	20d. per diem for field work
20 Oct. 1658	Thomas Bancroft	"1 day gardening 0. 2. 0" 1AB, 246	2s. per diem for gardening
25 Oct. 1658	Jonathan Taylor	"Recd 4 days ½ worke 0. 9. 0" 1AB, 314	2s. per diem for field work
10 Nov. 1658	Anthony Dorchester	"Recd 8 days worke about the Tanhouse 0. 16. 0" "Recd 20 days work about my howse over the river 2. 0. 0" "Recd by 1 day carying and getting Thatch 0. 2. 0" 1AB, 296	2s. per diem for work 2s. per diem for work 2s. per diem for carrying and getting thatch
Nov. 1658	Miles Morgan	"Recd by sowing of 17 acre 0. 5. 6" 1AB, 266	4d. per acre for sowing
Late 1650s	Rowland Stebbins	"Recd 51 days work/40 of them at 18d., and 11 of them at 16d., all is 3. 14. 6" 1AB, 110	16d. and 18d. per diem for field work
26 Mar. 1659	Francis Pepper	"Recd by worke . . . 16 weeks winter worke 6. 8. 0" "3 weekes Summer worke" 2AB, 121	8s. per week for winter work Payment for 3 weeks summer work
1659	James Taylor	"30 days worke, dyet allowed 1. 10. 0" 1AB, 250	1s. and meat and drink per diem for field work

FIELD WORK, *cont.*

Date	Name	Service	Rate
22 Aug. 1659	John Stebbins	"By 13 days worke at 2s. 6d. [is] 1. 12. 6" 2AB, 79	2s. 6d. per diem for field work
Nov. 1659	Francis Pepper	"By 16 days worke from the 25th of November to the 9 December, on which day he gave over working by the day having taken . . . 1. 1. 4" 2AB, 227	16d. per diem for winter work
20 Apr. 1660	Samuel Terry	"By worke as in Sam Terry's booke to this 20th April (60) 2. 3. 0" 2AB, 201	£2 3s. for field work
1660	Francis Pepper	"By 33 weekes and ½ worke at 10s. per week 16. 15. 0" "By 6 weekes worke at 8s. [is] 2. 8. 0" 2AB, 227	10s. per week for summer work 8s. per week for winter work
10 Dec. 1660	James Taylor	"To 4 weekes at freshwater brook 1. 12. 0" "To 4 weeks at home at 6s. per weeke 1. 4. 0" 2AB, 121	8s. per week for winter work 6s. per week for winter work
1661	Francis Pepper	"By allowance to 84 days when you helped Goodman Griswald [?] 8. 0" "By 15 weekes worke since your keeping sheep, viz. the Nov. 10th to this 1st March, at 8s. per weeke comes to £6 abate 8 days [when not working for JP]" "By 5 weekes and ½ worke last Spring before you went to keep sheep at 10s. per weeke 2. 15. 0" 2AB, 227	Payment for 84 days of field work 8s. per week for winter work 10s. per week for summer work

FIELD WORK, *cont.*

Date	Name	Service	Rate
1661	Charles Ferry	"By 3 days bogging Mr. Glover's meddow 0. 5. 0" 2AB, 261	20d. per diem for bogging
1661	Reice Bedortha	"Recd by 30 days about my house this summer 1661, and 6 days about my chimy . . . 4. 4. 0"	£4 4s. for unspecified work
		"Recd as above by your worke about my house all is 6. 9. 0" 2AB, 43	£6 9s. for unspecified work
18 Nov. 1661	Richard Sikes	"Recd by 60 days worke at . . . 8[?] 5. 0"	Payment for 60 days of field work
		"Recd by 42 days worke 5. 5. 0"	2s. 6d. per diem for field work
	Richard Sikes (son Increase)	"Recd by 3 days Increase 0. 2. 6" 2AB, 28	10d. per diem for youth's field work
Jan. 1661/62	James Taylor	"By 2 weekes at 6s. per week 0. 12. 0"	6s. per week for winter work
		"By 30 weeks worke from the 4th of March to the last of Sept. 1661 at 7s. per weeke 10. 10. 0"	7s. per week for summer work
		"By 7 weekes from the 18th October to the 18th Nov 1660 at 6s. per week 2. 2. 0"	6s. per week for winter work
		"By 6 weeks from the 18th Nov 1660 to this 1st of Jan 1661 at 5s. per week 1. 10. 0"	5s. per week for winter work
		"Abate out of this by the above: 1 week at 7s. for Traveling, 2 days and 1 weeke at 6s. for wedding, and more 1 weeke at 5s.; in all there is to be taken out 18s. and 11s. for your	Abatement for days not worked

FIELD WORK, *cont.*

Date	Name	Service	Rate
		dyet these weekes, all which abates 29s."	
		"Agreed with James to allow him for his dyet and 7s. a week from March till 29 September and thereafter 6[?]s. per weeke till 18 Nov. from [then] on to 18 Feb., 5s. per week and then . . . " 2AB, 121	6s. and 7s. and meat and drink per week for summer work 5s. and meat and drink per week for winter work
3 Jan. 1661/62		"By 4 weekes last winter before this, viz. from the middle of February till mid March all at 5s. per week 1. 0. 0"	5s. per week for winter work
		"By 24 weeks from the middle of March last yeare till Sept. middle at 7s. is 8. 8. 0" 2AB, 337	7s. per week for summer work
1662	Francis Pepper	"By 32 weekes worke and half [some days abated] at 10s. per weeke 16. 5. 0"	10s. per week for summer work
		"By 8 weekes want one day at 8s. per weeke 3. 2. 8" 2AB, 227	8s. per week for winter work
25 Sep. 1662	James Osborne	"By 6 days worke 0. 10. 0" 2AB, 277	20d. per diem for field work
5 Dec. 1662–3 Apr. 1663	Richard Sikes	"By 38 days ½ worke 4. 16. 3"	2s. 6d. per diem for field work
		"By 3 days Nathaniel at 18d. [is] 0. 4. 6" 2AB, 187	18d. per diem for field work
May 1663	Daniel Arnold	"Worke with me Just 25 days wch at 18d. per day cometh to 1. 17. 6" 2AB, 373	18d. per diem for field work

FIELD WORK, *cont.*

Date	Name	Service	Rate
5 Nov. 1663	Samuel Terry	"By 6 days worke 0. 12. 0" 2AB, 201	2s. per diem for field work
20 Nov. 1663	Francis Pepper	"By 29 weeks to the 10 November 1663 [is] 14. 10. 0" "By 2 weeks almost to this 20th November 1663 at 8s. per weeke 0. 13. 0" 2AB, 227	10s. per week for summer work 8s. per week for winter work
21 Nov. 1663	James Taylor	"By 8 Months and a weeke, that is in all 33 weeks of Summer worke, and your days that you worked not I abate all besides Summer worke, I allow you besides your dyet per week for 33 weeks to this 21 November 1663 [is] 11. 11. 0" 2AB, 337	7s. and meat and drink per week for summer work
20 Jan. 1664/65	Francis Pepper	"Owing to him for 17 days worke before he set in to the sheep 1. 2. 8"	16d. per diem for winter work
		"For 8 Months worke from the 1st March to November 1664 at 20d. per day comes to £17 10s."	20d. per diem for summer work
		"For 64 days worke from 1st November to this 20 Jan. 1664 at 16d. per day 4. 5. 0" 2AB, 229	16d. per diem for winter work
		"By account made up as in old Booke: this 20th Jan. 1664/65, and for all his worke to this day, I owe him the sum of 49. 0. 9"	£49 9d. for unspecified work
		"More By 20 weekes sumer worke at 10s. and 1 day 10. 01. 6"	10s. per week for summer work
		"By 7 weeks winter [work] at 2. 14. 0" 3AB, 139	7s. 8½d. per week for winter work

FIELD WORK, *cont.*

Date	Name	Service	Rate
May 1665	Joseph Crowfoot	"By 2 days work about the fence, gardening and shovelling the dung 0. 4. 0" 3AB, 187	2s. per diem for gardening and shoveling dung
1665	Richard Sikes	"By 20 days worke of Goodman Sikes, his worke Ano 63 Ano 64 [is] 2. 10. 0" 3AB, 83	18d. per diem for field work
1665	Rowland Stebbins	"To 1 day worke you promised to give toward supply of his Majesty's fleete at Barbados 0. 1. 6" 3AB, 104	18d. per diem for field work
1665	Jonathan Ball	"By 15 days worke 1. 10. 0" 3AB, 129	2s. per diem for field work
1660s?	John Kilum	"By clearing 3 acres Land . . . at 26s. per acre 3. 18. 0" 4AB, 87	26s. per acre for clearing land
1666	Francis Pepper	"By worke ano 1666 In the Spring 6 weeks, 2 days at 20d. [is] 3. 3. 4" 3AB, 139	20d. per diem for summer work
1666	Samuel Ball	"By 21 days worke of Samuel Ball at 18d. [is] 1. 11. 6" 3AB, 129	18d. per diem for field work
4 Jan. 1666/67	Francis Pepper	"By 18 days work this last summer at 20d. per day 1. 10. 0" 3AB, 139	20d. per diem for summer work

FIELD WORK, *cont.*

Date	Name	Service	Rate
23 Sep. 1667	Samuel Stebbins	"Recd by 19 days worke 1. 18. 0" 3AB, 22	2s. per diem for field work
		"5 days carying dung 10s." 3AB, 25	2s. per diem for carting dung
1667–1668	Francis Pepper	"By 44 days work part of last winter and some of this winter, winter days at 16d. per day 2. 18. 8"	16d. per diem for winter work
		"By 89 days worke summer at 20d. per day This summer past 7. 8. 4" 3AB, 139	20d. per diem for summer work
18 Apr. 1668	Peter Swinck	"By Stubbing and clearing 5 acres at 16s. per acre, abate for 10 Rod wanting measure 12d., and 4s. for Francis Pepper helping cleare off the stubs 2 days" 3AB, 167	16s. per acre for stubbing and clearing
3 Jun. 1668	Thomas Copley	"Agreed with Thomas Copley to Stub, Cleare, and Plow up my Peice of land betwixt Robert Ashley's and Brother Holyok, land that he bought of Thomas Day, being about Nine acres more or less what ever it bee: that whole parcel of land . . . all of it he is well to stub it and cleare it and likewise to break and Plow it up well, it being all compleated and well Plowed, I am to allow him Twenty Pounds (and also 2 pair of Stockens which are already delivered to him and recd by him); He is to	44s. 5d. per acre for stubbing, clearing, and plowing [additional considerations of two pair of stockings]

FIELD WORK, *cont.*

Date	Name	Service	Rate
		doe this work wholy to fin- ish the breaking and Plow- ing of it all by the middle of Aprill next come twelve Months, and at least five acres of it to be cleared and Plowed by the middle of Aprill next: and all to be very well Plowed, as wit- ness his hand" 3AB, 122–123	
7 Jul. 1668	Increase Sikes	"Agreed with Increase Sikes to Stub, Cleare, and Plough up Sixe acres of Ground in my land com- only called Sheepes Pasture at the hither end of side next to my ditch there, and so from this hither end all along by the ditch to the brow of the hill by the 3 corner meddow; he is to goe that length, and then in Breadth so much as to make up Sixe acres: for which well Stubbed and cleared and likewise well plowed and broken up, I am to allow and pay him the sum of Eleven Pounds, and one worsted pair of stockens which are already delivered him and Re- ceived by him: He is to doe this worke—wholly to fin- ish the Stubbing and Ploughing of it all up by the 25th of Aprill next come 12 Months, and at least halfe of it is to be done and well plowed by the 25th of Aprill next and	36s. 8d. per acre for stubbing, clearing, and plowing [addi- tional considerations of one pair of stock- ings]

FIELD WORK, *cont.*

Date	Name	Service	Rate
		All to be very well Plowed as witness his hand this 7th of July 1668" Apr. 1669 "I have accounted for all this 6 acres, though 2 acres of it is yet to doe, which he will performe and it is not to be reckned then" 3AB, 83, 172–173	Payment for stubbing, clearing, and plowing
22 Apr. 1669		"Agreed with Increase Sikes to Stub, cleare, and plow up the rest of my ground at round hill next to that he was to doe by former bargaine; He is to cleare and Plow up all the remainder to the top of the hill where the cart way goes down to the plaine, till it comes almost a point, viz. till it be but 8 rod long from the brow of the hill next to the Plaine meddow to the Round hill, for all which well stubbed and cleared and Plowed up, I am to allow and pay him Three and thirty shillings per acre, and one stubbing hoe already delivered him and Received by him: he is to doe this worke by the 25th of . . . Aprill next come 12 Months: and 4 acres of it is to be done and well Plowed by the 25th of Aprill next Spring: All to be well stubbed, as witness his hand This 22th of April 1669" 3AB, 173	33s. per acre for stubbing, clearing, and plowing [additional considerations of one stubbing hoe]

FIELD WORK, *cont.*

Date	Name	Service	Rate
20 Mar. 1669/70		" The Ground he Stubbed and plowed at the Round hill, I paid him for 6 acres and 9: all is 15 acres which as already accounted as above, you think it is somewhat above halfe an acre more: But be it more or less we now agreed that you should have 15s. more for it, and you are to stub it [all to] the further end the . . . and to Plow it up all to the goeing downe the hill and so I am to allow you 15s. more than is already accounted" "By Stubbing, clearing, and Plowing 9 acres of ground by my Round hill 14. 17. 0" 5AB, 161	30s. per acre for stubbing, clearing, and plowing £14 17s. for stubbing, clearing, and plowing 6 acres
6 May 1669	Samuel and Joseph Harmon	"Agreed with Sam and Jos Harmon to Stub, cleare, and plow up that parsell of land I have at the round hill betwixt my ditch and Serjeant Stebbing, all they are well to stub and to cleare and to doe it as well as formerly . . . and Plow it up all well, for which I am to allow and pay them 40s. per acre and 6 pounds of Cotton woole and one quart of Liquers: halfe of which [is to be] done and broken up by the middle of Aprill next and the other halfe by the middle of April next and come 12 months . . . they are also to	40s. per acre for stubbing, clearing, and plowing [additional considerations of stubbing hoe and 6 pounds of cotton]

FIELD WORK, *cont.*

Date	Name	Service	Rate
		have in a stubbing hoe in the Bargain" 3AB, 99	
1669	John Mun	"By 6 days ½ work for Mr Whiting 0. 13. 0" "By worke for Mr Whiting, 22 days to this 6 Nov. 69 [is] 2. 4. 0" 3AB, 97	2s. per diem for field work 2s. per diem for field work
15 Nov. 1669	Robert Butterworth	"By 48 days worke for Mr Whiting at 20d., is £4" 3AB, 219	20d. per diem for field work
13 Dec. 1669	Francis Pepper	"By 43 days worke this summer and some of them barning last winter, making Brooms being accounted at 5s., viz. 3 days; Also Packing or Salting my Porke accounted: all to this 13 December 1669 all is 3. 11. 8" 3AB, 139	5s. per diem for making brooms while "barning"
12 Jan. 1669/70	Increase Sikes	"Agreed with Increase to Stub that Plough Ground by my 3 corner meddow under the hill . . . all being well done by March come 2 yeare if not before; I am to allow and pay him 47s. per acre and 1 pair of Gloves of 4s. price already delivered him" 3AB, 173	47s. per acre for stubbing [additional considerations of one pair of gloves valued at 4s.]
		20 Nov. 1674 "By stubbing and Plowing 2 acres ½, Plowing 2 acres ½, and 30 rod at 47s. per acre 6. 14. 0" 5AB, 417	£6 14s. for stubbing, clearing, and plowing 2½ acres

FIELD WORK, *cont.*

Date	Name	Service	Rate
8 Oct. 1670	Samuel Stebbins	"By 1 Month work in harvest per agreement at 2. 6. 0"	£2 6s. per month for reaping
		"By 8 days ½ work afterward at 2s. [is] 0. 17. 0" 5AB, 173	2s. per diem for field work
24 Jan. 1670/71	James Taylor	"By breaking up 2 acres of land and stubbing one 2. 5. 0"	£2 5s. for clearing and plowing
		"By 5 days worke 0. 10. 0" 5AB, 55	2s. per diem for field work
1 Feb. 1670/71	James Osborne	"By . . . 15 days worke this summer 1. 10. 0" 3AB, 101	2s. per diem for summer work
1671	Samuel Harmon	"By Stubbing and clearing and Plowing 4 acres of new ground in the Round hill . . . 8. 0. 0"	40s. per acre for clearing and plowing
		"By stubbing and Plowing the Ground with Tho Copley . . . 20. 0. 0" 5AB, 165	£20 for stubbing and clearing
15 Jan. 1671/72	James Osborne	"By 8 days worke 0. 16. 0" 5AB, 121	2s. per diem for field work
7 May 1672	Isaac Morgan	Agreement between JP and Morgan for Morgan to bog and clear 3 acres of meadow for 30s. per acre 5AB, 189	30s. per acre for bogging and clearing
1672	John Stebbins, Jr.	"By 3 week worke for John . . . 1. 16. 0" 5AB, 279	12s. per week for field work
1 Nov. 1672	Nathaniel Harmon	"By 5 days ½ worke 0. 11. 0" 5AB, 165	2s. per diem for field work

FIELD WORK, *cont.*

Date	Name	Service	Rate
1673	Francis Pepper	"By worke several days, and barning, and also the worke since we last accounted till this mid-summer day 1673: comes to 6. 18. 4" 5AB, 159	£6 18s. 4d. for unspecified work
Jul. 1673	Luke Hitchcock	"By one fortnight's worke ending 20th April 1673 [is] 0. 14. 0" 2AB, 89	7s. per week for summer work
Aug. 1673	Henry Stiles of Windsor	"By worke 3 days the 1st weeke 0. [?] 8. 0" "And next week 4 days and ½ all is 7 days ½ at 2s. 6d. per day is 0. 18. 6" 5AB, 283	2s. 8d. per diem for field work? 2s. 6d. per diem for field work
Oct. 1673	Thomas Copley and Jonathan Ball	"By 6 days stubbing at 2s. 6d. per day" 3AB, 14	2s. 6d. per diem for stubbing
22 Nov. 1673	Pelatiah Morgan	"Agreed with Pelatiah Morgan to stub and cleare and throw in of ditch of my land at 3 corner meddow which Increase Sikes is to clear and plow, all the Rest Pelatiah is to stub and cleare and throw in the ditch at the end [for] 50s." 5AB, 185	Contract for stubbing, clearing, and plowing
12 Dec. 1673	Joseph Bedortha	"Agreed with Joseph Bedortha to Stubb, cleare, and Plough up Three acres of New Ground in my 3d Devision; for which 3 acre of ground . . . cleared and well broken up by him	26s. 8d. per acre for stubbing, clearing, and plowing

FIELD WORK, *cont.*

Date	Name	Service	Rate
		next May or June, I am to pay him foure Pounds: Three pounds whereoff is . . . in a young steere already delivered him, being that I had of Edmund Pringdrays, and the other 20s. I am to allow him on acot when the ground is broken up" 5AB, 29	
22 Dec. 1673	Richard Waite	"Agreed with Richard Waite to Bogg and cleare my meddow on the other side of the hill by the old ditch, 8 rod broad [for] 22s."	22s. for bogging and clearing 132-foot meadow
		"Also agreed with him to Bogg one acre in the meddow above Sam Holyoke's [for] 28s., and to procure him a bogging hoe, he paying what it cost" 5AB, 391	28s. per acre for bogging
28 Mar. 1674	Pelatiah Morgan	"Agreed with Pelatiah to bog for me 2 acres in my meddow above the . . . for which I am to pay him 23 bushels of Indian corne" 5AB, 185	11½ bushels of corn per acre for bogging
15 Apr. 1674	John Harmon, Jr.	"Agreed with John Harmon to cleare 2 acres of ground at the further end of the bogy meddow . . . for 30s . . . to be done before winter" 5AB, 123	15s. per acre for clearing ground
28 Apr. 1674	Henry Stiles of Windsor	"Agreed with Henry Stiles at Stony River to cleare all	£3 for clearing meadowland

FIELD WORK, *cont.*

Date	Name	Service	Rate
		the ground from the Plaine betwixt the River and over the Broke . . . for £3, to cleare fit for Mowing" 5AB, 283	
4 May 1674	John Holtum	"Agreed with John Holtum to Bog me Three acres in my meddow, viz. 6 rod wide, to run through the meddow . . . [for £4]" 5AB, 355	26s. 8d. per acre for bogging
Jun. 1674	Richard Waite	"By 4 days worke at stony River 0. 8. 0" "For burning Boggs 1 day ½ . . . 0. 3. 0" 5AB, 391	2s. per diem for field work 2s. per diem for burning bogs
1674	Francis Pepper	"By Bogging 4 acres at 30s. [per acre] 6. 0. 0" 5AB, 159	30s. per acre for bogging
Jul. 1674	James Mun	"By 1 weeke's work at stonny River 0. 13. 6" 5AB, 99	13s. 6d. per week for field work
30 Dec. 1674	Samuel Stebbins	"By 3 days worke at stony River 0. 6. 0" "5 days work at stony River 0. 12. 6" "By 3 days worke at stony River 0. 6. 0" 5AB, 173	2s. per diem for field work 2s. 6d. per diem for field work 2s. per diem for field work
18 Feb. 1674/75	Thomas Spofford	"By 8 weeke's work to this 18 Feb 74, at 3s. per weeke (your dyet and horsekeeping included) is 1. 4. 0" "By his tyme to this 28 Aug 75 [is] 6. 10. 0" 5AB, 447	3s., meat and drink, and horsestabling per week for field work £6 10s. for field work

FIELD WORK, *cont.*

Date	Name	Service	Rate
11 Mar. 1674/75	Nathaniel Bliss, Jr.	"By 1 day spreading dung 0. 2. 0" 5AB, 35	2s. per diem for spreading dung
Mar. 1674/75	Francis Pepper	"By clearing my Meddow, By help in carting dung, and by other days worke, all the worke to this March 1674/75 is 4. 7. 0" 5AB, 159	£4 7s. for clearing meadow, carting dung, and other work
17 Apr. 1675	James Osborne	"By 20 days worke: last year . . . 1674 [is] 2. 0. 0" 5AB, 121	2s. per diem for field work
30 Apr. 1675	Pelatiah Morgan	"Agreed with Pelatiah to stub and clear fit for plowing the Peice of New ground . . . [for] 8s." 5AB, 185	8s. for stubbing
1675	John Holtum	"By Bogging one acre in my meddow 1. 10. 0" 5AB, 491	30s. per acre for bogging
Dec. 1675	James Mun	"By 6 days worke finding dung and etc., all to this Dec 1675 [is] 0. 12. 0" 5AB, 99	2s. per diem for gathering dung
1675–1676	Richard Waite	11 days work 1. 4. 0 5AB, 391	2s. 2d. per diem for field work
11 Dec. 1676	Francis Pepper	"By the allowance for this summer worke till this 11 Dec 76 . . . 5. 0. 0"	£5 for summer work
1677		"By worke bogging the meddow 22 days at 20d. [is], 1. 16. 0"	20d. per diem for bogging
		"By bogging (besides the 22 days) 4 acres ½ of stray	28s. per acre for bogging and burning

FIELD WORK, *cont.*

Date	Name	Service	Rate
		boggs at 28s. per acre and Burning them is 7[?]. 0. 0" "2 acres ½ bogging at 25s. [is] 2. 0" 5AB, 159	25s. per acre for bogging
1678	Jonathan Bush	"By 20 days worke in Summer 2. 10. 0" 5AB, 513	2s. 6d. per diem for summer work
22 Nov. 1678	Samuel Roe of Suffield	"He engages to Stub, cleare, and Plow up one acre of land [for 45s., by following May]" 5AB, 301	45s. per acre for stubbing, clearing, and plowing
24 Jan. 1678/79	John Burbank	"Agreed with Goodman Burbank to stub and cleare 2 acres of Ground for me in my lot in feather streete . . . which he is to stub and cleare in the Spring, one acre of it is to be done by the last of April . . . and the other acre is to have cleared and done by the 15 of May next . . . [at] 30s. per acre . . . in Indian Corne"	30s. per acre for stubbing and clearing
		"Agreed for 3 acres more at 30s. per acre" 5AB, 287	30s. per acre for stubbing and clearing
9 Apr. 1680	Hugh Roe of Suffield	"Agreed with Goodman Roe well to stub and cleare it and also to fall and clear all the Trees and likewise . . . well to Plow up Two Acres of Ground in my lot [for] £5"	Contract for stubbing, clearing, and plowing
		"By breaking up 2 acres of land with clearing 5. 15. 0" 5AB, 483	57s. 6d. per acre for stubbing, felling trees, clearing, and plowing

FIELD WORK, *cont.*

Date	Name	Service	Rate
1680	John Clark	"By 4 days at fresh water River this Spring 1680 [is] 0. 8. 0" 5AB, 115	2s. per diem for field work
1680	John Warburton	"By 26 days at 12d. in December and January 1. 6. 0" "By 12 days to this 9th Feb 0. 18. 0" 5AB, 403	1s. per diem for winter work 18d. per diem for winter work
1680	John Burbank	"He promised to stub 2 acres ¼ for me at freshwater River for £4, and to go toward the grinding of flour" 5AB, 287	35s. 7d. per acre for stubbing and clearing
1680	Joseph Trumble	"By Breaking up Ground at Stony Brooke, 1 acre ¾ . . . 0. 12. 6" 5AB, 343	7s. 2d. per acre for breaking ground
1 Feb. 1680/81	John Peirce	"Agreed with John Peirce well to Stub and cleare 4 acres of ground in my lot at Enfield, fit for plowing, which he is [to receive] Three Pounds" 5AB, 547	15s. per acre for stubbing and clearing
31 Dec. 1681	Isaac Morgan	"Agreed with Isack Morgan well to stub and break up with Plough 2 acres of land in my lot at Enfeild; That is to say, all the bredth of my lot there and 14 rod in the length of it, and the place where he is to doe this is agreed to be about 40 rod from the	30s. per acre for stubbing, clearing, and plowing [additional considerations of one stubbing hoe]

FIELD WORK, *cont.*

Date	Name	Service	Rate
		front of my home lot there, at . . . Three Pounds and a stubbing hoe" 5AB, 421	
29 Jan. 1682/83	Richard Waite	"7 days worke in 1682 [is] 0. 18. 0"	2s. 7d. per diem for field work
Jun. 1683		"More by 22 days worke to this 4th June 1683 [is], 2. 4. 0"	2s. per diem for summer work
1683		"By 5 days worke 0. 10. 0" 5AB, 391	2s. per diem for field work
Feb. 1683/84	Francis Pepper	"By 46 days Summer worke at 20d." "36 days winter at 15d." 5AB, 159	20d. per diem for summer work 15d. per diem for winter work
14 Jan. 1684/85	Samuel Kent	"Agreed with Samuel Kent to Stub, Clear, and well Plow or breake up that acre of New Ground . . . [for] 50s. per acre" 6AB, 71	50s. per acre for stubbing, clearing, and plowing
21 Nov. 1687	John Bagg, Jr.	"By 15 days worke and ½, 3 days of wch goe for the sieth, and so I have 12s. to allow for at 2s. 6d. per day" 6AB, 208–209	2s. 6d. per diem for field work
6 Apr. 1688	Thomas Remmington of Suffield	"By 3 days worke 0. 7. 0"	2s. 4d. per diem for field work
		"9 days 1. 0. 0"	2s. 3d. per diem for field work
		"1 month worke 2. 10.[?] 0"	50s.? per month for field work
		"19 days worke 2. 6. 0"	2s. 5d. per diem for field work

FIELD WORK, *cont.*

Date	Name	Service	Rate
		"By 5 days worke 0. 11. 6"	2s. 4d. per diem for field work
		"22 days 2. 11. 4"	2s. 4d. per diem for field work
		"By 4 days worke 0. 9. 0" 5AB, 201	2s. 3d. per diem for field work
27 Mar. 1690	Robert Pease of Enfield	"By one Month's worke 30s., and more 3 weeks is 22s. 6d. [is] 2. 11. 0" 6AB, 227	30s. per month for field work
1692	John Kilum	"By 37 days worke, 18 of them at 2s. 6d. per day and [rest] at 2s. [is] 4. 3. 0" 6AB, 229	2s. and 2s. 6d. per diem for field work
Spring 1694	Timothy Hale	"2 days worke hand labor 0. 5. 0" 5AB, 323	2s. 6d. per diem for field work
6 Apr. 1695	Thomas Parsons	JP agreed with Parsons to work for JP the next summer for 6 or 7 months (23s. per month), abated if growing season shorter 6AB, 170	23s. in specie per month for field work
15 Jul. 1695	Timothy Hale	"By 32 days worke [at] 2s. 6d. [is] 4. 0. 0" "By 6 days worke at Suffeild 0. 15. 0" 5AB, 323	2s. 6d. per diem for field work 2s. 6d. per diem for field work
18 Mar. 1695/96 [?]	Thomas Parsons	JP agreed for Parsons to work for him again for the next summer, 6 months at £7 in specie. Parsons failed to appear on time and the agreement voided 6AB, 171	£7 in specie for 6 months work

FIELD WORK, *cont.*

Date	Name	Service	Rate
1695–1696		"By one monthly service beginning 4 April ending the 4th May as wee agreed 0. 10. 0" 4AB, 139	10s. and bed and board per month for work
1695–1696	William Anthony	"William Anthony Wages he assigns to me viz. 21 weekes . . . 6. 6. 0" 6AB, 33	6s. per week for field work
20 Dec. 1700	Thomas Day, Jr.	"By 12 days ½ worke 1. 17. 6" "By 13 days his Boy 0. 14. 0" 6AB, 217	3s. per diem for field work 1s. 1d. per diem for youth's field work

GLAZING

Date	Name	Service	Rate
18 Oct. 1655	John Gilbert	"Recd by mending my glass window 0. 17. 7" 1AB, 189	17s. 7d. for mending glass windows
3 Nov. 1663		"By work glasing my windows and etc. 3. 3. 3" 2AB, 357	£3 3s. 3d. for glazing

GROOMING

Date	Name	Service	Rate
30 Dec. 1680	Joseph Bedortha	"By bringing a horse, breaking and keeping him till Spring 0. 17. 0" 5AB, 187	17s. for breaking horse to saddle and stabling
Jul. 1696	Josias Beamon	"By looking after my horse to this day being 7 days and ¼ [is] 0. 15. 0"	2s. per diem for grooming horses

GROOMING, *cont.*

Date	Name	Service	Rate
		"By 2 days about my horses 0. 4. 0"	2s. per diem for grooming horses
		"2 days about my horses 0. 4. 0"	2s. per diem for grooming horses
		"By [currycombing?] my horses 0. 5. 0" 4AB, 133	5s. for currycombing? horses

ITINERANT CRAFTSMEN

Date	Name	Service	Rate
30 Aug. 1662	Samuel Bewell	"By 17 days worke reckening his coming up and goeing downe a day 2. 11. 0"	3s. per diem for carpentry
		"[Work past] 3. 16. 0"	£3 16s. for carpentry
		"By 27 days ½ worke 4. 2. 6"	3s. per diem for carpentry
		"[T]old Goodm Bewell his work about the gallery (besides his dyet) comes to 4. 5. 0, more due him for 3 days worke . . . setting up the Pillar 0. 11. 0" 2AB, 365	3s. 8d. per diem for carpentry
30 Oct. 1662	Thomas Hubbard	"By a fortnight's worke 2. 0. 0"	20s. per week for carpentry
		"By 5 weeks [work] 6. 0. 0"	24s. per week for carpentry
		"By 2 months work . . . at 24s. per week 9. 4. 0"	24s. per week for carpentry
		"By your Boy . . . 42 days 2. 2. 0"	1s. per diem for apprentice's carpentry
7 Jan. 1662/63	•	"Accounted and rests due to Goodman Hubbard . . . 8. 0. 0, and his boy's worke for this day being Wednesday the 7th of Jan. is reckoned and allowed for; I agreed with Goodman	4s. per diem for carpentry 1s. per diem for apprentice's carpentry 2s. abatement of board for wife at ordinary

ITINERANT CRAFTSMEN, *cont.*

Date	Name	Service	Rate
		Hubbard for this tyme to allow him besides his 4s. per day and his boy 12d., more 2s. per weeke toward the charge of his wife at the ordinary" 2AB, 363	
6 Feb. 1662/63	Samuel Bewell	"By 16 days worke this April 1663 [is] 2. 8. 0" "By ½ day work 0. 1. 6" 2AB, 365	3s. per diem for carpentry 3s. per diem for carpentry
24 Feb. 1662/63	Thomas Hubbard	"By 36 days worke himself to this 24th Feb. 1662 [is] 7. 4. 0" "By 37 days and ½ [is] 7. 17. 0" "By allowance toward his wife being at the ordinary 0. 14. 0"	4s. per diem for carpentry 4s. 2d. per diem for carpentry 2s. per week abatement of board
Oct. 1663		"More due to Goodman Hubbard for a fortnight's worke in May last as per his letter Recd October 1663; he written it, being worke which did not goe off a hand: I should allow him as I pleased But I set downe 3s. 4d. per day for ... 12 days is 2. 0. 0" 2AB, 363	3s. 4d. per diem for carpentry

LOGGING

Date	Name	Service	Rate
14 Apr. 1646	James Osborne	"5 days cutting wood at 16d. [is], 0. 6. 8" WPAB, 32	16d. per diem for cutting wood

LOGGING, *cont.*

Date	Name	Service	Rate
9 Jul. 1655	Francis Pepper	"By cutting 15 load of wood at 10d. [is] 0. 12. 6" 1AB, 203	10d. per load of wood cut
16 Nov. 1657	Nathaniel Pritchard	"Recd 575 foote loggs at 6d. [is] 1. 14. 9" 1AB, 118	6s. per 100 feet of logs
1660	Rowland Thomas	"By falling Timber for my howse 1660, 56 Trees containe 133 foote at 3d. per foote 1. 13. 3" "7 days hewing Timber 0. 17. 6" 2AB, 159	3d. per foot for felling trees 2s. 6d. per diem for hewing timber
27 Nov. 1660	John Bagg	"By worke at freshwater Brooke, 950 of log Pole at 6s. per 100 [is] 2. 17. 0" "Agreed with John Bagg to get and deliver me at the wharf 5 [?] hundred of good substantial Log Poles full 6 foote Long and of a sufficient [length] and breadth . . . [for] £4; (I am to lend him the Boate, he paying for it) . . . Also he is to deliver me at the wharfe 500 of good substantial broad Rayls, 11 foote and ½ long for which I am to give him 12s. per 100 [to be done by] March next" 2AB, 81	6s. per 100 feet for log poles 12s. per 100 feet for 11 ½-foot wharf rails
3 Dec. 1660	William Brooks	"Agreed with William Brooks to deliver me a pole wharfe by the end of next March; 500 of good broad and substantial Rayls 11 foote and ½ long, halfe [of?] oake and 500 of good	12s. per 100 feet for 11½ wharf rails, half to be of oak 8s. per 100 feet for 6-foot wharf rails 4s. per 100 feet for 6-foot wharf posts

LOGGING, *cont.*

Date	Name	Service	Rate
		broad and Substantial log rayle [?] of a good . . . and full 6 foote long . . . for which I am to allow him 12s. per 100 for the Rayle and 8s. per 100 for the logs . . . Also he is to get and deliver me at the wharfe 500 good cut oake Posts 6 foote longe . . . for which I am to pay him 4s. per [100] posts" 2AB, 34 1663, Pd. for "100 Rayls at the wharfe 0. 8. 0" 2AB, 215	Payment for 100 wharf rails
5 Dec. 1660	Thomas Miller	"Agreed with Thomas Miller for 100 of Rayls, good white oak Rayls at 7s. per 100, to be delivered within ½ a Mile of the great River, and on this side of the 2 brake going to chikkuppy: also for 20 Rod of log Rayles at 10d. per rod" 2AB, 145	7s. per 100 feet for white oak rails 10d. per rod for log rails
Jan. 1660/61	Samuel Bewell and Timothy Trawler	"Agreed with Sam Bewell and Timothy Trawler to doe the hewing for the House of Correction, and to hew the Timber for my New house for which I am to give you 3s. 8d. per diem and to allow you 2 hands a couple of days to cut them up: to pay them the one half in Comoditys and the other half in corne unless I can give them their content in commodi-	3s. 8d. and meat and drink per diem for hewing timber, JP to supply 2 hands for 2 days for work on his house

LOGGING, *cont.*

Date	Name	Service	Rate
		tys; If I pay any of their Sawer, that pay it is to be set off for so much wheate, and I am to find their dyet"	
		"By hewing Timber for the house of Correction 5. 10. 0"	£5 10s. for hewing timber for house of correction
		"By hewing Timber for my house 2. 14. 0" 2AB, 279	£2 14s. for hewing timber for JP's house
1661	Charles Ferry	"150 logg Poles, 9 rayles . . . 0. 11. 0" 2AB, 261	11s. for poles and log rails
18 Mar. 1661/62	John Bagg	"Recd 500 of log Poles [to be] narrowed 1. 15. 0" 2AB, 81	7s. per 100 for squaring logs
26 Dec. 1662	Rowland Thomas	"By falling the Timber for the howse of correction 1. 0. 6" 2AB, 159	20s. 6d. for felling timber for house of correction
20 Nov. 1663	Richard Excell	"By 450 of Rayls 1. 7. 0" 2AB, 329	7s. per 100 feet for hewing rails
28 Nov. 1665	Rowland Thomas	"4 days falling Timber for the dam 10s." "Falling Timber 40 foote at 3d. [is] 10s." 3AB, 159	2s. 6d. per diem for felling timber 3d. per foot for hewing timber
1666	Increase Sikes	"By 100 logs for saw mill at 8d. per log 3. 6. 8" 3AB, 83	8d. per log for (but not delivered to) saw-mill
1666–1668	Thomas Copley	"By Timber for Boards, 16 logs, 4 of them at 2s. 6d. [is] 10s. and 12 at 2s. [is] 1. 4. 0" 3AB, 123	2s. and 2s. 6d. per log delivered to saw-mill

LOGGING, *cont.*

Date	Name	Service	Rate
7 Dec. 1666	Samuel Ball	"By 20 load of wood 1. 0. 0" 3AB, 129	1s. per load of fire-wood cut
1667	Joseph Leonard	"By 47 days worke about my Mill dam and hewing the Timber for the dam 6. 6. 0" 3AB, 57	2s. 8d. per diem for hewing timber
27 Jan. 1667/68	John Bagg	"By 100 Rayls he says, but Joseph went for them in the morning and they were but 87 and 5 we had before is 92 Rayls, which is 8 wanting of 100 so that all come to but 11s." 3AB, 161	12s. per 100 feet for [wharf?] rails
28 Jan. 1667/68	Samuel Ball	"By 26 load of Wood Cutting 1. 6. 0" 3AB, 93	1s. per load of fire-wood cut
9 Dec. 1668	Samuel and Joseph Harmon	"By 50 loggs Sam and Joseph Harmon are to log by my Saw Mill, for which I am to allow 2s. 8d. per log is 6. 13. 4" 3AB, 127	2s. 8d. per log delivered to sawmill [Logging contracts usually made in winter]
21 Dec. 1668	Timothy Cooper	"Agreed with Timothy Cooper for 120 loggs fit for my Saw Mill, for length betwixt 12 foote and 25 foote: all the 12 foote loggs are to be at least 21 Inches at the smale end without the Barke, none of them under but mostly above, viz. 2 foote or 2 foote and ½: and the longer Loggs the least to be 18 Inches at the smale end without the	8d. per 12 to 25-foot log for (but not delivered to) sawmill, diameter to be at least 18 inches

LOGGING, *cont.*

Date	*Name*	*Service*	*Rate*
		Bark: and some loggs to be of all the lengths: all the loggs to be straite: and for this 120 Loggs I am to allow him 8d. per log one with another: In all £4; In case some few of the loggs that are long prove but 17 Inches at the smale end I promise not to refuse them for 8 or 10 Loggs; All these loggs to be got ready and fit for carting by the middle of March next" 3AB, 55	
28 Feb. 1668/69	Joseph Harmon	"Agreed with Joseph for 100 logs for my saw Mill, for length betwixt 12 foote and 25 foot, all the 12 foote logs are to be at least 21 Inches within the Barke at the smale end, none of them under but mostly above, viz. 2 fote or a foot and ½; And the longer logs the least to be 18 Inches within the Barke at the smale end, but generally above 18 Inches; some logs to be of all the lengths and all the logs to be straite, and to be cut off at both ends plaine for the saw: and to be delivered at my Saw mill, all being sound and good, for which logs being carted by [him] and laid by my Mill: I am to give 2s. 8d. per log: all which they are to cart to my Mill by the middle of November next" 3AB, 99	2s. 8d. per 12 to 25-foot log delivered to sawmill, diameter to be at least 18 inches

LOGGING, *cont.*

Date	Name	Service	Rate
6 Apr. 1669	Edmund Prin-gridays	"By 200 Rayls at 12s." 3AB, 177	12s. per 100 feet for [wharf?] rails
1669	Increase Sikes	"By 20 loggs (more than the 100 accounted above) at 8d. [is] 0. 13. 4" 3AB, 83	8d. per log for (but not delivered to) saw-mill
		"By 120 loggs at 8d. per log those Received; but you are to make up so many besides 100 formerly 4. 0. 0" 3AB, 172	8d. per log for (but not delivered to) saw-mill
1 Feb. 1670/71	John Harmon, Jr.	"By 3 Loggs to my sawmill 0. 6. 0"	2s. per log delivered to sawmill
		"By 50 loggs, at 2s. 8d. per log 6. 13. 4" 5AB, 123	2s. 8d. per log deliv-ered to sawmill
6 Mar. 1670/71	James Warrinar	"By 7 oake Logs for the ship 1. 13. 0" 5AB, 93	4s. 8½d. per oak log
14 Jul. 1671	John Hitchcock	"By 7 oake logs for Plank at 10s. per log comes to £3 10s., abating 5s. on a de-fective log, halfe of which to you, is 1. 13. 0" 5AB, 89	10s. per oak log
20 Dec. 1671	Thomas Steb-bins, Jr.	"By 5 loggs at 3s. 6d. per logg 0. 18. 0" 5AB, 163	3s. 6d. per log deliv-ered to sawmill (pays 3s. 7d.)
Feb. 1672/73	John Hitchcock	"Agreed with John Hitch-cock to get the Logs at 16 feet long and 18 inches at the smale end, for all which I am to allow him 3s. per log . . . I am to give him . . . 2s. 6d. per log laid all at the saw mill." 5AB, 89	2s. 6d. and 3s. per 16-foot log delivered to sawmill, diameter to be at least 18 inches

LOGGING, *cont.*

Date	Name	Service	Rate
1673	Rowland Thomas	"By 3 loggs of oake to the Saw Mill 0. 9. 0" 5AB, 15	3s. per oak log delivered to sawmill
1673	Joshua Willys of Suffield	"By 50 loggs at Stony Brooke at 10d. per logg . . . 2. 3. 6" 5AB, 403	10d. per log for (but not delivered to) sawmill
1673	Abraham Phelps of Windsor	"By 50 loggs at Stony Brooke at 10d. per Log 2. 1. 8" 5AB, 407	10d. per log for (but not delivered to) sawmill
28 Nov. 1673	Benjamin Parsons	"By 21 loggs, and carted to the sawmill at 2s. 6d. [is] 2. 12. 6" 5AB, 127	2s. 6d. per log delivered to sawmill
5 Mar. 1674/75	Samuel Bliss, Jr.	"Agreed with Samuel Bliss and Nathaniel Bliss to get and cart to my Sawmill 30 logs . . . of 20 foot long and 2 foot at the small end, except when the Barke on, some but 22 Inches: these at 4s. and other some of the logs in length 16½ and some 18 feet and 21 Inches at the smale end, these at 3s. per log, this if he can make wages otherwise I am to allow him wages" 5AB, 131	4s. per 20-foot log delivered to sawmill, diameter to be at least 22 inches 3s. per 16½ to 18 foot-logs delivered to sawmill, diameter to be at least 21 inches [Wage guarantee]
1675	Victory Sikes	"By 2 days hewing Timber for my Corne Mill 0. 5. 0" 5AB, 357	2s. 6d. per diem for hewing timber

LOGGING, *cont.*

Date	Name	Service	Rate
24 Apr. 1676	Samuel Kent	"By cutting wood this winter 7 load at 10d. [is] 0. 5. 10" 5AB, 345	10d. per load of firewood cut
1677	Joshua Willys	"By your halfe of 31 . . . loggs you cut with John Lenard at 8d., your halfe is 0. 10. 0" 5AB, 403	8d. per log for (but not delivered to) saw-mill
1678	Jonathan Bush	"By cutting 20 load of wood 1. 0. 0" 5AB, 513	1s. per load of firewood cut
16 Jan. 1678/79	Samuel Jones	"Agreed with him also for 100 of good white oake Posts . . . delivered at my house by March next, for which . . . 4d. per Post, well hoaled for 5 Rayle" 5AB, 459	4d. per white oak post mortised for 5-rail fence and delivered to JP's house
Feb. 1678/79	Samuel Stebbins	"By 4 days worke getting loggs 0. 10. 0" 5AB, 173	2s. 6d. per diem for getting logs
1683	Richard Waite	"By cutting 13 load of firewood 0. 13. 0" 5AB, 391	1s. per load of firewood cut
8 Feb. 1683/84		"By cutting 19 load of wood 0. 19. 0" "By 6 load of wood" "By 9 days getting posts and Rayles 1. 1. 0" 6AB, 75	1s. per load of firewood cut Payment for 6 loads of wood 2s. 4d. per diem for getting posts and rails
7 Aug. 1686	John Warner	"A sled log 0. 1. 0" "By sled Logs betwixt us 4s. 6d., my halfe 0. 2. 3" 5AB, 335	1s. per sled log 4s. 6d. for sled logs

LOGGING, *cont.*

Date	Name	Service	Rate
12 Aug. 1686	John Harmon, Jr.	"By loggs to my Sawmill John Warner gives me ac-cot this 12 Aug. 1686 . . . 1. 4. 0" 6AB, 109	24s. for logs for saw-mill

MEETINGHOUSE WORK

Date	Name	Service	Rate
1651–1652	Richard Sikes	"Recd by sweeping the Meeting House and Ring-ing the bell for the year 1651 [is] 2. 0. 0" "For the year 1652 [is] 2. 12. 0" 1AB, 87	40s. per annum for sweeping meeting-house and ringing bell 52s. per annum for sweeping meeting-house and ringing bell
1661	Benjamin Mun	"By what I allow for you for the Towne for your ringing the Bell Ano 1661 [is] 21s." 2AB, 63	21s. per annum for ringing bell
Jan. 1678/79	Lieutenant Thomas Steb-bins	"Six pound above men-tioned was set off with Leifftenant Stibings for sweeping the meeting house the year 79 and 80" 1TR, 422	£3 per annum for sweeping meeting-house

MILLING

Date	Name	Service	Rate
10 Feb. 1652/53	Anthony Dor-chester	"Agreed with Anthony Dorchester for the Tole of the Mill for a yeare . . . He is to allow us Thirteene Pounds for our Share of the Tole of the Mill, the which Thirteene Pounds	£13 for rent of grist-mill, one-half toll on JP's cornmeal

MILLING, *cont.*

Date	*Name*	*Service*	*Rate*
		he is to pay us in such Corne as he grinds: quarterly he is to pay it: he is to maintaine all Coggs and Rounds fit for grinding and to leave the Mill in as good repaire as he found it . . . This thirteen Pound he is to pay us besides in valuation to what corne the Plantation grinds: what percent corne I may grind into meale to Send out of Towne: he is to allow us half the Tole of that besides, and so Hee [is] to have half the profit of such corne according as I may agree with him for grinding it" [Mill rented from JP and Elizur Holyoke] 1AB, 128	
1654		"Anthony Dorchester desires we would accept £13 10s. for our share of the Toll of the Mill for this yeare 1654, which we yielded to" 1AB, 296	£13 10s. for rent of gristmill
14 Jan. 1655/56	Richard Sikes	"Recd by grinding 392 bushels of wheate at 1d. and ½ per bushel (the other half of your Toll being due) 2. 9. 0"	3d. per bushel of wheat ground
		"Recd by grinding 280 bushels at 3d. [per bushel] Because we promised you the whole part of it 3. 10. 0" 1AB, 329	3d. per bushel of wheat ground

MILLING, *cont.*

Date	Name	Service	Rate
10 Oct. 1656	Anthony Dor-chester	"And more for the tole of the mill of the rests to me 9. 5. 0" 1AB, 297	£9 5s. for grinding
17 Jan. 1664/65	Richard Sikes	"Agreed with Richard Sikes to Tend my Mill by well and Careful Grinding all the Corne shall be brought to it for one whole yeare: from [Monday 22 Jan. 1664/65] for which he is to have one half of the Tole and to allow me the other halfe of all the Tole; he is to mend cogs and Rounds and buckets except when a whole new Set of Coggs and Rounds are needful, then I allow 10s. toward it, he to take the care of the stopping breeches, scour-ing and etc., but I to pay for the clearing and scour-ing of ditches" 3AB, 22	One-half of toll for tending gristmill
Sep. 1666	Joseph Rogers	"Joseph Rogers to tend my Mill for a yeare: . . . and because noe house and the Rate and etc., For the first halfe yeare I am to [pay] him £10, for which he is well and Care Fully to [tend] the Mill and to at-tend to grind all the Corne shall be brought, and also to tend my Bolting Mill to Bolt into flowre what I shall have occasion for . . . and he is to keep all things in repair and to looke to the dam; Latter halfe yeare	£10 for tending grist-mill £12 for renting bolt-ing-mill

MILLING, *cont.*

Date	*Name*	*Service*	*Rate*
		he is to have all the Tole of the Mill [and] allow me £12 for it and doe ale the re-pairs . . . that belong, and he to take care of the dam. The 8th of January his tyme begins" 3AB, 322	
6 Mar. 1666/67		"Recd by almost 2 Months, viz. 7 weeks Tending my Mill 3. 0. 0" 3AB, 20	8s. 6d. per week for tending gristmill
24 Nov. 1673	John Artsell	"Agreed with John Artsell to tend my Sawmill at Stony River till May next, and for Sawing I am to al-low him 12d. per 100 for Bords and Planks [and 14d. for slitwork]" 5AB, 381	1s. per 100 feet for sawing boards and planks 14d. per 100 feet for slitwork
15 Nov. 1676	John Warner	JP agreed with Warner for Warner to have JP's mill at Quabaug one year at halves "he to tend it well and grind all the Corne that comes to it, and allow-ing me one halfe of the Tole" and performing all necessary maintenance. Half of toll: "1677 (4 months) 10. 4. 6" "1677 (rest of year) 23. 2. 0" "1678 [?] 24. — —" 5AB, 337	One-half of toll for tending gristmill £10 4s. 6d., JP's share of toll £23 2s., JP's share of toll £24, JP's share of toll
19 Nov. 1677–1678	Richard Sikes	"Rent of mill lot in neck for 1677, his half 2. 0. 0" "Rent of mill lot in neck for 1678, his half 2. 0. 0" 5AB, 135	40s. per annum for leasing mill lot 40s. per annum for leasing mill lot

MILLING, *cont.*

Date	Name	Service	Rate
24 Jan. 1677/78	Increase Sikes	JP and Sikes agree that Sikes will tend JP's sawmill for £12 a year. 5AB, 546–547	£12 per annum for tending sawmill
1695	Thomas Copley	"Tending Saw Mill 9. 19. 0" 6AB, 49	£9 19s. [per annum?] for tending sawmill

MILL LABOR

Date	Name	Service	Rate
Apr. 1646	Richard Sikes	"in winter 9 days at the mill at 20d. [is] 0. 15. 8" WPAB, 46	20d. per diem for mill work (pays 21d.)
17 Oct. 1648	Thomas Barber	"Recd in worke at the Mill 5 weeks (want one day) at 14s. per week 3. 7. 8" WPAB, 183	14s. per week for mill work
1663	Cornelius Williams	"By 5 weekes worke about my dam 5. 0. 0" 3AB, 311	20s. per week for mill work
Feb. 1663/64	Reice Bedortha	"By 28 days at the Mill . . . Trench 2. 16. 0" 3AB, 147	2s. per diem for mill work
6 Feb. 1664/65	Richard Sikes	"By looking after . . . the Trench, and getting help to doe it 5 days ½ [is] 0. 11. 0" "By stopping breeches againe and again 1. 0. 0" "By 24 days of Increase about the Mill at severall tymes 2. 8. 0" 3AB, 83	2s. per diem for mill work 20s. for repairing breaches 2s. per diem for mill work
1 Mar. 1664/65	Thomas Bancroft	"By 4 days ½ at the old Mill 0. 9. 0"	2s. per diem for mill work

MILL LABOR, *cont.*

Date	Name	Service	Rate
		"By floaring my Milstones 2. 0. 0" 3AB, 75	40s. for flooring mill-stones
1665	Jonathan Ball	"By 11 days worke at the Mill 1. 2. 0" 3AB, 129	2s. per diem for mill work
1660s?	Benjamin Mun	"By worke 43 days all to about 6 or 7 days at the Mill worke 4. 6. 0" "By John Mun 6 days Hay-making and 6 days at Mill 0. 18. 0" 3AB, 97	2s. per diem for mill work 18s. for mill work and field work
1660s	Thomas Steb-bins	"By 12 days worke at the mill 1. 4. 0" "By 21 days of Sam at the Mill 2. 2. 0" "By Joseph 8 days at the Mill 0. 12. 0" "By 4 days Sam at the Mill breech this Spring 0. 8. 0" 3AB, 131	2s. per diem for mill work 2s. per diem for mill work 18d. per diem for youth's mill work 2s. per diem for mill work
28 Nov. 1665	Rowland Thomas	"By 36 days at the Mill Trench, By 4 days about the Dam 5. 10. 0" 3AB, 159	2s. 9d. per diem for mill work
5 Dec. 1665	Nathaniel Prit-chard	"By 18 days at the Mill 36s." 3AB, 97	2s. per diem for mill work
18 Jan. 1665/66	Thomas Miller	"By 7 days worke and ½ at the Mill 0. 15. 0" 3AB, 191	2s. per diem for mill work
6 Feb. 1665/66	Richard Sikes	"By worke at the old mill Ano 63, 64 Stopping breeches, 8 days 1. 0. 0" 3AB, 83	2s. 6d. per diem for mill work

MILL LABOR, *cont.*

Date	Name	Service	Rate
Feb. 1665/66	Joseph Crow-foot	"By 10 days worke at the Mill at 2s. 6d. whereof 2 days he give . . . more 12 days worke at 2s. per day 2. 4. 0" 3AB, 187	2s. and 2s. 6d. per diem for mill work
28 Feb. 1665/66	Thomas Ban-croft	"Tho Bancroft acots worke don for me at the Mill stoping the former breach and mending this last breach in all that I am to pay him for 6 days 0. 12. 0" 3AB, 75	2s. per diem for mending breach in dam
1666?	Samuel Har-mon	"By 7 days worke about the Timber for the dam 0. 14. 0" "By 5 days at the Mill Trench 0. 10. 0" "By 6 days about the dam raising 0. 12. 0" 3AB, 99	2s. per diem for dam work 2s. per diem for trench work 2s. per diem for dam raising
1666	Richard Sikes	"By 10 days at the New Mill this 1666 [is] 1. 0. 0" 3AB, 83	2s. per diem for mill work
1666	Increase Sikes	"By 10 days worke at the New Mill whereoff 3 days you give towards it: so tis 7 day 0. 14. 0" "By 15 days want a little about mill worke 1. 9. 0" 3AB, 83	2s. per diem for mill work 2s. per diem for mill work
1666	Francis Pepper	"By 46 days at the Mill at 20d. [is] 3. 16. 8" 3AB, 139	20d. per diem for mill work

MILL LABOR, *cont.*

Date	Name	Service	Rate
1666	Edward Foster	"By 26 days ½ worke at the Mill Trench at 2s. 6d. and . . . 3. 6. 0" 3AB, 185	2s. 6d. per diem for mill trench work
Summer 1666	John Clark	"By work at the Mill Trench this summer 1666: 35 days himself and 45 days his son as he says all is 80 days at 2s. [is] 8. 0. 0" 3AB, 107	2s. per diem each for mill work for father and son
3 Oct. 1666	Lawrence Bliss	"By 15 days worke at the Mill 1. 10. 0" 3AB, 103	2s. per diem for mill work
Dec. 1666– Sep. 1667	Sam Ball	"By 20 days worke digging at the Mill Trench 2. 0. 0" "By 14 days at the Saw Mill trench 1. 8. 0" 3AB, 129	2s. per diem for mill trench work 2s. per diem for mill trench work
28 Dec. 1666	Benjamin Mun	"By 32 days at the Mill Trench 3. 4. 0"	2s. per diem for mill work
1666–1667		"By worke in the Mill Trench helping Goodman Mathews 36 days 3. 12. 0" 3AB, 129	2s. per diem for mill work
1666–1667	Jonathan Taylor	"By 10 days at the Mill, whereof 3 given so tis 7 days 0. 14. 0" 3AB, 175	2s. per diem for mill work
16 Jan. 1666/67	John Bagg	"By 18 days worke at 2s. 6d. per day at the mill trench" 3AB, 160	2s. 6d. per diem for mill trench work
1667	Joseph Crowfoot	"By 1 day worke at the Mill dam [at] 2s."	2s. per diem for mill dam work

MILL LABOR, cont.

Date	Name	Service	Rate
		"By 15 days worke before Harvest about saw mill Trench 1. 10. 0" 3AB, 187	2s. per diem for mill trench work
23 Dec. 1667	Samuel Harmon	"By 11 days worke about the Mill and fence and etc. 1. 2. 0" 3AB, 99	2s. per diem for mill work
27 Dec. 1667	Joseph Harmon	"By Joseph 32 days ½ whereoff 22 days ½ of them were at the Mill 3. 5. 0" 3AB, 99	2s. per diem for mill work and field work
27 Dec. 1667	John Harmon, Jr.	"By 46 days worke John Harmon, whereoff 22 days of them were at the mill all comes to 4. 12. 0" 3AB, 99	2s. per diem for mill work and field work
1 Mar. 1667/68	Rowland Thomas	"By 20 days worke at the Mill breach formerly 2. 3. 0"	2s. 2d. per diem for mill breach work
19 Apr. 1669		"By 2 days, almost another making the way to the saw mill 0. 6. 0" 3AB, 159	2s. per diem for clearing path to mill
24 Jan. 1670/71	James Taylor	"By 7 days worke at the mill trench of old 0. 14. 0" 5AB, 55	2s. per diem for mill trench work
1671	Corporal Richard Coy	"By 25¼ days worke at the Mill dam" 5AB, 327	Payment for 25¼ days of mill work
1671	Samuel Warner of Quabaug	"By 8 days worke at the mill trench at 2s. 6d. per	2s. and 2s. 6d. per diem for mill trench

MILL LABOR, *cont.*

Date	Name	Service	Rate
		diem and 2 days at 2s. per day 1. 4. 0" 5AB, 335	work
15 Jul.–24 Nov. 1671	Rowland Thomas	"By 8 days worke at Quabaug last tyme 1. 0. 0"	2s. 6d. per diem for mill work
29 Dec. 1671		"By 3 weeks at Stony River Saw Mill 3. 0. 0" 5AB, 15	20s. per week for mill work
15 Jun. 1672	Samuel Stebbins	"By 2 days worke at the Trench 4s., 1 day at the mill 2s., 4 days ½ scouring ditch above 9s." 5AB, 173	2s. per diem for mill work
1672	John Stebbins, Jr.	"By 1 weeke at the dam howse at stony River 0. 12. 0" 5AB, 279	12s. per week for mill work
20 Dec. 1672	Judah Trumble	"By 13 days at Mill Trench 1. 12. 0" "By worke with Sam Cross, 4 days mending dam 0. 8. 0" 5AB, 343	2s. 6d. per diem for mill trench work 2s. per diem for mill dam work
29 Apr. 1673	Rowland Thomas	"By 24 days worke at Quabaug Mill Trench with your Journeys thither 1st and 2d, all is 24 days at 2s. 6d. [is] 3. 0. 0"	2s. 6d. per diem for mill trench work
1673		"By 22 days and ½ at Stony River 3. 0. 0" 5AB, 15	2s. 8d. per diem for mill work
Aug. 1673	Henry Stiles of Windsor	"By filling up 4 Bays of the Dam at Stony River up to the top 4. 0. 0" 5AB, 283	20s. per dam bay filled

MILL LABOR, *cont.*

Date	Name	Service	Rate
18 Nov. 1673	John Stebbins, Jr.	"By daming at Stony Brooke in the Night[?], By worke helping fill stony brooke in the Dam, and helping daub the chimney 0. 6. 0" 5AB, 279	6s. for mill work and daubing
28 Apr. 1674	Henry Stiles of Windsor	"By 10 days ½ worke at my corne mill at Suffield 2. 11. 3" 5AB, 283	5s. per diem for skilled mill work (pays 4s. 10½d.)
24 Nov. 1674	Richard Sikes	"By 2 days ½ mending a breach at Mill 0. 5. 0" 5AB, 135	2s. per diem for mill work
1675	Victory Sikes	"By 23 days ½ about my corne mill 3. 17. 0" 5AB, 357	3s. 3d. per diem for mill work
Mar. 1675/76	Thomas Copley	"By worke about my Mill in all now to this 28 March 1676: 5 weekes worke wanting 2 days at 16s. per weeke 3. 14. 8" 5AB, 271	16s. per week for skilled mill work
1677	Samuel Cross	"By 38 days worke about the mill dam and etc. 4. 10. 0" 5AB, 441	2s. 4½d. per diem for mill dam work
5 Mar. 1677/78	Thomas Copley	"By 20 days your teame [at the mill] 3. 0. 0" "By 30 days worke at the Mill 4. 10. 0" 5AB, 171	3s. per diem for team at the mill 3s. per diem for skilled mill work
3 Feb. 1678/79	Nathaniel Bliss, Jr.	"By 3 days worke at Saw mill fresh water brooke, laying the foundation and 1 day raising 0. 8. 0" 5AB, 35	2s. per diem for mill work

MILL LABOR, *cont.*

Date	Name	Service	Rate
Nov. 1679	John Pengilley	"By 1 day worke with Joseph Lenord, 3 days with Goodman Thomas, and 5 days with Thomas Copley, all is 9 days att my mill 1. 2. 6" 5AB, 395	2s. 6d. per diem for mill work
7 Jan. 1679/80	Thomas Bancroft	"By floaring Millstones 2. 10. 0" 5AB, 233	£2 10s. for flooring millstones
1680	Benjamin Thomas	"By 5 days at fresh water River getting Timber for the Dam 0. 12. 0" "By 1 day ½ . . . making my Raft 0. 4. 0" 5AB, 449	2s. 5d. per diem for mill dam work 2s. 8d. per diem for making raft
1680	Hugh Roe of Suffield	"By 5 days at the Mill 0. 12. 6" "By 1 day about the mill 0. 2. 0" 5AB, 483	2s. 6d. per diem for mill work 2s. per diem for mill work
24 Mar. 1680/81	Judah Trumble	"By worke at the Mil formerly . . . Goodman Thomas: with Joseph Leonard and also with Goodman Coply 1681, all is 5 days 0. 10. 0" "By 5 days at my mill 0. 10. 0" 5AB, 343	2s. per diem for mill work 2s. per diem for mill work
1681	Thomas Hucksley	"By 14 days worke at my Mill at Suffeild in Ano 1681 . . . 1. 17. 6" 6AB, 47	2s. 8d. per diem for mill work
1681	Samuel Graves	"By the Sawmill worke 5. 0. 0" 5AB, 373	£5 for sawmill work

MILL LABOR, *cont.*

Date	Name	Service	Rate
1681	John Pengilley	"By 8 days formerly with Goodman Thomas 1. 0. 0" "By 6 days with Goodman Lenord 0. 12. 0"	2s. 6d. per diem for mill work 2s. per diem for mill work
21 Nov. 1681	Edward Pengilley	"By 21 days worke of Edward about the cog wheale and etc., and I paid for his dyet 14 or 15 days to Joseph Trumble 2. 12. 0"	2s. 6d. per diem for mill work
	John Pengilley	"By 5 days worke now 1681 with Thomas Copley 0. 12. 6"	2s. 6d. per diem for mill work
3 Feb. 1681/82		"By 18 days worke at my mill at beginning of Winter 1682, as Thomas Copley gives me account this feb 1682 [is] 2. 5. 0"	2s. 6d. per diem for mill work
1682		"By 23 days at my mill 1682 as Thomas Copley gives account 2. 17. 0" 5AB, 395	2s. 6d. per diem for mill work
1682	Thomas Hucksley	"By 12 days (with Thomas Copley) Ano 1682, and 2 days your lad 3s. [is] 1. 13. 0" 6AB, 47	2s. 6d. per diem for mill labor 18d. per diem for youth's mill work
29 Jan. 1682/83	Richard Waite	"By 6 days at the mill . . . 0. 12. 0" 5AB, 391	2s. per diem for mill work
1683	Thomas Copley	"By 32 days at my Mill to this 28 June 1683 [is] 4. 16. 0"	3s. per diem for skilled mill work
25 Aug. 1684		"By 12 days worke . . . at my mill[s?] to this 25 Aug. 1684 [is] 1. 10. 0" 6AB, 49	2s. 6d. per diem for mill work

MILL LABOR, *cont.*

Date	Name	Service	Rate
1680s[?]	Nathaniel Warner of Quabaug	"By 12 days worke at the Mill Trench . . . 1. 5. 0" 5AB, 333	2s. 1d. per diem for mill trench work
Spring 1685/86	Benjamin Parsons	"By 4 days ½ worke at my mill dam . . . Spring 1685/86 [is] 0. 9. 0" 6AB, 65	2s. per diem for mill work
1686	John Warner	"By worke at my mill since 1684: 2 days 0. 4. 0" "1 day more 0. 2. [?]0" "2 days at the dam 0. 5. 0" 5AB, 335	2s. per diem for mill work 2s. per diem for mill work 2s. 6d. per diem for mill work
1686	Richard Waite	"[2] days at Mill dam" "By 1 day more at the Mill dam 0. 2. 0" "By 4 days worke at the . . . Corne Mill 0. 8. 0" 6AB, 75	Payment for 2 days mill work 2s. per diem for mill dam work 2s. per diem for mill work
Feb. 1690/91	John Pengilley	"By 23 days ½ worke at Suffeild Mill to Feb. 1691 [is] 2. 17. 0" 5AB, 395	2s. 5d. per diem for mill work
1691	Nathaniel Horton	"By 3 days worke at my Mill, 2 of them last Spring at 2s. per day, and 1 day now Sept. 1691 at 2s. 6d. . . . 0. 6. 0" 6AB, 187	2s. and 2s. 6d. per diem for mill work
1691	Edward Smith of Suffield	"By 2 days worke at my mill 1691 about lumber and etc. 0. 5. 0" 5AB, 401	2s. 6d. per diem for mill work

MILL LABOR, *cont.*

Date	Name	Service	Rate
1692	Joseph Stebbins	"By 11 days worke at the Mill Dam in June 1692 [is] 1. 7. 6" 6AB, 161	2s. 6d. per diem for mill work
1692	John Warner	17 days at JP's mill 2. 2. 0 6AB, 11	2s. 6d. per diem for mill work
1692	Thomas Hucks-ley	"By worke at my Mill per Richard Austin's account this 24th of February 1691/92, 80 days worke and ½, whereof you gave 3 days so its 77½ [12 days more subtracted] 65 days ½ [is] 8. 2. 0"	2s. 6d. per diem for mill work
1693		"6 Months [worke], less 4 weeks 6. 10. 0"	24s. per month for mill work
1695		1696, "13. 3. 0" 1697, "25. 5. 0" 1698, "18. 10. 0"	£13 3s. for mill work £25 5s. for mill work £18 10s. for mill work
		"By 66 days and ½ Mill dam House to 1698 [is] 8. 6. 3" 6AB, 47	2s. 6d. per diem for mill work
1695	Timothy Hale	"By 16 days worke now at my Mill 2. 0. 0" 5AB, 323	2s. 6d. per diem for mill work
1695	Peter Mills	"By worke at my grist mill at Suffeild, in all 67 days worke 10. 1. 0" 6AB, 225	3s. per diem for skilled mill work
1695	Thomas Mighill of Suffield	For work at JP's mill in Suffield, 67 days 10. 1. 0 6AB, 224–225	3s. per diem for skilled mill work

MILL LABOR, *cont.*

Date	Name	Service	Rate
28 Feb. 1695/96	Samuel Parsons	"By 1 day worke at my Mill . . . 0. 2. 6" "By 2 days at Enfield getting Millstones 0. 5. 0" "3 days at Enfield Mil Dam 0. 7. 6" 6AB, 65	2s. 6d. per diem for mill work 2s. 6d. per diem for getting millstones 2s. 6d. per diem for mill dam work
20 May 1696	George Norton, Jr.	"By 29 days (and ½) worke at 2s. 6d., at my mill in Suffeild . . . 3. 12. 0"	2s. 6d. per diem for mill work
1697	Ensign George Norton of Suffield	"Accounting with Mrs. Norton . . . about her husband's worke at my Mill at Suffeild 25. 0. 0" "In another place 67 days and 2 days carting 10. 10. 0" 6AB, 35	£25 for skilled mill work 3s. per diem for skilled mill work
5 Mar. 1697/98	Edward Smith of Suffield	"By work at Suffeild Mill with Captain Norton . . . 39 days at 3s. [in 1696] 5. 7. 0" 5AB, 401	3s. per diem for skilled mill work (pays 2s. 9d.)

MILLWRIGHT

Date	Name	Service	Rate
Apr. 1646	Richard Sikes	"For coggs and rungs at mill 0. 5. 0" WPAB, 46	5s. for building cogs and rungs
31 Jan. 1665/66	John Webb, Sr. of Northampton	"John Webb Senior, for a debt which he owes me being between £30 and £40, Did Ingage Payment by next Michalstide; and for that Bound over 2 mares . . . which are to be	Agreement to pay £30-£40 debt to JP with pair of millstones

MILLWRIGHT, *cont.*

Date	Name	Service	Rate
		mine in case he doe not pay me the said debt, part of it in a pair of Millstones which he Ingages to deliver in the Spring, and the other to my Contract by Michalstide or else the mares to be mine, and they are hereby really and truly made over to me, John Pynchon, and I am to take them with the millstones for my debt unless he shall otherwise sattisfie my debt to continue" 3AB, 28	
6 Feb. 1665/66	Richard Sikes	"By mending Gudgeons, Spindle and Mill Bills 1. 2. 0"	22s. for mending mill mechanism
1666		"By Coggs and Round 1. 4. 0" 3AB, 83	24s. for building cogs and round
1666	William An-drews of New Haven	"By making my Mill £70, his halfe 35. 0. 0" "By making Bolting mill and other worke, his halfe 7. 17. 0"	£70 for building mill
12 Nov. 1666	William An-drews of New Haven, and Cornelius Wil-liams	"Agreed with Mr. Andrews and Cornelius Williams to build me a Saw Mill, and I give them for the whole worke compleated, well and substantial all work-menlike and set to sawing, the sum of £45, and they set a roofe over it fit for covering; the sawmill to be done with Planks 60 foot	£45 for building sawmill

MILLWRIGHT, *cont.*

Date	Name	Service	Rate
		long, I doe the digging, Carting, and Ironworke" 3AB, 311	
		"By your making the Saw mill, the whole worke 45. 0. 0" 3AB, 313	Payment for building sawmill
1666		"Memorandum: £45 was theire owne asking and I give them what they asked at the conclusion of all, I told them they must Plank it on both sides the trench from the Saw Mill to the Sluce which they in part yeilded to, I finding the Plank; there words were that if they had a good Bargain that they did not lose by it they would doe it into the Bargaine" 3AB, 311	Agreement for planking mill sluice
1668	Cornelius Williams	"By lengthening out the carriage at the End of the Saw mill, 2 days worke he pays Jonathan Burt, and finding Timber 0. 8. 0" "By ½ day helping taping the Gudgeon of the Saw Mill 0. 1. –" "By 270 foote of Plank for the Saw mill fleame 1. 4. -" 3AB, 313	8s. for two days mill work and finding timber
1668	John Barker	"By my Mill house 15. 0. 0" 3AB, 57	£15 for building mill house
27 Apr. 1669	John Webb, Sr. of Northampton	"By making of a pair of Millstones and delivering them to my Mill at £21,	£21 for hewing and delivering a pair of millstones

MILLWRIGHT, *cont.*

Date	*Name*	*Service*	*Rate*
		whereoff halfe is Zachary Feild's and halfe yours: viz. 10. 10. 0" 3AB, 211	
	Zachariah Field	"By making a pair of Mill-stones and delivering them at my mill for £21" 3AB, 223	Payment for mill-stones
6 Jan. 1669/70	Cornelius Williams	"By worke at Quabaug Mill which I allow you 8. 12. 6"	£8 12s. 6d. for skilled mill work
		"By a set of Coggs for the Mill and some the worke at the mill 0. 14. 6"	14s. 6d. for cogs and mill work
		"By getting the Iron of the old Mill 0. 1. 6"	18d. for getting iron from the old mill
1670		"By 1 day fastoning the Gudgeon at the Mill and mending 0. 3. 0" 3AB, 313	3s. per diem for skilled mill work
3 Nov. 1670	William Pritchard	"By what I am to pay him on account about Quabaug Mill, as per account 8. 15. 7"	£8 15s. 7d. for skilled mill work
		"By what I am to allow you for building the house over the Mill according to agreement 2. 1. 8" 5AB, 329	£2 1s. 8d. for building portion of mill house
5 Feb. 1672/73	John Webb, Jr.	Webb to make JP a pair of millstones and additional products for £23 (£21 if they are not delivered to the corn mill at Stony Brook) and 1 gallon of rum 5AB, 253	£23 and 1 gallon of rum for hewing and delivering a pair of millstones

MILLWRIGHT, *cont.*

Date	Name	Service	Rate
20 Mar. 1672/73	Victory Sikes	"By work about Cogs, rounds, and mending the water wheele for my Corne Mill 0. 11. 0" 5AB, 357	11s. for repairing cogs, rounds, and waterwheel
1673	John Artsell	Making JP's sawmill at Stony River £55 Building a house there £12 Making cogs, rounds, etc. for mill £3 5AB, 381	£55 for building saw-mill £12 for building mill house £3 for making cogs, rounds, etc.
1675	Victory Sikes	"By worke about Cogs and rounds 0. 10. 0" "By worke at the Sawmill 0. 5. 0" "Making the [saw] carriage 0. 11.[?] 0" "Work at the sawmill 0. 1. 6" 5AB, 357	10s. for repairing cogs and rounds 5s. for skilled mill work Payment for making saw carriage 18d. for skilled mill work
29 Jun. 1675	Medad Pomery	"By a Crank for my Saw-mill 5. 0. 0" 5AB, 263	£5 for building crank for sawmill
21 Dec. 1676	Isaac Gleason	Gleason to build house over JP's mill for 1¼ acre of ground and £7, to be completed by the end of May 1677 5AB, 518–519	£7 and 1¼ acre of land for building mill house
1677	John Artsell	For his half of fee for building JP's gristmill £45 "For Building and making my corne mill at Suffield £50" 5AB, 211	£90 for building gristmill £50 for building gristmill

MILLWRIGHT, *cont.*

Date	Name	Service	Rate
2 Nov. 1678	John Webb, Jr.	Webb to make JP a pair of millstones for £12 and 2 quarts of Rum 5AB, 252–253	£12 and 2 quarts of rum for hewing a pair of millstones
12 Dec. 1678	Victory Sikes	"By worke about Coggs and Rounds, and etc. for the saw mill 1. 3. 0" "By work at sawmill 0. 3. 0" 5AB, 357	23s. for repairing cogs, rounds, etc. 3s. for skilled mill work
10 Nov. 1679	William Pritchard	"By 22 days worke at my Mill at Suffield making wheels, cogs and rounds at 3s. [is] 3. 3. 0" 5AB, 329	3s. per diem for making wheels, cogs, and rounds for mill (pays 2s. 10d.)
7 Jan. 1679/80	Thomas Bancroft	"By floaring and laying my millstones at Stony brook, and I paid for his dyet 3. 0. 0" 5AB, 233	£3 and board for laying and flooring millstones
25 Jun. 1680	John Artsell	"By building the Saw mill at Freshwater the whole agreement is £45" 5AB, 211	£45 for building sawmill
22 Nov. 1680	Thomas Colton	"By 3 days at freshwater Mill laying the foundation 0. 9. 0"	3s. per diem for laying mill foundation
14 Mar. 1680/81		"By carting all the Timber for the dam, sluice, wheel and etc., all is 1 day is 0. 6. 0" "By 2 days ½ worke helping to lay the timber and raising 0. 6. 0" 5AB, 397	6s. per diem for carting mill materials 2s. 5d. per diem for mill raising

MILLWRIGHT, *cont.*

Date	Name	Service	Rate
1 Apr. 1681	Isaac Gleason	£11 for building house over JP's mill 5AB, 518–519	£11 for building house over mill
1681	Increase Sikes	"By mending Sawmill new carriage . . . Timber for Coggs 2. 0. 9" 5AB, 417–418	£2 9d. for skilled mill work
9 Jan. 1682/83	John Hirman and Jonathan Bush	"Agreed with John Hirman and Jonath Bush to . . . Build a Sawmill at freshwater Brook . . . 46 fote long, 14 feete across . . . [for] 6 [?] Pounds, and 6 hands a day or 4 hands a day and 2 another as they shall need the hands" 5AB, 509	46 × 14-foot sawmill at Freshwater brook
1683	Isaac Gleason	"By worke at my Mill this Spring past in March 1682/83, and mending the water wheele all is 1. 0. 0" "By 2 days worke about Cog wheele Spring 0. 6. 0"	20s. for skilled mill work 3s. per diem for mill-repair work
2 Apr. 1684		JP paid Gleason £9 7s. for work about his sawmill at Schonunganick "By the Running geare for my Mill all being . . . £10" 5AB, 471	£9 7s. for skilled mill work £10 for building running gear for mill
1 Apr. 1687		"Agreed with Isack Gleason (letting all former agreements fall) that he is to Build me a house over my mill 25 foote long and 20 foote wide [for] . . . £11 [and some land] paid" 5AB, 519	£11 and land for building 25 × 20-foot mill house

MILLWRIGHT, *cont.*

Date	Name	Service	Rate
8 May 1693		"By 25 days . . . at my Mill [at 3s. 6d.]"	3s. 6d. per diem for skilled mill work
		"By 8 days worke at the mill at 4s. 6d. per day 1. 16. 0" 6AB, 221	4s. 6d. per diem for skilled mill work
Nov. 1693	Nathaniel Burt, Jr.	"By Building my Grist Mill, the frame wholy new, and al the Running Geare and etc., all compleate and done, agreed at 26. 0. 0" 6AB, 53	£26 for building gristmill

MINING

Date	Name	Service	Rate
30 Mar. 1659	Edward Foster	"The £3 which Edward Foster owes me below he engages to pay me out of his worke at the lead mines [with] William Deins" 1AB, 217	Agreement for £3 work mining
24 Oct. 1698	Samuel Ely	"Agreed with Sam Ely for Twenty Load of good Coale for the Iron workes . . . for which I am to pay him £12 in Money" 6AB, 61	12s. in specie per load of coal

MISCELLANEOUS LABOR

Date	Name	Service	Rate
Mar. 1648	Henry Burt	"Recd in making . . . bush malt at 8d." WPAB, 188	8d. per bushel for making malt
6 Feb. 1651/52		"Recd by 1 day drying cloth 0. 1. 0" WPAB, 193	1s. per diem for drying woven cloth

MISCELLANEOUS LABOR, *cont.*

Date	Name	Service	Rate
3 Apr. 1654	David Chapin	"Recd by bottoming 3 chairs 0. 2. 0" 1AB, 8	8d. per chair for bottoming
28 Nov. 1655	Rowland Thomas	"Recd by gathering apples 0. 2. 0" 1AB, 234	2s. for gathering apples
16 Nov. 1663		"By Trimming hedge 0. 1. 6" "By 1 day Trimming Trees 0. 2. 6" 2AB, 159	18d. for trimming hedge 2s. 6d. per diem for trimming apple trees
21 Dec. 1664		"Trimming my Hedge 0. 3. 0" 3AB, 159	3s. for trimming hedge
Mid-1660s		"By 3 days Trimming Trees in my orchard 0. 7. 6" 3AB, 197	2s. 6d. per diem for trimming apple trees
28 Nov. 1665		"By Triming the hedge 0. 0. 8" 3AB, 159	8d. for trimming hedge
1666–1667	Jonathan Taylor	"By milking my Cows last year" "Milking my Cows this yeare 6 weeks" 3AB, 175	Payment for milking cows 1 year Payment for milking cows 6 weeks
9 Jan. 1670/71	Rowland Thomas	"By 5 days ½ Triming my orchard and making the way to . . . 0. 11. 0"	2s. per diem for trimming apple trees and clearing path to orchard
29 Dec. 1671		"By Triming my Apple Trees 0. 3. 0" 5AB, 15	3s. for trimming apple trees

MISCELLANEOUS LABOR, *cont.*

Date	Name	Service	Rate
May 1672	Thomas Cooper	"By lime (of old) about 3 bushels 0. 7. 0" 5AB, 69	2s. 4d. per bushel of lime
Mar. 1672/73	Rowland Thomas	"By 2 days Trimming my orchard now 0. 5. 0" 5AB, 15	2s. 6d. per diem for trimming apple trees
1674	Isaac Morgan	Agreement with Morgan for him to dig clay for chimney, etc., for house he is to lease from JP 5AB, 189	Contract for digging clay
8 Feb. 1683/84	Richard Waite	"By 4 days tending my cattle 0. 4. 0" 6AB, 75	1s. per diem for tending cattle
16 Sep. 1686		"To your Marriage 0. 5. 0" 6AB, 74	5s. for JP's performing marriage ceremony

MOWING AND REAPING

Date	Name	Service	Rate
1645–1646	Abraham Mundyne	"Mowing 2 acres ½ at 2s. 2d. [is] 0. 5. 5" WPAB, 27	2s. 2d. per acre for mowing
1645–1649	Thomas Reeves	"Recd in mowing 6 acres in my muxy meadow at 2. 2d. [is] 0. 13. 0" "On the other side 7 acres at 2s. [is] 0. 14. 1" WPAB, 44	2s. 2d. per acre for mowing 2s. per acre for mowing
1646	John Stebbins	"Mowing 4 acres, want alitle 0. 7. 8" WPAB, 55	2s. per acre for mowing

MOWING AND REAPING, *cont.*

Date	Name	Service	Rate
4 Sep. 1646	Rowland Thomas	"Recd 1 day [½] reaping 0. 3. 0" WPAB, 124 (first of 2 p. 124s)	2s. per diem for reaping
16 Oct. 1646	William Vaughan	"Recd Sam 3 days harvest 0. 4. 0" "2 days himself 0. 4. 0" WPAB, 112	16d. per diem for youth's reaping 2s. per diem for reaping
1 Nov. 1648	Thomas Stebbins	"2 days reaping 0. 4. 0" "9 days worke about hay 0. 15. 0" WPAB, 200	2s. per diem for reaping 20d. per diem for mowing
22 Nov. 1648	Richard Excell	"For mowing barley . . . 3 days and ½ [is] 0. 7. 0" WPAB, 136	2s. per diem for mowing barley
1649	George Alexander	"2 days mowing 0. 4. 0" "2 days reaping 0. 4. 0" "1 day worke 0. 1. 0" WPAB, 216	2s. per diem for mowing 2s. per diem for reaping 1s. per diem for field work
1650	Benjamin Mun	"Recd in mowing 4 acres . . . 0. 9. 9" "And 8 acres over the River 0. 16. 0" "3 days to mowing 0. 6. 0" WPAB, 60	2s. 5d. per acre for mowing 2s. per acre for mowing 2s. per diem for mowing
1652	Thomas Bancroft	"Recd by mowing 6 acres ½ in ano 1652 [is] 0. 13. 0" "Mowing 3 acres last yeare 0. 6. 0" 1AB, 147	2s. per acre for mowing 2s. per acre for mowing
5 Sep. 1652	Roger Pritchard	"Recd 9 days ½ haymaking at 18d."	18d. per diem for haymaking

MOWING AND REAPING, *cont.*

Date	Name	Service	Rate
19 Feb. 1652/53		"Recd 7 days and ½ at haying, 3 days reaping 0. 16. 0" 1AB, 135	18d. per diem for mowing and reaping
22 Feb. 1652/53	Richard Excell	"Recd by mowing 8 acres ¾ over Agawam . . . 3s. 6d., bec the grass is so thick [?] 8. 0"	3s. 6d. per acre for mowing thick grass
		"2 days Mowing over the great River 0. 4. 0"	2s. per diem for mowing
		"2 days Mowing Barley 0. 4. 0"	2s. per diem for mowing barley
		"1 day reaping 0. 2. 0" 1AB, 85	2s. per diem for reaping
1654	Francis Pepper	"By 10 days worke harvest at 2s. 5d. [is] 1. 0. 0"	2s. 5d. per diem for reaping (pays 2s. 2d.)
9 Jul. 1655		"By cutting up 3 acres of Pease 0. 6. 0"	2s. per acre for mowing peas
		"By cutting of 1 acre and ½ of Boggs 1. 17. 6"	25s. per acre for mowing marshland
		"By cutting 5 acres of Boggs 5. 0. 0" 1AB, 203	20s. per acre for mowing marshland
11 Feb. 1655/56	Richard Excell	"Recd mowing oates at home 0. 2. 0" 1AB, 85	2s. per diem for mowing oats
6 Jul. 1656	Samuel Terry	"Recd by 5 days at Hay-making"	Payment for 5 days haymaking
		"1 day reaping (yesterday) 0. 2. 0" 1AB, 240	2s. per diem for reaping
6 Oct. 1656	Thomas Ban-croft	"Recd by mowing 8 days 0. 16. 0" 1AB, 245	2s. per diem for mowing

MOWING AND REAPING, *cont.*

Date	Name	Service	Rate
9 Oct. 1656	Benjamin Mun	"2 days reaping this summer, and 2 days mowing 0. 8. 0" 1AB, 94	2s. per diem for mowing and reaping
11 Nov. 1657	Richard Excell	"1 day reaping and 1 day your boy 0. 4. 0" 1AB, 86	2s. per diem each for reaping for father and son
16 Nov. 1657	Thomas Bancroft	"Recd by mowing 5 acres at hom [and] 2 acres over river 0. 14. 10" 1AB, 245	2s. 1½d. per acre for mowing
20 Oct. 1658		"Recd by mowing 5 acres ¾ at 2s. 9d. [is] 0. 13. 0" "By mowing over Agawam, weeds and grass 0. 3. 3" 1AB, 246	2s. 9d. per acre for mowing (pays 2s. 3d.) 3s. 3d. for mowing weeds and grass
26 Oct. 1658	Rowland Stebbins	"Recd 8 days worke haymaking and reaping 0. 12. 0" 1AB, 262	18d. per diem for mowing and reaping
Nov. 1658	Miles Morgan	"Recd by making 4 acres of hay at 5s." 1AB, 266	5s. per acre for mowing hay
15 Dec. 1658	Jonathan Taylor	"Sold to Jonathan Taylor 12½ [year old] flax steere, for which he Ingages and promises me to reape and shock 2 acres of wheate and to cut one acre of pease when I call for it to be done next harvest, and to doe it upon 2 days [notice]" 1AB, 314	12½-year-old steer for reaping and shocking 2 acres of wheat and one acre of peas

MOWING AND REAPING, *cont.*

Date	Name	Service	Rate
12 Jan. 1658/59	Rowland Stebbins	"Recd 10 days ½ . . . haying at 16d. [is] 0. 14. 0" "Recd 2 days at harvest, and other worke 0. 2. 8" 1AB, 262	16d. per diem for mowing Payment for reaping and unspecified work
1659	James Warrinar	"By 3 days Mowing 0. 7. 0" 2AB, 143	2s. 4d. per diem for mowing
6 Sep. 1659	Joseph Crowfoot	"By 1 day cutting Pease 2s." 2AB, 171	2s. per diem for mowing peas
Nov. 1659	Jonathan Taylor	"By 10 days worke, to this 22th Sept. 1663 . . . at 2s. [is] 1. 0. 0" "By 1 day ½ reaping this last harvest (which you say is besides the former 10 days) 0. 3. 0" "By reaping ¾ of an acre 0. 5. 0" 2AB, 229	2s. per diem for reaping 2s. per diem for reaping 6s. 8d. per acre for reaping
22 Jan. 1660/61	Rowland Stebbins	"Recd by 4 days reaping 0. 6. 8"	20d. per diem for reaping
24 Nov. 1662		"Recd 3 days work haying in harvest 0. 4. 6" 2AB, 14	18d. per diem for mowing
13 Nov. 1663	Thomas Bancroft	"Agreed with Thomas Bancroft to mow my five acres peice next yeare, for wch I am to [pay him] 2s. [?] per acre But if he mow it well and close to the ground I promise to give him 2s. 6d. pr acre" 2AB, 117	2s. 6d. per acre for close mowing [Incentive clause]

MOWING AND REAPING, *cont.*

Date	Name	Service	Rate
1663?	Hugh Dudley	"By cutting 5 acres of Pease at 3s. per acre 0. 15. 0" "By 1 day taking up oats and rye 0. 2. 0" 2AB, 221	3s. per acre for mowing peas 2s. per diem for mowing oats and rye
26 Jun. 1664	Joseph Leonard	"Agreed with Joseph Leanord well to mow and make and cart and rake, all to be well done, of 10 acres of grass over Agawam, for 6s. per acre" 2AB, 314	6s. per acre for mowing, raking, and carting hay
24 Oct. 1664	John Dumble-ton	"By 1 day Mowing Oates 0. 2. 0" 3AB, 181	2s. per diem for mowing oats
15 Apr. 1665	Joseph Crow-foot	"By mowing oates 2s. 6d." 3AB, 187	2s. 6d. for mowing oats
1665	James Taylor	"By 16 days worke in Hay tyme and Harvest 1. 12. 0" 3AB, 121	2s. per diem for mowing and reaping
1665	Samuel Terry	"By 1 day reaping last year 0. 2. 0" "By 4 days worke and ½ this yeare making Reeke and Reaping 0. 9. 0" 3AB, 145	2s. per diem for reaping 2s. per diem for hay-making
1660s?	Thomas Cooper, Jr.	"By Mowing, making, Raking, Carting, Cocking, and etc., all my grass and hay over Agawam River at 5s. 6d. per acre, 8 acres of it, and the other 2 acres at 5s. [is] 2. 14. 0" 3AB, 285	5s. and 5s. 6d. per acre for mowing, raking, carting, and cocking hay

MOWING AND REAPING, *cont.*

Date	Name	Service	Rate
1666	Samuel Terry	"By worke making Reeke and fetching Hay and etc. this summer 66 [is] 0. 6. 6" 3AB, 145	6s. 6d. for haymaking
1666–1667	Jonathan Taylor	"By 2 days reaping and 1 day your boy 0. 5. 0" 3AB, 175	2s. per diem for reaping 1s. per diem for youth's reaping
1667	John Petty	"By 5 days Mowing 0. 10. 0" 3AB, 155	2s. per diem for mowing
16 Sep. 1667	Sam Ball	"By 5 days mowing 0. 10. 0" "1 day reaping 0. 2. 0" 3AB, 129	2s. per diem for mowing 2s. per diem for reaping
9 Mar. 1668/69	Timothy Cooper	"Agreed with Timothy Cooper to mow and make it that my meddow over Agawam River, being about 10 acres for mee; He is well to mow it and make it well and Rake it, also to cart it to the River side and Recke it well to save it till a boat fechs it; he is likewise to Rake after the cart: and to do all well and make it good hay and doe it all in Season, for which I am to allow him 6s. per acre (if about an acre of it remeane he is to let that alone)" 3AB, 55	6s. per acre for mowing, raking, carting, and ricking hay
12 Jan. 1669/70	Increase Sikes	"Agreed with Increase Sikes to mow and make into Hay next summer all	5s. 6d. per acre for mowing, raking, carting, and ricking

MOWING AND REAPING, *cont.*

Date	Name	Service	Rate
		my 10 acres of meddow over Agawam; . . . he is to cut it all well and close and make it good hay and Rake it all up and cock it up . . . also to cart it and Rake after the carts and to set it on a Reeke by the River side fit for the Boate to fetch, and to Rike it well to secure it from the Raine, and all this to doe in season that I may have good hay, at least halfe of it to be done before Harvest, if not all, for all which I am to allow and pay him 5s. 6d. per acre"	
		"By Mowing making and carting 9 acres of meddow at 5s. 6d. [is] 2. 9. 6" 3AB, 173; 5AB, 161	Payment for mowing and ricking 7 acres
6 Mar. 1670/71	James Warrinar	"By 1 day worke mowing 0. 2. 0" 5AB, 93	2s. per diem for mowing
17 Jun. 1672	Benjamin Dunnidge	"Agreed with Benjamin Dunnedge well to mow my Ten acres of grass over Agawam and also to make it hay; he being to doe it well, to Rake it well and Cock it well to secure it from the Raine, and all being well done . . . I am to allow him 6s. per acre" 5AB, 193	6s. per acre for mowing, raking, and cocking hay
1672	John Stebbins, Jr.	"By 1 Month worke at harvest this Sumer 2. 8. 0" "By 3 days reaping, mowing . . . 0. 7. 6" 5AB, 279	£2 8s. per month for harvest work 2s. 6d. per diem for mowing and reaping

MOWING AND REAPING, *cont.*

Date	Name	Service	Rate
24 Feb. 1672/73	Robert Ashley	"By Haymaking and rye 7 days ½ [is] 0. 15. 0" 5AB, 77	2s. per diem for mowing
Summer 1675	James Osborne (son James)	"By your son James, 24 days at Haymaking and about Pease this Summer 1675, ½ at 2s. and ½ at 18d. per day 2. 2. 0" 5AB, 121	18d. and 2s. per diem for mowing hay and peas
27 Jan. 1677/78	Edward Foster	"By worke this Last Summer Mowing, and about my Mill Dam and carting . . . and etc., 12 days 1. 4. 0"	2s. per diem for mowing and carting
2 Jan. 1678/79		"By 8 days Mowing last Summer 0. 16. 0" 5AB, 475	2s. per diem for mowing
1679	Richard Waite	"[21 days] mowing . . . harvest . . . cutting . . . 2. 3. 0" 5AB, 391	25d. per diem for mowing
Aug. 1679	John Burbank	"By mowing and etc. about 5 weeks 2. 9. 0"	10s. per week for mowing [Weekly wage]
1680		"By mowing this year 1680, in all 27 days, at 21d. [is] 2. 7. 3"	21d. per diem for mowing
10 Aug. 1681		"By 16 days Mowing and ½ at 21d. [is] 1. 15. 0" 5AB, 287	21d. per diem for mowing (pays 2s. 2d.)
18 Dec. 1681	Samuel Bedortha	"By 1 day Mowing 0. 2. 0" 5AB, 295	2s. per diem for mowing
1682	John Burbank	"By mowing to this 15 Aug of 1682 . . . 0. 15. 0" 5AB, 287	15s. for mowing

MOWING AND REAPING, *cont.*

Date	Name	Service	Rate
1683	Richard Waite	"By 2 weeks Mowing and etc., 10 days . . . 6 days . . . 23 days . . . 4. 2. 0" 5AB, 391	Payment of £4 2s. for mowing
Jul. 1684	Symon Booth, Sr. of Enfield	"By 12 days Mowing 1. 10. 0"	2s. 6d. per diem for mowing
16 Aug. 1684		"By Mowing To your selfe and Son, all is 9 days at 2s. 6d. [is] 1. 2. –" 6AB, 91	2s. 6d. per diem for both father and son mowing
16 Aug. 1684	John Beamon, Jr.	"By Mowing your selfe, 2 days ½ at 2s. 6d. [is] 0. 6. 3" 5AB, 349	2s. 6d. per diem for mowing
7 Aug. 1686	Symon Booth, Sr.	"By 25 days ½ worke, Mowing, Reaping, and etc. . . . yourself and sons 3. 3. 9" 6AB, 91	£3 3s. 9d. for mowing and reaping
1686	John Warner	"More 25 days more, some at 2s. and some at 2s. 6d., mowing and etc. 2. 19. 0" 5AB, 335	2s. and 2s. 6d. per diem for mowing
1690	Benjamin Jones	"By 12 days working, Mowing . . . at 2s. 6d. per day 1. 10. 0" 6AB, 205	2s. 6d. per diem for mowing

NAILMAKING

Date	Name	Service	Rate
8 Nov. 1669	John Aires	"Delivered Goodman Aires 500 of 10d. Nayls [and] 500 of 8d. Nayls [and] 300 of Sixpenny Nails [all is] 0. 15. 0" 3AB, 27	10d. per 50 nails 8d. per 50 nails 6d. per 50 nails

NAILMAKING, *cont.*

Date	Name	Service	Rate
1 Jul. 1678	Obadiah Cooley	"By Nailes I had of him 2400, at 4d., 1350 at 6d. [is] 1. 8. 0" 5AB, 195	4d. per 50 nails 6d. per 50 nails

NAVAL STORES PRODUCTION

Date	Name	Service	Rate
1661	Edward Griswald of Windsor	"By 3 barrels of Tar 2. 8. 0"	16s. per barrel of tar
Apr. 1663		"By 1 Barrel of Tarr 0. 16. 0" 2AB, 237	16s. per barrel of tar
29 Sep. 1670	Thomas Cooper	"To Tar, 10 Barrells which Goodman Dorchester delivered at Jonathan Gilbert's warehouse for you ano 1670 [is] 8. 5. 0" 3AB, 52	16s. 6d. per barrel of tar
Late 1660s?	Lieutenant Walter Fyler	"Recd by Leuit Fyler 6 Barrels tar, £4 10s., and freight of them paid 11s. [all being] . . . £5" 3AB, 286	15s. per barrel of tar
20 Mar. 1670/71	Anthony Dorchester	"By 10 Barrells of Tar 7. 10. 0" 5AB, 133	15s. per barrel of tar
26 Aug. 1674	John Clark	"By 10 barrels of Tar 7. 0. 0" 5AB, 115	14s. per barrel of tar
15 Apr. 1692	John Harris	"Agreed with John Harris for 7 months service upon the Rosin designe [for] 42s. per Month, in Corne, In-	42s. per month and housing for resin design work

NAVAL STORES PRODUCTION, *cont.*

Date	Name	Service	Rate
		dian Pease, and some part Rye and Pork . . . (and also to Let him have the use of my house)" 6AB, 199	
1693	Charles Ferry, Jr.	"The Burning about the Pine Trees at Rosin Hall costs Goodman Ferry 5 hands or 5 days, and such and my selfe, that is my hands 3 days; and such sore worke as Goodman Ferry said he would not doe that for 3s. a day in money" 6AB, 267	3s. per diem in money for resin work inadequate given the difficulty of the tasks
11 Apr. 1694	Thomas Mir-rick, et al.	"Luke Hitchcocke, Thomas Miricke Junr., Thomas Gilbert, Samuell Ely, Samuell Day, and George Webster desiring that the Town would grant them Liberty to make use of the pine Trees for the getting of Turpentine for Rosin; The Town did grant them Liberty of the Pine Trees from the Brow of the great hil to Goose Pond hil, and from the Bay path downwards to the path called Log Path for the Space of four yeers, provided they hinder no person the taking of any Tymber or Candle wood in the Compass therin improved. Also Samuel Bliss with his Partners being desirous to se what they can do at getting	Free use of town pine stand for naval stores production

NAVAL STORES PRODUCTION, *cont.*

Date	Name	Service	Rate
		of Turpentine for Rosin, is allowed to have with those his Partners that Joine with him, The use of the Pine Trees from the said log path to the mil River on the like Condition as abovesaid" 2TR, 284	
20 Oct. 1695	Roco	JP agreed with Roco that he and his wife would pay JP 25 barrels of turpentine and 21 barrels of tar for their freedom 6AB, 260–261	25 barrels of turpentine and 21 barrels of tar for freedom for 2 slaves

NURSING

Date	Name	Service	Rate
1653	Goodwife Taylor	"Recd by Nursing my child 3 months 1. 16. 0" 1AB, 126	12s. per month for nursing
11 Feb. 1655/56	Hannah Excell	"Recd by nursing my child 4 months, as 12s. per month is 2. 8. 0" 1AB, 85	12s. per month for nursing

PERSONAL TRANSPORTATION AND MESSENGER SERVICE

Date	Name	Service	Rate
Jul. 1657	David Wilton	"By your Journey to Road Island and Expenses 4. 10. 0" 1AB, 155	£4 10s. for journey to Rhode Island
1659	Richard Fellows	"By himself and 3 horses to fort Aurania 6. 0. 0" 2AB, 95	£6 for journey to Albany with 3 horses

PERSONAL TRANSPORTATION AND MESSENGER SERVICE, *cont.*

Date	Name	Service	Rate
May 1662	George Colton	"By a Journey to Fairfield himself and horse 2. 5. 0" "By a Journey himself and horse to Hartford 0. 8. 0" 2AB, 247	£2 5s. for journey to Fairfield 8s. for journey to Hartford
Mid-1660s	Samuel Terry	*Dr.* "To payment of your Passadge to England at 7. 0. 0" 3AB, 144	£7 for passage to England
1664–1665	James Taylor	"By a Journey to the Bay when I went to England 1. 0. 0" "By a journey to Bay, Ano. 1664 [is] 0. 15. 0" "By a Journey to Bay with my wife 1. 8. 0" "By 2 Journeys this summer to Hartford 0. 8. 0" "By a Journey to New London your selfe and horse being gone 18 days 3. 0. 0" 3AB, 121	20s. for journey to Boston 15s. for journey to Boston 28s. for journey to Boston with JP's wife Amy 4s. for journey to Hartford £3 for 18-day round trip to New London
9 Oct. 1666	John Bliss	"By a Journey to Bay with my wife 1. 10. 0" "By fetching Mary Pynchon from Hartford 0. 8. 0" 3AB, 89	30s. for journey to Boston with JP's wife Amy 8s. for fetching Mary Pynchon from Hartford
11 Mar. 1666/67	Timothy Cooper	"By a Journey to Stonington, himself and horse 1. 8. 0" 3AB, 55	28s. for journey to Stonington
1667	Joseph Crowfoot	"By a Journey to Hartford for my Chares 0. 8. 0" 3AB, 187	8s. for journey to Hartford to get JP's chairs

PERSONAL TRANSPORTATION AND MESSENGER SERVICE, *cont.*

Date	Name	Service	Rate
16 Feb. 1668/69	John Bliss	"By a Journey to Hartford, your Selfe and horse carrying my wife 0. 8. 0" 3AB, 89	8s. for journey to Hartford with Amy Pynchon
1660s or 1670s	Symon Lobdell	"By a Journey to Stonington 1. 0. 0" 3AB, 291	20s. for a journey to Stonington
21 Jan. 1671/72	James Taylor	"By a Journey to Albany of old 2. 10. 0" 5AB, 55	£2 10s. for journey to Albany
1672	Aaron Cooke	"By a Journey to Boston with the votes 1. 10. 0" 5AB, 197	30s. for journey to Boston with voting results
17 Feb. 1672/73	John Holtum	"To a Journey to New London last winter 1. 0. 0" "To a Journey to Boston in September last 1. 10. 0" 5AB, 355	20s. for journey to New London 30s. for journey to Boston
Apr. 1673	Aaron Cooke	"By a Journey to Boston with the votes, April 1673 [is] 1. 10. 0" 5AB, 197	30s. for journey to Boston with voting results
26 Apr. 1673	Timothy Cooper	"By allowance to you from Albany for going to Northampton for the 2 Indian Murderers 0. 8. 0" 5AB, 85	8s. for journey to Northampton to get accused Indians
1674	Jonathan Morgan	"By 20 days your selfe and horse at 4s. per day with Mr. Saron to Albany about Running the Line 4. 9. 0" 5AB, 383	4s. 5d. per diem for accompanying surveyor
Jun. 1674	Benjamin Dunnidge	"By 20 days with M. Saron to Albany 4. 1. 0" 5AB, 193	4s. 1d. per diem for accompanying surveyor

PERSONAL TRANSPORTATION AND MESSENGER SERVICE, *cont.*

Date	Name	Service	Rate
20 Jun. 1677	John Mun	"By a Journey to Albany, himselfe and horse which he shod at his own change in Aprill 1677 [is] 1. 10. 0" 5AB, 241	30s. for journey to Albany
22 Jun. 1677	John Hawkes	"By your Journey to Albany 0. 18. 0" 5AB, 467	18s. for journey to Albany
Sep. 1677	John Mun	"By Carying Cousin Davis to Boston, I agreed with you at 20s." 5AB, 241	20s. for bringing JP's cousin Benjamin Davis to Boston
Jul. 1682?	James Mun	"By a Journey to Boston Sept. 1683 when I was sick, 30s." 5AB, 99	30s. for journey to Boston
1685	Sam Ely	"By his voyage to Antigua from June 1683 to March 1684 and sallary . . . and for his paying his Passage Home 35. 0. 0" 6AB, 61	£35 for journey to Antigua
1694	Samuel Lamb	"A Journey to Boston 1. 5. 0" "By a Journey to Boston 1. 0. 0" 4AB, 95	25s. for journey to Boston 20s. for journey to Boston

PLOWING AND HARROWING

Date	Name	Service	Rate
1645–1646	Jonathan Taylor	"For Plowing 1 acre ½ [is] 0. 10. 0" "Plowing 1 acre" WPAB, 12	6s. 8d. per acre plowed

PLOWING AND HARROWING, *cont.*

Date	Name	Service	Rate
Apr. 1646	Richard Sikes	"Plowing 3 acres ¼ and 16 Rod [is] 1. 0. 0" WPAB, 46	6s. 1d. per acre plowed
22 Feb. 1646/47		"Ploughing ½ an acre 0. 3. 0" WPAB, 47–49	6s. per acre plowed
1648	James Bridge-man	"Plowing 2 acres and ½ [is] 0. 16. 8" WPAB, 72	6s. 8d. per acre plowed
1648	Benjamin Cooley	"Plowing 4 acres at 7s." WPAB, 119	7s. per acre plowed
22 Sep. 1648	Nathaniel Brown	"Plowing 4 acres at 6s. 8d. [is] 1. 6. 8" WPAB, 119A	6s. 8d. per acre plowed
1 Nov. 1648	Thomas Steb-bins	"Due to Thomas Stebbins for worke . . . for going with the plow after, 18d. an acre allowed him 2. 0. 0"	18d. per acre for driving plow
		"For Plowing 5 acres and ½ [is] 1. 16. 8"	6s. 8d. per acre plowed
		"And 2 acres of new ground 1. 0. 0" WPAB, 200	10s. per acre of new ground plowed
5 Feb. 1648/49	William Brooks	"William Brooks owes for 8 days Plowing, 3 acres ¾ at 6s. 8d." WPAB, 192	6s. 8d. per acre plowed
1649	James Bridge-man	"Plowing 1 acres ¾ at 6s. 8d." WPAB, 72	6s. 8d. per acre plowed
1649	Richard Sikes	"Plowing 2 acres 0. 13. 4"	6s. 8d. per acre plowed
		"Plowing 4 acres 1. 6. 8" WPAB, 47–49	6s. 8d. per acre plowed

PLOWING AND HARROWING, *cont.*

Date	Name	Service	Rate
27 Sep. 1649	Symon Beamon	"Plowing 4 acres, as Symon gives in the account at 6s. 8d. [is] 1. 6. 8" WPAB, 210	6s. 8d. per acre plowed
13 Oct. 1649	Rowland Thomas	*Dr.* "Plowing 1 acre 0. 6. 8" WPAB, 218	6s. 8d. per acre plowed
9 Dec. 1649	Henry Chapin	"Plowing 2 acres ¼ [is] 0. 15. 9" WPAB, 40	7s. per acre plowed
Dec. 1649	Griffith Jones	"Plowing 3 acres at 6s. 8d." WPAB, 212	6s. 8d. per acre plowed
15 Aug. 1650	Miles Morgan	"Plowing 9 acres and ½ at 6s. 8d. [is] 3. 3. 4" WPAB, 27	6s. 8d. per acre plowed
14 Dec. 1654	Thomas Stebbins	*Dr.* "Plowing 3 acres and ¼ at 7s. [is] 1. 2. 9" 1AB, 253	7s. per acre plowed
10 Oct. 1656	John Harmon	"Recd Plowing 7 acres 2. 9. 0" "5 acres [plowed] at 9s. per acre 2. 4. 0" 1AB, 328	7s. per acre plowed 9s. per acre plowed
10 Oct. 1656	Rowland Thomas	"Recd by 10 days and ½ your cattle and your selfe Harrowing my ground for grass 2. 2. 0" 1AB, 236	4s. per diem for harrowing with workman's team
1661	Thomas Stebbins (son Sam)	"26 days Sam driving Plow 1. 14. 8" 2AB, 299	16d. per diem for driving plow
1661	Samuel Ball	"By Sam Ball's worke in Plowing at the Spring and	18d. per diem for plowing [driving?]

PLOWING AND HARROWING, *cont.*

Date	Name	Service	Rate
		this fall, all is 37 days at 18d. per day, 2. 15. 6" 2AB, 63	
1669	John Mun	"Plowing 1 acre of Ground 0. 15. 0" 3AB, 97	15s. per acre plowed
30 Sep. 1670	Jonathan Morgan	"By 4 days plowing 0. 10. 0" 5AB, 175	2s. 6d. per diem for plowing
29 Apr. 1671	Rowland Thomas (son Joseph)	"6 days Plowing and Leveling the Lot I brought of Day 0. 12. 0"	2s. per diem for plowing and leveling homelot
1671		"By 2 days Joseph holding plow for . . . 0. 3. 0" 5AB, 15	18d. per diem for holding plow
Aug. 1671	Benjamin Parsons	"By plowing 2 acre and ½ of ground 0. 14. 0" 5AB, 127	5s. 7d. per acre plowed
15 Jan. 1671/72	John Clark	"By Plowing up 1 acre and ¾ of New ground on this side Robert Ashley's at 7s. [is] 0. 12. 3" 5AB, 115	7s. per acre of new ground plowed
30 Jan. 1671/72	John Ashley (youth)	"By Plowing 8 acres ¼ [is] 2. 16. 0" 5AB, 77	6s. 9½d. per acre plowed
May 1672	John Taylor	"By breaking up 2 acres of Land . . . for son Whiting 1. 14. 0" 5AB, 249	17s. per acre broken up
Jul. 1673	Aaron Cooke	"By Plowing up 12 acres of New Ground in July 10. 0. 0" 5AB, 197	16s. 8d. per acre of new ground plowed

PLOWING AND HARROWING, *cont.*

Date	Name	Service	Rate
27 Jun. 1674	William Pixly	"By Plowing at Pacomtuck as he says, 5 acres ½ and 30 rod, If not 40 rod, at 18s. per acre, and my homelot 2 acres ¾ and ½ at 21s. [is] 8. 0. 0" 5AB, 313	18s. and 21s. per acre plowed
24 Nov. 1674	Richard Sikes	"By Plowing 2 acres in the lot . . . 0. 18. 0" 5AB, 135	9s. per acre plowed
1675	William Pixly	"By Plowing up and clearing 4 acres of New ground at Pacomtuck this year 1675 at 18s. [is] 3. 12. 0" 5AB, 313	18s. per acre of new ground plowed
1678	Samuel Kent	"By Plowing 3 acres of Land for Burbank and Barber at 10s. per acre 1. 10. 0" 5AB, 345	10s. per acre plowed
1679	Thomas Remmington of Suffield	"By Plowing 3 acres per agreement 40s. more 30 rods 2. 3. 0" 5AB, 487	13s. 3d. per acre plowed
7 Sep. 1679	Samuel Terry	*Dr.* "I plowed an acre and 35 Rod as Roco tells me for Sam Terry (before his having my mare to Harrow it)" 5AB, 447	Notation that JP's slave plowed 1 acre and 35 rods
1680	Joseph Trumble	"By plowing [1¾ acre] 0. 14. 6" 5AB, 343	8s. 3d. per acre plowed
1683	Richard Waite	*Dr.* "To plowing [1½ acre] 0. 7. 6" 6AB, 74	5s. per acre plowed

PLOWING AND HARROWING, *cont.*

Date	Name	Service	Rate
Aug. 1684	John Beamon, Jr. (son Edmund)	"By your Son Edmund 5 days driving plow at 12d. [is] 0. 5. 0" 5AB, 349	1s. per diem for youth's driving plow

ROPEMAKING

Date	Name	Service	Rate
21 Feb. 1664/65	Anthony Dorchester	"By 6 pounds of hemp 0. 5. 0" 3AB, 85	10d. per pound of hemp
1666	Henry Chapin	"By making 5 halters 0. 2. 6"	6d. per halter
9 Nov. 1667		"By working 23 pounds hemp into Rope at 5d., the Rope for my Saw Mill 0. 9. 7"	5d. per pound of rope
1669		"By a Rope for my sawmill, viz. 30 pounds of yarn a little is left 0. 12. 6" 3AB, 157	5d. per pound of rope
23 Jan. 1673/74	Miles Morgan	"By 21 pounds of hemp at 9d. [is] 0. 15. 4" 5AB, 81	9d. per pound of hemp
28 Mar. 1674	Pelatiah Morgan	"By hemp 0. 0. 6" 5AB, 185	6d. for hemp
28 Jul. 1681	Isaac Morgan	"By making a cartrope: weigh 12 pounds" 5AB, 421	Payment for making 12 pounds of cart rope

SACKMAKING

Date	Name	Service	Rate
26 Jan. 1669/70	John Barber	"By 61 yards ½ yard which you allow in Sack[making]	2s. per yard of sacking

SACKMAKING, *cont.*

Date	Name	Service	Rate
		at 2s. per yard, which you have made into 20 sacks and allow the making into the Bargain 6. 2. 0"	
		"By 77 yards of Sacking made into 25 bags 7. 14. 0" 3AB, 295	2s. per yard of sacking
May 1674	Symon Lobdell	"By Baggs 37. 2. 0" 5AB, 433	£37 2s. for bags
23 Nov. 1676	John Barber	"By making 40 Baggs 0. 16. 6" 5AB, 43	5d. per bag
1681	Abraham Dibble	"For the debt of 11s. 8d., Goodman Dibble owes me we agreed he should allow me for it 2 baggs of about 6 yards and ¼ . . . and he is to make me more 4 baggs for which I allow— 20d. per yard and he to make them" 5AB, 399	20d. per yard of sacking
19 Jun. 1682	Symon Lobdell	"By making 13 baggs 0. 4. 0" 5AB, 433	3⁷⁄₁₀d. per bag

SAWING BOARDS

Date	Name	Service	Rate
1645–1646	Miles Morgan	"Recd in sawing 135 foote slitworke, oake Bords 536 foote, Pine bords 309 fote, . . . 320 fote at 4s. 4d. per 100" WPAB, 24	4s. 4d. per 100 feet of boards
Nov. 1647	Henry Burt	"Recd In sawing bords with Francis Ball, 867 foote at 3s. 8d. [is] 1. 11. 9"	3s. 8d. per 100 feet of boards

SAWING BOARDS, *cont.*

Date	Name	Service	Rate
		"In sawing slit work 118 foote at 4s. 4d. [is] 0. 5. 1"	4s. 4d. per 100 feet of slitwork
		"Recd 210 foote board at 5s. 6d."	5s. 6d. per 100 feet of boards
		WPAB, 158	
8 Dec. 1647	Rowland Thomas	"Recd of Rowland and Miles [Morgan] 910 foote boards, abating 10 foote for cracks, Rowland's ½ is 450, which at 5s. 6d. per [100] foote comes to above 1. 4. 9" WPAB, 156	5s. 6d. per 100 feet of boards
12 Feb. 1647/48	John Clark	"Recd . . . 751 foote of Bords" WPAB, 142	Payment for 751 feet of boards
17 Mar. 1647/48	John Stebbins	"Recd . . . 300 [feet of] fether edged boards at 5s. 6d. is 0. 16. 0" WPAB, 186	5s. 6d. per 100 feet of feather-edged boards
19 Apr. 1648	Henry Burt	"Recd in sawing with Francis Ball, Goodman Burt's halfe is 0. 18. 5"	18s. 5d. for sawing
		"Recd 210 foote of boards at 5s. 6d. [per 100] 0. 11. 6" WPAB, 159	5s. 6d. per 100 feet of boards
8 Aug. 1648	John Lumbard	"by Sawing . . . 505 foot of slit work at 4s. 4d. per 100 . . . [is] 1. 1. 10½" WPAB, 166	4s. 4d. per 100 feet of slitwork
22 Feb. 1648/49	John Stebbins	"In sawing lath with John Clark, his halfe is 100¾ at 4s. 4d. [is] 0. 7. 6" WPAB, 186	4s. 4d. per 100 feet of lath (each man)

SAWING BOARDS, *cont.*

Date	Name	Service	Rate
24 Nov. 1649	John Clark	"Recd in sawing . . . with Jo Stebbins 250, your half 0. 5. 0"	5s. for sawing
		"Sawing with . . . Nappen 0. 3. 6" WPAB, 143	3s. 6d. for sawing
23 Jan. 1649/50	Anthony Dorchester	"Recd of Anthony 300 of board at 5s. 6d. [is] 0. 16. 6" WPAB, 242	5s. 6d. per 100 feet of boards
24 Jan. 1652/53	John Lumbard	"Recd . . . 5 boards, 62 foote ½ [is] 0. 3. 5" 1AB, 135	5s. 6d. per 100 feet of boards
1653?	Jonathan Burt	"Recd . . . 640½ [feet of boards]"	Payment for 640½ feet of boards
		"Recd 198 fote old boards 0. 12. 0"	6s. per 100 feet of boards
13 May 1654		"Recd by 330 foote of boards at 5s. 6d. [is] 0. 18. 0" 1AB, 133–134	5s. 6d. per 100 feet of boards
1654	Anthony Dorchester	"280 foote of Planks 1. 2. 0"	7s. 10d. per 100 feet of planks
		"Recd 360 foote of planks for the mill at 6s. per 100 is 23s., your halfe is 0. 11. 6" 1AB, 129–130	6s. per 100 feet of planks (pays 6s. 6d.)
1655	Jonathan Burt	"Recd 200 of boards . . . " 1AB, 133–134	Payment for 200 feet of boards
11 Feb. 1655/56	Richard Excell	"5 days ½ Sawing at 20d. [is] 0. 9. 2" 1AB, 85	20d. per diem for sawing

SAWING BOARDS, *cont.*

Date	Name	Service	Rate
5 Jul. 1658	James Warrinar	"Recd by Boards, 600 foote . . . 2. 0. 6" 2AB, 32	6s. 9d. per 100 feet of boards
Aug. 1658	Jonathan Burt	"By 30 days worke and ½ hewing, framing, sawing and etc. [is] 3. 1. 0" "By 10 days worke shingling, hewing, [?] reaping and etc. 1. 0. 0" 2AB, 82–83	2s. per diem for hewing, sawing, and joining 2s. per diem for general woodworking
20 Oct. 1658	John Lumbard	"Recd by 12 days Sawing over the river 1. 4. 0" 1AB, 242	2s. per diem for sawing
16 Sep. 1659	James Warrinar	"By 1 day Sawing and ½ [is] 0. 3. 6" "By 14 days ½ Sawing 1. 15. 0" 2AB, 143	2s. 4d. per diem for sawing 2s. 5d. per diem for sawing
Jan. 1659/60	John Harmon	"Recd by 500 of boards at 7s. [is] 1. 18. 0" 2AB, 35	7s. per 100 feet of boards (pays 7s. 7d.)
15 Mar. 1659/60	George Alexander and James Wright	"Agreed with Goodman Alexander and James Wright to doe all the Sawing for the howse of Correction, both Pine and Oake, for ale the sawing worke they are to doe Except Boards and planks for wch I am to allow them the sum of seven pounds, Ten shillings and find them dyet while they are doeing it; they are to doe all the work by the middle of August" "It was expressed the	£7 10s. and board for 2 workers for sawing for 36 × 18-foot house of correction

SAWING BOARDS, *cont.*

Date	Name	Service	Rate
		howse to be 36 foote Long and 18 foot wide." 2AB, 1	
1660	George Alexander	"By sawing worke for the howse of Correction £7 10s., your half is 3. 15. 0" 2AB, 250–251	
Jun. 1660	Deacon Samuel Wright	"By your halfe for the Sawing of the Timber for the Correction house 3. 15. 0"	£7 10s. for sawing timber for house of correction
		"By 18 days Sawing for my New house 2. 5. 0" 2AB, 223	2s. 6d. per diem for sawing
1660–1661	George Alexander	"By 37 days himself and son at 2s. 6d. [is] 4. 12. 6" "By 8 days Sawing"	2s. 6d. per diem for sawing
		"By 11 days sawing at 2s. 6d. [is] 1. 7. 6" 2AB, 250–251	2s. 6d. per diem for sawing
18 Sep. 1660	Thomas Salmon	"By 8 days Sawing at 2s. 6d., and the day going home [to Northampton] 2s. [is] 1. 2. 0" 2AB, 254	2s. 6d. per diem for sawing
19 Oct. 1660	Charles Ferry	"By 4 days Sawing 0. 8. 0" 2AB, 261	2s. per diem for sawing
Jan. 1660/61	John Harmon	"By 86 foote of Boards 0. 6. 6"	7s. 6d. per 100 feet of boards
		"By 5 days ½ Sawing . . . 0. 13. 9" 2AB, 293	2s. 6d. per diem for sawing
1661	Charles Ferry	"Recd by 86 foote of bords 0. 6. 6" 2AB, 261	7s. 6d. per 100 feet of boards

SAWING BOARDS, *cont.*

Date	Name	Service	Rate
3 Jan. 1661/62	James Taylor	"10 [days] sawing 1. 0. 0" 2AB, 337	2s. per diem for sawing
Mar. 1661/62	Thomas Roote of Northampton	"By 28 days your Son Thomas Sawing, but 26 days because of 2 wet days at 2s. 6d. per day 3. 5. 0" 2AB, 225	2s. 6d. per diem for sawing
29 Mar. 1662	Thomas Salmon	"By Sawing 13 days and 2 days coming and going [from and to Northampton] . . . 1. 16. 0" 2AB, 254	2s. 6d. per diem for sawing (pays 2s. 5d.)
29 Mar. 1662	George Alexander	"13 days Sawing at 2s. 6d. [is] 1. 12. 6" "By 2 days coming and going 0. 4. 0" 2AB, 251	2s. 5d. per diem for sawing 2s. per diem for travel time
31 Mar. 1662	Samuel Wright	"By 28 days worke in Sawing, at 26 days because of 2 wett days . . . 3. 5. 0" 2AB, 223	2s. 6d. per diem for sawing
2 Apr. 1662	Anthony Dorchester	"By 950 [feet] of boards at 7s. [is] 3. 6. 6" 2AB, 137	7s. per 100 feet of boards
19 Oct. 1662	Thomas Salmon	"By 11 days sawing to this 19th October 1662 [is] 1. 7. 6" 2AB, 254	2s. 6d. per diem for sawing
Nov. 1662	Edward Foster	"By 127 foote of boards 0. 8. 11" 2AB, 209	7s. per 100 feet of boards
26 Dec. 1662	Rowland Thomas	"By 450 Boards 1. 11. 6" 2AB, 159	7s. per 100 feet of boards

SAWING BOARDS, *cont.*

Date	Name	Service	Rate
6 Jan. 1662/63	Thomas Salmon	"By 14 days Sawing over the River (with Goodman Alexander) at 2s. 6d. [is] 1. 14. 0" 2AB, 254	2s. 6d. per diem for sawing (pays 2s. 5d.)
Apr. 1663	Henry Chapin	"By 655 foote of boards at 7s. 6d. [is] 2. 8. 0" 2AB, 243	7s. 6d. per 100 feet of boards (pays 7s. 2d.)
19 Oct. 1663	James Warrinar	"By 300 of boards 1. 1. 0" 2AB, 143	7s. per 100 feet of boards
21 Feb. 1664/65	Anthony Dor-chester	"By sawing 400 [is] 1. 0. 0" "7 days ½ Sawing (2 hands) 1. 10. 0" 3AB, 85	5s. per 100 feet of boards 4s. per diem for pit sawing
Mar. 1664/65	Thomas Copley	"Rest due to me 2. 6. 7, Which he is to pay me in Boards, I having agreed with him for 1000 feete of Good white wood Boards, full inch thick, sound and free from cracks, for which I allow him 55s. at fresh-water River and he ingages to saw them instead and deliver them me by the middle of May next at fresh water" "Recd by Bords 702 feet 1. 18. 0" 3AB, 4	5s. 6d. per 100 feet of boards 5s. 5d. per 100 feet of boards
1665	Jonathan Ball	"By 2 days worke sawing 0. 5. 0" 3AB, 129	2s. 6d. per diem for sawing
23 Mar. 1665/66	Samuel Wright	"By Sawing Board for the house of Corection 3. 1. 0.	£3 1s. for sawing for house of correction

SAWING BOARDS, cont.

Date	Name	Service	Rate
		I pay you James Wright by Nathaniel Ely's order whom the County Cort Impowered to see that house finished" 3AB, 195	
23 Mar. 1665/66	Thomas Roote	"By sawing, as per Nathaniel Ely's Note for the house of correction 3. 2. 6" 3AB, 219	£3 2s. 6d. for sawing for house of correction
16 Aug. 1666	Thomas Copley	"1710 [foot of planks] and 115 foote . . . he is to deliver me and I am to allow for all 10. 0. 0" "By 325 foote of Plank 1. 15. 0" "By [1310] Sawing for the Mill house, slit work at 5s. per hundred, your halfe 3. 5. 6" 3AB, 123	£10 for planks [and boards?] 10s. 9d. per 100 feet of planks 5s. per 100 feet of slitwork
28 Mar. 1668	Thomas Stebbins	Dr. "To sawing 940 foote of your owne Timber at 2s. 9d. but your being the first at 2s. 6d. per 100" 3AB, 164	2s. 6d. and 2s. 9d. per 100 feet of boards at sawmill
21 Apr. 1668	Cornelius Williams	"To Cornelius sawing 924 foote of Boards at 2s. 9d. [per 100 feet] 1. 5. 6" 3AB, 198	2s. 9d. per 100 feet of boards at sawmill
22 Apr. 1668		"To Cornelius account of sawing for [Robert Ashley] 791 foote viz. boards 491 [feet] at 2s. 9d. [per 100 feet] and slit work 300 foot at 3s. 4d. [is] 1. 3. 6" 3AB, 170	2s. 9d. per 100 feet of boards at sawmill 3s. 4d. per 100 feet of slitwork at sawmill

SAWING BOARDS, *cont.*

Date	Name	Service	Rate
1669?	Richard Sikes	"To [what] I paid the Towne to Goodman Sikes [for] Sawing the Timber for the frame 3. 10. 0" 3AB, 27	£3 10s. for sawing timber for meeting-house
1671	John Artsell	"By Sawing Bords for the dwelling house 0. 7. 0" "Worke Sawing Bords 11. 15. 0" "By 12 days worke at the Saw Mill 1. 16. 0" "By filing and setting a Saw 1. 0. 0" "By Sawing Bords 4000 at 8d. . . . 2. 4. 0" 5AB, 181	7s. for sawing boards for a dwelling house £11 15s. for sawing 3s. per diem for sawing at mill 20s. for filing and setting saw 8d. per 100 feet of boards at sawmill, JP's servant (pays 13d.)
1674		"By sawing 3000 of Bords and Planks this winter 1. 10. 0" "Formerly 7000 and better 1000 and half 5. 0. 0" 5AB, 211	1s. per 100 feet of boards and planks at sawmill 1s. 2d. per 100 feet of boards at sawmill
29 Jun. 1675	Medad Pomery	"Agreed with Medad Pomery for 180 of good oake Planks, Inch and quarter thick when sawne, to be delivered at the foote of the falls [for] 7s. 6d. per 100" 5AB, 263	7s. 6d. per 100 feet of boards, white oak planks delivered at the foot of the falls
13 Mar. 1675/76	Thomas Miller	"By 626 foote of Bords at 5s. 6d. for my mill 1. 15. 0" 5AB, 289	5s. 6d. per 100 feet of boards
1677	Philip Matoone	"By sawing 5600 [feet] 2. 16. 0" 5AB, 537	1s. per 100 feet of boards at sawmill

SAWING BOARDS, *cont.*

Date	Name	Service	Rate
1677	Samuel Cross	"8000 [feet] of Bords at 10s. [per 1000 feet] 4. 0. 0" 5AB, 441	1s. per 100 feet of boards at sawmill
28 Jan. 1677/78	Anthony Austin	4350 "sawing of wch at 10s. per [1000] is 2. 3. 0" 5AB, 523	1s. per 100 feet of boards at sawmill
25 Jun. 1680	John Artsell	"By sawing Boards formerly in April 1680, 7500 of at 12d. [is] 3 15. 0" 5AB, 211	1s. per 100 feet of boards at sawmill
7 Aug. 1686	John Warner (son Daniel)	"By your son Daniell his Sawing formerly accounted for to this 12 Aug. 1686 11,045 feet Bords at 10d. per 100 is . . . 4. 12. 0"	10d. per 100 feet of boards at sawmill, youth sawing
		"And 5725 [feet] of slit-work at 14d. [is] 0. 6. 8" 5AB, 335	14d. per 100 feet of slitwork at sawmill
1687	Philip Matoone	"By Sawing 4000 of Bords 2. 0. 0" 6AB, 199	1s. per 100 feet of boards at sawmill
1694	Samuel Terry, Jr.	"By 1000 [feet] of Bords for my Corne mill at Enfield which you say you brought to the mill at 2. 5. 2" 6AB, 203	45s. per 1000 feet of boards delivered to gristmill
14 Jan. 1697/98	Thomas Geares of Freshwater	"Goodman Geares came to me and brings an account of worke done for me as followeth . . . By sawing (for me) in the year 1690: 9000 and 500 foote of Bords at 12d. per 100 is 4. 15. 0"	1s. per 100 feet of boards at sawmill
		"By sawing 545 foote . . . at	10d. per 100 feet of

SAWING BOARDS, *cont.*

Date	Name	Service	Rate
		10d. [is] 0. 15. 6" "By sawing 1525 feet for my farmers in the yeare 1691 [is] 5. 5. 3" 5AB, 349	boards at sawmill

SCHOOLTEACHING

Date	Name	Service	Rate
Nov. 1653	Pentecost Mathews	"Recd by worke schooling my child . . . as in John Mathews booke to this 2 November 8. 2. 9" 1AB, 127	£8 2s. 9d. for schooling JP's child
1659		"John Mathews Wife, By schooling of Elizur 2 years and Hannah till this November 1659 in all 35s."	35s. for schooling 2 children
12 Dec. 1661		"By schooling and keeping of Marriage Bans for which I agreed to allow you £3" 2AB, 99	£3 for schooling, and keeping marriage bans
2 Nov. 1663	Mrs. Warhan	"By Mary Pynchon's Tabling and schooling halfe a yeare 6. 0. 0" 2AB, 373	£12 per annum for schooling and board
8 Apr. 1682	Daniel Denton	"By schooling Joseph and Mary 0. 19. 6" 5AB, 473	19s. 6d. for schooling 2 children

SERVICE, FEMALE

Date	Name	Service	Rate
1645	Sarah Chapin	"Recd 25 days worke and ½ before her tyme began at 6d. [is] 0. 12. 9"	6d. per diem for service

SERVICE, FEMALE, *cont.*

Date	Name	Service	Rate
		"Sarah tyme begins the 1 of November 1645" "Recd her yeares wages 3. 10. 0" "Recd since then for washing 0. 3. 0" WPAB, 38	£3 10s. per annum for service 3s. for washing
1653	Mary Copley	"Agreed with Mary to take wages instead of finding her cloathes; I am to allow her 50s. a yeare: her yeare begins in September 1653" 1AB, 224	£2 10s. per annum for service, no apparel
1653	Jonathan Taylor	"Due for you wife's being here ten days 1. 0. 0" 1AB, 126	2s. per diem for service
Oct. 1655	Patience Burt	"By Patience's yeares service £5; abate 4s. 6d. for 1 pair shoes 4. 15. 6" 3AB, 81	£5 per annum for service
1656	Mary Copley	"Due to Mary for 3 years, to September 1656, 50s. per anum 7. 10. 0" 1AB, 224	£2 10s. per annum for service
14 Aug. 1669	Elizabeth Waite	"Agreed with Sam Ely for to have the service of my maid Elizabeth Waite, which she hath to Serve, being neare 2 yeares; it wants about three weeks of 2 yeares, all which service that is yet due from her shee is now to performe to Sam Ely, and he accepts of it, shee likewise declares her selfe willing and desirous to serve out her tyme with him, her consent	Service agreement for approximately 2 years

SERVICE, FEMALE, *cont.*

Date	*Name*	*Service*	*Rate*
		being to it which shee expressed before him. Sam Ely Ingages to allow me for her tyme 40s. which 40s. he is to pay me in wheate and Porke by spring come 12 Months and to sattisfie his old debt first or else to allow and pay me 50s. in all he pay it not all by Spring come 12 Month and Moreover he is to allow and pay 40s. to Elizabeth at the end of her tyme and to cloathe and provide for her during the tyme and at her goeing from him as is the custome and befitting such a servant" 3AB, 69	
Feb. 1671/72	John Lamb	"By your daughter's help 3 weekes 0. 10. 0" 5AB, 75	3s. 4d. per week for service
10 Apr. 1673	Hannah Morgan	"Agreed with Serjeant Miles Morgan for his Daughter Hannah [to] Live with us a yeare, to begin [the] 1st of May which day shee is to come to us [I will] give her £6 for the yeare"	£6 per annum for service
		"By her yeare's wages to the 5th of May 1674 [is] 6. 0. 0"	Payment for 1 year of service
		"By a weeke worke after her tyme out 0. 3. 0" 5AB, 4–5	3s. per week for service
2 Dec. 1673	Sarah Dumbleton	"By one yeare's wages ending December 2d. 1673 [is] 6. 0. 0" 5AB, 183	£6 per annum for service

SERVICE, FEMALE, *cont.*

Date	Name	Service	Rate
12 June 1675	Margaret Wyard	"Agreed with her to live with us one yeare viz. from the 12th of June 1675 to the 12th of June 1676 for which yeares service I am to allow her Six Pounds" 5AB, 480–481	£6 per annum for service
Jul. 1675	Hannah Bagg	"Hannah Bagg came to us July 3, 1675 and staid about 10 weeks" 5AB, 25	Payment for 10 weeks service
25 Nov. 1675	Sarah Dumble-ton	"Sarah came to us November 25, 1675" "By Sarah's service from March and ½ more her service about 4 months ½ from 25 November to 10th April 5. 0. 0" 5AB, 183	Service schedule £6 per annum for service
11 Mar. 1675/76	Hannah Bagg	"Hannah Bagg came to us in July; shee is to have two pair shoes . . . [and] 1 pair of stockens . . . shee came to us againe the 18 or 19th of February and went away about the 20th of [Sep.?]" 5AB, 25	Servant's apparel
1676	Mary Tilton	"Mary Tilton came to us on Friday the 24th of November 1676 at Night" "By her yeare's wages Ending November 25, 1677 [is] 6. 0. 0" 5AB, 512–513	£6 per annum for service Payment for 1 year of service
Mar. 1677/78	Joanna Lamb	"Joanna Lamb came to us in March 1677/78, and went away at the halfe	£6 per annum for service

SERVICE, FEMALE, *cont.*

Date	*Name*	*Service*	*Rate*
		yeares end Recd by her halfe a yeares Service 3. 0. 0" 5AB, 349	
Oct. 1678	Abigail Dibble	"Abigail Dibble came to us the 1st day of October 1678, and we are to give her £6 for a yeare service" 5AB, 398	£6 per annum for service
10 Apr. 1679	Sarah Hunter	"To Sarah Hunter who came to us Aprill 10th, 1679 and went away June 15, 2 mo. and a week at 2s."	2s. per week for service
5 Jul. 1679		"Recd by 10 weekes service 1. 5. 0" 5AB, 31	2s. 6d. per week for service
9 Apr. 1680	Ruth Beamon	"Ruth Beamon came to us Aprill 9th 1680 for a yeare at sixe Pounds, as my wife told me" 5AB, 19	£6 per annum for service
29 Sep. 1681	Hester Spencer	"Recd by 5 weekes service Hester 0. 10. 0" 5AB, 543	2s. per week for service
Jul. 1683	Sarah Jeffreys	"I agreed with Goodman Jeffrey for his daughter Sarah to live with us a yeare. I propounded her wage to be £5 10s., but he said it must be £6 . . . Shee came to us on Thursday afternoon the 5th day of July 1683"	£6 per annum for service

SERVICE, FEMALE, cont.

Date	Name	Service	Rate
Jan. 1683/84	Hannah Jeffreys	"Goodwife Jeffreys being here and proffering her daughter Hanah to come to us: I treated with her and shee yeilded to our having her (whom she says is 12 years old and since August last) till shee be 18 yeares old. I sending her cloathes which shee now needs to weare . . . [and to give her a pair of shoes] and so shee is to live with us till shee be 18 yeares of age, and I cloathing her and providing well for her" 5AB, 461	Twelve-year-old to remain as a domestic servant until age eighteen
23 Dec. 1687	Sarah Stevenson	"By 1 yeare wages £6" "By halfe a yeare 3" 5AB, 321	£6 per annum for service £6 per annum for service
1690–1691	Susannah Ponder	"Recd by 2 yeares Service at £6, is £12" 5AB, 219	£6 per annum for service
30 Jun. 1692	Hannah Holeman	Holeman to live with JP "as a Servant faithfully and dilligently ought to doe" for a year at £6 6AB, 248–249	£6 per annum for service
1693	Susannah Ponder	"Sue Ponder her wages ½ yeare to this 10 February 1693 [is] 3. 10. 0" 5AB, 218–219	£7 per annum for service
7 Sep. 1695	Priscilla Warner	"Priscilla Warner came to dwel with us for a yeare, and for her yeares service I am to allow her £7 10s. in pay or £5 in money" 6AB, 23	£7 10s. per annum for service

SERVICE, FEMALE, *cont.*

Date	Name	Service	Rate
1696	Sarah Bagg	Came to service October 1696, stayed ¼ year, 1. 4. 0 6AB, 208–209	£5 per annum for service [in specie?]
1699	Alice Beamont	Alice Beamont to live with JP for five months, at £6 per annum 6AB, 250	£6 per annum for service

SERVICE, MALE

Date	Name	Service	Rate
1638	William Warri-nar	"Agreed with William War-rener for three quarters of a yeare, and his tyme to begin the 12 of June 1638 and to end on the 12 March 1638 and he is to receive for the said tyme eight pounds" WPAB, 3	£10 13s. per annum for service
2 Oct. 1640	Thomas Miller	Apprenticed to WP as a servant. Discharged 22 May 1648, 4 months before his time ran out. Was paid 40s. for time. WP supplied him with "suit and appar-rel" CVHM, Ms.	Service agreement
21 Apr. 1646	Nathaniel Brown	"Nathaniel Browne came to my father the 21 of Aprill 1648 at night, he came from Hartford and I agreed with him at Hart-ford for £4 19s. for 6 months [to] 22 of October 1646"	£10 per annum for service
		"Nathaniel Browne was ab-sent from . . . service about his own occasions, 4 days	Abatement for days not worked

SERVICE, MALE, *cont.*

Date	Name	Service	Rate
		and ½ at Hartford, and . . . days in the Bay more . . . days" WPAB, 120	
31 Jul. 1646	Francis Pepper	"Agreed with Francis [to serve] from the 12 of September 1645 till 1 November 1645 he is to have 1.[?] 11. 0"	Service schedule
		"And from the 1 of November till April 1646 [?] he is to have 4. 10. 0"	£4 10s. for service
		"more due to him from the first of Aprill to the end of July which is 4 months at 20s. per mo. is £4" WPAB, 29	20s. per month for service
11 Nov. 1647	Nathaniel Brown	"Recd by a yeare and ½ wages 13. 5. 0" WPAB, 119A	£8 16s. 8d. per annum for service
1647–1648	Francis Pepper	"Recd ¾ years service at £8 10s. a year 6. 7. 6"	£8 10s. per annum for service
		"Recd a yeare's wages to 25 Sept. 1648 [is] 9. 0. 0" WPAB, 30	£9 per annum for service
8 Feb. 1648/49		"Recd 4 months winter at 12s. per month is 2. 8. 0" WPAB, 198	12s. per month for winter service
28 Aug. 1650		"Recd in what is due to Francis for 4 months service in winter last 2. 2. 0" WPAB, 197	10s. 6d. per month for winter service
Jun. 1653	Symon Beamon	"For service from May till the 20th of September for, which tyme I was to allow him 4. 16. 0" 1AB, 197	24s. per month for summer service

SERVICE, MALE, *cont.*

Date	*Name*	*Service*	*Rate*
10 Jan. 1653/54	Francis Pepper	"Agreed with Francis Pepper to serve me to the end of March nexte for which tyme I am to allow him 2. 5. 0" 1AB, 203	18s. per month for winter service
1 Feb. 1654/55	James Taylor	"I agreed with James Taylor for him to take wages instead of my finding him clothes: from this tyme till the 10th of next October I am to allow him 55s., and then from the 10th till his tyme be out I am to allow him £4 per annum, out of which he is to find himself that clothing which otherwise I was to allow him and this according to James his desire and he fully consenting with it" 1AB, 250	£4 per annum for service, servant to find his own apparel
1658		"By agreement with him for one yeare, to Serve me from the 3d December 1658 to the 3d of December 1659 for which yeare Service I am to allow him £9, 1 pair of shoes, and 1 pair of Stockens"	£9, shoes, and stockings per annum for service
		"By 8 months service 8. 5. 0" 2AB, 121	£8 5s. for 8 months service
Jul. 1661	John Earle	"John Earle came to my work July 1st (61) his foote being swelled he did nothing and again a day of him and James goeing to the long meddow for . . . again a day of James going to	Method of docking for days missed

SERVICE, MALE, *cont.*

Date	Name	Service	Rate
		Windsor and 2 days him, all make 6 days which will abate a week and so I must count his work from the 8 July (61)" "Againe take out 2 days goeing to Windsor after your sonne when Goodman Colton went, because he reaped in his tyme, and 2 days of James goeing at the same tyme, and 4 days, and 1 day he was after the swine, before the Court, a Sabbath falling out in this tyme, and so it is all one as if he came to me but the 14th of July" 2AB, 294	
15 Sep. 1663		"By John Earle by me 9 Months at freshwater River as Goodman Colton [says?] is 6. 15. 0" 2AB, 294–295	£9 per annum for service
21 Mar. 1664/65	Jonathan Ball	"Jonathan Ball came to me the 21 March 1664 and he is to be with me 2 month for which I am to allow 20s. per Month" 3AB, 129	20s. per month for service
10 Nov. 1665	Richard Waite	"Agreed with Benjamin Parsons to have my youth Richard Waite 2 years, from the 10th day of this present November 1665, he is to allow him fitting food, lodging, and apparell, and to allow and pay me 50s. Each yeare for his service, and to Send him	50s. and food, lodging, and apparel per annum for youth's service

SERVICE, MALE, *cont.*

Date	*Name*	*Service*	*Rate*
		home to me as well apparelled as he is now By his owne Consent and so this is put to John Bliss rent" "This lad was turned over to John Bliss" 3AB, 94	Notation of servant's transfer
1665		"Richard Waite had when he went to Benjamin Parsons: 1 good sute of kersy at 7s. per yard, viz. Coate and breaches and 1 Red cotton wastcote somewhat worne, and 1 doblet and breeches old, 1 pair Drawers and an old pair more, 2 pair New white Cotton Stocken, his shooes wore bad but Henry promised him a New pair more, which he had after he was there, 3 Shurts, Bande, and etc." 3AB, 95	Servant's apparel
2 Apr. 1667	John Ponder	"Recd by 8 months worke 7. 0. 0" 3AB, 18	£10 10s. per annum for service
1673–1674	Jacop, the Dutch lad	"Jacob the Dutch Lad: Agreed with him to dwell with me one yeare as a servant, for which I am to allow him £12 for the yeare's service. This yeare begins the 12th of March 1673/74" "[Absent 5 weeks]"	£12 per annum for service
6 Mar. 1674/75		"I agreed with Jacob to live with me and serve me one yeere more after this yeare	£13 10s. and stabling for a mare per annum for service

SERVICE, MALE, *cont.*

Date	Name	Service	Rate
		. . . which will be the 20th of April next, for which yeares service . . . I am to allow him Thirteen Pounds, Ten shilling and the keeping of his mare"	
		"By his first yeares service ending the 20 of April 1675 [is] 12. 0. 0"	£12 per annum for service
		"By about 2 Months tyme of his last yeare till he went to Albany 2. 3. 0" 5AB, 428–429	£12 per annum for service
1675	Thomas Scot	"By your service at Squeak-eag, 1 month 1. 4. 0" 5AB, 454	24s. per month for service
9 Nov. 1676	Jonathan Bush	"Agreed with Jonath Bush to dwell with me one yeare . . . [for] Nine Pounds" 5AB, 512–513	£9 per annum for service
22 Oct. 1687	John Weathers	"Agreed with John Weathers to live with me a yeare [beginning Mon., 24 Oct.] I am to allow and pay him Nine Pounds [is] 9. 0. 0"	£9 per annum for service
1688		"9. 0. 0" 6AB, 75	£9 per annum for service
21 Oct. 1689	William Willoughby	To live with JP for 5 months for £4 and "helping him in such things as he needs"	£9 12s. per annum for service
		"By his 5 Months service 4. 3. 2" 6AB, 232–233	£4 3s. 2d. for 5 months service
21 Feb. 1689/90	Benjamin Sitton	JP agreed for Sitton to come and live with JP for ½ year at wages of £6 10s.	£13 and 4 barrels of gunpowder per annum for service

SERVICE, MALE, *cont.*

Date	Name	Service	Rate
		and 2 pounds of powder. 6AB, 220–221	
13 Oct. 1690	John Hunter	One year's service £10 6AB, 240–241	£10 per annum for service
Aug. 1692	William Cheney	"By his Service according to agreement . . . 8. 0. 0" 6AB, 249	£8 for service
12 Feb. 1694/95	Samuel Edwards	"Agreed with Samuel Edwards for a yeare's service . . . He is to live with me and doe [for] Thirteen Pounds [and bed and board] paid" 6AB, 69	£13 per annum for service
Mar. 1694/95	John Humphreys	"John Humphrey came to me on Friday noon the 24th of March 1692/93. I account his time to begin: March 25, 1693 and am to allow him for the yeare he accounted in my service the whole yeare £11 in Pay and £4 in Mony" "By your yeares service to the 25 of March 1694, besides wintering your Horse and £4 in Money more" 6AB, 71	£11 in pay and £4 in specie per annum for service
Mar. 1694/1695	Mathew Copley	"Mathew Copley came to me on Munday Night, March 9th" 6AB, 49	Service schedule
6 Apr. 1695	Joseph Williston	"Agreed with Joseph Williston to allow him £20 in Pay for a yeare To cut and	£20 per annum for cutting and carting firewood, making

SERVICE, MALE, *cont.*

Date	*Name*	*Service*	*Rate*
		cart my firewood, make Fire and Tend my cattle . . ." 6AB, 265	fire, and tending cattle
26 Feb. 1696/97	Samuel Palmer	"Agreed with Samuel Palmer to Live with me . . . Halfe a year." 6AB, 59	Service agreement for ½ year
12 Mar. 1696/97	Jedediah Bart-let	JP agreed that Bartlet would get his firewood for a year, from April to April. To cart it home and cut it up. To tend cattle, carry corn meal to and from mill, and do all necessary chores for £20 in pay	£20 per annum for cutting and carting firewood and doing chores
Mar. 1697/98		Similar agreement for £12 in specie 6AB, 259	£12 in specie per annum for cutting and carting firewood and doing chores

SHEPHERD

Date	*Name*	*Service*	*Rate*
6 Oct. 1656	Francis Pepper	"Recd from Francis by his keeping my Sheepe the yeare 1656 in all 5. 2. 6"	£5 2s. 6d. per annum for keeping sheep
7 Oct. 1656		"Recd 14 days worke at 18d. per diem, Recd 28 days worke at 20d. [for keeping sheep] 2. 15. 0"	18d. and 20d. per diem for keeping sheep
1657		"Recd by keeping the Sheep Ano 1657 [is] 5. 10. 0" 1AB, 208	£5 10s. per annum for keeping sheep

SHEPHERD, *cont.*

Date	Name	Service	Rate
26 Mar. 1659		"Recd by keeping sheep in the year 1658 [is] 5. 14. 0" 1AB, 209	£5 14s. per annum for keeping sheep
2 Nov. 1659		"By keeping my sheep this 1659 [is] 6. 10. 0"	£6 10s. per annum for keeping sheep
1660		"Keeping my sheep 1660 [is] 7. 10. 0"	£7 10s. per annum for keeping sheep
1661		"By keeping of my sheepe this yeare to 1661 by agreemt at 2s. 10d. [is] 7. 10. 0"	£7 10s. per annum for keeping sheep [2s. 10d. per diem]
		"By 15 weekes work since your keeping sheep, viz. from the Nov. 10th to this 1st March at 8s. per weeke comes to £6" 2AB, 227	Schedule for sheep-keeping [Sheep-keeping ends 10 November]

SHEEP SHEARING

Date	Name	Service	Rate
10 Oct. 1656	Benjamin Parsons	"1 day shearing sheepe 0. 2. 0" 1AB, 282	2s. per diem for shearing sheep
26 Mar. 1658	Benjamin Cooley	"Recd 2 days sheering sheep Recd 2 days other worke 0. 7. 0" 2AB, 23	7s. for shearing sheep and unspecified work
1658–1659	Benjamin Parsons	"By 1 day sheepe shearing 0. 2. 0" 2AB, 61	2s. per diem for shearing sheep
1659	Samuel Marshfield	"By one day sheep shearing this year (59) 0. 2. 0" 2AB, 109	2s. per diem for shearing sheep

SHEEP SHEARING, *cont.*

Date	Name	Service	Rate
1659	Benjamin Parsons	"By 1 day sheepe sheering 0. 2. 0" 2AB, 61	2s. per diem for shearing sheep
18 Nov. 1661	Benjamin Cooley	"By 2 days work shearing 0. 4. 0" 2AB, 305	2s. per diem for shearing sheep
12 Nov. 1663	Benjamin Parsons	"By 1 day sheering sheepe 0. 2. 0"	2s. per diem for shearing sheep
3 Sep. 1664		"By shearing 30 sheepe 0. 2. 6" 2AB, 273	1d. per sheep sheared
1665		"By shearing sheepe Ano 1665 [is] 0. 2. 6"	2s. 6d. for shearing sheep
1666		"By Shearing Sheepe Ano 1666 [is] 0. 2. 6" "By Shearing Sheepe last summer 0. 2. 2" 3AB, 95	2s. 6d. for shearing sheep 2s. 2d. for shearing sheep
Aug. 1671		"By shearing of sheape 0. 2. 0"	2s. for shearing sheep
28 Nov. 1673		"By Twice shearing of sheepe 0. 4. 4" 5AB, 127	2s. 2d. for shearing sheep
Jun. 1675		"By shearing sheepe 0. 1. 6"	1s. 6d. for shearing sheep
1677		"Shearing sheep 0. 1. 0" 5AB, 413	1s. for shearing sheep

SHINGLING AND LATH WORK

Date	Name	Service	Rate
2 Dec. 1657	Samuel Grant	"Agreed with him to shingle my howse over the River: he is to heap and lay the shingles, as also to lay the lath and make the rafter feet and put them on, which are to be made long that the eves may be long and deep to safeguard the house, as also [to see that] shingles may come over the end, all to be done well and with good shingles, the bad ones he is to throw aside—and this is to be done by the middle of march, for which I am to allow him £4 15s." 1AB, 181	£4 15s. for shingling house
25 Oct. 1658		"I agreed with Sam Grant to shingle my howse about 23 foote long and 16 foote wide with 3 [foot] shingle, he to lay all the lath, and hew and lay the shingle to make and put on the [house], for which I [am] to allow him 58s., and so I am to allow him though the house be wide 24 foote long"	£2 18s. for laying lath and 3-foot shingles for 23 × 16-foot house
Mar. 1659/60		"Agreed with Sam Grant to shingle my new house of 42 foote long and 21 [foot] wide, with foote and half shingles, to lay [all] Boards on which the shingles are to be laid, and to lay [all] planks for gutters and to make all the gutters . . . for the Porch . . . "	£10 for laying lath and 18-inch shingling on 42 × 21-foot house

SHINGLING AND LATH WORK, *cont.*

Date	Name	Service	Rate
		25 Oct. 1661 "Recd by shingling my house 10. 0. 0" 2AB, 122–123	Payment for shingling house
		"By laying the lath and shingling my house for the Cyder press 1. 1. 4" 2AB, 123	£1 1s. 4d. for laying lath and shingles for cider press house
25 Oct. 1661		"Recd by shingling my stair case -. 15. 0" "Recd ½ day lifting bords 0. 1. 6" 2AB, 122	Payment for shingling staircase 3s. per diem for lifting boards
25 Oct. 1661	John Stebbins	"Agreement [with] Goodman Stebbins for shingling the house of correction, he is to lay all the lath and shingles, and to hew the shingles and to fit and put ... the rafter feete on, for which I am to allow him £6, and for what he is to allow me 12s. per 100 ... to be done next Spring with 18 Inch shingle, the lower rafters to be 40 foote long"	£6 for shingling house of correction with 1½ foot shingles, lower rafters to be 40 feet long
		"By shingling the house of correction 6. 0. 0" 2AB, 79	Payment for shingling house of correction
5 Nov. 1663	John Lamb	"By puting up the [400] shingles 0. 4. 0" 2AB, 352–353	1s. per 100 shingles laid
17 Jul. 1667	Joseph Leonard	"Agreed with Joseph Leanord to shingle my howse at the Mill with 3 foote shingles, I finding the shingles and laying them by the	1s. per 100 siding shingles laid, JP to saw lath, 14d. if sawmill unavailable

SHINGLING AND LATH WORK, *cont.*

Date	*Name*	*Service*	*Rate*
		house . . . then Joseph is to lay them well, and he is to get and lay all the Lath: he getting the lath which I am to cart, he providing the lath except carting as aforesaid, and taking my shingle and laying them well and workemanlike: the whole covering being com-pleated by him of both the roofes. I am to pay him for the whole covering com-pleated and well done: by the hundred, for every hundred of shingle layd I am to allow him 12d. and to saw the lath at my saw mill, which he is to get and lay and doe all the Cover-ing for 12d. per 100, which he is to goe about as soon as the house is ready for covering, and is then forth-with to Cover it out of hand. In case of my Saw mill failing, that I cannot saw the lath, then he is to rend and hew them and the laying of them with the shingle on them is to goe at 14d. per 100 . . . " 3AB, 57	
3 Jun. 1668	John Stebbins	"By shingling Mr. Whit-ing's house at Westfield with the back Roome 13. 10. 0"	£13 10s. for shingling house
		"By allowance on shingling, you saying you had a hard Bargaine 3. 10. 0"	£3 10s. additional payment for shin-gling due to difficulty of task

SHINGLING AND LATH WORK, *cont.*

Date	Name	Service	Rate
		"By shingling the addition to the Back Roome 3. 10. 0" 3AB, 223	£3 10s. for shingling back room addition
1672	John Stebbins, Jr.	"By shingling my gutter at home 0. 10. 0" "By shingling the howse at Stony River which John Artsell is to allow 3. 10. 0" "By covering my house 3. 0. 0"	10s. for shingling gutter £3 10s. for shingling house £3 for shingling roof
15 Oct. 1673		"Agreed with John Stebbing to lath my house at Stony River, he to get the Lath (I finding Nayles) which worke he doe next weeke and I to give him 8s. for it; he did not finish it and so I allow but 0. 6. 0" 5AB, 279	8s. for laying up lath
1673–1674	Jonathan Morgan	"By shingling my house at the Round hill and laying the Bords 4. 0. 0" 5AB, 383	£4 for shingling house
Aug. 1675	George Norton of Suffield	"By 4 days ½ shingling 0. 5. 0"	13⅓d. per diem for shingling
1677		"By worke about the Meetinghouse laying the Bords, shingling, clapboarding, . . . and covering . . . Planks for the floore 6. 5. 0" 5AB, 463	£6 5s. for shingling, clapboarding, and floor work
1677	John Pope	"By shingling and clapboarding the Meetinghouse (and shaving and Joining . . . clapboards) 3. 5. 0" 5AB, 527	£3 5s. for shingling, clapboarding, and joining

SHINGLING AND LATH WORK, *cont.*

Date	Name	Service	Rate
Dec. 1678	Philip Matoone	"By worke shingling over my ox house 0. 17. 0" "By covering my share of the Mill 0. 12. 0"	17s. for shingling ox house 12s. for shingling JP's share of mill
1 Mar. 1678/79		Matoone to shingle JP's 51 × 24-foot barn in Round Hill for £6 10s. and all the leftover shingles 5AB, 537	£6 10s. and leftover shingles for shingling 51 × 24-foot barn

SHINGLEMAKING AND CLAPBOARDMAKING

Date	Name	Service	Rate
24 Oct. 1649	John Mathews	"Recd 1900 of shingles 3. 0. 0" WPAB, 105	3s. 2d. per 100 shingles
20 Sep. 1658		"200 of Clapboards 0. 10. 0" 1AB, 270	5s. per 100 clapboards
6 Nov. 1658		"Agreed with John Mathews to get me Thirteen hundred and halfe of good sound Three foote shingles an inch thick . . . for £3" 2AB, 99	4s. 5d. per 100 3-foot shingles
15 Dec. 1658	Thomas Miller	"By shingles for my howse over the River . . . 4. 5. 0" 2AB, 145	£4 5s. for shingles for house
1659	John Mathews	"By 100 of Long shingles 0. 4. 0" "By hewing 700 of shingle 0. 7. 0" "By 200 and halfe of 3 foote shingles 0. 13. 0" "By 12,000 of shingles 11. 0. 0" 2AB, 99	4s. per 100 3-foot shingles 1s. per 100 18-inch shingles, for hewing only 5s. 2d. per 100 3-foot shingles 1s. 10d. per 100 [18-inch?] shingles

SHINGLEMAKING AND CLAPBOARDMAKING, *cont.*

Date	Name	Service	Rate
31 Dec. 1659	Thomas Miller	"Agreed with Thomas Miller to deliver at my howse eight thousand of good shingles 18 inches Long . . . to be delivered at my howse by the end of March next for which I am to allow him 20s. per thousand" 2AB, 145	2s. per 100 18-inch shingles
1659–1660	Nathaniel Pritchard	"Recd by 100 of Clapboard 0. 6. 0" 2AB, 107	6s. per 100 clapboards
5 Dec. 1660	Thomas Miller	"Agreed with him for 100 of 5 foote clapboards . . . at 8s." 2AB, 145	8s. per 100 5-foot clapboards
25 Oct. 1661	Samuel Grant	"Recd by hewing . . . shingles you and Thomas Barber 2. 14. 0" 2AB, 122	£2 14s. for hewing shingles
Apr. 1663	Thomas Miller	"By 2000 of 3 foote shingles at 40s. [is] 4. 0. 0" "By shingles . . . 0. 3. 0" "By Long shingles for the gutter of my [house] 0. 2. 0" "Shingles for my howse 6. 0. 0" "By shingles for howse of correction 3. 0. 0" 2AB, 145	4s. per 100 3-foot shingles 3s. for shingles 2s. for 3-foot shingles £6 for shingles £3 for shingles
20 Aug. 1663	Nathaniel Ely	"By 200 of clapboards 0. 2. 6" 2AB, 249	15d. per 100 clapboards, for hewing only
5 Nov. 1663	John Lamb	"By hewing 4000 of shingles 3. 0. 0" 2AB, 353	18d. per 100 shingles, for hewing only

SHINGLEMAKING AND CLAPBOARDMAKING, *cont.*

Date	Name	Service	Rate
5 Nov. 1663	John Bagg	"John Bagg is to get me 2000 of good 3 foote shingles at 40s. per 1000"	4s. per 100 3-foot shingles
		"By 2000 of 3 foote shingle at 40s. per 1000 [is] 4. 0. 0"	4s. per 100 3-foot shingles
		2AB, 347	
1 Mar. 1664/65	Thomas Bancroft	"By 400 of Clapboard 1. 0. 0"	5s. per 100 clapboards
		3AB, 75	
1665	Nathaniel Pritchard	"By clapboards 800 [is] 2. 5. 0"	5s. 7d. per 100 clapboards
		3AB, 97	
1677	Philip Matoone	"By 6 days worke shaving shingles 0. 15. 0"	2s. 6d. per diem for shaving shingles
		5AB, 537	
18 Jan. 1677/78	Nathaniel Foote	"By 1000 of shingles 1. 3. 0"	2s. 4d. per 100 shingles
		"By 2 days shaving of shingles 0. 5. 0"	2s. 6d. per diem for shaving shingles
		5AB, 451	
8 Dec. 1684	Increase Sikes	"By 10,500 of shingles for my house 10. 0. 0"	2s. per 100 [18-inch?] shingles
		5AB, 416–417	
1696		"By 8000 of shingles 7. 10. 0"	2s. per 100 [18-inch?] shingles
		6AB, 121	

SHOEMAKING AND COBBLING

Date	Name	Service	Rate
7 Nov. 1646	Samuel Wright	"Mending and making shoes 0. 15. 0"	15s. for making and mending shoes
		WPAB, 84	

SHOEMAKING AND COBBLING, *cont.*

Date	Name	Service	Rate
12 Oct. 1647		"Mending and making shoes 0. 8. 7" WPAB, 85	8s. 7d. for making and mending shoes
29 Dec. 1648		"In making 7 pair shoos at 12d. [is] 0. 7. 0"	1s. per pair of shoes
		"3 pair at 6d. [is] 0. 1. 6"	6d. per pair of shoes
		"4 pair of heeles 0. 0. 8"	2d. per pair of heels
		"Above is Recd in shoe making 1. 8. 4"	28s. 4d. for shoemaking
		"Recd in mending shoes and making 2 pair formerly 0. 7. 0" WPAB, 86	7s. for making and mending shoes
24 May 1653		"1 pair shoes . . . 0. 6. 4" 1AB, 111	6s. 4d. per pair of shoes
27 Jan. 1660/61	Thomas Day	"Shoes for John Pynchon [Jr.] 3s. 6d."	3s. 6d. per pair of boy's shoes
		"My wife's shoos 0. 4. 8"	4s. 8d. per pair of woman's shoes
		"Pair for my wife 0. 4. 6"	4s. 6d. per pair of woman's shoes
		"For Miriam's shoos 0. 2. 8"	2s. 8d. per pair of woman's shoes [maid]
		"By abatement on sole leather . . . you say some of it proved not good 0. 9. 0" 2AB, 157	9s. abatement for poor quality of sole leather
16 Jan. 1665/66		"A shoe for Mary Pynchon 0. 2. 6"	5s. per pair of woman's shoes
		"Mending Beltes, shoes 0. 1. 9"	1s. 9d. for mending belts and shoes
		Mending JP, Jr.'s, shoes 0. 1. 6	1s. 6d. for mending boy's shoes
		"A Scabberd for a sword 0. 2. 0"	2s. for a sword scabbard
		"1 pair shoes for Mary Pynchon 0. 5. 0"	5s. per pair of girl's shoes
		"1 pair shoes for Miriam 0. 4. 3"	4s. 3d. per pair of woman's shoes

SHOEMAKING AND COBBLING, *cont.*

Date	Name	Service	Rate
3 May 1666		"By worke: making and mending shooes and wheat and else as in Goodman Day's Booke: the whole . . . [is] 12. 1. 6"	£12 1s. 6d. for cobbling, shoemaking, and wheat
30 Aug. 1667		"To 5 hides of sole leather from N. London" *Dr.* "To 6 hides £9 5s., a small one"	Payment for 5 hides 30s. 10d. per hide of sole leather [Sole leather from New London]
9 Dec. 1667		"To 6 smale hides at Jonathan [Gilbert's] warehouse, which I gave a note this 9 Dec. 1667 for you to Call for them and Receive them all at 3. 10. 0"	11s. 8d. per small hide
1668		"By 1 pair shooes for John 0. 7. 6" "By 1 pair shoes my wife 5s., 1 pair of John 7s. 6d. [is] 0. 12. 6"	7s. 6d. for JP, Jr.'s shoes 5s. for Amy Pynchon's shoes 7s. 6d. for JP, Jr.'s shoes
		"By 1 pair shoos my wife 0. 5. 0" "By 4 pair Shoes"	5s. for Amy Pynchon's shoes Payment for 4 pairs of shoes
		"By 1 pair shooes [for] John Artsell, 8s. 6d." "By mending my Boots 0. 1. 9" "By 1 pair shoes mysefe 0. 8. 3" 3AB, 151	8s. 6d. per pair of man's shoes 1s. 9d. for mending boots 8s. 3d. for JP's shoes
1660s or 1670s	Symon Lobdell	"By 12 pair shoos [size] 10s at 5s. is £3, 4 pair of them, 11s at 5s. 6d. and 8 pair of Today, 12s at 6s. [is] 6. 10. 0"	5s. per pair of size 10 shoes 5s. 6d. per pair size 11 shoes 6s. per pair size 12 shoes

SHOEMAKING AND COBBLING, *cont.*

Date	Name	Service	Rate
		"By Shoos Mending, shooes, and etc., as in Symon Lobdell's account . . . 7. 17. 9"	£7 17s. 9d. in cobbling and shoemaking
		"Here is accounted a pair of shoes for myself which I had but the day before the reckning with Hides [?] for shoostrings and Joseph's shooes not to be made" 3AB, 291	Payment for 1 pair of shoes
4 Jan. 1669/70?	Thomas Day	"By 1 pair shooes for my wife 0. 7. 0"	7s. for Amy Pynchon's shoes
May 1670		"By making a Boote for a lame horse 0. 2. 6" 3AB, 161	2s. 6d. for making boot for lame horse
29 Aug. 1670	Symon Lobdell	"By shooes, 6 pair of 12s and 6 pair 11s, abate 20d. as per [him?] 3. 3. 3" 3AB, 291	5s. 6d. per pair of size 11 shoes 6s. per pair size 12 shoes
4 Jan. 1670/71		"By shooes [8 pair] and 2. 0. 9"	5s. 1d. per pair of shoes
		"By severalls brought from old Booke 17. 4. 0"	£17 4s. for shoemaking
		"By your account of worke for me: shooes making and etc., all is 6. 12. 6"	£6 12s. 6d. for shoemaking
		"By mending shooes £3 15s. 1d. . . . "	£3 15s. 1d. for cobbling
21 Mar. 1671/72		"By [16] pair shoes . . . £4 16s."	6s. per pair of shoes
22 Apr. 1672		"By mending shooes and else as in Symon's Book 2. 10. 7" 5AB, 105	£2 10s. 7d. for cobbling

SHOEMAKING AND COBBLING, *cont.*

Date	Name	Service	Rate
Dec. 1672	Thomas Day	"By 1 pair shooes for Sarah Dumbleton 0. 7. 0" "By 1 pair shooes for my wife 0. 6. 0" 5AB, 107	7s. per pair of girl's shoes 6s. for shoes for Amy Pynchon
7 Aug. 1674	John Holton	"Mending shoes Roco and . . . 0. 1. 0" 5AB, 355	1s. for mending shoes
1675		"By mending shoes 18d. Roco's, 2s. my Boots [is] 0. 4. 0" "By 1 pair shooes for Ruth[?] 1 pair for Hester[?] 0. 12. 0" "By 1 pair of shoes for Hanah Bagg 0. 6. 6" 5AB, 491	4s. for mending shoes 6s. per pair of woman's shoes 6s. 6d. per pair of woman's shoes
29 Jun. 1680	John Norton	JP and Norton agree "to make my leather into shoes." JP to provide leather and flax; Norton to do the work and JP to "pay him for 10s, 11s, and 12s, Two shillings a Paire for Plaine shoe: and 2s. 6d. a pair for french heeles; he to take his Pay out of the shoes and french heeles at 8s. 6d. pair and plaine shooes from 10 to 12s at 6s., for womens shoes from 6 to 8 . . . at 6s. a pair"	2s. for making plain shoes, size 10-12 2s. 6d. for making French heels. Takes pay in plain shoes size 10-12 and woman's shoes, sizes 6-8 at 6s., or in French heels at 8s. 6d.
1682		"By shoes mending and etc. 6. 6. 0"	£6 6s. for cobbling
1684		"More by making 24 pair of shooes 2. 17. 6" 5AB, 551	2s. 4d. per pair of shoes

SHOEMAKING AND COBBLING, *cont.*

Date	Name	Service	Rate
24 Nov. 1684		Works for JP at wages of 7s. 6d. per week 6AB, Index, 12	7s. 6d. per week for shoemaking
5 Jan. 1685/86		"By shooes, mending and etc. . . . 9. 3. 0"	£9 3s. for cobbling
1687		"By mending shooes and other things as in John Norton's Booke 3. 7. 0" 5AB, 551	£3 7s. for cobbling
8 Feb. 1687/88	Thomas Day, Jr.	"By 1 pair shoes for John Weathers 0. 8. 6" "By 1 pair shoes for Sue 0. 8. 0" 5AB, 267	8s. 6d. per pair of man's shoes 8s. per pair of woman's shoes
29 Jun. 1691	Ebenezer Parsons	"By shoes mending [and making] 8. 10. 3"	£8 10s. 3d. for cobbling and shoemaking
Sep. 1694		"8. 0. 6" 6AB, 247	£8 6d. for cobbling and shoemaking

SLAUGHTERING, GELDING, AND DRESSING

Date	Name	Service	Rate
1645–1646	Miles Morgan	"Recd of Miles his worke in killing 6 hoggs and 2 goates 0. 1. 0" "For killing 8 hoggs . . . 0. 4. 6" WPAB, 23	1s. for killing hogs and goats 6¾d. per hog killed
30 Oct. 1648		"Killing a cow 0. 1. 8" "Dressing of a bullock 0. 1. 8" "Killing and dressing a sow 0. 0. 8" WPAB, 26	20d. per cow killed 20d. per bullock dressed 8d. per sow killed and dressed

SLAUGHTERING, GELDING, AND DRESSING, *cont.*

Date	Name	Service	Rate
30 Dec. 1648	Thomas Cooper	"½ a day helping about the dressing a bullock that was killed by Francis Ball 0. 0. 10" WPAB, 202	20d. per diem for dressing bullock
15 Aug. 1650	Miles Morgan	"Killing a cow 0. 2. 0" "Killing 2 hoggs 0. 1. 0" "Killing two calves 0. 1. 0" WPAB, 28	2s. per cow killed 6d. per hog killed 6d. per calf killed
26 Apr. 1653	Thomas Cooper	"By dressing 8 bundles of Bever 0. 4. 0" 1AB, 78	6d. per bundle of beaver dressed
14 Dec. 1654	Thomas Stebbins	"By 10 days dressing Bever 1. 0. 0" 1AB, 253.	2s. per diem for dressing beaver
Nov. 1658	Miles Morgan	"Recd by killing an ox . . . 0. 2. 6" 1AB, 266	2s. 6d. per ox killed
May/Jun. 1661		"By killing 5 hogs 0. 3. 4" "By killing 2 calves 0. 1. 4"	8d. per hog killed 8d. per calf killed
17 Jul. 1661		"For killing 2 cows 0. 4. 0" "By killing 10 hoggs 0. 6. 8" 2AB, 131	2s. per cow killed 8d. per hog killed
1661	Thomas Stebbins	"3 days dressing Bever 0. 6. 0" 2AB, 299	2s. per diem for dressing beaver
28 Dec. 1664	Miles Morgan	"By killing 10 swine 0. 6. 8" 2AB, 339	8d. per hog killed
22 Aug. 1665	Samuel Terry	"By killing 5 hoggs 0. 3. 4" 3AB, 145	8d. per hog killed

SLAUGHTERING, GELDING, AND DRESSING, *cont.*

Date	Name	Service	Rate
1660s	Thomas Stebbins	"2 days dressing Bever 0. 4. 0" 3AB, 131	2s. per diem for dressing beaver
23 Mar. 1666/67	Jedediah Strong	"By cutting and docking 3 horses at 3s. 6d. [is] 0. 10. 6"	3s. 6d. per horse gelded and docked
		"By docking a wild Mare in to the bargaine"	Payment for docking a wild mare [shortening the tail]
		"By Blooding 3 Cows 18d."	6d. per cow blooded
		"By spaying 6 Sows 3s."	6d. per sow spayed
10 Apr. 1668		"By Spaying 9 sows and halfe spaying one 0. 5. 0" 3AB, 205	6³⁄₁₀d. per sow spayed
10 Mar. 1668/69	Miles Morgan	"By killing 9 swine 6s., 1 Cow 2s."	8d. per hog killed 2s. per cow killed
		"By cutting severall boares, smale Pigs 0. 1. 6"	1s. 6d. for gelding boars and pigs
		"By killing 2 swine 0. 1. 4" 3AB, 241	8d. per hog killed
12 Mar. 1668/69	Jedediah Strong	"By cutting and docking a horse 0. 3. 6" 3AB, 205	3s. 6d. per horse gelded and docked
15 Nov. 1669	Miles Morgan	"Killing 6 Cattle, Cutting 10 boars, Killing 5 Calves" 3AB, 247	Payment for gelding, killing, cattle and hogs
9 Apr. 1670	Jedediah Strong	"By cutting a horse and spaying 2 Sows 0. 3. 6" 3AB, 205	3s. 6d. for gelding and spaying
28 Nov.–30 Dec. 1670	Miles Morgan	"By killing 3 cattle 0. 7. 6"	2s. 6d. per head of cattle killed
		"By cutting a Bull 0. 1. 6" 5AB, 81	1s. 6d. per bull gelded

SLAUGHTERING, GELDING, AND DRESSING, *cont.*

Date	Name	Service	Rate
1671	Jedediah Strong	"By spaying 8 sows 0. 4. 0" "By spaying 4 smale Piggs 0. 1. 6" 3AB, 205	6d. per sow spayed 4½d. per piglet spayed
21 Feb. 1672/73	John Hitchcock	"By killing 14 hoggs . . . 0. 8. 0" 5AB, 89	7d. per hog killed
23 Jan. 1673/74	Miles Morgan	"By killing 2 calves 0. 1. 0" "By killing a cow 0. 2. 0" "By killing a hog 0. 0. 8" 5AB, 81	6d. per calf killed 2s. per cow killed 8d. per hog killed
1674–1675	Isaac Morgan	"Cutting calves . . . cutting a Bull . . . killing sheep . . . killing 2 cattle . . . killing hoggs" 5AB, 423	Payment for gelding, killing, cattle and hogs
Feb. 1674/75	Miles Morgan	"By killing 1 cow, 3 hogs" "By killing 2 hogs 1s. 4d." 5AB, 81	Payment for killing 1 cow and 3 hogs 8d. per hog killed
1678	Joseph Trumble	"By cutting 26 hoggs now this Spring at 8d. per hogg 1. 5. 9" 5AB, 343	8d. per hog gelded (pays 1s.)

SOAPMAKING

Date	Name	Service	Rate
6 Jul. 1667	Henry Glover	"By 12 firkins of sope at 17s. [is] 10. 4. 0"	17s. per firkin of soap [firkin = 8 gallons]
		"By Goodman Morgan's boate, 3 firkins of sope at 17s. is 2. 11. 0"	17s. per firkin of soap
1668		"To 30 firkins of sope at 17s., one of which is the	17s. per firkin of soap

SOAPMAKING, *cont.*

Date	Name	Service	Rate
		firkin which you are to pay more for Mr. Gilbert, so it is but 29 firkins at 17s. [is] 24. 13. 0"	
Jun. 1670		"By 20 firkins of sope: 4 whereof were broken out the heads and not half full: so I account but 18 firkins which at 16s. [is] 14. 8. 0"	16s. per firkin of soap
1671		"By 10 firkins of sope 8. 0. 0" 3AB, 53	16s. per firkin of soap

STABLING

Date	Name	Service	Rate
13 Oct. 1649	Rowland Thomas	"For Sam keeping Cows for us while they were downe the falls 6 days 0. 10. 0" "Recd in keeping 10 cows, 2. 6. 8" WPAB, 218	20d. per diem for keeping cows £2 6s. 8d. for keeping cows
24 Sep. 1656	Samuel Wright, Jr.	"Recd wintering 2 Horses 24s., one of the horses to your father's account, so it is but one 0. 12. 0"	12s. per winter for stabling horse
Jul. 1657		"Wintering my Mare 0. 12. 0" 1AB, 218	12s. per winter for stabling horse
5 Jul. 1658	James Warrinar	"Recd by payment toward cowkeeping 0. 17. 0" 2AB, 32	17s. for keeping cows
30 Apr. 1659		"By keeping of my Cows is remaining 0. 12. 3" 2AB, 142–143	12s. 3d. for keeping cows

STABLING, *cont.*

Date	Name	Service	Rate
1659	Richard Fellows	"By wintering of 4 cattle at 12d. per weeke, which he had 7 weeks is 7s. for each" 2AB, 95	1s. per week for stabling head of cattle
10 Feb. 1659/60	John Scot and John Henryson	"By wintering Major Hawthorne's horse 0. 5. 0" 2AB, 25	5s. per winter for stabling horse
1667	Elizur Holyoke	"By wintering a sheep 0. 4. 0" 3AB, 43	4s. per winter for stabling sheep
26 Jan. 1666/67	John Petty	"I sent 3 Colts to John Petty to keep till Spring . . . 1. 0. 0" "By wintering a yoake of Steeres at 15s. pce 1. 10. 0" 3AB, 155	6s. 8d. per winter for stabling colt 15s. per winter for stabling steer
1666–67?	Rowland Thomas	"By keeping 5 horses in the spring at 8d. per week 0. 8. 8" 3AB, 197	8d. per week for stabling horse in spring
1667?	Zachariah Field	"By wintering 4 horses, 6 weeks at 12d. per weeke, each horse is 1. 4. 0" 3AB, 7	1s. per week for stabling horse
20 Sep. 1667	James Kellogg	"Agreed with James Kellog to winter my 2 horses at 15s. peice, which he [is to] take care of as his own 1. 10. 0" 3AB, 281	15s. per winter for stabling horse
1670	John Keepe	"By keeping 2 young heifers from March 14 to April 14 at 8d. per weeke 0. 5. 4" 3AB, 67	8d. per week for stabling heifer

STABLING, cont.

Date	Name	Service	Rate
1670	John Dumbleton	"By wintering 3 bullocks winter 1670 [is] 2. 0. 0" 5AB, 51	13s. 4d. per winter for stabling bullock
Dec. 1670	John Petty	"By 3 cattle wintering 2. 5. 0"	15s. per winter for stabling head of cattle
		"By 1 yerling wintering 0. 10. 0" 5AB, 63	10s. per winter for stabling yearling
29 Dec. 1670	George Colton	"By 5 cattle wintering almost 5 weeks 1. 2. 6" 5AB, 147	1s. per week for stabling head of cattle
13 Jan. 1670/71	Samuel Ely	"By wintering 3 cattle a month last yeare 0. 12. 0" 5AB, 151	4s. per month for stabling head of cattle
24 Jan. 1670/71	James Taylor	"By wintering and breaking my white horse and the sorrel horse at 3s. piece [per week?] 3. 0. 0" 5AB, 55	30s. per winter for breaking [to saddle, plow, both?] and stabling horse
29 Apr. 1671	Rowland Thomas	"By keeping horses . . . in winter 8 weeks at 6s. per horse 1. 10. 0" 5AB, 15	15s. per winter for stabling horse
1671	John Dumbleton	"By wintering 2 steere now let to Goodman Taylor, and by wintering 2 calves sent the other day keeping until Spring 2. 10. 0" 5AB, 51	£2 10s. for stabling steers and calves
31 Jan. 1671/72	John Petty	"By wintering 3 cattle winter 1671 at 14s. [is] 2. 2. 0"	14s. per winter for stabling head of cattle
		"By part wintering a mare 0. 5. 0"	5s. for stabling mare part of winter

STABLING, *cont.*

Date	Name	Service	Rate
1673		"By wintering 2 cattle ano 1673 (the other 2 wintering went on the Bargaine of the farme)" 5AB, 63	Payment for stabling 2 cattle
1674	John Dumble-ton	"By wintering 3 cattle 1 year, and 2, another 5; only I wintered one of yours . . . 3. 10. 0" 5AB, 51	£3 10s. for stabling cattle
1674–1675	John Allyn	"By wintering 2 Mares and a Colt at Pacomtuck Winter 1. 4. 0" 3AB, 231	24s. for stabling horses
10 Mar. 1674/75	George Colton	"By wintering 3 cattle 2. 5. 0" 5AB, 147	15s. per winter for stabling head of cattle
1675	John Petty	"By wintering 3 cattle ano 1675 [is] 1. 16. 0"	12s. per winter for stabling head of cattle
		"Cattle ano 1676 [is] 0. 6. 0" 5AB, 63	6s. for stabling cattle
Feb. 1675/76	Edward Foster	"By wintering 2 beasts, viz. a hereford and a calfe; your being to keep them out all the winter 1. 0. 0"	10s. per winter for keeping head of cattle
Jan. 1676/77		"By wintering a steer . . . 0. 12. 0" 5AB, 59	12s. per winter for stabling steer
1 Jul. 1678	Obadiah Cooley	"By wintering 4 head cattle, 3. 0. 0." 5AB, 195	15s. per winter for stabling head of cattle

STABLING, cont.

Date	Name	Service	Rate
1681	Nathaniel Burt	"By winter feeding a yoake of cattle £5, and Summer feeding them £2 [is] 7. 0. 0" 5AB, 155	£5 for winter feeding yoke of steers £2 for summer feeding yoke of steers
1 Dec. 1681	Nathaniel Bliss, Jr.	"By keeping my steers a fortnight and yoaking them 0. 8. 0" 5AB, 35	4s. per week for stabling and breaking oxen to yoke

STONEMASONRY

Date	Name	Service	Rate
1648	Rowland Thomas	"Recd 24 load of stones for my sellre at 20d., but he allows of 2 load more because he had 20 load; all is 26 load 3. 0. 0" WPAB, 155	20d. per load of cellar stones (pays 28d.)
13 Oct. 1649		"Recd in fetching some stones from the upper falls 0. 4. 5" WPAB, 218	4s. 5d. for carting stones from upper falls
6 Jan. 1653/54		"Recd by putting stones under my cobhouse 0. 0. 6" 1AB, 74	6d. for underpinning cob house
10 Oct. 1656		"Recd by Stones for Griffith Joane's Tanning 0. 13. 9" 1AB, 236	13s. 9d. for stones
1659	Thomas Bascomb and son	"By 14 days worke himself and son 2. 16. 0" "By 15 days worke hewing stones for me 2. 10. 0" 2AB, 149	4s. per diem for stonemasonry, father and son 3s. 4d. per diem for hewing stones

STONEMASONRY, *cont.*

Date	Name	Service	Rate
1660	Rowland Thomas	"By 50 load of Stone from the hither stone place at 15d. per load 3. 2. 6" "2 days almost about underpinning and daubing 0. 3. 6" "By getting stones, 100 load from the sixteen acres, Stone at 12d. per load is 5. 0. 0" 2AB, 159	15d. per load of stones from hither stone quarry 2s. per diem for stonemasonry 1s. per load of stones from Sixteen Acres
9 Sep. 1660	Thomas Bascomb and son	"By 18 days worke hewing stone 3. 12. 0" "By 18 days your son 2. 5. 0" 2AB, 149	4s. per diem for hewing stones 2s. 6d. per diem for youth's hewing stones
1661	Edward Griswald of Windsor	"By hewing stone and etc., 3 days 0. 4. 0" 2AB, 237	16d. per diem for hewing stones
3 Apr. 1663	Thomas Bascomb and son	"By worke hewing and Carying stone: my kitchin floore, hearth, and etc., 18 days himself at 4s. per day 4. 12. 0 [and] 12 days his son at 2s. 6d. [is] 1. 10. 0" 2AB, 149	4s. per diem for adult's hewing and carting stones 2s. 6d. for youth's hewing and carting stones
16 Nov. 1663	Rowland Thomas	"By 10 load of stone 0. 10. 0" 2AB, 159	1s. per load of stones
23 Nov. 1663	Thomas Bascomb	"Recd by his worke to the last day of November, 19 days, that is to say with this week £3 16s. So I shall owe Goodm Bascomb if he worke out this week 25s." "There's more due for his owne and Son's work, 6 days—19s. 6d. So all is £2	4s. per diem for stonemasonry £2 4s. for stonemasonry, father and son

STONEMASONRY, *cont.*

Date	Name	Service	Rate
		4s. -d." [paid in cotton cloth] 2AB, 148	
21 Dec. 1664	Rowland Thomas	"By 8 days worke in orchard and underpinning 1. 0. 0" 3AB, 159	2s. 6d. per diem for stonemasonry
Mid-1660s		"By worke at Westfeild for my son Whiting, 24 days the first about getting stone, and 20 days when stonning the cellar . . . 63 days worke in all at 65 days for loss in goeing and coming at 2s. 6d. [is] 8. 2. 6"	2s. 6d. per diem for stonemasonry
		"By 36 load of stone (besides) at 12d. [is] 1. 16. 0" 3AB, 197	1s. per load of stones
1665	Nathaniel Pritchard	"By 6 load of Stones at 4s. 6d. [is] 1. 7. 0" 3AB, 97	4s. 6d. per load of stones
28 Nov. 1665	Rowland Thomas	"By worke underpinning the Cowhouse 0. 0. 8" 3AB, 159	8d. for underpinning cow house
24 Apr. 1667	Thomas Bascomb	"By worke as above in Bakerfeld about stones 4 days at 3s. 6d. [is] 0. 14. 3" "Recd as above for worke for the Prison house 3. 9. 0" 3AB, 4	3s. 6d. per diem for stonemasonry £3 9s. for stonemasonry for house of correction
Apr. 1667?		"To 8 weeks worke and halfe, is 51 days, In how many letting days, I suppose all may be 48 days Current"	Payment for 48 days stonemasonry

STONEMASONRY, *cont.*

Date	*Name*	*Service*	*Rate*
1667?		"By Mr. Glover, 18 days Qx done of the days you workt for . . . 8. 8. 0"	£8 8s. for stonemasonry
		"By 24 days worke, the 2d Tyme at 22 days 3. 17. 0" 3AB, 35	3s. 6d. per diem for stonemasonry
4 Jan. 1667/68	Joseph Warrinar	"By 3 days digging stones at Bancroft's Lot 0. 10. 6" 3AB, 132	3s. 6d. per diem for stonemasonry
1 Mar. 1667/68	Rowland Thomas	"By worke about stones (besides your weekes allowance for and etc.) 0. 1. 3" 3AB, 159	15d. for stonemasonry
10 Oct. 1668	Thomas Bascomb	"By 44 days worke at my mill house to this 24th of Nov. 1668 at 3s. 6d. per day [is] 7. 14. 0" 3AB, 35	3s. 6d. per diem for stonemasonry
19 Apr. 1669	Rowland Thomas	"By digging stones 1. 4. 0" 3AB, 159	24s. for digging stones
15 Nov. 1669	Thomas Bascomb	"By worke for Mr. Whiting about stoning his cellar and chimny in all to this 15th Nov. 1669, 35 days at 3s. 6d. [is] 6. 2. 6" 3AB, 35	3s. 6d. per diem for stonemasonry
Late 1660s	Rowland Thomas (and son Joseph)	"By 10 days about the well and 10 days Joseph 2. 1. 0" 3AB, 197	£2 1s. for stonemasonry
Jul.–Nov. 1671	Rowland Thomas	"By 1 day underpining my old Parler 0. 2. 6"	2s. 6d. per diem for underpinning parlor
29 Dec. 1671		"By underpinning my litle Room 0. 3. 9"	3s. 9d. for underpinning small room

STONEMASONRY, cont.

Date	Name	Service	Rate
		"By 5 days ½ underpinning Mr. Glover's house 0. 13. 9" 5AB, 15	2s. 6d. per diem for underpinning
11 Mar. 1674/75	James Stevenson	"By 9 load of stones to the wharfe and 6 load at Pacosuck . . . This according to Ben Knowlton . . . your halfe is 0. 13. 6" "By 6 load of stone . . . your halfe is 0. 3. 9" 5AB, 321	21½d. per load of stones 15d. per load of stones
Jun.–Jul. 1675	Thomas Bascomb	"22 days working with stones at 3s. 6d. [is] 3. 17. 0" 3AB, 35	3s. 6d. per diem for stonemasonry
1678	Benjamin Parsons	"By 20 load of Stones to my Mill from Smale Brooke 3. 15. 0" 5AB, 413	3s. 9d. per load of stones from Small Brook
1679	Robert Old of Suffield	"Worke about Suffeild Mill stonning the house and . . . 15 days at 5s." 5AB, 445	5s. per diem for stonemasonry

SURVEYING

Date	Name	Service	Rate
1645	Samuel Hubbard	"Recd in measuring 26 acres of ground in the Long meadow, his half is 0. 1. 1" WPAB, 75	1d. per acre for surveying
29 Dec. 1664	Nathaniel Ely	"By measuring 130 acres of land at freshwater brooke 0. 12. 0" 3AB, 109	9/10d. per acre for surveying

SURVEYING, *cont.*

Date	Name	Service	Rate
21 Apr. 1668		"By 1 day to measure land at Woronoak 0. 3. 0"	3s. per diem for surveying
		"By measuring land at Mill River 0. 3. 4" 3AB, 199	3s. 4d. for surveying
1671	Corporal Richard Coy	"By measuring out my Land, 50 acres and one 3d part of . . . 0. 10. 0" 5AB, 327	10s. for surveying

TAILORING

Date	Name	Service	Rate
31 Jan. 1645/46	William Vaughan	"Recd in Taylery work, himself and his wife making Some cloathes 0. 3. 0"	3s. for tailoring by both husband and wife
		"Making 10 Indian coates 0. 15. 0"	18d. per Indian coat
		"More 10 days worke himself, and . . . Sam 0. 15. 0"	18d. per diem for tailoring by both father and son
		"Recd 8 pair Stockens, Recd 16 pair Stockens . . . 1646 . . . more 2 dozen pair stockens 0. 7. 0"	21d. per dozen pair of stockings
		"Recd 6 days worke himself and Son 0. 9. 0" WPAB, 112	18d. per diem for tailoring by both father and son
25 Jul. 1646	John Dible	"Recd 3 Coates making 0. 4. 6"	18d. per coat
		"Recd 2 coats this 26 July 1646 [is] 0. 3. 0"	18d. per coat
		"2 caps 0. 1. 0" WPAB, 77	6d. per cap
16 Oct. 1646	William Vaughan	"Recd 44 Coates at 18d. [is] 3. 6. 8"	18d. per coat
		"For a wastecoate makeing 0. 1. 0"	1s. per waistcoat

TAILORING, *cont.*

Date	Name	Service	Rate
		"Recd 9 days worke himself and 9 days Sam 0. 15. 0"	20d. per diem for tailoring by both father and son
		"More 1 day himself 0. 1. 0"	1s. per diem for tailoring
		"More Recd 4 days himselfe and 1 Sam 0. 1. 8[?]"	Payment for 5 days tailoring
30 Oct. 1646		"[26½ days] 0. 17. 6"	8d. per diem for tailoring
		"Recd 10 Coate 0. 15. 0"	18d. per coat
27 Nov. 1646		"Recd 27 Coates at 18d. [is] 2. 0. 6"	18d. per coat
		"Recd 28 [0?] coates . . . 18. 8. 0"	£18 8s. for coats
		"5 coates, 10 capps 0. 18. 6"	18s. 6d. for coats and caps
		"13 capps 0. 6. 0" WPAB, 112	5½d. per cap
15 Jun. 1647		"Recd 9 caps at 6d. [is] 0. 4. 6"	6d. per cap
		"Recd 8 coates 0. 12. 0" WPAB, 146	18d. per coat
20 Mar. 1647/48?	Thomas Stebbins	"Recd making 4 dozen ½ wastcoates at 8d. [is] 1. 16. 0"	8d. per waistcoat
		"8 dozen pair of stockens . . . 2. 0. 0"	5s. per dozen pair of stockings
		"8 pair childrens stockens at 2s. 6d. per dozen 0. 1. -"	2s. 6d. per dozen pair of children's stockings
		"Recd 8 days work taylering 0. 8. 0"	1s. per diem for tailoring
29 Mar. 1648		"For making 2 coates at 18d. and 1 at 16d. [is] 0. 2. 10" WPAB, 139	16d. and 18d. per coat

TAILORING, *cont.*

Date	Name	Service	Rate
30 Jun. 1648	Samuel Marshfield	"Recd 25 days worke Taylering ... abate 12d. [is] 1. 4. 0" WPAB, 182	1s. per diem for tailoring
1 Nov. 1648	Thomas Stebbins	"Making a divinity sute for Sam 0. 3. 0"	3s. for divinity suit
		"Making 7 caps green kersey laced 0. 7. 0"	1s. per cap, green kersey laced
		"Making 1 dozen and 3 pair of stockens 0. 6. 0"	4s. 10d. per dozen pair of stockings
		"5 days Taylering 0. 5. 0"	1s. per diem for tailoring
		"Recd in making 3 dozen and 3 wastcoates, 6 of them being Red, the rest white cotton at 8s. per dozen 1. 6. 0"	8s. per dozen cotton waistcoats, red and white
		"Recd heming 12 straight coates and 2 pair brechers 0. 2. 6" WPAB, 200	2s. 6d. for tailoring
21 Apr. 1649	Samuel Marshfield	"Recd 11 days worke in Taylering 0. 11. 0" WPAB, 182	1s. per diem for tailoring
2 May 1650	Thomas Stebbins	"Recd ... 17 Red Coates, 20 blew Coates, 12 white Coates, 8 Red coates, in all 57 coates [is] 4. 15. 0"	20d. per coat
24 Aug. 1650		"2 blue wastecoats 0. 1. 0"	6d. per waistcoat
		"6 wastecoates 0. 4. 0" WPAB, 214	8d. per waistcoat
28 Aug. 1652		"By making 12 wastecoates 0. 8. 0"	8d. per waistcoat
		"By 10 dozen of Caps, at 6s. per dozen 3. 0. 0"	6s. per dozen caps
		"By 11 dozen and 9 of wastecotes at 8d. [is] 4. 14. 0"	8d. per waistcoat

TAILORING, *cont.*

Date	Name	Service	Rate
		"By 4 Coate and 3 smale coate 0. 10. 0"	10s. for coats
		"By 3 dozen and 1 Coate 3. 2. 0"	19d. per coat
		"By 1 dozen stockens . . . 0. 5. 0"	5s. per dozen pair of stockings
		"By 3 days mending harness 0. 5. 0"	20d. per diem for mending harness
		"2 days Taylering 0. 2. 0" 1AB, 91	1s. per diem for tailoring
1653	Samuel Marshfield	"Recd by Taylery Worke at about 4. 4. 4"	£4 4s. 4d. for tailoring
		"Recd by more Taylery worke, and several days worke, in all 2. 6. 4" 1AB, 108	£2 6s. 4d. for tailoring
14 Dec. 1654	Thomas Stebbins	"Recd by making 3 dozen coates 3. 5. 0"	22d. per coat
		"Recd by 11 dozen of wastecoates 4. 8. 0"	8d. per waistcoat
		"By 6 dozen and 4 caps 1. 18. 0"	6d. per cap
		"Recd by Taylery worke, mending, Saddlry 0. 16. 0" 1AB, 253	16s. for tailoring and mending tack
1 Oct. 1656		"Recd by making Indian Coats and wastecotes and caps 12. 5. 8" 1AB, 254	£12 5s. 8d. for making waistcoats and caps for Indian trade
9 Oct. 1656	Thomas Noble	"Recd by Taylering as in Thomas Noble's booke 8. 6. 6"	£8 6s. 6d. for tailoring
		"Recd more by Taylering as in Thomas Noble his booke, all this work being accounted 2. 18. 6" 1AB, 317	£2 18s. 6d. for tailoring

TAILORING, *cont.*

Date	Name	Service	Rate
20 Nov. 1658		"By Taylery worke to this 20th Apr. 1659 [is] 10. 11. 2" 2AB, 97	£10 11s. 2d. for tailoring
1661	Thomas Stebbins	"By making drawers 2 pair 0. 2. 0" "By 1 Pettycote making 0. 1. 6" "4 days worke Taylering 0. 5. 0" 2AB, 299	1s. per pair of drawers 18d. per petticoat 15d. per diem for tailoring
Jul. 1662	Thomas Noble	"By worke Taylering as in Thomas Noble's Booke . . . 23. 0. 2" 2AB, 333	£23 2d. for tailoring
Dec. 1663		"By work Taylering in Thomas Noble's Booke 5. 17. 8" "By more worke Taylering 0. 13. 8" 3AB, 135	£5 17s. 8d. for tailoring 13s. 8d. for tailoring
1660s	Thomas Stebbins	"Mending Harness 2 days 0. 4. 0" "8 days Taylering at 18d. [is] 0. 12. 0" "3 pair drawers making 0. 3. 0" "Making John Holden's leather breeches 0. 2. 0" "3 pair and else 0. 3. 0" "Making 3 men's wastcotes 0. 4. 0" "2 Petticotes for Miriam [Waite] 0. 1. 6" "9 pair Stockens 0. 4. 6" "By making my wife's Petticote 1. 0. 0"	2s. per diem for mending harness 18d. per diem for tailoring 1s. per pair of drawers 2s. for pair of leather breeches 3s. for tailoring 16d. per waistcoat 9d. per petticoat 6d. per pair of stockings 20s. per petticoat for Amy Pynchon

TAILORING, cont.

Date	Name	Service	Rate
		"Making 2 worsteds 0. 2. 0"	1s. per worsted
		"Drawers 0. 1. 0"	1s. per pair of drawers
		"Indian wastcotes 0. 1. 6" 3AB, 131	18d. for making waistcoats
1666	Joseph Warrinar	"By making Rich's sute 4s."	4s. per suit
		"By making my wife's silk Peticote 0. 3. 0"	3s. per silk petticoat
		"Making John Holden's Jacket 3s." 3AB, 133	3s. per jacket
16 Mar. 1668/69	"John Waite the Taylor"	Dr. "To 200 Needles 0. 5. 0"	2s. 6d. per 100 needles
		"To 100 best Needles 0. 2. 6"	2s. 6d. per 100 "best" needles
		"By 9 days worke, and 9 days is 18 days at 2s. 9d. [is] 2. 9. 6"	2s. 9d. per diem for tailoring
		"By 2 days each Comeing and Goeing" 3AB, 31	Payment for 4 days travel time
1669	Thomas Noble	"By worke Taylering as in Thomas Noble's Book, the particulars to the Sum of 8. 13. 3" 3AB, 137	£8 13s. 3d. for tailoring
27 Dec. 1669	Joseph Warrinar	Dr. "Tayler's Sheeres, Buttons, and Gallome 0. 3. 6" 3AB, 132.	3s. 6d. for tailor's tools
27 Nov. 1671	Thomas Stebbins, Jr.	"By worke Taylering and etc., all to the 20th of December 1671 [is] 9. 16. 4" 5AB, 163	£9 16s. 4d. for tailoring
7 Aug. 1672	Thomas Noble	"By worke Taylering (of old) as in Goodman No-	£2 18s. for tailoring

TAILORING, *cont.*

Date	Name	Service	Rate
		ble's Booke 2. 18. 0" 5AB, 221	
1679	Thomas Remmington of Suffield	"By 13 days Taylering at 2s. [is] 1. 6. 0" "By 9 days Taylering 0. 18. 0" "By worke making drawers 0. 1. 6" 5AB, 487	2s. per diem for tailoring 2s. per diem for tailoring 1s. 6d. for making drawers

TANNING

Date	Name	Service	Rate
7 Feb. 1662/63	Griffith Jones	"By Tanning 16 ox hides at 14s., 9 Cow hides at 8s. [is] 14. 16. 0" 2AB, 173	14s. per ox hide tanned 8s. per cow hide tanned
16 Dec. 1664–30 Oct. 1667	Returne Strong	"Dressing 13 hides and 2 small ones 7. 0. 0" "Dressing a horse skine 0. 5. 0" "By dressing 5 hides 3. 17. 0" "By taning 4 hides and a horse skin and a small hide 2. 1. 0" "By taning 6 hides 2. 1. 0" "By taning 3 hides 1. 16. 0" "By taning a horse skin 0. 5. 0" "By taning 5 hides 3. 17. 0" "By taning 7 hides 5. 0. 0" "By taning 3 hides 2. 2. 0" "There are 4 hides that are allmost redy that will come	£7 for dressing hides 5s. per horse hide dressed 15s. 5d. per hide dressed £2 1s. for tanning hides 3s. 6d. per hide tanned 12s. per hide tanned 5s. per horse hide tanned 15s. 5d. per hide tanned 14s. 3d. per [ox?] hide tanned 14s. per [ox?] hide tanned 14s. or 15s. per [ox?] hide tanned

TANNING, *cont.*

Date	Name	Service	Rate
		to 14 or 15 shillings apese, if you please to pay it what is coming to me now; Cr . . . Gilbert, I owe him 7 pounds, he calls very hard for it. I would intreat you to pay it to with speade" 3AB, 219½	
9 Dec. 1667	Thomas Day	"To 6 smale hides at Jonathan [Gilbert's] warehouse which I gave a note this 9 Dec. 1667 for you to call for them and Rec them all at 3. 10. 0"	11s. 8d. per small hide
8 Jun. 1668		"To 3 hides by Returne Strong delivered to Goodman Morgan, Thomas Day to pay for them in good wheat sometime next winter 5. 2. 0" 3AB, 150	34s. per [ox?] hide
Nov. 1668	John Strong, Jr.	"By leather to Symon Lobdell 4. 18. 0" 3AB, 209	£4 18s. for leather
19 Nov. 1668	John Strong, Sr. (from Symon Lobdell's debit account)	"To a Moose hide Elder Strong Tanned (which you say is the best of all) and yet I sell it to you for 0. 14. 0"	14s. per moose hide
		"To 3 hides of Sole leather from Goodm Ford's 5. 10. 0"	£1 16s. 8d. per hide of sole leather
		"To a parsell of leather from Elder Strong's 4. 18. 0"	£4 18s. for leather
		"To a parsell of Leather of mine from New London 14. 9. 0"	£14 9s. for leather

TANNING, *cont.*

Date	Name	Service	Rate
		"Q 10 Hides come to about £14 9s." 3AB, 12	28s. 10d. per hide
26 Mar. 1669	John Scot	"By a hide weigh . . . 49 pounds" "By a dry hide 20s. and ½ at 6d. per pound is 0. 10. 3" 3AB, 189	Payment for a 49-pound hide 6d. per pound of dry hide tanned
21 Aug. 1669	John Strong, Sr.	"These were Hides which Elder Strong Tand of mine . . . To 4 hides at 24s. pce, 1 ox hide 36s., the Bull hide 27s. [is] 7. 19. 0" "To a Smale hide Torne with wolves 0. 5. 0" "To a parcel of leather came from New London viz., 5 sole leather hides at about 30s. piece, 5 uppers leather, 2 of them at 40s., 3 of them about 10s. piece, all at 11. 10. 0"	24s. per hide 36s. per ox hide 27s. per bull hide 5s. per torn hide 30s. per hide of sole leather 40s. per hide 10s. per uppers hide
11 Oct. 1669		"To payment for a parcel of Leather to Mr. Haughton £16 6s. 0d. on which you are to allow me 20s. all is £17 6s." 3AB, 290	£17 6s. for leather
20 Nov. 1669	John Scot	"This November 20, my wife says the account brought a hide of about 30 pounds; But it was so holy it [was worth but] 4s. [is] 0. 4. 0" 3AB, 189	4s. for a damaged hide

TANNING, *cont.*

Date	Name	Service	Rate
1660s or 1670s	Symon Lobdell	"By a hide 42 pounds to Mr. Haughton [?] 0. 10. 6" 3AB, 291	3d. per pound for [green?] hide
5 May 1670	John Strong, Sr.	"1 Sole leather hide 49 or 50s. and uppers leather hides from Elder Strong you say 4. 16. 0" 3AB, 290	49s. or 50s. for hide of sole leather 23s. for uppers hide
20 Mar. 1670/71		"By Taning 6 and 8 Moose hides at 5s. [is] 3. 10. 0" "By Taning 2 hides, 1 11s. 6d., a smale hide 2s. 6d. . . . 1. 14. 0" "Taning 4 hides 2. 8. 0" "Taning 3 great ox hides 3. 10. 0" "And 2 Cow hides 1. 4. 6"	5s. per moose hide tanned 34s. for tanning 12s. per hide tanned 23s. 4d. per ox hide tanned 12s. 3d. per cow hide tanned
May 1671		"By Taning per agreement (ox hides at 13s. and Cow hide at 8s. apiece), 7 sole hides at 13s. pce is £4 11s. and 9 upper leather hides at 8s. is 3. 12. 0 [all is] 8. 3. 0" "By 1 horse hide which you say is now ready 0. 8. 0" 3AB, 209	13s. per ox hide tanned 8s. per cow hide tanned 8s. per upper hide tanned 8s. per horse hide
Dec. 1685	Thomas Sweatman	"By Tanning and Currying 1 hide . . . 0. 19. 6" "By Tanning and Currying 4 hides Goodman Norton had 3. 4. 6" 6AB, 171	19s. 6d. per hide tanned and curried 16s. 1d. per hide tanned and curried

THATCHING

Date	Name	Service	Rate
1652	John Lumbard	"2 days thatching, 1 day thatching 0. 4. 0" 1AB, 135	16d. per diem for thatching
Jan. 1652/53	John Stiles of Windsor	"Recd by 6 days thatching ... yourselfe and son my cowhouse and Barne 1. 0. 0"	3s. 4d. per diem for thatching by both father and son
5 Nov. 1655		"Recd by thatching 24 days himself at 2s." "And your son 24 days at 20d. [is] 2. 0. 0"	2s. per diem for thatching 20d. per diem for youth's thatching
16 Dec. 1657		"Agreed with John Stiles of Windsor to thatch my barne over the great River (which Goodman Barber is to build); I am only to lay the thatch in place and he [is] to doe all the other worke [well and substantial and workmanlike for] five pounds Ten shillings; and Thatching to be done [before] English harvest next" 1AB, 151	£5 10s. for thatching barn
1658–1659		"By getting Thatch for my Barne over the River about 17 or 18 day and about pressing Cyder 1 day ½ all is 19 days worke 2. 0. 0" 2AB, 91	2s. per diem for getting thatch
1659–1660	Nathaniel Pritchard	"By 3 days almost getting Thatch 0. 5. 4" 2AB, 107	2s. per diem for thatching
Jan. 1663/64	Benjamin Parsons	"By ½ day Thatching 0. 1. 0" 3AB, 95	2s. per diem for thatching

THRESHING AND WINNOWING GRAINS, BREAKING FLAX

Date	Name	Service	Rate
14 Apr. 1646	James Osborne	"Recd 5 days threshing 0. 6[?] 0" WPAB, 32	Payment for 5 days threshing
5 Feb. 1652/53	Benjamin Cooley	"By fanning and cleaning Corne [1 day] 0. 2. 0" 1AB, 131	2s. per diem for fanning and cleaning wheat
20 Mar. 1657	James Osborne	"6 days threshing" 1AB, 249	Payment for 6 days threshing
Nov. 1659	Francis Pepper	"By threshing and cleaning 180 bushels of wheat at 5d. per bushel is 3. 17. 3" "By threshing and cleaning bushels Pease 1. 5. 3" "By 56 bushels ½ of oates and cleaning them out at 2d. ½ per bushel 0. 11. 8" 2AB, 227	5d. per bushel for threshing and cleaning wheat (pays 6½d.) £1 5s. 3d. for threshing and cleaning peas 2½d. per bushel for threshing and cleaning oats
1660	Benjamin Mun	"By fanning 36 bushels of wheate at 1d. per [bushel] 0. 4. 6" "Fanning of oates and winnowing of wheat [at] 18d. [per diem] 0. 5. 4" 2AB, 63	1d. per bushel for fanning wheat (pays 1½d.) 18d. per diem for fanning oats and winnowing wheat
1660	Francis Pepper	"By threshing and cleaning of 126 [?] bushels of winter wheate at 6d. per bushel, and 55 bushels of Summer wheate at . . . per bushel 4. 2. 0" "By threshing and cleaning oates and Pease . . . 1. 13. 0"	6d. per bushel for threshing and cleaning winter wheat (pays 4⅖d.) 33s. for threshing and cleaning oats and peas
1661		"By threshing and cleaning 50 bushels and ½ of wheate at 5d. per bushel,	5d. per bushel for threshing and cleaning wheat

THRESHING AND WINNOWING GRAINS, BREAKING FLAX, *cont.*

Date	Name	Service	Rate
		and 140 bushels of oates and Pease at 2d. ½ [is] 2. 10. 2"	2½d. per bushel for threshing and cleaning oats and peas
1662		"By Threshing and cleaning 139 bushels wheat at 5d. [is] 2. 17. 11"	5d. per bushel for threshing and cleaning wheat
		"By Threshing and cleaning 69 bushels Pease, 110 bushels oates, 20 Barley 199 at 2d. ½ per bushel 2. 1. 6" 2AB, 227	2½d. per bushel for threshing and cleaning peas, oats, and barley
20 Jan. 1664/65		"I owe Frances for threshing and cleaning 229 bushels of wheat at 5d. per bushel . . . 4. 14. 0"	5d. per bushel for threshing and cleaning wheat
		"Threshing and cleaning oates and Pease 17 bushels at 2d. ½ per bushel 1. 18. _" 2AB, 229	2½d. per bushel for threshing and cleaning oats and peas
1666	John Keepe	"By fanning wheate 5 days 0. 10. 0"	2s. per diem for fanning wheat
		"Fanning Barley and oates 4 days 0. 8. 0" 3AB, 67	2s. per diem for fanning oats and barley
20 Feb. 1668/69	Benjamin Parsons	"By 30 pounds of flax 1. 10. 0" 3AB, 95	1s. per pound of flax
Nov. 1670	James Osborne	"By 6 days Threshing last winter"	Payment for 6 days threshing
1 Feb. 1670/71		"3 days threshing accounted" 3AB, 101	Payment for 3 days threshing

THRESHING AND WINNOWING GRAINS, BREAKING FLAX, *cont.*

Date	Name	Service	Rate
1675–1681	Miles Morgan	"Swingling 10 pounds flax" 5AB, 489	Payment for swingling 10 pounds of flax
1677	Francis Pepper	"By 12 days threshing 0. 16. 0" 5AB, 159	16d. per diem for threshing
26 Dec. 1681	Benjamin Knowlton	"Agreed with Benjamin Knowlton well to Brake and swingle 60 pounds of flax at 3d. per yard and I am to pay [15s.]" 5AB, 415	3d. per yard for breaking and swingling flax
8 Feb. 1683/84	Richard Waite	"By Swingling 5 pounds of flax . . . 0. 1. 3" 6AB, 75	3d. per pound for swingling flax

WAMPUM STRINGING

Date	Name	Service	Rate
1645	Josias Moxon	"Recd by Josias stringing 52 fadam and ½ of wampum" "Recd by Josias stringing 93 fadam . . . 0. [?].7" WPAB, 5	Payment for stringing 52½ fathoms of wampum Payment for stringing 71 fathoms of wampum
15 Nov. 1645	Henry Burt	"Recd by the stringing of 71 fatham of wampam at 1d. . . . 0. 8. 10" WPAB, 88	1d. per fathom of wampum strung (pays 1½d.)
1645–1648	Henry Smith	"Recd by stringing 112 fadam 0. 14. 0" WPAB, 11	1½d. per fathom of wampum strung
15 Jul. 1647	Henry Burt	"Stringing 326 fadam wampam at 1d. [is] 2. 0. 9" WPAB, 90	1d. per fathom of wampum strung (pays 1½d.)

WAMPUM STRINGING, *cont.*

Date	Name	Service	Rate
19 Apr. 1648		"Due to him for stringing 461 fadam of wampam at 1d. . . . 2. 17. 0" WPAB, 159	1d. per fathom of wampum strung (pays 1½d.)
1648	John Stebbins	"Recd in stringing 404 fadam wampam 2. 10. 6" WPAB, 185	1½d. per fathom of wampum strung
3 Jan. 1648/49	Josias Moxon	"Recd in Josias stringing wampam 277 fadam and ½ at 1d. [is] 1. 14. 9" WPAB, 206	1d. per fathom of wampum strung (pays 1½d.)
Jun.–Dec. 1649	John Stebbins	"404 fadam wampan" WPAB, 250	Payment for stringing 404 fathoms of wampum
16 Nov. 1649	Henry Burt	"46 fadam" WPAB, 251	Payment for stringing 46 fathoms of wampum
12 Dec. 1649		"Recd in stringing 96 fadam wampam . . . 0. 22 [?] 0" WPAB, 193	Payment for stringing 96 fathoms of wampum
21 Mar. 1649/50	Benjamin Stebbins (son of John)	"Measured of Benjamin stringing 79 fadam"	Payment for stringing 79 fathoms of wampum
30 Mar. 1650		"35 fadam"	Payment for stringing 35 fathoms of wampum
		15 Jul. 1650 "11 fadam" WPAB, 245	Payment for stringing 11 fathoms of wampum
30 Mar. 1650	John Stebbins	"Recd in stringing . . . 225 fadam and ½ at . . . 1. 8. 4" WPAB, 243	1½d. per fathom of wampum strung

WAMPUM STRINGING, *cont.*

Date	Name	Service	Rate
1650		"Recd of John Stebbins stringing this day [15 May 1650] . . . I measured his wampam, and it is 162 fadam"	Payment for stringing 162 fathoms of wampum
		"Recd the 21 May 1650, I measured 70 fadam"	Payment for stringing 70 fathoms of wampum
		"June 12, blue wampam 66 fadam"	Payment for stringing 66 fathoms of wampum
		"June the 18, white wampum 181 fadam"	Payment for stringing 181 fathoms of wampum
		"July 12, 1650 . . . 89½"	Payment for stringing 89½ fathoms of wampum
		"July 15, 16" WPAB, 245	Payment for stringing 16 fathoms of wampum
1650	Benjamin Smith	"316 fadam	Payment for stringing 316 fathoms of wampum
	Goodman Burt	"273 fadam"	Payment for stringing 273 fathoms of wampum
	Benjamin Smith	"186 fadam"	Payment for stringing 186 fathoms of wampum
	Josiah Moxon	"154 fadam"	Payment for stringing 154 fathoms of wampum
	Goodman Burt	"35½ fadam" WPAB, 260–261	Payment for stringing 35½ fathoms of wampum
6 Feb. 1651/52	Henry Burt	"Recd by stringing wampam, in all to this 6 Feb. 1651, Just 1251 fadam . . . [is] 7. 16. 4½" WPAB, 193	1½d. per fathom of wampum strung

WAMPUM STRINGING, *cont.*

Date	Name	Service	Rate
1652		"Recd by Stringing 969 fadam of wampum last summer at 1d. per fadam is 6. 1. 1" 1AB, 114	1d. per fathom of wampum strung (pays 1½d.)
12 Feb. 1652/53	John Stebbins	"Recd by stringing 117 fadam and ½ of wampam at 1d. ½ per fad 0. 14. 8" "Recd in wampam bead 7. 15. 4" 1AB, 103	1½d. per fathom of wampum strung £7 15s. 4d. in wampum beads
26 Apr. 1653	Thomas Cooper	"Recd by stringing 212 fadam and ½ wampam 1. 6. 6½" "stringing 181 fadam ½ of wampam 1. 2. 8" 1AB, 78	1½d. per fathom of wampum strung 1½d. per fathom of wampum strung
Oct. 1653	David Burt	"Recd by stringing 969 fadam of wampam last summer at 1d. ½ per fadam is 6. 1. 1" 1AB, 114	1½d. per fathom of wampum strung
1653–1654	John Stebbins	"Recd by stringing 160 fadam wampam 1. 0. 0" 1AB, 104	1½d. per fathom of wampum strung
1654	Rowland Stebbins	"Recd by stringing 160 fadam of wampam 1. 0. 0" 1AB, 104	1½d. per fathom of wampum strung
7 Aug. 1655	Samuel Chapin	"Recd by stringing 240 [?] fadam of wampam 1. 10. 10" 1AB, 294	£1 10s. 10d. for stringing wampum
19 Sep. 1655	Henry Burt	"Recd by stringing of wampam, 671 fadam at 1d. pr. [is] 4. 3. 10" 1AB, 238	1d. per fathom of wampum strung (pays 1½d.)

WAMPUM STRINGING, *cont.*

Date	Name	Service	Rate
9 Apr. 1656	Samuel Chapin	"Recd by stringing 15 fad ½ wampam 0. 1. 11" 1AB, 295	1½d. per fathom of wampum strung
30 Sep. 1656	John Stebbins	"Recd by stringing 155 fadam wampam 0. 19. 4" 1AB, 243	1½d. per fathom of wampum strung
10 Oct. 1656	Henry Burt	"Recd by stringing 853 fadam of wampam . . . 5. 6. 0" 1AB, 238	1½d. per fathom of wampum strung
Nov. 1657	John Stebbins	"Recd by stringing 93 fadam 0. 11. 5" "Recd by wampam (the whole parcel) 51. 16. 0" 1AB, 244	1½d. per fathom of wampum strung £51 16s. for wampum
Aug. 1658	Henry Burt	"Recd by Stringing 601 fadam of wampam . . . 3. 15. 0" 1AB, 283	1½d. per fathom of wampum strung
Jun. 1663	John Stebbins	"By stringing wampam 640 fadam 4. 0. 0" 2AB, 79	1½d. per fathom of wampam strung
31 May 1665		"By stringing . . . [519 fathom at 1d. ½ per fathom is] 3. 4. 10 (395 fadam white . . . 124 fadam blue)"	1½d. per fathom of wampum strung
3 Jun. 1668		"By stringing 292 fadam Wampam 1. 16. 6" 3AB, 223	1½d. per fathom of wampum strung

WEAVING

Date	Name	Service	Rate
Feb. 1678/79	Charles Ferry	"By 63 yards weaving 1. 11. 6"	6d. per yard of cloth woven
1684		"weaving 1. 1. 1" 5AB, 485	21s. 1d. for weaving
1691	Charles Ferry, Jr.	"By weaving 42 yards at 8d. [is] 1. 8. 0"	8d. per yard of cloth woven
1693		"By weaving 51 yards of Teere Cloth at 6d. ½ [is] 1. 7. 0"	6½d. per yard of "Teere Cloth" woven [calico]
Jan. 1693/94		"By weaving 26 yards at 7d. [is] 0. 15. 2" 6AB, 235	7d. per yard of cloth woven
11 Aug. 1699?		"By weaving cloth: for Ruth 0. 2. 7" 4AB, 79	2s. 7d. for weaving

WELLMAKING

Date	Name	Service	Rate
1692	John Kilum	"By making my well 2. 10. 0" 6AB, 229	£2 10s. for making well

WHEELWRIGHT

Date	Name	Service	Rate
5 Nov. 1663	John Lamb	"By mending Cart 6s. "axle True 1s. 8d."	6s. for mending cart 1s. 8d. for truing axle
		"Mending the Tumbler 0. 1. 6"	1s. 6d. for mending tumbler
5 Sep. 1664		"Cart wheels repaired 1. 9. 0"	29s. for mending cart wheels
		"Mending cart and axle 0. 2. 0"	2s. for mending cart and axle

WHEELWRIGHT, *cont.*

Date	Name	Service	Rate
Mid-1660s		"Mending cart codder 0. 1. 0" 2AB, 353	1s. for mending cart cotter
30 Nov. 1665		"By worke wheeles, and from John Lamb's Book . . . 5. 6. 3"	£5 6s. 3d. for wheelwright work
1667		"By worke wheeles, and etc., from John Lamb's Booke . . . 2. 19. 0" "By cariage for my Great Gun 1. 12. 0"	£2 19s. for wheelwright work £1 12s. for building cannon carriage
15 Dec. 1669		"By worke cart making, wheels, and carting, his Lad's, himselfe, and etc." 3AB, 149	Payment for wheelwright work on cart
May 1671		"By worke in John Lamb's Booke, days worke mending wheeles, making wheeles, and a Plow, carting, loading Boats, and etc., all this to this 25 May 1671 [is] 7. 15. 0"	£7 15s. for wheelwright work
Feb. 1671/72		"Making axles and etc." 5AB, 75	Payment for making axles
30 Mar. 1675	Samuel Wright (estate inventory)	"To wheelwright tools 3. 1. 0" "Sithes, weges, forkes 0. 19. 0" "Saw, grindstone, Loome 3. 1. 0" 1HCPCR, 170	Tools Tools Tools

Wage Ordinances

SPRINGFIELD WAGE ORDINANCES, FEBRUARY 1649/50

"Husbandmen and ordinary Labourers:"
"from the first day of November not take above 16d. by the day wages, for the other 8 months they shall not take above 20d. by the day, except in tyme of harvest for reapinge and mowinge or for other extraordinary works as are sufficient, workmen are allowed 2s. per day"
"Carpenters, Joyners, wheel wrights, or such like Artificers:"
"from the first of November to the first of March, shal not take above 20d. per day wages And for the other 8 months not above 2s. per day"
"Tailors:"
"not to exceed 12d. per day through the yeare"
"Teames consistinge of 4 Cattell with one man:"
"shall not take above 6s. per day wages: from May till October: to worke 8 howers, and the other part of the yeare 6 howers for theyr days worke"
"And it is further ordered that whosoever shall either by givinge or takinge exceede these rates, he shall be Lyable to be punished by the magistrate according to the quality and nature of the offence"
  Source: 1TR, pp. 203–204

MASSACHUSETTS BAY COLONY WAGE ORDINANCES, 1670–1672

  Bill introduced in the General Court on May 17, 1670:
"Labourers by the daye from the end of September to the end of March dyeting themselves .... 1s. 3d. per day
    From the end of March to the end of June .... 1s. 8d.
    From the end of June to the end of September they workeing 10 houres in the daye besides repast .... 2s.
  Taske worke. One Acre of salt marsh, and one Acre of English grasse well mowen .... 2s. per acre
    one Acre of wheat well reapeing .... 4s.
    one Acre of Rye well reapeing .... 3s.
    one Acre of Barly, and one Acre of oats, each well moweing .... 1s.
    one Acre of peas, cutting .... 3s.
    one Coarde of woode, cutting, and well Coarding .... 1s. 3d.
    This wages is allowed as above to workemen Dyeting themselves.
  Carpenters and Masons and Stonelayers, from 1 March to 10
    of October .... 2s. per day and all worke

taken by the great or peice by Carpenters, masons, joyners, or shinglers, is to be apportioned according to the equitie of the value of Daye's worke as above, they dyeting themselves.

Master Taylors, and Such as are fully workmen of that Trade for one daye's worke of 12 hours .... 1s. 8d.

    Apprentices to that trade the first 4 yeares, the like daye .... 1s.

And all weavers for thier worke at 12 hours per day, are to have the like wages as Taylors.

All men and women Servants shall in their respective wages be moderated according to the proportion of labour above limitted.

No person shall pay, neither shall any Shoemaker receave, more than 5s. for men's Shoes of elevens or twelves, nor for women's Shoes of Seavens or Eights more than 3s. 8d.

    And all bootes and shoes of other Sizes proportionable to the rates abovesaide.

Coopers shall not receave nor any person pay for a thight barrel of 32 gallons above 2s. 8d., and other Cooper's worke proportionable in price to barrels.

Smythes Shall not take nor any person paye for great worke, as for Ships, Mills, plough Irones, all Irones for Cart wheeles well layd upon the wheeles, and other the like great worke, above 5d. per lb. For smaller worke as Chaynes and other the like Solde by weight, not above 6d. per lb. For the largest horse shoe well set with 7 nayles, not above 6d. per shoe. For removeing a horse shoe, 2d. For an ordinary felling axe, 3s. 6d. For one broade axe, 5s. 6d., one broade hoe 3s., all being good and well steeled, and all other Smithe's worke not named to be proportioned according to the prices above Said."

Source: Morris, *Government and Labor*, pp. 65–66

    Comparison between 1670 bill and bill introduced in the General Court in 1672:

1670		1672
"One acre of wheat 'well reapt'	4s.	5s.
One acre of peas, cutting	3s.	2s. 6d.
Shoemakers, for shoes of elevens or twelves	5s.	4s.
for women's shoes of sevens and eights	3s. 8d.	3s.
Smiths, for iron work	5d. per lb.	4½d. per lb.
for smaller work such as chains	6d.	5½d.
for the largest horseshoe	6d.	5½d.
for removing a horseshoe	2d.	1½d.
for an ordinary felling axe	3s. 6d.	3s.
for a broad axe	5s. 6d.	4s. 6d.
for a broad hoe	3s.	2s. 6d."

Source: Morris, *Government and Labor*, p. 68, n.45

NEW HAVEN WAGE ORDINANCES, 1640–1641

		Maximum Wages	
		1640	1641
"Skilled workmen	Summer:	2s. 6d.	2s.
	Winter:	2s.	20d.
Journeymen in skilled trades	Summer:	2s.	20d.
	Winter:	20d.	16d.
Farmers and laborers	Summer:	2s.	18d.
	Winter:	18d.	14d.

Sawing		
by the hundred, for boards	4s. 6d.	3s. 8d.
for planks	5s.	4s.
for slitwork	5s. 6d.	4s. 6d.
by the day, top man or foreman (summer)	2s. 6d.	2s.
pit man, less skill (summer)	2s.	18d.
Felling of timber, 2 feet or more	3d. per foot	2½d. per foot
between 18 inches and 2 feet	2d. per foot	1½d. per foot
Hewing and squaring of timber, at least 15 in. sq.	18d. tun girt measure	15d.
Sills, beams, plates, etc.	1d. per foot	
Mowing, by the acre, salt marsh	3s.	3s. 6d.
fresh marsh	2s. 6d.	3s.
Thatchers	2s. 6d. per diem	
Fencing, with pales (pales and carting not included)	2s. per rod	18d.
with five rails	2s. per rod	18d.
with three rails	18d. per rod	14d.
Lime, by the bushel	9d.	7d.
by the hogshead	5s.	4s."

Source: Morris, *Government and Labor*, pp. 79–80

CONNECTICUT COLONY ORDINANCES, 1677

Shoemakers	
Plain and wooden-heeled shoes (all sizes above men's sevens)	5s. 6d.
French heels, well wrought	7s. 6d.
Tanners	
Tanning hides	
green hides	2d. per lb.
dry hides	4d. per lb.
Sale of hides	
green hides	3d. per lb.
dry hides	6d. per lb.

Source: Morris, *Government and Labor*, p. 82

Crop Valuation Table

Crop	Range of Value	Citations
Apples	2s. 6d. per bushel	3AB, 155
Barley	3s.–4s. per bushel	2AB, 239; 3AB, 319
Beaver	8s.–9s. 4d. per pound	1AB, 78
Beef	2¾d. per pound	1AB, 300
Cider	6d. per quart, 16s. per barrel	3AB, 97, 199
Corn	2s. 4d.–2s. 6d. per bushel	1AB, 266; 3AB, 123
Dung	8d. per cartload	1AB, 100
Hemp	9d.–10d. per pound	3AB, 97; 5AB, 81
Oats	2s. per bushel	5AB, 59, 71
Peas	2s. 6d. per bushel	5AB, 77, 83
Pork	2½d.–3d. per pound	2AB, 255; 3AB, 107B
Salt	5s.–8s. per bushel	3AB, 114
Sugar	8d.–1s. per pound	3AB, 114
Tar	14s.–16s. 6d. per barrel	3AB, 97
Turnips	1s.–16d. per bushel	3AB, 97
Turkeys	4s. 6d. per fowl	5AB, 81
Wheat	3s. 6d.–3s. 10d. per bushel	1AB, 95, 297

Population Table, 1636–1776

Year	Population
1636	8
1640	45
1646	100
1665	288
1672	304
1685	540
1690	750
1738	1,692
1765	2,755
1776	1,974